*For
Benjamin E. Mays
and
Howard Thurman*

# The SHAPING of BLACK AMERICA

Lerone Bennett, Jr.

Illustrated by Charles White

 Johnson Publishing Company, Inc.    Chicago, 1975

Copyright © 1969, 1970, 1971, 1972, 1973, 1974, 1975 by Johnson Publishing Company, Inc. *Illustrations copyright © 1975 by* Johnson Publishing Company, Inc.

*The ten chapters of the present work appeared originally in somewhat abridged version, as articles in* EBONY *Magazine, under the series title* The Making of Black America, *between June 1969 and February 1974. Each article has been rewritten, altered or added to by the author for this book.*

All rights reserved, including the right to reproduce this book or any portion thereof in any form.

Library of Congress Cataloging in Publication Data
Bennett, Lerone, Jr., 1928-
   The Shaping of Black America
E185.B43     917.3'06'96     74-20659
ISBN 0-87485-071-1

*Book design and cover by* Norman L. Hunter.

*Production Coordinator:* Janice Bek.

*Cover illustration by* Charles White.

*Janson Linotype, 12/14.*

*Manufactured in the United States of America.*

# Preface

This is an essay toward a new understanding of the long and continuing attempts of Africans and African descendants to possess themselves and the new land. This essay in historical reconstruction grows organically and chronologically out of an earlier book, *Before The Mayflower*. But there are several differences between this study and *Before The Mayflower*. First of all and most important of all, this is a developmental history instead of a chronological history. I have been interested here in the forces and events that made black America what it is today. And since black America was of central importance in the shaping of white America, I have dealt at some length with some of the forgotten pages of white history and Indian history.

I have been interested also in the creation of a new conceptual envelope for black American history. It should be clear by now to almost everyone that understanding the black experience requires new concepts and a radically new perspective. I have tried here to advance the work of conceptual reconstruction. I have tried to give concrete content to the notion that "blacks lived a different time and a different reality in this country."*

The book is divided into two sections. The first section—Foundations—begins with the first generation of African-Americans and contains chapters on the black founding fathers, the white semi-slaves of America, and the vitally important story of the relations between blacks and Indians. There is also a chapter on the black pioneers, who created a new historical form, in part African, in part European, in part X.

The second section—Directions—focuses on the history of black labor and black capital (not black capitalism) and ends with the central paradoxes of the political economy of blackness. There is no final chapter: the final chapter is being written by men, women and children who are groping for new directions in one of history's hard places.

---

* Lerone Bennett, Jr., *The Challenge of Blackness* (Chicago: Johnson Publishing Company, 1972), p. 39.

## PREFACE

*I* owe a debt of gratitude to many people, including Publisher John H. Johnson, Doris E. Saunders, Norman L. Hunter, Charles White, Beverly Adams, Basil Phillips, Jan Bek, Carmel Tinkchell, Pamela Cash, Betty Carter and the personnel of the Hall Branch Library and the Newberry Library. I am also indebted to my wife Gloria, who provided administrative assistance and support.

*Lerone Bennett, Jr.*

Chicago, 1974

# CONTENTS

*Part One: Foundations*

    I. The First Generation . . . . . . . . . . . 5

    II. White Servitude . . . . . . . . . . . 39

    III. The Road Not Taken . . . . . . . . . . . 61

    IV. Red and Black . . . . . . . . . . . 83

    V. The Black Founding Fathers . . . . . . . . . . . 113

    VI. The World of the Slave . . . . . . . . . . . 145

    VII. Jubilee . . . . . . . . . . . 169

*Part Two: Directions*

    VIII. System . . . . . . . . . . . 207

    IX. The Black Worker . . . . . . . . . . . 233

    X. Money, Merchants and Markets . . . . . . . . . . . 285

    *Appendix* . . . . . . . . . . . 340

    *Bibliography* . . . . . . . . . . . 343

    *Index* . . . . . . . . . . . 351

# ILLUSTRATIONS

| | |
|---|---|
| The First Generation | 3 |
| White Servitude | 37 |
| The Road Not Taken | 59 |
| Red and Black | 81 |
| The Black Founding Fathers<br>　*Paul Cuffee, Richard Allen* | 111 |
| The World of the Slave<br>　*Harriet Tubman* | 143 |
| Jubilee | 167 |
| System<br>　*Frederick Douglass,*<br>　*W. E. B. DuBois* | 205 |
| The Black Worker | 231 |
| Money, Merchants and Markets | 283 |

*All illustrations by Charles White rendered in monochromatic oil on boards.*

# The SHAPING of BLACK AMERICA

# Part One

# FOUNDATIONS

# The First Generation

*I*N August, when the shadows are long on the land and even the air oppresses, the furies of fate hang in the balance in black America. It was in August, in the eighth month of the year, that three hundred thousand men and women marched on Washington, D.C. It was in August that Watts exploded. It was in August, on a hot and heavy day in the nineteenth century, that Nat Turner rode. And it was in another August, 344 years before the March on Washington, 346 years before Watts, and 212 years before Nat Turner's war, that "a Dutch man of Warr" sailed up the river James and landed the first generation of black Americans at Jamestown, Virginia.

No one knows the hour or the day of the black landing. But there is not the slightest doubt about the month. John Rolfe, who betrayed Pocahontas and experimented with tobacco leaves, was there; and he said, in a letter to his superior, that the ship arrived "about the latter end of August" in 1619. Rolfe had a nose for nicotine, but he was obviously deficient in historical matters, for he added gratuitously that the ship "brought not anything but 20 and odd Negroes." Concerning which the most charitable thing to say is that John Rolfe was probably pulling his superior's leg. For in the context of the meaning of America, it can be said without exaggeration that no ship ever called at an American port with a more important cargo. In the hold of that ship, in a manner of speaking, was the whole gorgeous panorama of black America, was jazz and the spirituals and the Funky Broadway. Bird was there and Bigger and Malcolm and millions of other X's and crosses, along with Mahalia singing, Gwendolyn Brooks rhyming, Duke Ellington composing, James Brown grunting, Paul Robeson emoting, and Sidney Poitier walking. It was all there in embryo in the 160-ton ship.

The ship that sailed up the James on a day we will never know was the beginning of America, and, if we are not careful, the end. *That* ship brought the black gold that made capitalism possible in America; it brought slave-built Monticello and slave-built Mount Vernon and the Cotton Kingdom and the graves on the slopes of Gettysburg. It was all there, illegible and inevitable, on that August day. That ship brought the *blues* to America, it brought *soul*, and a man with eyes would have seen it, would have said that the seeds of an Alcindor are here, would have announced that a King was coming and that a Du Bois would live and die, would have foretold agonies and pains and funerals, would have predicted four hundred years of Sundays and Saturday nights. A man with eyes, I say, would have seen all that in the twenty black seeds planted that day and in the bad faith of whiteness that would manure them. He would have seen it all, and he would have stood up and announced to his startled contemporaries that this ship heralds the beginning of the first Civil War and the second.

As befitting a herald of fate, the ship was nameless, and mystery surrounds it until this day. Where did this ship come from? It came from some unidentified spot on the high seas where she robbed a Spanish frigate of a cargo of Africans destined for the West Indies. In this piratical venture, which was really a robbery within a robbery, the so-called

Dutch man-of-war was associated with the *Treasurer*, a Virginia-based ship sailing under the commission of the Duke of Savoy.

Although the evidence is tantalizingly vague, there are indications that the Jamestown Landing was, as James C. Ballagh said, "the result of a deliberate commercial design." To grasp all the ramifications of this point, one must pause for a moment and consider the backdrop and the chain of causes. Important as the Jamestown Landing was, it was only an episode in a larger drama that continued for almost four hundred years and cost the lives of some forty million Africans.

This drama, which is known as the African Slave Trade, had been going on for more than one hundred years when the Virginia colony was founded in 1607. By that time European slave traders had transported tens of thousands of blacks to the New World to work in the Spanish West Indies, Brazil, Cuba, and other colonies. By that time, too —as we shall see later—Europeans had forced hundreds of blacks to accompany them in the pioneering explorations of the American continent. For reasons that need not detain us here, the English were late starters in this sinister drama. In the years immediately preceding the Jamestown Landing, the slave trade and the colonization movement were dominated by the Spanish, Portuguese, and Dutch. This naturally displeased the English, who launched a series of raids on Spanish shipping. One of the minor functionaries in this struggle was Samuel Argall, the governor of the newly-settled English colony of Virginia. In April, 1618, Argall sent one of the colony's ships, the *Treasurer*, to the West Indies "under pretense," it was said, "of getting salt and goats for the colony." But it was noted then and afterwards that the ship was manned by "the ablest men of the colony" and was loaded with "powder, shott, wast, clothes, ordynaunce, streamers, flagges and other furniture ffitt for the man of warre."

Somewhere in waters of the West Indies, this ship linked up with another vessel, which was manned chiefly with English sailors and pretended to sail under the commission of the Duke of Orange, although it was uncommissioned and hence a pirate. The two ships later attacked and captured a Spanish frigate loaded with one hundred or more Africans. The *Treasurer* and the Dutch man-of-war appropriated the Africans at gunpoint and sailed for Virginia. But they were separated, according to contemporary accounts, during a violent storm, which shook the ships and terrified their passengers. During the struggle to save the ships, the land that was to become America claimed its first African victims. Several Africans, we are told, died during the storm, probably of hunger, and were unceremoniously thrown overboard. Finally, after a delay of several weeks, the Dutch man-of-war sailed into Hampton Roads. The captain of this vessel, a shadowy figure named Jope, "ptended," John Rolfe noted that he was in need of food, and he offered to exchange black flesh for "victualle." The deal was arranged, and twenty black men and women debarked and looked around to see what shore the tide of fate had brought them.*

They could not have been impressed with what they saw. Jamestown was a mean, dank, primitive place, precariously perched on the western end of a low, marshy peninsula. The town consisted of a row of timber houses in various states of disrepair. There was also a wooden, barn-like building which housed the Church of England and the recently established House of Burgesses. The town was enclosed with a wooden stockade and at the western bulwark a gun platform had been erected. There were other settlements, equally nondescript, on both sides of the James. There were scarcely one thousand persons in the whole colony, and most of them were servants or former servants.

It would not have escaped the new immigrants that fate had made them a party to an uncertain and illegal adventure. There was something fragile, something furtive about this community. And yet there was also an air of anticipation that was doubtlessly related to the stirring events that coincided with the arrival of the Jamestown Twenty. In the months preceding their arrival, the colony had installed the new House of Burgesses, shipped its first big load of tobacco to England, formalized a new system of white servitude, inaugurated a new system of private property, and welcomed a shipload of brides, who were promptly purchased at the going rate of 120 pounds of tobacco each. Thus, white servitude, black servitude, private property, "representative democracy," and bride purchase were inaugurated in America at roughly the same time.

Despite or perhaps because of all this activity, Virginia, in August, 1619, was a community of fear. The white settlers were doing something wrong, and they knew it. They were systematically appropriating the land of the Americans, i.e., the Indians, who had greeted them with civility and had provided most of the provisions that had enabled them

---

* The *Treasurer* apparently arrived shortly thereafter and landed one black woman, Angelo.

## THE FIRST GENERATION

to survive. And so they were consumed with anxieties and vague fears, tending, as contemporary reports indicate, to see an enemy or a potential enemy behind every bush and in every shadow. It was not for nothing that stockades enclosed Jamestown and other settlements and that the law required settlers to "bringe their pieces [guns] to the church uppon payne for every offense." There were other fears as well, the fear of sex, the fear of passion, the fear of art; and these fears, vague and benumbing, would enter into and color the white man's dialogue with the new immigrants.

It was across the high voltage lines of these fears and in the context of a socioeconomic situation defined by labor scarcity that black confronted white for the first time in English America.

Centuries later, the historian must view the first meeting of these two groups with an astonishment equivalent to their own. The scene flickers with a hundred ironies and invites a thousand idle reflections. What was the first word to pass between black and white? What did the whites think of the blacks? And what—pray tell—did the blacks think of the whites? What did the blacks think, what did they feel there on the bank of the James River in the wilderness of North America? On these and other matters, the meager record is vexatiously silent, giving us neither the faces nor the passions of the first black Americans. We know from other sources that the group was composed of roughly the same number of males and females. We also know that most of the immigrants had Spanish names. Three of the men were named Antonio or Antoney, and one of the women was named Isabell. One man, however, retained his African identity. His name or at least the English approximation was Jiro.

In years to come an intricate controversy would develop over the meaning of that first meeting on the James. Certain scholars, reading twentieth-century preoccupation into the minds of the first white settlers, would say, without a figleaf of evidence, that the first white settlers saw black and immediately started painting Jim Crow signs. The record does not support that view. On the contrary, the record clearly shows that the first sign black people saw in America was a welcome sign. The colonists needed labor. They were unconcerned at that point about its color or national origin. The twenty black immigrants represented labor power. And it was as labor, indentured labor, that blacks entered the world that was to become the United States of America.

Let it be said at the outset—though we shall return to this point later in greater detail—that there was nothing unusual about the mode of transportation or the price paid for the first black immigrants. Most of the first white settlers came the same way, and most of them were sold, as the first blacks were sold, by the captains of ships or the agents of captains of ships. To come right out with it, America—in the beginning—was a land of the hunted and the unfree. For almost two hundred years, the land was inhabited largely by a population of black, red, and white bondsmen. Most of these bondsmen, in the beginning, were indentured servants. That is to say, they were temporary slaves who sold themselves or were sold by others to the colonies or individual planters for a stipulated number of years (five, seven or more) in order to pay the cost of their passage. Finally, and most important, if hardest for us to understand, race did not have the same meaning in 1619 that it has today. The first white settlers were organized around concepts of class, religion, and nationality, and they apparently had little or no understanding of the concepts of race and slavery. It is certainly significant in this regard that English law in 1619 forbade the enslavement of baptized Christians. As an example, we might consider the first American court case relating to blacks. In November, 1624, a black man testified against a white man in a Virginia court. The court record notes: "John Phillip A negro Christened in England 12 yeers since, sworne and exam. sayeth, that beinge in a ship with Sir Henry Maneringe, they tooke A spanish shipp aboute Cape Sct Mary, and Caryed her to mamora." This case is especially instructive, not only because it defines the law of the time, but also because it bears directly on our next point. The names of most of the first black immigrants indicate that they had been baptized either in Spain or on the coast of Africa. For that reason, and for others that will appear in due course, it is virtually certain that the first black immigrants entered America as free men and women temporarily bound to service. American scholarship being what it is, the number of white scholars who deny this point is understandably large. But the proponents of this view are forced to argue the untenable theory that blacks were first enslaved and then raised to the status of indentured servants in the face of an ever-increasing demand for labor which almost led to the de facto slavery of white indentured servants. This is so patently absurd that we can safely consign it to the footnotes of small scholarly journals.

Two additional points stand out in this brief review of the legal status

# THE FIRST GENERATION

of the first black Americans. The first and possibly more significant point is that the Jamestown blacks were bought by the colony with public provisions. They were therefore servants not of individuals but of the state. And as servants of the state, they were assigned to officers of the colony and planters closely associated with the administration of the colony. In 1623, twenty of the twenty-three were listed as servants of representative planters and officers, including the governor, who controlled the largest number, eleven.

The second point is that the legal status of the black immigrants was, in theory, higher than the legal status of the first white indentured servants. The Dutch and English pirates who sold the black immigrants to the colony had, in fact, no legal rights of ownership they could exercise or transfer. "As the captives, not of warfare, but of piracy," James C. Ballagh wrote, "[the black immigrants] were under the protection of international law in maintaining their original status, and had they been citizens of a powerful civilized community they might have received it." We can safely ignore Ballagh's ideas on civilization. The key concept here—we will meet it again and again in this book—is power. In the seventeenth century, as in the eighteenth, nineteenth and twentieth centuries, it was a question of power. The Dutch and the English had the power, and they used that power to reduce the first black immigrants to temporary servitude.

From what I have already recorded, from the court records of the period, the official records of the Virginia Company, and the citation of authorities, it can be safely concluded that the first generation of blacks fell into roughly the same socioeconomic category as the first white immigrants. Not only in Virginia but also in New England and New York —as we shall soon see—the first blacks were integrated into a forced labor system that had little or nothing to do with skin color. That came later. But in the interim, a fateful forty-year period of primary importance in the history of America, black men and women worked side by side with the first generation of whites, cultivating tobacco, clearing the land, and building roads and houses. The work was hard, the rewards few, and the mortality rate frightful. Two out of every three white indentured servants died in the first year in the colonies, victims of hard work and the dreaded "Virginia sicknesse," which was probably malaria. But the first generation of blacks was made of sterner stuff. Not a single black died in the first three years.

*IN* the months and years that followed the Jamestown Landing, the black population of Virginia grew slowly and uncertainly. In 1621 the *James* arrived from England with a number of immigrants, including one black man, Antonio. The next year the *Margaret and John* brought Mary, another English sojourner. In 1623 the *Swan* brought still another black from England, John Pedro. By this time blacks had integrated six out of the twenty-three white settlements in Virginia.

According to census reports, which are not entirely reliable, there were twenty-two blacks out of a total white population of 1,275 in 1623. Eleven men and one "Negors woman" were at Fleur de Hundred, a settlement on the upper bank of the James. Two men and two women were at Wariscoyack (now Isle of Wight) on the south side of the James. Three women were living in Jamestown, and one man and one woman were living in Elizabeth City (now Hampton). One man was reported at the neck of land which joined Jamestown to the mainland, and another man was listed at a plantation on the west bank of the Powhatan River opposite Jamestown.

At this juncture or slightly later—the record is not clear—there occurred three events of pivotal importance. The first event was mournful. On some unspecified date between April, 1622, and February 16, 1623, the first black person died in English America. It is significant that we know neither the name nor the sex of the victim nor the circumstances of the death. The cold and careless record simply lists the death of "one Negar" at West and Sherlow Hundred, a small settlement on the north side of the James in the vicinity of Charles City. Although a certain mystery still hangs over the event, it is obvious that the reported death of "one Negar" was significant. It was the first drop of pain, the first drop of blood, in a dry basin that would become a river and then an ocean.

Of equal or perhaps greater concern were the other two events. In late 1623 or early 1624, Antoney and Isabell, two of the first black arrivals, brought what might have been a shipboard romance to a significant conclusion by marrying. Isabell was soon brought to bed with what was probably the first black child born in English America. The child, a boy named William, was taken from his home in Elizabeth City to Jamestown and baptized before the cedar chancel in the Church of England. William apparently had no last name. He enters the record thus, the first of a long black line of youth defined by X's and question marks. Philip Alexander

Bruce, a white authority on Colonial Virginia, made a dubious observation about this birth. Said he: "While the mind cannot contemplate the birth of the first negro [sic] on North American soil with the same emotions as those aroused by the birth of Virginia Dare [the first white child born in North America], the event nevertheless was one which cannot be regarded without a feeling of the profoundest interest when we reflect upon its association with the great events which were to come after."

Racism apart, there is no reason why we cannot contemplate this birth with equal or even greater interest than we give to the birth of Virginia Dare. For when we brood over the train of events that followed the birth of William ?—slavery, the capital that provided the take-off fuel for the American economy, the Civil War and so forth—it is an open question as to which birth was more significant.

There occurred a postscript to this event that throws additional light on the methodology of some white historians. In an early edition of J. C. Hotten's *Lists of Emigrants to America*, the first black family in America was correctly identified as "Antoney Negro: Isabell Negro; and William theire Child Baptised." But in the second edition of the work, the entry was modified to read "Anthony, negro, Isabell, a negro, and William her child, baptised." Thus, with a stroke of the pen, Negro was reduced in importance, the black family was eliminated ("theire" becomes "her") and black reality was forced into the preconceived molds of the chronicler's mind.

All this—the train of events that followed the birth of William and the peculiar problems of some white historians—was far in the future in 1624 when William ? increased the black population of Virginia by some 5 percent. At the time of the first detailed census in 1624–25, there were twenty-three blacks in Virginia—eleven males, ten females, and two children.* These men, women and children constituted some 2 percent of the total population of 1,227 (487 white and Indian indentured servants and 608 "free" white men and women). The black inhabitants were living in six of the twenty-three settlements and were apparently the servants of seven planters, five of whom were officers of the colony.

---

* The second child is not identified by name. There is no indication in the record that the child was born in Virginia. It is possible that this child was born on the ship. James C. Ballagh identifies the child as Peter and says his mother was named Frances, but he does not identify his authority.

The newlyweds, Antoney and Isabell, and their son William were still living in Elizabeth City. John Pedro, a thirty-year-old black man, lived nearby on the company land beyond the Hampton River. There were three unidentified black men and five unidentified black women on a tract of public land in Jamestown. On the neck of land to the west of Jamestown was Edward, a solitary black figure in a white settlement of 126 males and 19 females. On the south side of the James, at Wariscoyack, were Antonio and Mary, who would later distinguish themselves as the leading black family in the colony. Four black men, two black women and an unidentified black child were listed on the plantation of Abraham Piersey, the wealthiest man in the colony. With the significant exceptions of Antoney, Isabell and William, the blacks are listed with whites as "servant's." The fact that Antoney, Isabell, and William are not listed specifically as servants probably indicates that they were to all intents and purposes free people in 1624. The further fact that they were permitted to marry, a privilege generally denied servants, argues strongly in favor of this theory.

The names and locations listed above are preserved in the *Musters of the Inhabitants in Virginia*, an important historical document that should be quoted directly on the first generation of blacks.

Pierseys hundred.

The MUSTER of m'ABRAHAM PIERSEYS Servant's.

. . . . . . . . . . . . . . . . . . . . .

NATHANIELL THOMAS aged 23 yeres in the *Temperance* 1621
RICHARD BROADSHAW aged 20 yeares in the same Shipp
ROBERT OKLEY aged 19 yeares in the *William & Thomas* 1618

Negro ⎫
Negro ⎬ 4 Men
Negro ⎪
Negro ⎭

ALLICE THOROWDEN ⎱ maid servant's arrived in the
KATHERINE LEMAN   ⎰ *Southampton* 1623

Negro Woman.
Negro Woman and a yong Child of hers.

# THE FIRST GENERATION

James Citty

    The MUSTER OF Sʳ GEORGE YEARLY Kᵗ &ct

. . . . . . . . . . . . . . . . . . . . .

    Servant's at JAMES CITTY

. . . . . . . . . . . . . . . . . . . . .

THEOPHILUS BERISTON 23 in the *Treasuror* 1614
Negro Men. 3
Negro Woemen. 5.
SUSAN HALL in the *William & Thomas* 1618

. . . . . . . . . . . . . . . . . . . . .

James Citty

    THE MUSTER OF CAPᵀ WILLIAM PIERCE

. . . . . . . . . . . . . . . . . . . . .

ESTER EDERIFE a maid servant in the *Jonathan*
ANGELO a Negro Woman in the *Treasuror*.

. . . . . . . . . . . . . . . . . . . . .

Neck of Land nere
    James Citty.
        Servant's

. . . . . . . . . . . . . . . . . . . . .

EDWARD a Negro
ISBELL PRATT in the *Jonathan*

. . . . . . . . . . . . . . . . . . . . .

Wariscoyack.

    The MUSTER OF m'EDWARD BENNETT'S servant's

. . . . . . . . . . . . . . . . . . . . .

WASSELL WEBLING
        in the *James* 1621
ANTONIO a Negro

. . . . . . . . . . . . . . . . . . . . .

MARY a Nergro Woman in the *Margrett & John* 1622

Elizabeth Cittie

CAPT WILLIAM TUCKER his MUSTER

. . . . . . . . . . . . . . . . . . . . . .

PEETER PORTER aged 20 in the *Tyger* 1621.
WILLIAM CRAWSHAW an Indean Baptised.
ANTONEY Negro: ISABELL Negro: and WILLIAM theire Child Baptised


A MUSTER of the Inhabitente of ELIZABETH CITTIE beyond Hampton River. Beinge the Companyes land.

CAP<sup>T</sup> FRANCIS WEST his MUSTER

. . . . . . . . . . . . . . . . . . . . . .

REINOULD GODWIN aged 30 in the *Abigall* 1620
JOHN PEDRO a Neger aged 30 in the *Swan* 1623


This record is of considerable importance, for it is the earliest evidence of the status of the black inhabitants, who are clearly identified with a number of whites as "servant's." It is to be noted that some of the blacks are not identified by name and that others do not have family names. This was not at all unusual in that day and time. Many whites in the document are listed in the same way. For example: "Mary, a maid," "Thomas, a Boye," "James, a French Man," "Two Frechmen," "Henry," "Peter."

Across the years that followed the official muster, the black population grew by natural additions and importations. In 1625 Brase, another victim of piracy, was brought into the colony by Captain Thomas Jones. This triggered the first public fight over the disposition of a black. After a short and sharp legal controversy, the General Court decided that Brase was a prize of war and belonged not to an individual but to the state. He was later assigned as a servant to the governor. Four years later, in 1629, there was a substantial increase in the black population when the first ship from Africa arrived at Port Comfort, bringing blacks captured from a Portuguese ship off the coast of Africa. These captives were exchanged for eighty-five hogsheads and five butts of tobacco. In the 1630s and 1640s, approximately 160 blacks were imported. By 1649 officials were able to report that "there are in *Virginia* about fifteene thousand English, and of *Negroes* brought thither, three hundred good servants."

## THE FIRST GENERATION

*B*Y mid-century the "three hundred good servants" were integral parts of an evolving social system which had chosen neither its name nor its orientation. The colony still consisted of a series of settlements along the James and isolated cabins and huts stockaded against the environing forests and the Indians beyond. Most of the inhabitants lived in isolated independence, each group huddling within the confines of palisaded forts in the midst of dense swamps and belts of trees that separated them from the next settlement. By all early accounts, most of the people were a hard-drinking, refractory lot, driven to the edge of desperation by unceasing toil and constant danger. This was a hard and brutal age, and the pleasures of the age reflected the pressures of the environment. Almost everyone "drank tobacco," in the current phrase, and it is said that the women were foremost in drinking and smoking.

There were other problems, not the least of which was the dangerous imbalance of the sexes. The inevitable result was that the predominantly male population was involved in an astonishing number of sexual irregularities. Things reached such a pass that the Assembly had to legislate against English women who "contracted themselves to several men at one time, whereby much trouble doth grow between parties, and the Governor and Council of State much disquieted."

At that point and for several years thereafter, the colony was defined by what can only be called pious greed. This contradictory phenomenon manifested itself in the unrelenting encroachment on the land of the Indians and the evangelical quest for workers to tend the land thus appropriated for the greater glory, it was said, of God. There was not enough labor to cut down the trees, build the houses and cultivate the tobacco; and the men who ran the colony were constantly maneuvering to increase the number of laborers and the amount of work done by the laborers. What gave this quest a special twist was the insatiable European demand for the new weed, tobacco. This demand had triggered a get-rich boom in the colony, and it was reported that even "the marketplace and streets, and all other spare places are planted with Tobacco."

One of the most striking features of this colony, from our standpoint, was the relative absence of color consciousness. From the surviving evidence it appears that the first white colonists had no concept of themselves as *white* men. The legal documents identified whites as Englishmen and Christians. The word *white*, with all its burden of guilt and arrogance, did not come into common usage until the latter part of the century. To be sure, blacks were identified in early records as Negroes or Negers. But *Negro* was a national rather than a racial designation. In fact, the early records identify the *nationality* of all non-Englishmen (Irish, Scotch, French, etc.). It is scarcely necessary to say that there were prejudiced individuals in Virginia. But there is a world of difference between prejudiced individuals and a social system institutionally committed to prejudice. It is to be observed too that the prejudice we find in the records is largely class prejudice, which was distributed without regard to race, color, or national origin. The fundamental division in society at that time was not between blacks and whites but between servants and masters—and there were blacks and whites on both sides of the line.

The evidence in favor of this point falls into three categories. First of all, and perhaps most importantly, white masters held the black and white laboring classes in equal contempt and exacted the same tributes and the same work from both groups. To contemporary readers this may sound odd, not to say outlandish. But it was not at all unusual in those days for a white master to force a white woman servant to marry a black male servant. Nor was it unusual for a white master to give a black man a position of authority over white male and white female servants. There is incontrovertible evidence that one master hired a black overseer to drive his white female and male servants. There is also a legal record of a master who freed his black male servant in his will and directed that he should serve as the legal guardian of a white female servant. On this issue it is possible to cite numerous documents and any number of authorities. Historian John Fiske said that the general condition of the white indentured servant "seems to have been nearly as miserable" as that of black servants. More unequivocal is the statement of Philip A. Bruce, who said that "the life which the slaves followed as agricultural laborers could not have differed essentially from that of the white servants engaged in the performance of the same duties; the tasks expected of both were the same, and in the fields, at least, no discrimination seems to have been made in favor of the latter. During the greater part of the seventeenth century, the negro [sic] was regarded as a mere servant for life, and as a laborer differed in that particular alone from the white person who was bound for a period of years." Bruce added: "Side by side in the field, the white servant and the slave were engaged in planting, weeding, suckering, or cutting tobacco, or sat side by side in the barn manipulating the leaf in the course of preparing it for market, or plied their axes to the same trees in clearing away the forests to extend the new grounds. The same holidays were allowed to both, and doubtless, too, the same privilege of cultivating small patches of ground for their own private benefit." This statement, which carries additional weight because it comes from a conservative historian with little compassion for blacks, is accurate at least for the first decades of the seventeenth century. During that period white masters proved to be remarkably color blind when the claims of color contradicted their fundamental economic interests. Later, when the economic interests of Colonial masters changed, their eyesight improved considerably.

If white masters were, in the beginning, ecumenical in their intolerance, white servants were even more broadminded in their identification with nonwhite servants who shared their lot. They worked with black servants in the field; they drank persimmon beer with them on Saturday afternoon and Sundays; they frolicked with them on Christmas, "Pinkster" (Pentecost), and other holidays.

Sharing the same accommodations, the same situation, and the same enemy, the first black and white Americans, aristocrats excepted, developed strong bonds of sympathy and mutuality. There was no barrier between them, and circles of community and solidarity developed and widened. Of particular interest in this connection is the fact that black and white servants often made common cause against the master class. They often ran away together and on several occasions staged interracial revolts. As early as 1640 a Dutchman named Victor and "a Scotchman called James Gregory" attained a certain notoriety by running away in the company of a black man named John Punch. In the same year and in the same month, July, six of William Pierce's white servants ran away with a black named Emanuel. According to the court record, they "plotted to run away into the Dutch plantation . . . and did assay to put the same in Execution." They "had . . . taken the skiff of . . . Pierce . . . and corn, powder and shot and guns . . . which said persons sailed down . . . to Elizabeth river where they were taken." Others were not taken, and the flight of black and white conspirators continued throughout the Colonial period.

This happened not only in Virginia but also in New York and Massachusetts and other colonies, not only in the seventeenth century, but also in the eighteenth century. By way of illustration, we can cite the following advertisements which appeared in Colonial newspapers in the eighteenth century:

> Runaway in April last from Richard Tilgman, of Queen Anne county in Maryland, a mulatto slave, named Richard Molson, of middle stature, about forty years old and has had the small pox, he is in company with a white woman named Mary, who it is supposed now goes for his wife; and a white man named Garrett Choise, and Jane his wife, which . . . people are servants to . . . neighbors of Richard Tilgman. . . .
>
> Runaway from the subscriber the second of last month, at the town of Potomac, Frederick County, Maryland, a mulatto servant named Isaac Cromwell, runaway at the same time, an English servant woman, named Ann Greene. . . .

These advertisements are worth noting not only for the light they throw on the close relations which existed between blacks and whites, but also because they illustrate the third category of evidence, the large-scale interracial mating and marrying of blacks and whites. In the pioneer settlements and on the first plantations, black and white servants were "brought together," as one white historian put it delicately, "in intimate and close association." This naturally led to many informal and formal relationships. The grand outcome, as Peter Fonntaine, a contemporary witness, testified, was that Colonial Virginia "swarmed" with mulatto children. This was not solely, as some believe, the result of the casual exploitation of black women by white masters. On the contrary, as James Hugo Johnston proved in an excellent study, *Race Relations in Virginia and Miscegenation in the South*, "the larger part of such race mixture" was due to the union of the black male and the white female.

If we can believe contemporary court records, many white women were free of that "natural race prejudice" usually ascribed to the whites of the Colonial period. One instance out of many can be cited here, not so much because it illustrates racial mixing, but because it evokes the ambiguity of the racial picture at that time. This instance, cited by the Chester County, Pennsylvania, court, involved a constable named David Lewis who "returned a Negro man of his and a white woman for haveing a baster childe. . . . the Negro said she intised him and promised him to marry him; she being examined, confest the same . . . the court ordered that she shall receive twenty-one lashes on her beare backe ... and the court ordered the Negroe man never to meddle with any white woman more uppon paine of his life."

How did the white masters respond to all this?

Some, as the above example indicates, tried to stop it; others shrugged in indifference; still others promoted it. "In the seventeenth century," Johnston writes, "the association of the indentured servant and the slave was very close. They were often subjected to the same treatment and held by the master in the same esteem. Such associations led to many of the marriages that have been recorded. In those colonies where the numbers of the Negro slaves were comparatively few and when the master's only interest in his indentured servant was in the profits of his labor, many masters must have been little concerned to prevent the intermixture of the two races. Many instances of this lack of interest in race relations could, no doubt, be discovered throughout the entire Colonial period." Some of these instances were cited by Thomas Branagan, who visited Philadelphia in the eighteenth century. "Many respectable citizens," he wrote, "who are reduced in temporalities; on their decease their poor orphans are bound out in gentlemen's homes, where the maid servants are generally white, the men servants are black, and the employers allow the blacks as many liberties as they think proper to take; and no distinction is made between the white girls and black men...." Allowing, as we must, for some exaggeration, and remembering, as we must, the individual white masters and servants who projected phobic prejudices, usually as a function of their own personal problems, we can regard this testimony and the other evidence cited above as indications of the fluidity of the racial situation in the first decades of the founding of the republic.

In examining this record, one is struck not only by the widespread racial intermingling but also by the attempts to explain away a phenomenon that is too deeply etched in the record to deny. Philip A. Bruce, for example, commented with disapproval: "The class of white women who were required to work in the fields belonged to the lowest rank in point of character; not having been born in Virginia and not having thus acquired from birth a repugnance to association with Africans upon a footing of social equality, they yielded to the temptations of the situations in which they were placed." A more revealing comment came from a contemporary, Edward Long, who said that "the lower class of women in *England*, are remarkably fond of the blacks, for reasons too·brutal to mention...." Long's comments and the comments of others indicate that upper-class whites of that period and later had an ideological concept of lower-class whites that was definitely racist.

One has to make an effort to visualize the shape of this world. It seems somehow un-American, as undoubtedly it was, since it existed in America for only a brief spell and then by default. Within recent years, a number of scholars have addressed themselves to the issues raised by this period. Some of these men, ignoring evidence to the contrary, have contended that Englishmen had a sharp sense of color distinction from the very beginning. But the record they cite is not from the beginning. Not only that: they fail to tell us *which* Englishmen. As anyone who reads the record knows, there was a greater social gap between rich Englishmen and poor Englishmen than between poor Englishmen and poor Africans. Proponents of this view also commit a grave methodological error by citing the record of black bondage in isolation from the record of white bondage.

One must be careful, however, not to exaggerate. It is certain that there were fools and bigots then. And although it appears that the fools were class fools rather than race fools, the net effect in some instances was the same. It is also true that black servants were more exposed than white and Indian servants. Unlike the white and Indian servants, black servants did not have at their back the pressure and power of an organized group or nation. Nor was the Englishman bound by his own self-interest to recognize the claims of the Africans. It must also be remembered that some Africans did not speak English and that others were unfamiliar with the English Common Law and the white man's passion for private property. As a result, it was relatively easy in some cases to take advantage of African immigrants by extending their indentures. Yet, when all this is said, the fact remains that some Africans made the transition with extraordinary ease and exploited English subtleties on baptism and freedom with brilliance.

*WITHIN* the confines of this system of indeterminacy, which can only be called equality of oppression, blacks fared about as well as whites. Many black servants, like many white servants, worked for a specified number of years and were freed. Some blacks served longer terms than most whites, but some blacks also served shorter terms than the four-to-seven years required of most whites. An interesting and instructive case in point is

## THE FIRST GENERATION

that of Richard Johnson, a black carpenter who came to Virginia in 1651 as a free man and signed a contract of indenture. Within two years Johnson was a free man. Within three years he was acquiring property and servants—white servants—of his own. Another black servant who signed a contract of indenture for a relatively short period was Andrew Moore, who migrated to Virginia as a free man and bound himself out for a term of five years. In October, 1673, the General Court "ordered that the Said Moore bee free from his said master, and that the Said Mr. Light pay him Corne and Clothes according to the Customo of the Country and four hundred Pounds tobac and Caske for his service Done him Since he was free, and pay costs."

There are also records of black indentured servants who were bound for seven, ten, and even longer periods. In the following case, for example, the term of servitude specified was ten years. "Be it thought fitt & assented unto by Mr. Steph. Charlton in Court that Jno. G. Hamander Negro, his servant, shall from ye date hereof [1648] serve ye sd Mr. Charlton (his heyers or assns.) until ye last days of November wh shall be in ye year of our Lord . . . one thousand six hundred Fifty & eight and then ye sd Negro is to bee a free man."

Throughout this period and on into the eighteenth century, poor children—black and white—orphans, and children born out of wedlock were routinely bound out by the county parishes until their twenty-fourth or thirtieth birthday. A characteristic indenture of this type is listed below:

> This indenture witnesseth yt I Capt. Francis Pott have taken to service two Daughtgers of my negro Emanuell Dregis to serve & bee to me my heyers Exors. Adms. or Assigns. The one whose name is Elizabeth is to serve thirteene years whch will be compleat & ended in ye first part of March in ye yeare of our Lord God one thousand six hundred Fifty & eight. . . . And ye other child whose name is Jane Dregis (being about one yeare old) is to serve ye said Capt. Pott as aforesaid untill she arrive to ye age of thirty years old wh will be compleate & ended. . . . [May, 1674], And I ye said Francis Pott doe promise to give them sufficient meate, drinke, Apparel & Lodging and to use my best endeavor to bring them up in ye fear of God and in ye knowledge of our Saviour Christ Jesus. And I doe further testify yt the Eldest daughter was given to my negro by one who brought her upp by ye space of eight years and ye younger he bought and paid for to Capt. Robert Shephard (as maye bee made appear). In witness whereoff have

hereunto sett my hands & seale in ye 27th of May one thousand six hundred forty & five.

MR. FRANCIS POTT.

Witness the names of Thom. P. Powell & John Pott.

In the case of black servants, as in the case of white servants, masters were required to provide adequate food, shelter, and clothing. Not infrequently they were also required to provide religious instruction, education, and some training in a craft. One such indenture required the master to teach the young black indentured servant "to read ye bible distinctly also ye trade of a gunsmith that he carry him to ye Clark's office & take Indenture to that purpose." Another indenture "ordered that Malacai, a mulatto boy, son of mulatto Betty be, by the church wardens of this Parish, bound to Thomas Hobday to learn the art of a planter according to law."

Upon completion of the stipulated period of service, black servants were entitled to the same "freedom dues" granted whites, usually clothes and a year's supply of corn. Accompanying the freedom dues in most cases was a written discharge similar to the one granted Francis Pryne in Northampton County in 1656.

I Mrs. Jane Elkonhead . . . have hereunto sett my hand yt ye aforesd Pryne shall bee discharged from all hinderances of servitude (his child) or any [thing] yt doth belong to ye sd Pryne his estate.

JANE ELKONHEAD.

These familiar facts bestow a greater wealth of harmonics on the experiences of the first generation of Virginia blacks, many of whom worked out their terms of servitude and were freed. We have already commented on the probable status of Antoney and Isabell in 1624. We can also note the case of Anthony Longae, who was released from all servitude in Northampton County in 1635. We don't have a clear picture of Longae's later years, but we have undisputed proof that other freed blacks were soon accumulating capital.

Nothing could better illustrate the odyssey of the first generation of blacks than the life of Anthony Johnson, who came to America in 1621 from England. Before very many years passed, Johnson was released from servitude and married Mary Johnson, who also came to the colony from England and who also shared his servitude on the Bennett plantation in Wariscoyack. Obscurity covers Johnson's first years of freedom. But

# THE FIRST GENERATION

one can readily imagine him clearing a few acres, fencing them in, and planting corn and tobacco. He obviously prospered, for the year 1651 found him in Northampton County on the Eastern Shore, and here, for a tantalizing moment, the picture becomes clear. In that year Johnson imported and paid for five servants, some of whom were white, and was granted 250 acres of land on the basis of the headright system, which permitted planters to claim fifty acres of land for each individual brought to the colony. The abstract of the deed, as recorded in *Cavaliers and Pioneers*, reads as follows:

> ANTHONY JOHNSON, 250 acs. Northampton Co., 24 July 1651, .... At great Naswattock Cr., being a neck of land bounded on the S. W. by the maine Cr. & on S. E. & N. W. by two small branches issueing out of the mayne Cr. Trans. of 5 pers: Tho. Bemrose, Peter Bughby, Antho. Cripps, Jno. Gesorroro, Richard Johnson.

During the ensuing months, Johnson established America's second black community on the banks of the Pungoteague Creek in Northampton County.* In 1651 John Johnson, who was probably Anthony Johnson's son, imported eleven persons, most of them white males and females, and received headrights for 550 acres adjacent to his father. Three years later Richard Johnson bought two white indentured servants and received one hundred acres of land in the same area. Here are the records of the two deeds:

> JOHN JOHNSON, 550 acs. Northampton Co., 10 May 1652 ... At great Naswattocks Cr., adj. 200 acs. granted to Anthony Johnson. Trans. of 11 pers: John Edwards, Wm. Routh, Tho. Yowell, Fra. Maland, William Price, John Owen, Dorothy Rily, Richard Hemstead, Law. Barnes, Row. Rith, Mary Johnson.
>
> RICH. JNOSON (Johnson—also given as John), Negro, 100 acs. Northampton Co., 21 Nov. 1654, .... On S. side of Pongoteague Riv., Ely. upon Pocomock Nly. upon land of John Jnoson., Negro, Wly. upon Anto. Jnoson., Negro, & Sly. upon Nich. Waddilow. Trans. of 2 pers: Wm. Ames, Wm. Vincent.

Surrounded by black and white servants, Anthony Johnson and his Johnson allies and relatives prospered, but not without a certain dissension. The Johnsons were apparently a proud, contentious brood, and they were

---
* It seems from the record that the first black community was established in 1644 in Greenwich Village, New York, by free blacks of New Amsterdam (New York).

soon in court, suing each other over infringements of contract and property.

Although the outline of Anthony Johnson is vague, the few glimpses we are able to catch of him testify that he was enterprising and widely respected. On the debit side, it should be said that he seems to have accepted too readily the habits of his white neighbors. If the records are correct—and we have no reason to doubt them—he held another black man in lifetime servitude.

The luck of the Johnsons ran out in late 1651 when a fire destroyed their home. The next year Johnson petitioned the court for tax relief, which was granted in the following order:

> Upon ye humble pet[ition] of Anth. Johnson Negro; & Mary his wife; & their Information to ye Court that they have been Inhabitants in Virginia above thirty years consideration being taken of their hard labor & honoured service performed by the petitioners, in this County, for ye obtayneing of their Livelyhood And ye great Llosse they have sustained by an unfortunate fire with their present charge to provide for, Be it therefore fitt and ordered that from the day of the date hereof (during their natural lives) the sd Mary Johnson & two daughters of Anthony Johnson Negro be disingaged and freed from payment of Taxes and leavyes in Northampton County for public use.

Anthony Johnson was hardly atypical; other blacks owned substantial property in other counties. In 1656, for instance, Benjamin Doyle imported six persons and received a patent for three hundred acres of land in Surry County. In this same period some enterprising members of the first generation of blacks bought and leased land from whites. In 1668 John Harris bought fifty acres of land from a white man in New Kent County. Shortly after 1676 Phillip Morgan leased two hundred acres of land in York County for ninety-nine years.

One can hardly doubt, in the face of these examples, that the first generation of blacks had, as J. H. Russell pointed out, "about the same industrial or economic opportunities as the free white servant." Some members of this generation moved with ease and profit in the white marketplace. Some became big planters and dealt with other planters on a basis of substantial equality.

Scarcely less surprising is the fact that the first generation of blacks voted and participated in public life. It was not until 1723, in fact, that blacks were denied the right to vote in Virginia. According to Albert E. McKinley, blacks also voted in North Carolina until 1715, in South Carolina until 1701, and in Georgia until 1754. Blacks not only voted, but they also held public office. There was a black surety in York County, Virginia, in the first decades of the seventeenth century, and a black beadle in Lancaster County, Virginia.

What has been outlined above with reference to Virginia holds good also—though with slight modifications—of other colonies. The first blacks apparently arrived in Massachusetts from the West Indies in 1638 on the *Desire*, America's first slave ship. And although the record is not as firm as we could wish, it seems that they were assigned the status of indentured servants. In any case, there was a period of legal indeterminacy in Massachusetts as well as in Virginia. There is no better authority on this point than Lorenzo J. Greene, the author of *The Negro in Colonial New England*. "Freedom [in New England]," he writes, "was gained in several ways. Some Negroes had never been actual slaves, that is, bound to service for life; they were indentured servants. Not being used to chattel slavery, English colonists in the seventeenth century, as repeatedly asserted, were not familiar with the law and practice of perpetual bondage. It has also been shown that to a great degree the New Englanders, influenced by the Mosaic Law, regarded the slave as synonymous with the Hebrew 'servant,' who was to serve for six years and then go free. In fact, until almost the end of the seventeenth century the records refer to the Negroes as 'servants' not as 'slaves.' For some time no definite status could be assigned to incoming Negroes. Some were sold for a period of time only, and like the white indentured servant became free after their indenture...."

Somewhat similar factors appear to have been at work in New York, where the black landing preceded the English or even the name New York. When Peter Minuit negotiated the flagrantly fraudulent deal in which he "bought" Manhattan Island from the Indians for a handful of beads and trinkets, there were apparently some blacks in the Dutch population. At any rate, there are records from 1626 identifying eleven blacks —about 5 percent of the non-Indian population—who were listed as servants of the Dutch West India Company. We know the names of at least four of the eleven: Paul d'Angola, Simon Congo, Anthony Portuguese, and John Francisco. The eleven "pioneers by proxy," to use Roi Ottley's apt phrase, were all males; and they, like the first black Virginians, were apparently seized on the high seas from the Spaniards. Two years after the landing of the eleven males, the Dutch imported three black women who were identified as "Angolans." These were apparently the first non-Indian women in New York.

In New York, as in Virginia, the first generation of blacks worked on company land, clearing the timber, cultivating crops, and building roads and houses. They undoubtedly helped erect the wall which was built as a defense against expected attacks from the English and the Indians. This wall ran along a lane later named Wall Street.

In 1644, eighteen years after their arrival, the "Dutch Negroes," as they were called, staged the first black legal protest in America, filing a pointed petition for freedom. Unbelievable as it may seem in retrospect, the petition was granted. In February, 1644, the Council of New Netherland freed the eleven blacks because they had "served the Company seventeen or eighteen years" and had been "long since promised their freedom on the same footing as other free peoples in New Netherland." The eleven persons freed were Paul d'Angola, Big Manuel, Little Manuel, Manuel de Gerrit de Rens, Simon Congo, Anthony Portuguese, Gracia, Peter Santome, John Francisco, Little Anthony, John Fort Orange. All received parcels of land in what is now Greenwich Village.

It appears from the record that New York blacks stood on the same footing as white indentured servants from the very beginning. "They had almost full freedom of motion and assembly," James Weldon Johnson wrote; "they were allowed to marry; wives and daughters had legal protection against the lechery of masters, and they had the right to acquire and hold property." From other sources it may be learned that the first generation of New York blacks were "free and familiar." One Captain Graydon, who spent some time in the colony as a prisoner of war, said later that "their blacks, when they had them, were very free and familiar; sometimes sauntering about among the whites at meal time, with hat on head, and freely joining occasionally in conversation, as if they were one and all of the same household."

The New York and Virginia experiences were repeated, with minor variations, in other colonies, especially Pennsylvania, where the system of black indentured servitude was so deeply entrenched that there were probably more black indentured servants than black slaves at the time of the American Revolution.

# THE FIRST GENERATION

*I*T is very difficult to determine the precise number of blacks in these colonies in the first decades of the seventeenth and eighteenth centuries. According to the best estimates, there were some 375,000 whites and 58,000 blacks in the colonies in 1715. At that time there were 2,000 blacks and 96,000 whites in Massachusetts, 4,000 blacks and 27,000 whites in New York, 2,500 blacks and 45,800 whites in Pennsylvania, 9,500 blacks and 40,700 whites in Maryland, 23,000 blacks and 72,000 whites in Virginia, and 10,500 blacks and 6,250 whites in South Carolina.

Who were these black immigrants? Where did they come from? What did they want?

The answer to the first question is simple. They were Africans—of course. This is one of those facts so big that it is easily overlooked, or assumed without question; and yet it is the key to an understanding of the first generation of blacks. *They were Africans.* They were former citizens of states and principalities on the West Coast of Africa, displaced persons forcibly transported to a strange and hostile environment to do the dirty and unpleasant work. Not only were they Africans, but they were carriers of an African worldview. To be specific, they had ideas about social organization and the nature of the forces that controlled the world. They also had technical skills, particularly in the area of agriculture, which was well developed in Africa. "It ought not to be forgotten," Du Bois says with his usual acumen, "that each Negro slave brought to America during the four centuries of the African slave trade was taken from definite and long-formed habits of social, political, and religious life."

It is necessary to make this point with some force because it is so often overlooked or ignored. To be sure, some of the black immigrants were more than Africans and less than Africans. In other words, some of them were cosmopolites who had spent months or years wandering in the white roads of the West. Some, as we have seen, had been baptized into the Church of Rome or the Church of England or the Church of Amsterdam. Some were Muslims. Some had undergone the seasoning process—the process by which Africans were taught pidgin English and the rudiments of the English system—in the West Indies or England.

Nobody knows and nobody will ever know for sure precisely what country in Africa made the first sacrifices for America. But we can be reasonably sure that most of the first immigrants came from "Angola," that vague, omnibus term white slavers used to denote all the countries on the

West Coast of Africa. It should be noted, however, that certain of the first black immigrants were specifically identified as natives of Madagascar off the East Coast of Africa.

All of these points serve to press home the fact that the first black immigrants were far from homogenous. Not only did they come from different countries and different kinship groups, but they also spoke different languages and dialects and reflected different aspects of the African worldview. Most apparently were average citizens, but some were warriors, priests, noblemen, and even kings and queens. There are repeated references in the Virginia record to persons of high rank. A contemporary witness, Hugh Jones, tells us that Africans "that have been kings and great men [in their countries] are generally lazy, haughty, and obstinate." A remarkable case in point was reported by John Josselyn, an English traveler who was visiting Samuel Maverick of Massachusetts in 1639:

> The second of October, (1639) about 9 of the clock in the morning, Mr. Mavericks Negro woman came to my chamber window, and in her own Countrey language and tune sang her very loud and shrill, going out to her, she used a great deal of respect towards me, and willingly would have expressed her grief in English; but I apprehended it by her countenance and deportment, whereupon I repaired to my host, to learn of him the cause, and intreat him in her behalf, for that I understood before, that she had been a Queen in her own Countrey, and observed a very humble and dutiful garb used towards her by another Negro who was her maid. Mr. Maverick was desirous to have a breed of Negroes, and therefore seeing she would not yield by persuasions to company with a Negro young man he had in his house, he commanded him, wil'd she nill'd she, to go to bed with her, which was no sooner done, but she kicked him out again, this she took in high disdain beyond her slavery and this was the cause of her grief.

In the person of this bewildered queen of an unnamed country we catch a glimpse of the myriad persons of whatever rank who were the helpless victims of a human holocaust unleashed by desperate and ambitious men. In this same story we are witnesses to the inevitable but nonetheless tragic communications problems of the first generation of blacks, who were forced to sing their "own Countrey language and tune" in a strange land.

## THE FIRST GENERATION

We might observe, in passing, that the old records throw a revealing light on the controversy over African-American names. According to these records, the first African-Americans entered America with Spanish rather than English names. Antonio, for example, was exceedingly popular among males in the seventeenth century. Other popular names included Michaela, Couchaxello, Mingo, Pedro, Carlos, Dago, Andrewa, Sancho, Francisco, Jibina, Maria, Dando, Isaiah, Wortello, Tomora, Black Jack, Angola, Tony Kongo. The second generation of blacks generally discarded the Spanish and African names for more prosaic English words. By the end of the seventeenth century, there were substantial numbers of second-generation blacks named John, Mary, Sam, etc.

Of whatever name, of whatever rank, the carriers of this tradition resisted the illegitimate authority of Englishmen. It was difficult, we are told, to break in new black immigrants. Edward Kimber, an English traveler, said some Africans refused to yield to the requirements of the new system. "To be sure," he said, "a *new Negro*, if he must be broke, either from Obstinacy, or, which I am more apt to suppose, from Greatness of Soul, will require more hard Discipline than a young Spaniel; You would really be surpriz'd at their Perserverance: let an hundred Men shew him how to hoe, or drive a Wheelbarrow, he'll still take the one by the Bottom, and the other by the Wheel; and they often die before they can be conquer'd." The hoe was a widely used agricultural implement in West Africa, and the refusal of some Africans to use it properly in the new environment was an indication of that day-to-day resistance to servitude that became a permanent feature of the African arsenal.

There were other modes of resistance, including arson, suicide, and homicide. The most common mode of resistance, however, was flight. As early as 1640, as we have seen, there was a dramatic break for freedom in Virginia by John Punch and other indentured servants. From that year until the end of slavery, indentured servants and slaves repeatedly ran away from their masters. Some of these runaways settled in Indian villages and entered into a close and continuing entente with the first Americans. Several historians have remarked with interest that not a single black perished in the great Indian attack on Virginia in 1622. There is other evidence to indicate that the Indians generally killed all whites and spared all blacks.

For almost all Africans, the forced adaptation to Engish ways involved mind-boggling changes, including the enforcement of severe and unremitting toil, the banishment of African gods, and the destruction of the African family. In the descriptions that have come down to us from that period, no mention is made of the responses of Africans to the forced acculturation. It is necessary, therefore, to add these to the picture by reading between the lines of the standard sources. Despite the relatively fluid racial situation, one may be sure that black people, even then, wrestled with questions of identity. One observes with interest that many African customs survived and that black people gathered in large groups for "feasts and burials." In 1680 the Virginia Assembly said that "the frequent meetings of considerable numbers of negroe slaves under pretence of feasts and burials is judged of dangerous consequence." At a somewhat later date, Henry Knight witnessed a funeral in Virginia and wrote: "They sing and dance and drink the dead to his new home, which some believe to be in old Guinea." Along with these examples, it is to be noted that black immigrants amused themselves and others by telling stories and tall tales of Africa. One Senegambia, for instance, was justly celebrated in the Narragansett section of Massachusetts for her eloquence as a teller of tales.

It is obvious from all this that the first black Americans moved to the sound of distant drummers their contemporaries could neither hear nor see. On one level, the more superficial level, this expressed itself in the "strange" African songs and dances almost all commentators noted. But the sound of the drum, the curve of the melody, and the spasm of muscles possessed by waves of rhythm were only the tips of vast icebergs of culture that reached to unfathomable depths in the minds of the first blacks.

For most of the seventeenth century, most Africans apparently hoped for a miracle that would enable them to return to Africa. As the years passed, with no sign of a miracle, many abandoned hope and decided to make the best of a bad situation. Whatever the rationale, it is established beyond doubt that many made the transition with a facility that gives point to Kenneth Stampp's observation that the first generation of blacks were as prepared for freedom as the tenth generation. To the Virginia cases already cited, we might add the case of the black woman who became a full member of the church in Dorchester, Massachusetts, only three years after the arrival of the *Desire*. By that time, 1641, there were at least forty black members of the Bouweire Chapel in New Amsterdam. In the same year two Africans, Anthony von Angola and Lucie d'Angola, were married in the Dutch church in New Amsterdam. These cases are apropos—

as are several others—for the light they shed on the activities of the first blacks, who were slowly, painfully shaping the foundations of the black family of the nineteenth and twentieth centuries.

The transition was made with equal aplomb in the world of work. Most of the first generation of blacks were skilled farmers who made several innovations that were later credited to their white masters. An early example of this was reported in Virginia, where the governor ordered rice planted in 1648 on the advice of "our Negroes," who said that conditions in Virginia were as favorable to the production of the crop as "in their Country." This happened in so many cases that the skill of the first blacks became a part of the folklore, a fact noted by Washington Irving in the following satirical sketch: "These Negroes, like the monks of the Dark Ages, engross all the Knowledge of the place, and being infinitely more adventurous and more knowing than their masters, carry on all the foreign trade; making frequent voyages in canoes, loaded with oysters, buttermilk, and cabbages. They are great astrologers predicting the different changes of weather almost as accurately as an almanac. . . ."

Not all of the first generation of blacks were field hands by any means. Some were artisans, some were barbers and sailors, and some were professional men. One instance of a black professional man was reported in Connecticut, where one Primus served as an apprentice to a doctor. When the doctor died, Primus struck out on his own, becoming "extraordinarily successful throughout the country." Alice M. Earle, the chronicler of that area, said that "even his master's patients did not disdain to employ the black successor, wishing no doubt their wonted bolus and draught." Another pioneer black doctor was Lucas Santomee, a free black who was "well-known in the colony [of New Amsterdam] as a physician."

All in all, then, the first decades of the seventeenth century were decades of hope and some promise for blacks, who moved among the white inhabitants with a freedom that would be denied most of their descendants.

This situation began to change in the middle of the seventeenth century. As we have already indicated, there were individuals in the colonies who used any and every pretext to increase the burdens of their neighbors. In the 1620s and 1630s, these men invented a number of devices to increase the burdens of white indentured servants. Fortunately for the white servants and unfortunately for the black servants, a combination of circumstances isolated and exposed the increasingly large number of immigrants from non-European countries. What put steam into this movement and increased the dangers of black immigrants was the fact that it coincided with the interests of the rising class of planters, who had accumulated considerable capital by midcentury and were increasingly aware of the economic potential of gang labor on large plantations.

We can trace this development with some precision in Virginia, where there were scattered but unmistakable signs of a deterioration in the position of blacks in the 1630s and 1640s. The tension points (then and now) were sex and power. In September, 1630, for instance, a white man, one Hugh Davis, was "soundly whipt before an assembly of negroes [sic] and others for abusing himself to the dishonor of God and the shame of Christianity by defiling his body in lying with a negro. . . ." Ten years later, in October, 1640, another white man, Robert Sweat, was "whipt at the whipping post" for getting a black woman with child. In considering this record, one must be careful to remember, however, that similar punishment was meted out to whites for sexual transgressions with other whites.

Sex continued to be a problem in Colonial Virginia, not to the servants, who got on famously, but to the men of power, who were scandalized by the broad tolerance of the bulk of the white population. There were accordingly repeated attempts to establish a clear line of demarcation between Protestant Christians and non-Christians and Catholic servants, and to limit the opportunities and the potential power of Americans (Indians), Asians, and Africans. For reasons of state and power, Virginia declared in 1640 that all colonists except blacks were to arm themselves against the Indians. More ominously, the celebrated John Punch was sentenced, in the same decade, to lifetime servitude for running away from his master.

These developments, though suggestive, were not conclusive. As Oscar and Mary Handlin have pointed out in a perceptive essay, the laws relating to blacks were not at all unique before the 1660s.* Nor did they establish an irreversible trend. The same thing can be said of the scattered attempts of a handful of big planters to reduce individual blacks to slavery. Consider, for example, the case of one Manuel, who was sold "as a slave for-ever" by Thomas Bushrod. In September, 1644, the Assembly ruled that the "said servant was . . . no Slave and [was] to serve as other Christian servants do. . . ." Clearly, the situation was still open at that date. Some

---

*Immigrants from Ireland were banned from the militia in Maryland and other colonies. There was also widespread discrimination against the Scotch and Welsh. It should also be noted that a Massachusetts law of 1652 required blacks to serve in the militia. By the end of the century blacks were specifically barred in Massachusetts.

form of servitude was still a distinct possibility for all laborers; so was an open system of free labor for all. But as the years wore on, socioeconomic forces—the limited supply of poor whites, the political situation vis-à-vis the Indians, and the unprotected status of African-Americans—tilted the scales of fate in the direction of the black immigrants. The end result was a fateful national decision, a terrible and unchangeable moment of truth that would live on, deep in the psyche of the nation, giving the American story a new dimension and an aura of tragedy.

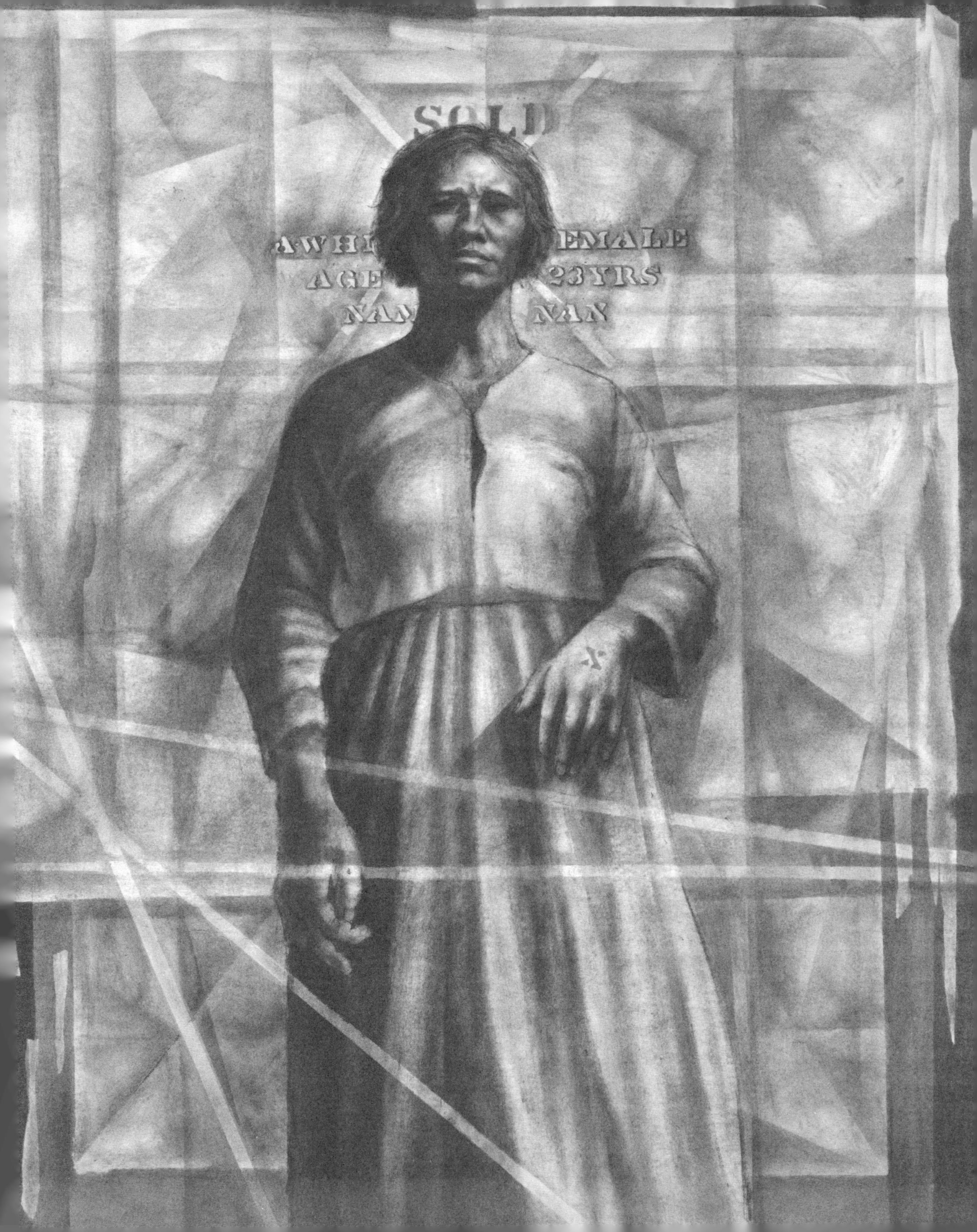
SOLD
AGE
23YRS
NAN

# *White Servitude*

*A*LTHOUGH great care has been taken to hide the fact, black bondsmen inherited their chains from white bondsmen, who were, in a manner of speaking, America's first slaves. And as America moved, in the middle of the seventeenth century, toward a fateful decision that would define it forever, increasing attention was directed to the status of these white bondsmen, who pioneered in both servitude and slavery. To understand what happened to blacks in the second half of the seventeenth century, one must first understand what happened to these whites in the first and second halves of the seventeenth century. For they ran the first leg of the marathon of American servitude before passing on the baton of anguish to the reds and the blacks.

The story of this succession, the story of how white bondsmen passed on the torch of forced labor to blacks and of how whites created a system of white servitude that lasted in America for more than two hundred years, has never been told before in all its dimensions.* For obvious reasons, the traditional embalmers of the American experience seem to find white servitude enormously embarrassing. In any case, they generally ignore it, dwelling instead on black servitude. But this maneuver—and it is precisely that—distorts both black bondage and the American experience. For white bondage and red bondage are the missing legs on the triangle of American servitude, a triangle that defines the initial American experience as an experiment in compulsion. Both red and white bondage were integral parts of that experiment, but white bondage was particularly important for two reasons. In the first place, white bondage lasted for more than two centuries and involved most of the first white immigrants to the American colonies. It has been estimated that at least two out of every three immigrants to the colonies south of New York worked for a term of years in the fields or kitchens as semi-slaves.

The second and possibly more important reason for the centrality of white servitude is that it was, as Eric Williams noted, "the historic base upon which Negro slavery was constructed." In other words, white servitude was the proving ground for the mechanisms of control and subordination used later in African-American slavery. The plantation pass system, the slave trade, the sexual exploitation of servant women, the whipping post and slave chain and branding iron, the overseer, the house servant, the Uncle Tom: all these mechanisms were tried out and perfected first on white men and women. Also tried out and perfected first on white men and women was the theory of racism. It is not the least of the paradoxes of this period that Colonial masters used the traditional Sambo and minstrel stereotypes to characterize white servants, who were said to be

---

* There has been an obvious attempt to play down or minimize the importance of white servitude. Few general books have been written on the subject, and most of these are out of print or hidden away in secluded scholarly nooks. Some textbooks and scholarly works manage to cover the entire Colonial period without mentioning white servitude. Others cover the subject in a line or two. See James C. Ballagh, *White Servitude in the Colony of Virginia*; E. I. McCormac, *White Servitude in Maryland*; C. A. Herrick, *White Servitude in Pennsylvania*; Eric Williams, *Capitalism and Slavery*; Abbot Emerson Smith, *Colonists in Bondage*.

good-natured and faithful but biologically inferior and subject to laziness, immorality, and crime. U. B. Phillips, who was wrong about so many things in the slave regime, was at least right about this. "In significant numbers," he wrote, "the Africans were latecomers fitted into a system already developed." Indisputably, and in view of that fact, it is plain that nothing substantial can be said about the mechanisms of black bondage in America except against the background and within the perspective of white bondage in America.

As was the case of black bondage, the controlling cause was not biology but economic demand as refracted through the peculiar prisms of European power groups with little or no sympathy for the poor and underprivileged. The opening of the New World gave a new twist to the peculiar perceptions of these groups and brought to the surface Europe's ancient (Athens) and enduring (the Third Reich) fascination with unfree labor. And it was this fascination, honed to a fine edge by the possibility of colossal profits, that condemned millions of blacks, reds, and whites to the horrors of extended servitude. The very important point here is that both black and white bondage grew out of and reflected the internal tensions of Europe. These tensions revolved around certain ideas about the proper subordination of *white* people, and a new milieu of competitive egoism growing out of the Renaissance and the Commercial Revolution. And out of this there finally emerged a new spirit of adventure and ruthlessness that included a certain contempt for all human beings and a willingness to use any and every expedient in the search for gold, glory, and conquests for God.

These mental attitudes reflected, in turn, certain material contradictions in Europe, which was a confused and afflicted place on the eve of colonial expansion. The situation was particularly turbulent in England, where the upper classes were engaged in the bloody process of driving the peasants from the land. One consequence of this process was that the relief rolls of the country, on the eve of the founding of the plantations of Virginia and Massachusetts, bulged with supplicants, and the roads swarmed with beggars, vagabonds, and thieves.

It was in this setting of social nightmare that England embarked on its career of colonialism. One of the main reasons for this departure was the idea that England needed a dumping ground for its undesirables. As Bacon put it in a state paper delivered to James I in 1606, colonization gave England "a double commodity, in the avoidance of people here, and in making use of them there." Five years later, in 1611, Velasco, the Spanish minister to England, said the same thing in different words. "Their principal reason for colonizing these parts is to give an outlet for so many idle, wretched people as they have in England, and thus prevent the dangers that might be feared of them."

Whatever the rationale, one thing is clear: the "idle, wretched" people became the first fodder of colonialism. And they played this role under a system of forced labor with deep roots in European experience. By this time, of course, the institution of slavery had virtually died out in Europe. But other forms of forced labor, including the apprenticeship system, were common. And when the opening of the New World created a demand free labor could not satisfy, European powerbrokers created a system of forced labor based loosely on the old apprenticeship system. Under the new system, called indentured servitude, a person sold himself or was sold for a specified number of years (usually from two to seven, although some were sold into lifetime servitude) to pay the cost of his transportation to America. The indentured servants, as the first white bondsmen were called, signed a contract of indenture in England or America. A typical indenture, signed in 1682/3, is reproduced below:

> This Indenture made the *21st February 1682/3* Between *Rich. Browne aged 33 years* of the one party, and *Francis Richardson* of the other party, witnesseth, that the said *Rich. Browne* doth thereby covenant, promise, and grant to & with the said *Francis Richardson* his Executors & Assigns, from the day of the date hereof, until h*is* first & Next arrival *att New York or New Jersey* and after, for and during the term of *foure* years, to serve in such service & imployment, as he the said *Francis Richardson* or his Assigns shall there imploy h*im* according to the custom of the Country in the like kind—In consideration whereof, the said *Francis Richardson* doth hereby covenant and grant to and with the said *Richard Browne* to pay for h*is* passing, and to find and allow h*im* meat, drink, apparel, and lodging, with other necessaries, during the said term, & at the end of the said term to pay unto *him according to the Custom of the Country*.
>
> In Witness thereof the parties above mentioned to these Indentures have interchangeably set their Hands and Seals the day and year above written.

There were other servants, called redemptioners, who were given transportation on the basis of their promise to pay the captain after arrival in an American port. If the redemptioner could not arrange to pay the captain, either by borrowing the money from friends or relatives or by selling himself or members of his family, he was sold by the ship captain.

This system did not spring full blown from the heads of the original settlers. It evolved, piece by piece, act by act, within the context of the colonial syndrome. The system was based at first on a voluntary contract that carried with it no implication of servility. But, as James C. Ballagh has shown, the system deteriorated and "tended to pass into a property relation which asserted a control of varying extent over the bodies and liberties of their person during service as if they were things." The indentured servant, in other words, tended to become a de facto slave for the length of the indenture. For all that, there were distinct and important differences between indentured servitude and slavery, which was *hereditary* and *perpetual*.

The system of white servitude evolved in America, but it evolved within a context of experience that came to America with the first white immigrants, most of whom were de facto slaves. Something of this comes out in the history of Virginia where, before 1619, as Ballagh has proved, practically every inhabitant was "a servant manipulated in the interest of the [Virginia] Company, held in servitude beyond a stipulated term." This caused no end of trouble between the company and the servants, who complained repeatedly that they were being treated like slaves. The complaints of the white servants were by no means groundless. For the residents were driven to work in gangs and punished severely for minor infractions. Anyone who missed church on Sunday was to "lye neck and heels that night" and be "a slave" for a week. For the third offense, the person was to be a slave for a year and a day.

Thus, the white founding fathers of Virginia.

They were hardly alone. For roughly the same thing happened in Massachusetts, where the Puritans began their famous crusade for democracy by reducing to servitude a relatively large number of white men and women. It was in 1628, eight years before the first evidence of Indian servitude and ten years before the first hint of black servitude, that white bondage began in the Puritan Commonwealth. In that year, 180 servants landed at Salem to prepare the food and homes for the pioneers of the history books, who came over a year later. When the celebrated *Mayflower* arrived, the principle of white unfreedom came with it. At least sixteen of the passengers were white indentured servants. There were parallel developments in other colonies. William Penn founded Pennsylvania on the rock of white servitude, and the same principle was made white flesh in South Carolina, Maryland, and the other original colonies.

Besides the men and women held to service or labor, several white pioneers were reduced to slavery within a few years of the first landing. In 1609 a Virginia colonist named Henry Spelman was apparently sold to the Indians by Captain John Smith. Spelman, who was rescued a year later, said: "I was carried by Capt. Smith, our President, to ye Fales, to ye litell Powhatan, wher, unknown to me he sould me to him for a town called Powhatan." This was apparently a fairly common occurrence in the early days. For we also read that in 1609 Admiral Newport gave Powhatan a boy named Thomas Salvage in exchange for an Indian servant.

Not only were white men bartered and exchanged, they were also openly sentenced to slavery for penal offenses. Such a case occurred in 1641 in Massachusetts, where William Andrews was condemned to slavery by the General Court for assaulting his master. In the same year, two other white men, John Haslewood and Giles Player, were sentenced to slavery for theft and housebreaking. By 1642 at least six white men had been condemned to slavery in Massachusetts for various offenses. (Some were apparently released before their death.) There is also the remarkable case of the Connecticut white man who was sold into slavery in Barbados because of "notorious stealing, breaking up and robbing two mills and living in a renegade manner in the wilderness."

Although some Indians were reduced to slavery and servitude in the first years of the English settlement, Colonial masters evinced a decided preference for the poor whites of Europe. From the start, poor white children from the streets and almshouses of London and Amsterdam were shipped to the colonies. There were also irregular shipments of laborers and maids, some of uncertain character. Beginning in 1619—a significant date—Colonial masters began to shape this irregular traffic into an organized system. Ironically enough, the first step on this road was taken at the first meeting of a representative political body in America. At its first meeting in Jamestown, in July, 1619, the Virginia House of Burgesses provided for the recording and enforcement of contracts of indenture, made it illegal for female servants to marry without the consent of their masters and authorized masters to whip their servants. These acts legalized indentured servitude in Virginia and provided for a statutory class of unfree laborers. Hence, representative democracy and servitude

—white servitude—were born together in America. To make sure everyone got the message, the legislature transformed itself into a high court and sentenced a refractory white servant to stand four days with his ears nailed to the pillory.

When the first blacks landed at Jamestown, they found the system of indentured servitude firmly established and most of the white population living in the shadow of chains. Writing from Virginia in that year, John Pory said that "our principall wealth consisteth in servants." This "wealth," to use the current phrase, increased dramatically in the following years. In 1627 some fifteen hundred kidnapped children were sent to Virginia. And their services were so satisfactory that authorities pleaded for another shipment of the "friendless boyes and girles." In 1636 there were some five thousand persons in Virginia, and it has been estimated that at least three thousand of them had come to the colony as servants. All in all, it is said that at least eighty thousand indentured servants were imported by Virginians in the Colonial period.

The story was very much the same in other colonies. Tens of thousands of displaced white persons streamed into Maryland, Pennsylvania, and the Carolinas. In one four-year period, some twenty-five thousand white servants were shipped to Philadelphia alone. Because of the nature of the white servant trade, it is very difficult to determine precisely how many indentured servants were shipped to the colonies. It appears, however—and this is a very conservative estimate—that at least 250,000 persons were indentured servants during the Colonial period. This figure, it is worth noting, does not include the sizeable number who died during the white Middle Passage.

*WHO* were these people? Where did they come from? How did they come?

The answers to these questions are to be found not in the myth of the pure white settlement, but in the short and simple annals of the poor and the oppressed. The cast of characters in this drama included victims of every imaginable description. There were political and military prisoners captured in war or rebellion. There were Quakers and Catholics fleeing Protestant oppression, Germans and Swiss Protestants fleeing Catholic oppression, and Jews fleeing Catholic and Protestant oppression. There were rogues, whores, orphans, convicts, and derelicts, all the mangled victims of the social and political upheavals of the time. "People of every age and kind," Abbot Emerson Smith wrote, "were decoyed, deceived, seduced, inveigled, or forcibly kidnapped and carried as servants to the plantations."

The servants came from all over Christian Europe—from Germany and Holland and Switzerland and Scotland. Most, however, came from England and Ireland.

They came, these Christian demi-slaves, the same way most blacks came, crammed shoulder to shoulder, toe to toe, the living and the dead side by side, in the unventilated holds of crowded ships. In this respect, as in others, there were striking similarities between the white servant trade and the black slave trade. (It was not for nothing that the trade in Irish servants was called the Irish Slave Trade.) The same techniques were used to capture Africans in Africa, Englishmen in England, and Germans in Germany; and the same ports (Bristol, Liverpool) were used by the same merchants and captains to transport them. It is a point of immense importance here that some of the big African slave traders acquired their experience and capital in the white servant trade.

As in the African Slave Trade, so in the European Servant Trade: the victims were recruited by fraud and violence. Most of the major traders and captains relied on hired agents, who were called "spirits" in England and newlanders in Germany. These agents, who were paid so much a head for each person recruited, scoured the countryside, distributing propaganda leaflets and trumpeting the virtues of life as a bonded servant in Virginia or Maryland or Pennsylvania. But when these methods failed, other forms of persuasion were used, including kidnapping and coercion, usually with the explicit or implicit sanction of the authorities. Hence, the name Spirit, which was defined as "one that taketh upp men and women and children and sells them on a shipp to be conveyed beyond the sea." Enticing children with candy, derelicts with rum, and the gullible with stories of the pot of gold awaiting them in the American colonies, Spirits entrapped tens of thousands. They also resorted to force and violence, kidnapping children and adults on the streets of Bristol and other cities and holding them in depots until the day of departure. We have a report on one of these depots by a man who was kidnapped and held in Wapping. He was carried into a room, he said, "where half a score were all taking Tobacco: the place was so narrow wherein they were, that they had no more space left, than what was for the standing of a small table. Methought their mouths together resembled a stack of Chimneys, being in a manner totally obscured by the smoak that came from them; for there was little discernable but smoak, and the glowing coals of their pipes. Certainly the smell of this room would have outdone *Assa Foetida*.... After I had been there awhile, the Cloud of their smoak was somewhat dissipated, so that I could discern two more in my own condemnation: but alas poor Sheep, they ne're considered where they were going, it was enough for them to be freed from a seven years Apprenticeship, under the Tyranny of a rigid Master ... and not weighing ... the slavery they must undergo for five years, amongst Brutes in foreign parts, little inferior to that which they suffer who are *Gally-slaves*. There was little discourse amongst them, but for the pleasantness of the soyl of that Continent we were designed for, (out of a design to make us swallow their gilded Pills of Ruine), & the temperature of the Air, the plenty of Fowl and Fish of all sorts; the little labour that is performed or expected having so little trouble in it, that it rather may be accounted a pastime than anything of punishment; and then to sweeten us the farther, they insisted on the pliant loving natures of the Women there; all which they used as baits to catch us silly Gudgeons...."

The bait was apparently effective, for thousands were spirited away. One man said he spirited away five hundred persons a year for twelve years. Another man, one William Thiene, was accused in 1617 of spiriting away 840 persons in a single year. As can be imagined, this was not a particularly good period for people who liked to walk the streets alone. In fact, things got so bad in London that one could precipitate a major riot by shouting, "Spirit!"

There were other strategems, equally successful. Some ship captains made a practice of visiting the Clerkenwell House of Corrections and plying the women prisoners with drinks. When the women were sufficiently drunk, the captains, with the connivance of the warden, would carry them off to America. The captains also recruited prostitutes. On November 17, 1692, one Narcissus Luttrell noted in his diary "that a ship lay in Leith going for Virginia, on board which the Magistrates had ordered 50 lewd women out of the houses of correction, and 30 others who walked the streets after 10 at night."

At different periods in the course of the servant trade, there were special projects like the controversial plan for sending one thousand young Irish girls to Jamaica for breeding purposes. No one seems to know what happened to this plan, but there is a letter of one Henry Cromwell which throws a curious light on the age. "Concerninge the younge women, although we must use force in takinge them up. Yet it beinge so much for their owne goode, and likely to be of soe great advantage to the publique, it is not in the least doubted, that you may have such a number of them as you shall think fitt to make use upon this account."

Since it was widely believed that colonization was of "soe great advantage to the publique," the courts were used to recruit white servants. One could be sentenced in this period to "transportation" and seven years exile in the colonies for a number of offenses, including petty theft, maiming and killing cattle, and trade union activity. Persons convicted of these and other crimes were shipped to the colonies and were known familiarly as His Majesty's Seven-Year Passengers. The best estimates suggest that at least fifty thousand convicts were shipped to the American colonies in this period and that most of them went to Virginia and Maryland, which were known, in some circles, as "penal colonies." Marcus W. Jernegan, author of *Laboring and Dependent Classes in Colonial America*, commented: "In this connection, it has been suggested that American genealogists in search of missing data to complete their family tree would find a rich mine of unexplored material in the archives of [the prisons of] Newgate and Old Bailey, the latter filling 110 manuscript volumes."

Also condemned for extended periods of servitude were Irish Catholic priests, Quakers, and Scottish and Irish soldiers taken in war or rebellion. In 1652, for instance, 270 Scotchmen captured at the Battle of Dunbar were sold in Boston. One year later one hundred Tories were transported from Ireland to be sold as slaves in America. Some of the political prisoners, as the last example indicates, were slaves condemned, in the language of the day, "to serve in our colonies in America during the term of their natural lives."

There was another penal category, an omnibus category, loosely identified as "rogues and vagabonds." These persons were identified in the famous language of statute 39, Eliz., c. 4, as:

> All persons calling themselves Schollers going about begging, all Seafaring men pretending losses of their Shippes or goods on the sea going about the Country begging, all idle persons going about in any Cuntry eyther begging or using any subtile Crafte or unlawful Games or Playes, or fayning themselves to have knowledge in Phisiognomye Palmestry or other like crafty Scyence, or pretending that they can tell Destenyes Fortunes or such other like fantasticall Imag-

ynacons; all persons that be or utter themselves to be Proctors Procurers Patent Gatherers or Collectors for Goales Prisons or Hospitalls; all Fencers Bearewards comon Players of Enterludes and Minstrells wandring abroade (other then Players of Enterludes belonging to any Baron of this Realme . . . ); all Juglers Tynkers Pedlers and Petty Chapmen wandring abroade; all wandring persons and comon Labourers being persons able in bodye using loytering and refusing to worcke for such reasonable wages as is taxed or comonly given in such Parts where such persons do or shall happen to dwell or abide, not having lyving otherwyse to maynteyne themselves; all persons delivered out of Gaoles that begg for their Fees, or otherwise do travayle begging; all such persons as shall wander abroad begging pretending losses by Fyre or otherwise; and all such persons not being Fellons wandering and pretending themselves to be Egipcyans, or wandering in the Habite Forme or Attyre of counterfayte Egipcians.

There were finally the partners and offsprings of unhappy or poverty-stricken families. It was not unusual in this day for aggrieved husbands and wives to contrive to have their spouses removed from the country. Nor was it unusual for desperate parents to conspire with Spirits to rid themselves of children they could not or would not care for. "Among those who repair to Bristol" for America, the mayor of Bristol said in 1662, "some are husbands that have forsaken their wives, others wives who have abandoned their husbands, some are children and apprentices run away from their parents and masters."

Runaway children, recreant husbands and wives, political prisoners, prisoners of war, prostitutes, religious dissenters, convicts, kidnapped waifs, rogues, vagabonds, dreamers—all were assembled, by fair means and foul, at ports of embarkation and packed like fish into the holds of ships for the eight-to-twelve week trip to America. Under the best circumstances, this trip was a harrowing experience. Under the conditions imposed on the servants, it was almost unendurable. There was little or no room for movement between decks, the food was poor, and the air foul. The plight of white servants was admirably illustrated by the case, cited in a petition to Parliament in 1652, of seventy-two servants who were locked up below deck during the entire voyage of some six weeks "amongst horses, that their souls, through hot and steam under the tropic, fainted in them." This was not exceptional, as the voluminous evidence on the servant trade indicates. Henry Laurens, the South Carolinian who bought and sold white and black flesh, said he "never saw an Instance of Cruelty in Ten or Twelve years experience in that branch [the African Slave Trade] equal to the cruelty exercised upon these poor Irish. . . . Self-interest prompted the baptized Heathens [captains] to take some care of their wretched Slaves for a Market, but no other care was taken of those poor Protestant Christians from Ireland but to deliver as many as possible alive on Shoar upon the cheapest terms." Sometimes, as Laurens and others testified, more than half of the servants died before the ships reached America.

When the ships arrived in American ports, the dead were thrown overboard, and the survivors were cleaned up for on-deck sale. In some cases both men and women were stripped naked and examined by prospective buyers.

"The servants were produced from their quarters," Abbot Emerson Smith wrote, "the prospective purchasers walked them up and down, felt of their muscles, judged their states of health and morality, conversed with them to discover their degrees of intelligence and docility, and finally if satisfied, bought them and carried them off home." He added: "The whole scene bore resemblance to a cattle market; a number of servants afterwards compared themselves to horses displayed for sale."

Like the slaves who followed them, the white servants were separated and sold with little or no regard for family connections. Husbands and wives were separated, and children under five were sold or given away until their twenty-first birthday.

"Many parents," Gottlieb Mittleberger, a contemporary witness said, "must sell and trade away their children like so many head of cattle."

The price of white flesh, like the price of black flesh, varied according to the time and place and the strength, age, and skill of the servant. But the average price for a healthy white man or a healthy white woman seems to have been from fifteen to twenty pounds in the first part of the seventeenth century.

One could, of course, make better deals. There is a record of a white man who was sold for four cows in Maryland in 1641. A century later a ship captain told a committee of the Irish House of Commons that he got about thirty-five barrels of pitch or turpentine for each Irishman sold in North Carolina.

The trade in white flesh was a big business, and the men who succeeded in that business used accepted merchandising and marketing skills, including newspaper advertisements. Here are some examples:

> Just imported from Ireland and
> to be sold on Board the Ship
> Virtue, John Seymour, Master, now
> in the Harbour of Boston, a parcel
> of healthy men Servants chiefly
> Tradesmen.

> JUST ARRIVED
> In the ship Sophia, Alexander Verdeen, Master, from
> Dublin, Twenty stout, healthy Indentured
> MEN SERVANTS
> Whose Indentures will be disposed of on reasonable
> Terms, by the Captain on board, or the
> subscribers

> Several very likely servants, tradesmen and
> husbandmen, lately arrived from Bristol; to
> be sold very reasonable by Captain Samuel Bromage
> or Mr. Thomas Sharpe

It was not unusual for merchants to sell blacks, whites, and Indians from the same auction block. In 1714 Samuel Sewall, a prominent Boston merchant, offered for sale

> several Irish Maid Servants time
> most of them for Five Years one
> Irish Man Servant who is a good
> Barber and Wiggmaker, also Four
> or Five Likely Negro Boys

Some enterprising and insensitive merchants, called "soul-drivers," bought servants in lots of fifty or more and drove them through the countryside, selling them by ones and twos to local planters.

It would be a mistake to assume that this was a subterranean business, condemned by men of substance and goodwill. On the contrary, the leading men of the colonies were engaged in it, both as buyers and sellers. George Washington bought white indentured servants; so did William Carter and Robert Beverly. Some of the leading Colonial planters and merchants, such as Carter and Beverly of Virginia, had a hand in the Indian, European, and African trade.

Once the sale was consummated, the servant became subject to the will, whim, and interest of another human being. In theory, as we have seen, he had limited legal rights, including the right of appeal to a court of masters. In practice, as almost every student of white servitude has pointed out, he was a de facto slave until the end of his indenture. "They became in the eyes of the law," said J. B. McMaster, "a slave and in both the civil and the criminal codes were classed with the Negro and the Indian. They were worked hard, were dressed in the cast off clothes of their owners, and might be flogged as often as the master and mistress thought necessary...." There is similar testimony from T. J. Wertenbaker, who said that "the indentured servants . . . were practically slaves, being bound to the soil and forced to obey implicitly those whom they served;" and C. A. Herrick, who said that "no matter how kindly they may have entered into the relation, as a class and when once bound, indentured servants were temporarily chattels."

*THE* laws defining the servant's rights and obligations varied from state to state, but there were common structures. As a rule, servants could not marry without the consent of masters and could not buy whiskey or engage in trade. They could not leave the plantation area without a pass or raise their hand against their master. Nor could they vote or hold office.

Like the slave, the servant could be bought, sold, borrowed, won or lost in a card game, given away as a prize, seized for a debt, pledged as security on a loan, and transferred in a will. The master, on the other hand, was obligated to feed and clothe the servant and to give him certain "freedom dues" (corn, clothes and, in some cases, land) at the end of his term. But there is plenty of evidence to indicate that masters did not always live up to their obligations. Some, in fact, did everything they could to extend the time of their servants, who were tricked, forced, or penalized into second and third terms.

Like most social systems, white servitude produced and reproduced itself. In the colonies, as in England, the courts manufactured servants by sentencing poor whites to servitude for relatively minor infractions and by increasing the time of rebellious servants.

As the system developed in America, other forms and styles of servitude sprang up. Children born out of wedlock and the children of the poor were routinely bound out until they were twenty-one. It was also common for poor whites to "voluntarily" sell themselves into servitude to pay medical expenses and other debts. In 1675 a Virginia white man named Lambert Groton "voluntarily" sold himself into lifetime servitude in order to satisfy a debt of 3,200 pounds.

Whatever the form, whatever the style, white servitude was a system designed to extract the maximum amount of labor power from poor whites. Some of these whites were artisans, and some were teachers, musicians, and bartenders. Most, however, were field hands, and most—male and female—worked the traditional slave hours from dawn to dusk. It is perhaps of parenthetic interest that white historians are virtually unanimous in denying that white women were forced to work in the fields. Contemporary witnesses, however, tell us in no uncertain terms that white women were forced to work in the fields, and there are records of a number of cases in which white women asked the courts to relieve them of this burden. The record on this point is as clear as it can be, and the only mystery is why so many competent white historians have been driven to the extremity of denying what the record so clearly affirms.

In the field and in the house, male and female white servants worked alongside black and red servants and slaves. Many lived with blacks and Indians in primitive huts they were forced to build. Occasionally, servants —black and white, male and female—lived in the same small house with the master.

Most of the white servants were illiterate, most of them were male, and most were relatively free of racial prejudice. Most, moreover, were divided by internal boundaries relating to religion and nationality. And it is worthy of note that white planters commented at length on the "racial" characteristics of the various "tribes" of white people. Most observers said the Scotch and German servants were the best servants and that the Irish were the worst. One must remember, however, that the evidence comes almost entirely from the white upper class. The servant, like the slave, left few records to tell his side of the story.

How did the servant fare under this system?

How did white masters treat white servants?

If we can credit contemporary witnesses and surviving records, white masters treated white servants the same way they treated black servants —and black slaves. That is to say, they drove them hard in the fields, lashed them unmercifully, and appropriated their labor power. In general, it can be said, on the basis of contemporary reports and the writings of scholars, that the lot of the white servant was often worse than the lot of the slave. In a letter written in 1770, William Eddis said that "Negroes being a property for life the death of slaves in the prime of youth and strength is a material loss to the proprietor. . . . They are therefore under more comfortable circumstances than the miserable Europeans over whom the rigid planters exercise an inflexible severity. . . . Generally speaking, they [white servants] groan beneath a worse than Egyptian bondage." This testimony is corroborated by another contemporary witness, Richard Lignon, who said he saw in Barbados "such cruelty done to Servants, as I did not think one Christian could have done to another."

There is additional evidence on this point from the servants, who complained repeatedly of cruel and abusive treatment. There was, for example, the case of the master who was carried to court for hanging a servant "up by the heels as butchers do beasts for the slaughter." This master, it was said, was "rebuked" by the court. But there were other masters who escaped punishment and admonition, although they were charged with beating servants to death. To all this must be added the fact that the law of white servitude, like the law of black servitude, was cruel and violent. It was customary, at least in the early days of white servitude, to nail the ears of offenders to the pillory. The law also sanctioned the removal of the ears of rebel servants and provided for the whipping of male and female offenders until the blood flowed. The laws relating to runaway servants—black and white—were exceedingly harsh. A Maryland law of 1639 said that a servant convicted of running away should be executed. Less extreme but no less oppressive was a Virginia law of 1642/3 that required a servant who ran away for the second time to be branded on the cheek or shoulder with the letter R. In view of all this, we should not be surprised to learn that white servant women were systematically exploited by white masters and overseers. "Many of this class of women," Philip A. Bruce wrote, "were exposed to improper advances on their master's part as they were by their situation, very much in the power of these masters, who, if inclined to licentiousness, would not be slow to use it." Many were so inclined, as the frequency of legislation on the subject proves.

From the outset white servants conspired and attempted to revolt. But most of the white conspiracies and revolts, like most of the black conspiracies and revolts, were betrayed by favorite servants—in this case, favorite white servants. Interestingly enough, white historians use the same conceptual apparatus in their explanation of the number of white and black revolts. Abbot Emerson Smith, for example, says that "a disposition to general rebellion seems scarcely to have existed among servants on the continent, perhaps because the chance of success was negligible as compared with that on a relatively small island." This statement should be taken with a grain of salt. For white resistance to the system developed early and continued throughout the Colonial period.

Like the slaves, white servants ran away repeatedly, leaving the plantations late at night, beating their way through the forests, swimming creeks and rivers, pursued all the while by posses and dogs. In a generally unsuccessful attempt to stop the flow of runaways, Colonial masters adopted the first fugitive servant/slave laws and filled Colonial newspapers with revealing evidence on the barbarity of the system. Here are some typical ads for runaway white servants:

> Run away about Two Years ago from Cecil County in Maryland, Nicolas Collings, small Statue, bushy Hair almost Grey: A Shoemaker by Trade. Whoever secures him, and gives notice therefore to Mr. Abel van Burkeloo of the said County, shall have Ten Shillings Reward.

> RAN AWAY, from the subscriber, living on Monocacy, Carroll's Manor, in Frederick County, 6 miles from Frederick-Town, on the 27th of December last, *an indented Irish* Servant *Man* known by the name of *Patrick Quigley*, a Shoemaker by trade, of middling stature, well set, of ruddy complexion, short black hair, about 5 feet 2 or 3 inches high, 24 years of age; had on and took with him when he absented a felt hat half worn, short blue sailor's jacket; red waistcoat, pair of white cloath breeches, a pair of white and a pair of black speckled milled stockings, and a pair of old shoes with steel buckles. Whoever takes up the Said Servant and brings him to the subscriber or secures him in any goal, so that his master may get him again shall have, if taken 20 miles from home, TWENTY SHILLINGS, if 30 miles, THIRTY SHILLINGS; if a farther distance THREE POUNDS, including what the law allows, and reasonable charges, if brought home to
>
> DANIEL HARDMAN.

January 8, 1785

Most of the advertisements were prosaic and matter of fact. Some, however, reflected creativity, if not compassion:

> Last Wednesday noon, at break of day
> From *Philadelphia* ran away
> An Irishman named John McKeoghn,

> To Fraud and imposition prone;
> About five feet five inches high,
> Can curse and swear as well as lie. . . .

In the matter of runaways, as these advertisements show, there was absolutely no difference between the institutions of slavery and white servitude. Significantly, some of the advertisements indicated that the white servants wore collar chains and were scarred and maimed, presumably by cruel treatment.*

Such, in broad outline, was the situation of the white indentured servants, as America approached a fateful fork in the road.

At this juncture, white servants constituted the economic base of the colonies, and it was widely believed, as the Council of Montserrat said in 1680, that "not one of these colonies ever was or ever can be brought to any considerable improvement without a supply of white servants and Negroes." In 1756 the president of the council of Pennsylvania told Governor William Shirley of Massachusetts that "every kind of Business here, as well among the Tradesmen and Mechanicks as the Planters & Farmers, is chiefly carried on and supported by the Labour of Indented Servants." At about the same time Governor Horatio Sharpe of Maryland said that "the planters Fortunes here consist in the number of their Servants (who are purchased at high Rates) much as the Estates of an English Farmer do in the multitude of Cattle."

Not only were white servants the basis of the wealth of the early colonies; they were also the basis of a huge and growing system of servility. By the last decade of the seventeenth century, servitude had become a part of the fabric of America, and the famous settler syndrome —arrogance, protofascism, insensitivity to human needs, and a tendency toward unreality—was well developed. "The system of indentured service in its social effects," Philip Bruce said, "differed but little, if at all, from

---

* Although there were periodic demands for the emancipation of white people, the system of white servitude survived in America until the third decade of the nineteenth century. Even the Revolutionary War, with its rhetoric of liberty and equality, failed to free the white bondsmen of America. As a matter of historical fact, some white Americans claimed at the time that keeping white servants was part of the inalienable rights of mankind. In 1778, for instance, a revolutionary committee of Cumberland County, Pennsylvania, adopted the following resolution: "Resolved that all Apprentices and servants are the Property of their masters and mistresses, and every mode of depriving such masters . . . of their Property is a violation of the Rights of Mankind."

the system of slavery. It really accentuated the social divisions among the whites more distinctly than the presence of the institution of slavery did. . . . It gave purely class distinctions a recognized standing in the colonial courts of law. It was not until the end of the century that Negro bondsmen became numerous on the plantations, and yet in social spirit the seventeenth century in Virginia did not differ from the eighteenth. The ever-increasing multitude of African slaves after 1700 simply confirmed the social tendencies which had previously been fostered by the presence of the indentured whites."

As one could expect, this state of affairs pleased some masters, and plans were afoot in the latter part of the seventeenth century to create a permanent system of white servitude. One need only read John Locke's *Fundamental Constitutions of Carolina* to realize the depth of this sentiment. This extraordinary document, which has received insufficient attention in the general literature, declared boldly for a hereditary aristocracy based on a permanent system of forced labor—black and white. This document is persuasive evidence in favor of the argument that the American colonies had not decided on their name or their orientation in 1669. But that decision could not be long delayed, and the mere adoption of such a drastic measure was a clear sign that the colonies were approaching a fork of truth.

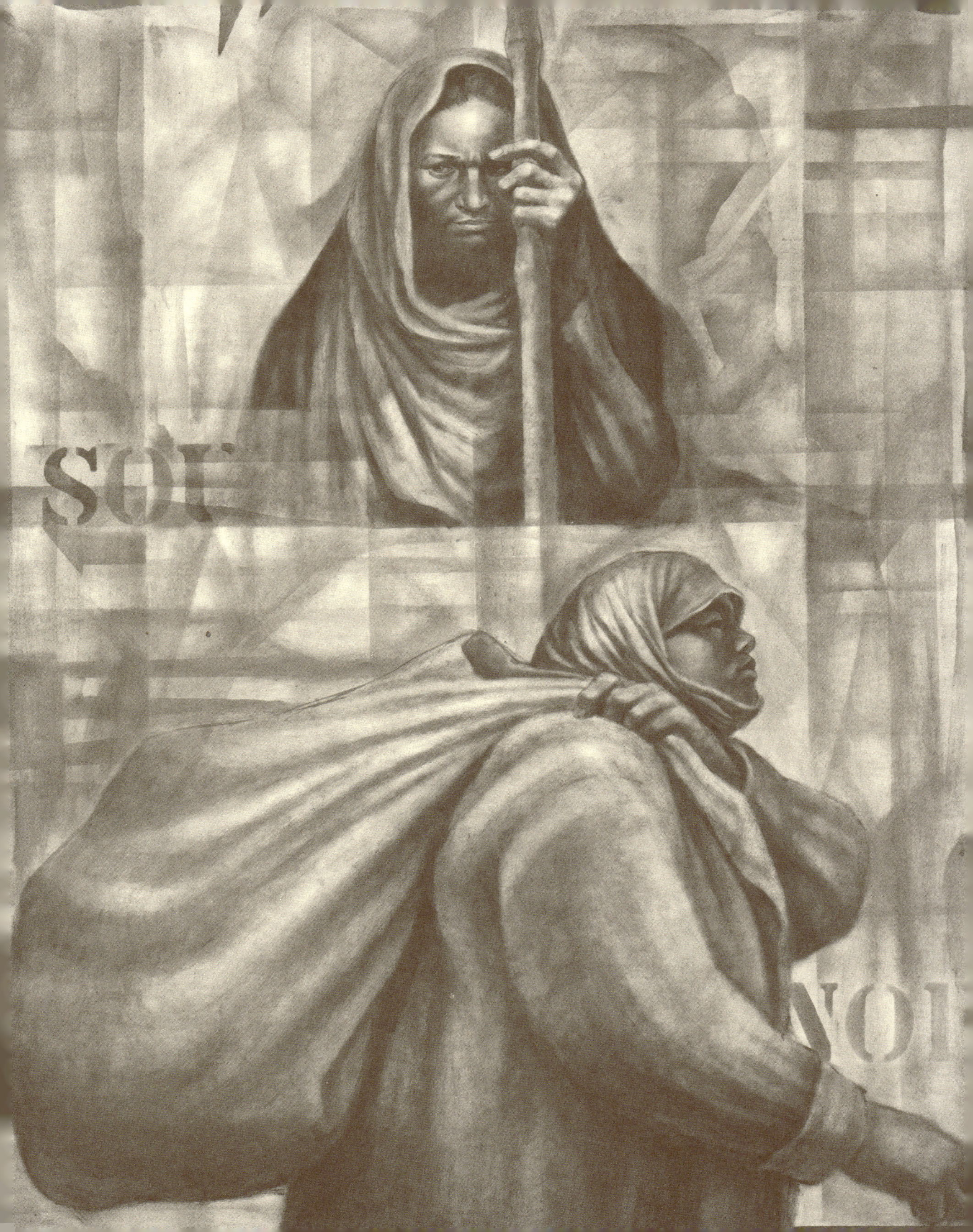
SOU
NOI

# *The Road Not Taken*

*A* nation is a *choice*. It chooses itself at fateful forks in the road by turning left or right, by giving up something or taking something—and in the giving up and the taking, in the deciding and not deciding, the nation *becomes*. And ever afterwards, the nation and the people who make up the nation are defined by the fork and by the decision that was made there, as well as by the decision that was not made there. For the decision, once made, engraves itself into the landscape, engraves itself into things, into institutions, nerves, muscles, tendons; and the first decision requires a second decision, and the second decision requires a third, and it goes on and on, spiralling in an inexorable processus which distorts everything and alienates everybody.

America became America that way.

Fork by fork, step by step, option by option, America or, to be more precise, the men who spoke in the name of America decided that it was going to be a white place defined negatively by the bodies and the blood of the reds and the blacks. And that decision, which was made in the 1660s and elaborated over a two-hundred-year period, foreclosed certain possibilities in America—perhaps forever—and set off depth charges that are still echoing and re-echoing in the commonwealth. What makes this all the more mournful is that it didn't have to happen that way. There was another road—but that road wasn't taken. In the beginning, as we have seen, there was no race problem in America. *The race problem in America was a deliberate invention of men who systematically separated blacks and whites in order to make money*. This was, as Kenneth Stampp so cogently observed, a deliberate choice among several alternatives. Slavery, he said, "cannot be attributed to some deadly atmospheric miasma or some irresistible force in the South's economic evolution. The use of slaves in southern agriculture was a deliberate choice (among several alternatives) made by men who sought greater returns than they could obtain from their own labor alone, and who found other types of labor more expensive...."

It didn't have to happen that way. Back there, before Jim Crow, before the invention of the Negro or the white man or the words and concepts to describe them, the Colonial population consisted largely of a great mass of white and black bondsmen, who occupied roughly the same economic category and were treated with equal contempt by the lords of the plantations and legislatures. Curiously unconcerned about their color, these people worked together and relaxed together. They had essentially the same interests, the same aspirations, and the same grievances. They conspired together and waged a common struggle against their common enemy—the big planter apparatus and a social system that legalized terror against black and white bondsmen. No one says and no one believes that there was a Garden of Eden in Colonial America. But the available evidence, slight though it is, suggests that there were widening bonds of solidarity between the first generation of blacks and whites. And the same evidence indicates that it proved very difficult indeed to teach white people to worship their skin.

All this began to change drastically in the sixth decade of the seventeenth century. The decade of the 1660s: this was the first great fork in the making of black America. For it was at this fork that certain men decided to ground the American economic system on human slavery. To understand that great fork, one must understand first the roads leading to it—roads that were not taken.

The first road—a road never seriously considered, although it was open, at least for a while—was the road of fraternal cooperation with the Americans, i.e., the Indians, in a program of free and creative development of the immense resources of the American continent. This obviously would have required consummate diplomacy and an abandonment of the peculiar European idea that Europeans were divinely ordained to appropriate the resources and alter the institutions of non-Europeans. It would have involved, in other words, the transformation of both Americans and Europeans and the creation of a new synthesis made up of the best elements of both configurations. This road—the only road to justice—was rejected out of hand by the white founding fathers, who adopted a policy of genocide.

The second road, also rejected, was a free and cooperative system of labor for all immigrants. This would have involved, at a minimum, an abandonment of the European principle of masters and servants and would have required all men to live by the sweat of their brow. Because the Europeans were already hooked on the master principle, because they could never somehow get over the idea that it was necessary for somebody else to work for them, this road was not taken. And the decision not to take that road left only two alternatives: temporary servitude and eventual freedom for all workers—red, black, and white—and the road of permanent servitude based on the work of one or possibly all three of the subordinate labor groups. This last road was taken, and one group was singled out for permanent servitude. Why?

To answer that question, we must back up again and consider the groups not selected.

First, the Indians. A popular idea to the contrary notwithstanding, the Indians were enslaved in all or most of the colonies. But Indian slavery and servitude created problems that the colonists preferred to deal with in other ways. To begin with, there was the problem of security. It was difficult to keep Indian servants and slaves from running away because they knew the country and could easily escape to their countrymen, who were only a forest or river away. Another and possibly more persuasive argument against large-scale enslavement of Indians was that the supply was relatively limited. Finally, and most importantly, Indian servants and slaves were members of groups with a certain amount of power. These groups could (and did) retaliate. For this combination of reasons, it was considered unwise to enslave large groups of Indians, who were usually sold into slavery in the West Indies.

From the standpoint of the masters, the poor whites of Europe presented equally serious problems. The supply of poor whites, like the supply of Indians, was limited; and poor whites, like Indians, but for different reasons, could escape and blend into the whiteness of *their* countrymen. The most serious problem, however, was that poor whites had tenuous but nonetheless important connections with circuits of power. There were pressure groups in England that concerned themselves with the plight of poor whites. This fact alone drastically limited the options of Colonial masters. For in order to safeguard the relatively limited supply of poor whites, it was necessary to make costly—from the standpoint of the masters—concessions to white servants and to improve their living conditions.

The last group—the group finally selected—did not have these disadvantages, as Oscar and Mary F. Handlin noted: "Farthest removed from the English, least desired, [the African] communicated with no friends who might be deterred from following. Since his coming was involuntary, nothing that happened to him would increase or decrease his numbers. To raise the status of Europeans by shortening their terms would ultimately increase the available hands by inducing their compatriots to emigrate; to reduce the Negro's term would produce an immediate loss and no ultimate gain. By midcentury the servitude of Negroes seem generally lengthier than that of whites; and thereafter the consciousness dawns that the Blacks will toil for the whole of their lives. . . ."

Unhappily for the Africans, they had none of the disadvantages of the Indians and poor whites, and they had—again from the standpoint of the planters—distinct advantages. They were marked by color and hence could not escape so easily. The supply seemed to be inexhaustible, and the labor of Africans was relatively inexpensive when compared with the cost of transporting and maintaining white indentured servants for a limited number of years. This last fact was decisive, and it was clearly understood by the colonists as early as 1645. It was in that year that

Emanuel Downing sent a famous letter to his brother-in-law John Winthrop, saying, among other things: "If upon a Just Warre the Lord shold deliver [Narragansett Indians] into our hands, wee might easily have men woemen and children enough to exchange for Moores, which wilbe more gaynefull pilladge for us then wee conceive, for I doe not see how wee can thrive untill we get into a stock of slaves sufficient to doe all our business, for our children's children will hardly see this great Continent filled with people, soe that our servants will still desire freedome to plant for themselves, and not stay but for verie great wages. And I suppose you know verie well how wee shall mayneteyne 20 Moores cheaper than one Englishe servant."

Twenty Africans for the price of one English servant—how could a Puritan resist such a deal! And how could he overlook the final and deciding factor: the Africans were *vulnerable*. There were no large power groups nearby to retaliate in their name. Nor did they have power groups on the international scene to raise troublesome questions. They were, in fact, naked before their enemies, and their enemies were legion.

As the pointer on the roulette wheel neared the African number, the power brokers of England suddenly and dramatically increased the odds against Africans by announcing a new policy of restricted white emigration and massive support of the African Slave Trade. With the formation of the Royal African Company (1672), the wheel of fate came to an abrupt halt before the black square. For henceforth, as James C. Ballagh has pointed out, it would be "the policy of the king, and of the Duke of York, who stood at the head of the [Royal African] Company, to hasten the adoption of slavery by enactments cutting off the supply of indented servants, at the same time that large importations of slaves were made by their agents."

But we must take care here to preserve perspective. Ballagh is suggesting, as others suggested before and after him, that history or some impersonal force decided for the colonists. But history is made by men and not by circumstances. And if history created the circumstances and the alternatives, it was still left to men in the colonies to choose between the alternatives. That happened, in the first instance, in isolated areas in the menacing decade of the 1640s. In that decade certain men in Maryland, Virginia, and Massachusetts began holding certain Africans in lifetime servitude. There are some indications that this was a deliberate gambit on the part of designing men who wanted to force a favorable legal decision in favor of slavery. If so, the gambit had its desired effect. For the first legal enactment in favor of slavery in the colonies came in 1641 in Massachusetts, which declared in its Body of Liberties that there "shall never be any bond slaverie, villinage or Captivitie amongst us, unless it be lawfull Captives taken in just warres, and such strangers as willingly sell themselves or are sold to us." This was, all things considered, a fateful and ominous "unless," for the following words clearly authorized African, Indian, and European slavery. Once the genie was out of the bottle, there was a more or less deliberate effort to create a legal structure for slavery, a fact noted by Herbert S. Klein, who said: "Once these first hints about the existence of a status of slavery within the colony [of Virginia] had been made by the legislature, there seems to have developed at this point a conscious effort on the part of the Virginians to create a statutory framework on which to firmly base this condition."

This effort unfolded, roughly, in four stages. The first stage, linked, in part, with the Massachusetts precedent, was the extension of the term of black servants from a specified number of years to life. Following Massachusetts on this point were Connecticut in 1650, Virginia in 1661, Maryland in 1663, New York and New Jersey in 1664, South Carolina in 1682, Pennsylvania and Rhode Island in 1700, North Carolina in 1715, and Georgia in 1755.

The second and more momentous stage, a stage that marked the institutional divergence of servitude and slavery, was the introduction of the principle of heredity. Virginia pioneered in this development, declaring in December, 1662: "*Whereas* some doubts have arisen whether children got by any Englishman upon a negro woman shall be slave or ffree, *Be it therefore enacted and declared by this present grand Assembly, that all children borne in this country shall be held, bond or ffree only according to the condition of the mother.* . . ."

This raised more questions and doubts than it answered. For what precisely was a Negro? And what was the child of a Negro man and a white woman? And what in the world was a white person? Was it a matter of blood or culture or Christianity?

The third phase of the process—defining slavery and providing a rationale for the system—was involved almost entirely with a farcical quest for answers to these questions. The first question requiring attention was the question of religion, for religion and not race was the first rationale for slavery. This caused no end of problems for Colonial masters, for it was an axiom of their faith that freedom in Jesus Christ was real. More to the point: the whole colonization crusade of the colonists was based on the idea of carrying the word to the "heathens." How then could they deny freedom to a "heathen" who had seen the light? The answer, as usual, was both practical and profitable. "Baptism," to quote Ballagh again, "thus involved a dilemma. If conferred it sealed the pious end of slavery but freed the Christian slave. On the contrary, if enfranchisement was a possible result, Christianization was certain to be retarded or completely stopped. The wisdom and the conscience of colonial assemblies were equal to the emergency. They held both to their justification and to their slaves. The Virginia Assembly in a law of 1667 presents but a typical example of general colonial action. It settled the question by the naive declaration, worthy of the metaphysician that rightly separates the spiritual person from bodily form, 'Baptisme doth not alter the condition of the person as to his bondage or freedom; in order that diverse masters freed from this doubt may more carefully endeavor the propagation of Christianity.'"

That settled that, but it did not settle the legal question of who could be enslaved. And in 1670 the Virginia legislature spoke again on the subject, saying: "All servants not being Christians imported into this country by shipping shalbe slaves for life." Whether by design or accident, this law excepted blacks who had been baptized in Africa, Europe, the West Indies, or other colonies. But this loophole was eliminated in the act of 1682 which declared that ". . . all servants except Turks and Moores . . . which shall be brought or imported into this country, either by sea or land, whether Negroes. . . . Mullattoes or Indians, who and whose parentage and native country are not christian at the time of their first purchase of such servant by some christian, although afterwards, and before such their importation . . . they shall be converted to the christian faith. . . . shall be judged, deemed and taken to be slaves. . . ." In plain English, this meant that all Jews, Asians, and Africans (except Turks and Moors) were subject to slavery in Virginia. It meant also that Virginia was embarking on the process (completed in the eighteenth century) of basing slavery on race rather than religion. (The Virginia legislature finally said that a Negro was anyone with one Negro grandparent.)

In this manner Virginia (and America) crossed a great divide, a divide that requires some elaboration. For what was involved here was the idea of racism, which is not an individual idea or peculiarity but an institutionalized ideology that commits the institutions of a society to the destruction of a people because of race. The idea developed by the Virginians (and Americans) was simple and profitable. The idea was that all whites were biologically superior to all blacks, who were infidels and heathens, a dangerous and accursed people who embodied an evil principle that made them dangerous to the morals and the politics of the community. The truth or falsity of this idea disturbed few men then (or now). The only thing that mattered was that this idea or something like it was necessary to justify past, present, and future aggression against blacks.

With the institutionalization of this idea, the structure of slavery was almost complete. There remained only the fourth phase, a phase that continued for two hundred years and involved the destruction of the legal personality of the slave.

The first step in this direction was the declaration that the slave was the property of the master. As such, the slave could not hold property or engage in trade or commerce. Nor could the slave as a piece of property *move* without the express consent of his master. He could not leave the plantation without a pass, he could not gather in large groups, he could not commit himself to a marriage vow. More ominously, he could not even defend himself. In the words of the codes, he was in the "condition of a natural person, in which, by the operation of law, the application of his physical and mental powers depend[ed] . . . upon the will of another. . . ."

BY these words and acts, and in these stages, the masters of Colonial America committed themselves and America to the institution of human slavery. Having made that decision, the masters had to make another decision, for neither the masters nor the servants had been prepared for the new script of roles in the statutes. Nature does not create masters or slaves. Nor does it create blacks or whites. In order to make masters and slaves, in order to make blacks and whites, it is necessary to kill them —it is necessary to separate them by rivers of blood. But terror alone is not enough. One must condition the mind and the eye and the heart. And the conditioning of one generation must be repeated in the next generation and on and on ad infinitum. The men who ran Colonial America did not shrink from these exigencies. Moving swiftly and ruthlessly, they began in the middle of the seventeenth century to separate blacks and whites and to create a race problem in America.

Curiously enough, there is no full-length treatment of this process. Most historians avoid the subject by positing a natural or cultural bias in the European psyche. But this maneuver fails to explain why this natural or cultural bias manifested itself in one way in 1619 and another way in 1819 or why it developed in one way in Maryland, another way in Massachusetts, and a third way in Brazil. Nor is it possible, from the traditional standpoint, to explain why the laws against blacks became progressively worse and differed significantly in different demographic and economic situations. From time to time, some historians admit, in so many words, that the traditional view is untenable. Stanley Elkins, for example, who has advanced a fanciful theory of slavery, said that "the interests of white servants and blacks were *systematically* driven apart." After reading the same evidence, the Handlins said that "the emerging difference in treatment [of blacks and whites] was *calculated* to create a real division of interest between Negroes on the one hand and whites on the other." [My emphasis]

No one reading the evidence can doubt this. Nor can it be doubted that blacks and whites had to be taught the meaning of blackness and whiteness. This is not to deny "differences" in color and hair formation, etc. It is only to say that perceptions had to be organized to recognize the differences and that men had to be organized to take advantage of them. The so-called differences were not the cause of racism; on the contrary, men seized on the differences and interpreted them in a certain way in order to create racism. Not only did they exploit "differences," but they also created "differences" and preserved them by force and violence. The differences, in other words, were rationalizations and excuses, not the causes of racism. Once established, however, the ideology of rationalizations assumed a calamitous autonomy and influenced the interests from which they derived.

Who was responsible for this policy?

The white founding fathers, the Byrds, the Mathers, and Winthrops, the Jeffersons, the Washingtons, *the heroes of all the Fourths of July:* they divided blacks and whites, they sowed the seeds of division and hate and blood. In an attempt to evade the implications of this fact, some men blame "the English" or "Colonial public opinion." But Colonial public opinion was the public opinion of the planter-merchant aristocracy. As

T. J. Wertenbaker, Philip A. Bruce, James Hugo Johnston and scores of other scholars have pointed out, the colonies were run by a closed set of men who monopolized political, ecclesiastical, and economic power. "The system of life built up in the agricultural colonies," James Hugo Johnston writes, "resulted in planter control. Both social and governmental institutions were devices wrought by the planters. The system of Negro slavery may have been thrust upon them by England, but the problems arising from it were first of all the planters' problems; and on the governing class is the responsibility for the system of slave institutions worked out in the colonies." There is corroboration on this point from another authority, Philip A. Bruce, who says that "the whole power of Virginian society even in the times when universal suffrage prevailed, was directed by the landowners. That society was composed entirely of the landed proprietors and their dependents. . . . The public sentiment was exclusively the sentiment of men who, like the landowners of England, looked to agriculture for the income which went to the support of their families, and whose only material interests were those associated directly with the soil."

Not only did the planters have the power; they also had a vested interest in black exploitation. It was on their plantations that the new system of black servitude was tried out for the first time, and by midcentury, as Elkins notes, blacks had accumulated in large enough parcels in the hands of the colony's big planters to develop in these men a vested interest in the new system. "The advantages of slave labor," Wertenbaker says, "were manifest to planters of the type of William Byrd or William Fitzhugh, men who had built up fortunes by their business ability. It is but natural that they should have turned early from the indentured servants to stock their plantations with the cheaper and remunerative African workers." Herbert S. Klein adds: "The Virginia planter, in his drive for a more economic system of labor, was the first to reduce the Negro to the status of a servant for life. But the judiciary and the legislature, which were uniquely representative of and in fact entirely composed of the members of the planter class, were not far behind in taking cognizance of this growing customary law governing the Negro's condition, and they early gave recognition to this whole body of practice." In the face of these testimonies, one can hardly escape the impression that it was the big planters and their allies who reduced the vulnerable and powerless black servants to slavery and enacted legislation that committed every white person and every white institution to support of the new order.

How was all this done?

It was done by the creation of a total system of domination, a system that penetrated every corner of Colonial life and made use of every Colonial institution. Nothing was left to chance. The assemblies, the courts, the churches, and the press were thrown into the breach. A massive propaganda campaign confused and demoralized the public, and private vigilante groups supplemented the official campaign of hate and terror.

It was all done deliberately, consciously, with malice aforethought. To mold the minds of whites, to teach them the new ideas, and to let them know who was to be loved and who was to be despised, the planter-merchant aristocracy used every instrument of persuasion and control. In every colony, from New York to South Carolina, the same mechanisms of separation and subordination were elaborated and imposed. From New York to South Carolina, the same penalties were used to keep blacks and whites apart, the same rewards were developed to make poor whites support a system that penalized them, the same statutes were elaborated to crush and diabolify blacks.

The statutes were designed to instill a sense of superiority in whites and a sense of worthlessness in blacks. They were designed to create stereotypes and invidious images. The language of these statutes ("abominable mixture," "barbarous," "savage") was instructive; it designated, pointed out, authorized, and it was a legal requirement, in many cases, for parsons and politicians to read the language at public meetings and church services.

What we are concerned to emphasize here is that the laws were the heart and center of a massive public education campaign. The best evidence in favor of this point is the extraordinary letter Governor William Ceech wrote to the English government, which had demanded explanation of a Virginia law denying the suffrage to free blacks. Governor Ceech wrote:

> [The] Assembly thought it necessary, not only to make the Meetings of Slaves very penal, but to fix a perpetual Brand upon Free Negroes and Mulattos by excluding them from the great Privilege of a Freeman, well knowing they always did, and ever will, adhere to and favour the Slaves. And, 'tis likewise said to have been done with design, which I must think a good one, to make the free Negroes sensible

that a distinction ought to be made between their offspring and the Descendants of an Englishman, with whom they never were to be Accounted Equal. This, I confess, may Seem to carry an Air of Severity to such as are unacquainted with the Nature of Negroes, and Pride of a manumitted Slave, who looks on himself immediately On his Acquiring his freedom to be as good a Man as the best of his Neighbours, but especially if he is descended of a white Father or Mother, lett them be of what mean Condition soever; and as most of them are the Bastards of some of the worst of our imported Servants and Convicts, it seems no ways Impolitic, as well for discouraging that kind of Copulation, as to preserve a decent Distinction between them and their Betters, to leave this mark on them, until time and Education has changed the Indication of their spurious Extraction and made some Alteration in their morals.

This is a significant document that has been too often ignored by historians. We don't have to speculate on the motives of the men who created the American race problem. They tell us clearly what they were doing and why they were doing it.

They were passing laws *to preserve a decent Distinction between* blacks and whites.

They were passing laws to fix *a perpetual Brand* upon blacks.

They were passing laws *with design . . . to make free blacks sensible that a distinction* should be made between their children and the children of Englishmen.

They were passing laws to break the *Pride* of blacks.

They were passing laws *to leave this mark on them.*

And it can be said, by inverting this language, that the laws were also passed to leave a mark on whites, who were instructed, under pain of punishment, how to act in relation to blacks. Under these laws whites of all classes were penalized for expressing human impulses. It therefore became very expensive for a white person to like black people or to love them. This was not, it should be emphasized, a matter of hints and vague threats. The laws were quite explicit. Symptomatic of this were the laws passed to punish whites who befriended blacks or ran away with them.

Masters were also disciplined. The right of the master to free his slave was curbed and finally eliminated. The master was also forbidden to teach his slaves or to permit them to gather in large assemblies. Winthrop Jordan, who argues that racism was a natural or cultural bias of Englishmen, contradicts himself on this point by saying that the laws were designed to *force* workers and masters to treat black people like slaves. He writes:

> While the colonial slave codes seem at first sight to have been intended to discipline Negroes, to deny them freedoms available to other Americans, a very slight shift in perspective shows the codes in a different light; they aimed, paradoxically, at disciplining white men. Principally, the law told the white man, not the Negro, what he must do; the codes were for the eyes and ears of slaveowners.... Members of the assemblies, most of whom owned slaves, were attempting to enforce slave-discipline by the only means available, by forcing owners, individually and collectively, to exercise it.

As the years wore on, and as the number of slaves multiplied, the laws increased in severity and scope. The first laws applied only to some blacks, primarily non-Christians. But by the middle of the eighteenth century, many of the laws applied to all blacks, free and slave, Christian and non-Christian.

Behind the legislator and the planter stood the writer, teacher, and priest. The perceptions of whites and blacks were organized and manipulated by churches, which were an integral part of the governing mechanism. In some cases churches were directly involved in carrying out laws relating to indenture and sexual irregularities. In other cases churches and ministers bought and sold slaves. In still other cases churches led the campaign of villification, openly identifying blacks with Ham and the Indians with the devil.

Equally important as an adversary was the press. The owners and writers of many of the first American newspapers had direct or indirect interests in slavery, and their journals were in the front ranks of the white crusade. It is not at all surprising therefore to learn that editorials and news stories accentuated antagonisms in the colonies and that advertisements for black runaways were to the first American newspapers what advertisements for deodorant and detergent are to the electronic media of the seventies. The *Boston News Letter*, the first permanent American newspaper, published slave advertisements almost from the first edition.

The whole system of separation and subordination rested on official state terror. The exigencies of the situation required men to kill some white people to keep them white and to kill many blacks to keep them black. In the North and South, men and women were maimed, tortured, and murdered in a comprehensive campaign of mass conditioning. The severed heads of black and white rebels were impaled on poles along the road as warnings to black people and white people, and opponents of the status quo were starved to death in chains and roasted slowly over open fires. Some rebels were branded; others were castrated. This exemplary cruelty, which was carried out as a deliberate process of mass education, was an inherent part of the new system.

*THE* thrust behind the drive for separation and subordination was overwhelming. Separation paid, and was paid for. And before long slavery and the slave trade were the twin fountains of the economic system of New England and the Southern colonies. The phenomenal growth of the slave trade, the development of the plantation system, the expanding drive against Indian land—all these factors created iron bands of interests that compelled every Colonial institution to support the politics of division.

Despite this fact, there was widespread opposition to the new order in the white community, particularly among poor whites, many of whom were still indentured servants or former indentured servants. What is amazing here and worthy of detailed examination is that so many whites openly flouted the new laws and conspired with blacks to evade them. How explain this? The explanation is simple: whites, in general, had not been prepared for the new departure. In the words of one white historian, opinion had not "hardened sufficiently" against black people. In the words of another, many whites "had not learned to hold the attitude toward the Negro" that the new script demanded. In addition to these purely passive considerations, there were positive and active links between blacks and white indentured servants, who continued to run away together and to conspire together. A point of considerable importance here is that slavery did not immediately displace white servitude. For more than one hundred years, the two systems existed side by side, mutually influencing one another. For almost as long a period, the white servant and the black slave continued to interact, threatening the stability of this dual system of servitude.

In order to preserve domestic tranquility, the leading groups in the colonies made it a matter of public policy to destroy the solidarity of the laborers. Laws were passed requiring different groups to keep to themselves, and the seeds of dissension were artfully and systematically sown.

Indians were offered bounties for betraying black runaways; blacks were given minor rewards for fighting Indians; and poor whites were used as fodder in the disciplining of both reds and blacks.

At the same time masters used Draconian measures to stop the mingling and mating of blacks and whites. From the last quarter of the seventeenth century to the end of the eighteenth century, policy-makers legislated against these practices. In the process white women were whipped, banished, and enslaved to keep them from marrying black men. "The increasing number of mulattoes, through intermarriage and illicit relationships," Lorenzo J. Greene writes, "soon caused alarm among Puritan advocates of racial purity and white domination. Sensing a deterioration of slavery, if the barriers between master and slaves were dissolved in the equalitarian crucible of sexual intimacy, they sought to stop racial crossing by statute." In this instance, as in so many others, it was necessary to teach whites the value of whiteness. Under the ground rules of the time, a master could virtually enslave a white woman who married a black man and could hold in extended servitude all the issue of such a marriage. In this situation, as might have been expected, Puritan greed triumphed over Puritan morals, and many masters encouraged or forced white women to marry black men. It finally became necessary to pass laws penalizing masters for forcing white women to marry black men. The Maryland law of 1681 said:

> Forasmuch as, divers free-born *English,* or white women, sometimes by the instigation, procurement or connivance of their masters, mistresses, or dames, and always to the satisfaction of their lascivious and lustful desires, and to the disgrace not only of the *English,* but also of many other Christian nations, do intermarry with Negroes and slaves, by which means, divers inconveniences, controversies, and suits may arise ... for the prevention whereof for the future, *Be it enacted:* That if the marriage of any woman-servant with any slave shall take place by the procurement or permission of the master, such woman and her issue shall be free.

Neither statute law nor terror stopped intermarriage and interracial dating, which continued for more than a century. Strange as it may seem today, there were even some open protests against the laws. The minutes of the Council of Virginia, May 11, 1699, contain "the petition of George Ivie and others for the repeal of the Act of the Assembly, Against English peoples marrying with Negroes, Indians or Mulattoes...."

In the 1690s and the decades that followed, the central task of the masters was changing—and distorting—the perceptions of George Ivie and men and women who shared his view. This was done slowly, methodically and painfully. It was done with the carrot and the stick. It was done by enticing some with promises and browbeating others into submission by threats and blows. We have already dealt at some length with the methodology of the stick, and we should note that the carrot was also a powerful and persuasive weapon. One manifestation of this was the new state policy of favoring poor white servants, who were systematically given preference over blacks and Indians. In the last decades of the seventeenth century and the first decades of the eighteenth, the laws became increasingly liberal toward white servants, and special efforts were made to accentuate the differences between blacks and whites. As the number of blacks increased, the heavy labor was shifted to blacks, whites were employed as overseers of the slave population, and sympathetic attention was given to the petitions of white artisans. At the end of the seventeenth century, white workers in New York City filed a complaint alleging that black labor had "soe much impoverisht them, that they Cannot by their labours gett a Competency for the Maintenance of themselves and Family's." Similar petitions were filed in Massachusetts, Pennsylvania, and other colonies. Responding to these fears, the South Carolina Assembly voted in 1743 that "no slaves that shall hereafter be brought up to any mechanic trades shall be suffered to be hired out or to work for any other than their own masters."

A corollary of the strategy of the carrot was the creation of a common white front. The planters needed the silence and/or support of the poor whites. To get this support, they manipulated symbols and sanctions in such a way as to persuade poor whites to identify with masters instead of their fellow workers. The designation of poor whites as a buffer class was a particular expression of this general policy. In some colonies, "Deficiency acts" were passed to increase the number of poor whites. These acts usually offered bounties to encourage white immigration and required planters to employ a certain number of poor whites. A 1698 law of South Carolina offered the captains of ships thirteen pounds for each white servant imported and required every owner of six black slaves to buy one white servant. This and similar acts said frankly that poor whites were needed not only for labor but also for protection. In 1711 a South Carolina governor asked the House of Assembly to import whites at public expense. He went on to say that the house should consider "the large quantities of Negroes that are daily brought into this Governt., and the small number of whites that comes amongst us, and how many are lately dead, or gone off. How insolent and mischievous the Negroes are become, and to consider the Negro Act doth not reach up to some of the crimes they have lately been guilty of."

As this language makes clear, poor whites were deliberately used to insure the social system against black rebellion. In the words of Abbot Emerson Smith, poor whites were viewed as a "defense against the Negro menace." A revealing example of this was a South Carolina act "for the better securing of this province from Negro insurrections & encouraging of poor people by employing them in the Plantations." This was, to a great extent, a ruse of the planters, who bought the cooperation of poor whites by throwing them crumbs from the table. But many, perhaps most, poor whites had neither the space nor the consciousness to look gift horses in the mouth. And so, many accepted the bait, never noticing, perhaps not even caring, that it was bait and that it covered a sharp steel hook. One of the by-products of this was that most poor whites were persuaded that they had a stake in the system and that it was working to their advantage. Steadily and inescapably, a new rhythm was imposed on them, and by the middle of the eighteenth century a solid white front was developing. A curious and crucial point here is that concerted action by blacks and whites virtually ceased after the creation of the white front. What is even more interesting is that white revolt against the system almost disappeared. "Significantly," Winthrop Jordan said, "the only rebellions by white servants in the continental colonies came before the firm entrenchment of slavery."

The impact of all this on blacks and whites was disastrous. The development of the slave system and the systematic separation of blacks and whites created a race problem in America, divided the working force, made it impossible to create a single American community, and laid the foundation for an anti-democratic, hierarchial police state, taut with tensions and fears. With the creation of this system, the number of African slaves increased dramatically. On the eve of the Revolution, blacks constituted 60 percent of the population of South Carolina, 40 percent of the population of Virginia, and 30 percent of the population of Maryland. By the first census there were 757,000 blacks in America, 19.3 percent of the population.

As it turned out, the emerging slave system had an immediate and disastrous impact on poor whites. Unable to compete with the large planters, poor whites retreated to the marginal land in the hills, where they eked out a hand-to-mouth existence. To the untutored mind of the poor whites, it seemed that blacks were the cause of their misery. They therefore began to hate black people with a passion. Notice the emphasis in the following passage from the conservative historian, T. J. Wertenbaker: "While not destroying entirely the little farmer class, it [slavery] exerted a baleful influence upon it, driving many families out of the colony, making the rich man richer, reducing the poor man to dire poverty. Against this unfortunate development the Virginia yeoman was helpless. Instinctively, he must have felt the slave was his enemy, and the hatred and rivalry which even today exists between the Negro and the lowest class of whites, the so-called 'poor white trash,' dates back to the seventeenth century." The poor white was wrong: slavery, not the slave, was his enemy. But it would take time—and blood—to see this.

It was against this background that the white identity in America was forged. American whites developed a sense of personality and nationality in response to the presence of blacks and Indians. They were *not* black, they were *not* red, they were *white*. Black and red, as Jordan has pointed out, "rapidly came to serve as two fixed points from which English settlers could triangulate their own position in America: the separate meanings of *Indian* and *Negro* helped define the meaning of living in America." What Jordan fails to mention and what is equally supported by the evidence is that the white sense of identity developed in response to the forced degradation of blacks. "When the Negro slave had supplanted the indentured servant upon the plantations of the colony," Wertenbaker wrote, "a vast change took place in the pride of the middle class. Every white man, no matter how poor he was, no matter how degraded, could now feel a pride in his race. Around him on all sides were those whom he felt to be beneath him, and this alone instilled into him a certain self respect. Moreover, the immediate control of the Negroes fell almost entirely into the hands of white men of humble means, for it was they, acting as overseers upon the large plantations, that directed their labors in the tobacco fields. This also tended to give them an arrogance that was entirely foreign to their nature in the seventeenth." What this means, if it means anything, is that white character structure underwent a fundamental transformation in the crucible of slavery.

As the seventeenth century ended and the eighteenth century began, white arrogance increased, and a yawning chasm opened up between blacks and whites.

One more decision in the history of black and white had passed, never to be called back, never to be erased, never to be forgotten.

What were blacks doing all this time?

They were retreating, going back to the wall, contesting, with all the resources at their command, every inch of the ground. And it was during this retreat that the African began to forge a New World personality. This personality was colored indelibly by the fact that blacks were deliberately pushed out of the circle of community. They were *in* but not *of* Colonial America. They were the colonial subjects of the colonial subjects of England. They were not being exploited by George III but by George Washington and his class.

Responding to this situation, blacks began to define themselves in opposition to whites, who were viewed as enemies and oppressors. Nothing shows this more clearly than the remarkable ferment that began with the imposition of slavery and continued for more than a century. In 1672, 1687, 1694, 1709, 1710, 1722, 1730, and 1741, blacks conspired or staged revolts. They also committed suicide, established maroon camps, poisoned masters, and fled to the Indians.

Beyond doubt blacks wanted freedom and fought for freedom. But, as we have shown, they were powerless, and their adversaries held all the high ground. For them and for the millions who would follow, this was one of history's hard places, one of those impossible historical situations that condemn people to centuries of horror with no hope of immediate escape or salvation. There *are* impossible historical situations, and this was one of them. There was no immediate possibility of escape for the black victims, and there was no immediate possibility of triumph. And there was nothing *in the world* they could do about it, except to play the cards history had dealt, waiting and watching, taking advantage of every opportunity, extending the lines of hope and organization.

It was done.

It was done not only by the black founding fathers who began to create a new synthesis in the wilderness of North America, not only by the underground priests who remembered the drums and made others remember, not only by the fathers and mothers who began to shape the foundations, real but shaky, of the black family, not only by the "black and unknown bards" who found strength in song and rhyme and gave others strength, not only by the rebels and outlaws who, waiting and watching, seized opportunities and made thieves pay for the crime of theft—it was done, it was splendidly done, not only by these, not only by the new priests and leaders and bards but also, and perhaps most importantly, by the millions of maintaining individuals who never rose to public attention but never sank to the level the masters demanded, the millions of maintaining individuals who looked horror full in the face and endured, leaving millions of black seeds on the hard white ground, seeds that would take root and, miraculously, grow.

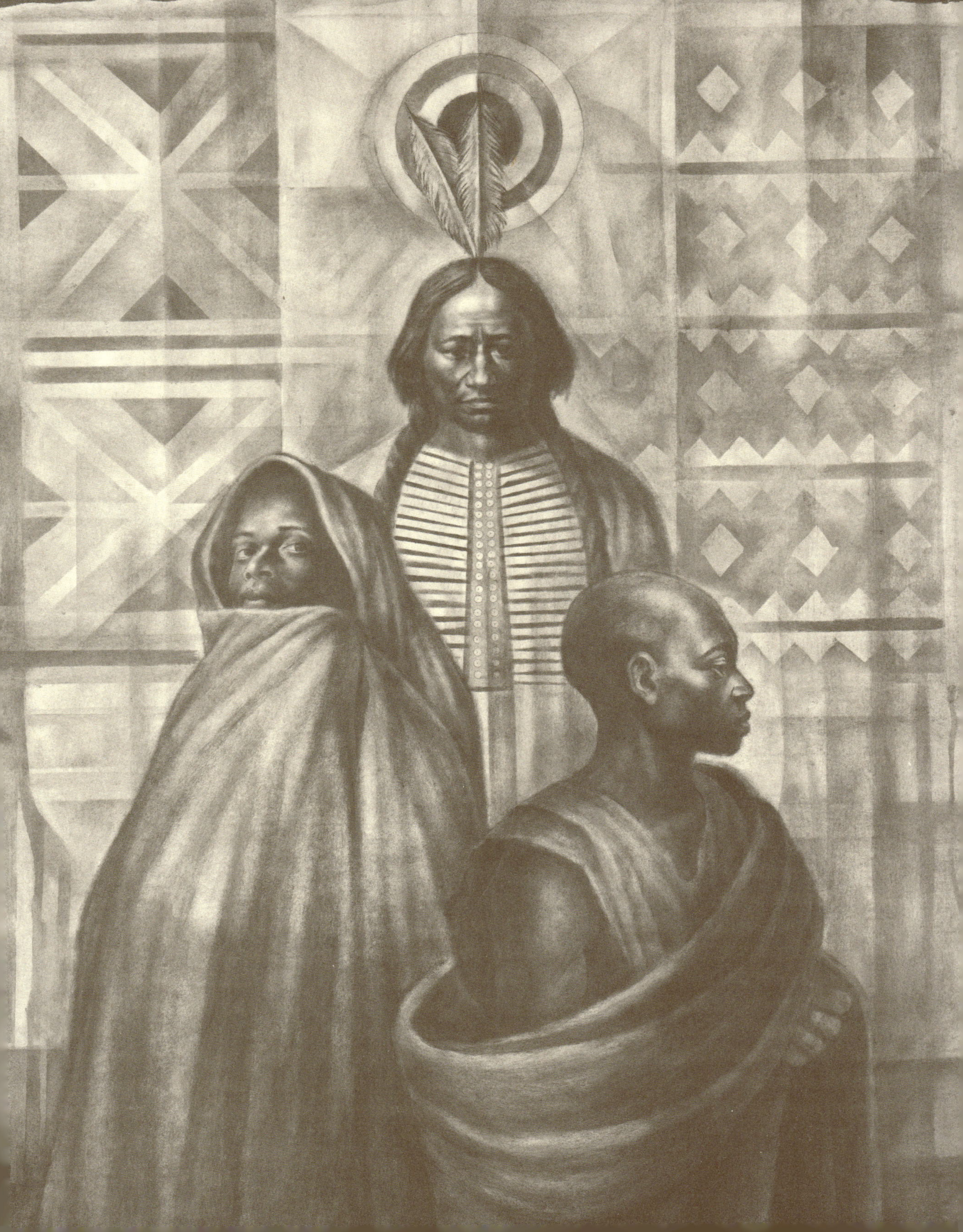

# Red and Black

*I*T was at a forking of worlds that the African and Indian met and became a part of each other and obverse reflections of each other's agony. Back there, centuries ago, at the turning of the worlds, the African had the labor, the Indian had the land, and the European had a plan—and the necessary firepower. The Plan, brutally stated, was to use the firepower to take the Indian's land and to make the African till it. There can be no understanding of the African or the Indian without some understanding of this fact. For it was in the crossfire of this plan that the African and Indian met and molded each other.

The story of their mutual molding, the story of their mutual and sometimes antagonistic attempts to avoid the hammer of fate, a story one seldom sees on television and almost never reads in standard textbooks, is one of the great chapters of American history and is central to an understanding of the red man and the white man and the black man. A number of sensitive men have deplored the habitual neglect of this poignant story. Some fifty years ago, in 1926, Melville Herskovits, the anthropologist, told us that black Americans "have .... mingled with the American Indian on a scale hithertoo unrealized." There is furthermore the testimony of Kenneth Wiggins Porter, the leading authority on black and Indian relations, who said that contact between Africans and Indians "has had as its main results, historically, the bringing about of two so-called Indian wars, one of great importance; and racially, the Africanizing of two of the principal Indian tribes, as well as of a number of Indian peoples of lesser importance, and the infusing into the blood of the American Negro of a perceptible and significant Indian element."

To understand the significance of these statements, we must go all the way back to the dawn of American history. For a growing body of research suggests that Africans were among the first permanent settlers of America. In fact, some scholars believe that it was an African explorer, and not Columbus, who made the first voyage to the New World. As evidence, they cite fragmentary but tantalizing references in the Spanish chronicles. Peter Martyr—to cite one of many examples—says Balboa found Africans in Darien when he landed in 1513. These Africans, some experts say, were probably shipwrecked pirates from Ethiopia.

Even more persuasive is the evidence cited by Dr. Leo Weiner (*Africa and the Discovery of America*), who suggested that African traders from Guinea founded, long before Columbus, a colony in Mexico, possibly on the site of Mexico City. Basing his theories on old Spanish chronicles and linguistic and archeological evidence, Dr. Weiner concluded that the influence of the African colonists extended from Canada in the North to the Maya, Aztec, and Inca civilizations in the South. It was his opinion that African culture was directly or indirectly the basis of Indian civilization, an opinion hotly contested by traditional white authorities.

Regardless of the ultimate outcome of this debate, it is certain that Africans arrived in the area of the present-day United States and made contact with the Indians long before the arrival of the first English settlers. Most of these Africans accompanied the first Spanish explorers as servants, slaves, and scouts; and it was through them, or some of them, that New World Indians made their first contact with the Old World. What better example can one find of this than Stephen Dorantes, also called Estevanico and Esteban, a brilliant and endlessly resourceful black man who accompanied Panfilo de Narvaez on his trip to Florida in 1528. Dorantes, who was about thirty at the time, was a slave or manservant of Andrew Dorantes, one of Narvaez's men. Dorantes was apparently only one of several Africans in the expedition of about five hundred persons. Shortly after the landing near Pensacola Bay in May, most of these persons were killed by the Indians or died of disease and hunger. Some, if we can credit the narratives, were killed by their hungry and terrified colleagues, who ate them. The survivors—a mere handful—hurriedly re-embarked in September and set out for Mexico. But most of them, including Narvaez, were drowned in a violent storm off the coast of Texas. The four survivors—three white men and the indestructible Stephen Dorantes—were captured and held in servitude by the Indians of western Louisiana or eastern Texas. They apparently impressed the Indians with their "magical powers," which consisted of a mishmash of Christian rituals, incantations, and minor surgery. In any case, we are told that Dorantes distinguished himself as a medicine man and interpreter and was "in constant conversation" with the Indians. "It was the Negro," Cabeza de Vaca, the Spanish leader, said, "who talked to them [the Indians] all the time; he inquired about the road we should follow, the villages—in short, about everything we wished to know."

Finally, after some six years of captivity, the four men escaped and succeeded, after some two years of wandering, in reaching the Spanish settlement in Mexico. Never bashful, never at a loss for the right word or the right approach, Dorantes soon became a hero in the settlement with stories of his exploits—doubtlessly embellished—in Indian territory. The Spanish were especially taken with Dorantes's stories of Cibola or "the Seven Cities of Gold." And so, in 1539, the governor dispatched an expedition to Cibola. The leader of this expedition was Father Marcos de Niza, and the guide and ambassador to the Indians was Stephen Dorantes. A Spanish historian says that "the Indians in those places through which they went got along with the Negro better because they had seen him before." For this reason, Dorantes was "sent on ahead to open up the way and pacify the Indians." He traveled, we are told, in great splendor, arrayed in the colorful regalia of a medicine man with "bels and featuers on his arms and legs," and accompanied by a large retinue of Indians, including a harem of beautiful women who swore by his magical powers. By prearrangement, Dorantes was to send back to the main party crosses of different sizes to indicate his position and his nearness to Cibola. "So the sayde Stephan [sic]," Father Marcos wrote later, "departed from mee on Passion-sunday after dinner; and within foure dayes after the messengers of Stephan returned unto me with a great Crosse as high as a man, and they brought me word from Stephan, that I should forthwith come away after him, for hee had found people which gave him information of a very mighty Province, and that he had sent me one of the said Indians. This Indian told me, that it was thirtie dayes journey from the Towne where Stephan was, unto the first Citie of the sayde Province, which is called Ceuola. Hee affirmed also that there are seven great Cities in this Province, all under one Lord, the houses whereof are made of Lyme and Stone, and are very great...."

At this point, it seems that Dorantes, a fearless and, some say, an arrogant man, overplayed his hand. Without waiting for Father Marcos and the main party, he strode into the pueblo and demanded the traditional tribute of "turquoises and women." The Indians, fearing his power and the power of the men he represented, imprisoned him. The next day, "when the sunne was a lance high," Dorantes tried to escape and died in a hurricane of arrows. This marked the ending of the expedition and the beginning of the Dorantes legend. To this day, Zuñi legends preserve the story of the "Black Mexican, a large man," who came from his abode "in Everlasting Summerland."

Thus ended the first documented contact between Africans and Indians in the United States. And it should be said, at least in passing, that Dorantes's role was shot through with ambiguity. Although we cannot conclude that he had the same motives as his patrons, the fact remains that he was a de facto agent of European colonization, and his relations with the Indians were tainted by the aims, conscious and unconscious, of his backers. For all his obvious faults, there remains a quality about Dorantes that, even from this distance, invites respect. He was daring, he was resourceful, and he was without fear. Personal qualities apart, he was certainly the first non-Indian to explore Arizona and New Mexico.

Another example showing still more clearly how blacks preceded Englishmen in the exploration of America comes from the East Coast where, in the summer of 1526, in the area of present-day South Carolina, Lucas Vasquez de Ayllon landed with five hundred Spaniards and one hundred Africans. Not long thereafter Ayllon died and the slaves revolted and ran away to the Indians. The Spanish survivors returned to Haiti, leaving the Africans with their Indian friends as the first non-Indian settlers in that area.

With the arrival of the first permanent English settlers—eighty-one years later—the casual and sporadic contacts of the exploration period gave way to the deeper and more complex relations of colonization. This did not immediately change the relations between Africans and Indians, who continued to communicate with one another on different wave lengths. There were many reasons for this. There was, as some scholars have pointed out, "a consciousness of kind" between Africans and Indians, who had, it is said, an "instinctive sympathy" for one another. This theory has been questioned by other scholars who say the Indian could hardly have felt "spontaneous sympathy" for the blacks "whom he beheld toiling side by side with the white servant in the tobacco fields which were encroaching more and more upon his hunting grounds. . . ." Concerning which, there is this further to be noted: the Indian also beheld the African toiling in the fields at the point of a gun. More importantly, the Indian also beheld other Indians toiling side by side with the black servant.

Another significant, though more diffuse, factor in the growing sense of identity between some Indians and some Africans was the cultural affinity between the two groups. There were, to be sure, obvious and marked differences between African culture and Indian culture, but there were also underlying similarities, particularly in the realm of the spirit. And these similarities became more consequential in the presence of European culture, which was perceived by both Africans and Indians as cold and superficial. Partly because of this, some Indians believed, from the beginning, that Africans lived in a primary relationship with the world of spirits and were therefore "good medicine." It is certainly significant that the first Indians called the first Africans *Manitto*, a word which "in their language signifies not only God but likewise the Devil."

Another and more tangible reason for the African-Indian bond was the common glue of slavery and servitude. As was shown in the first and second chapters, many Indians were captured and forced into extended servitude and slavery. These slaves and servants worked with blacks in the fields and were subject to the same laws and disabilities. As James Hugo Johnston has said, "The white man enslaved the Indian and debased the

Indian woman as he did the Negro woman." Given these and other common burdens, it was inevitable that bonds of sympathy and solidarity would develop between the two groups. Nor is it surprising to learn that Africans and Indians cooperated in many ways to lighten the burden of their common affliction. They traded information, worldviews, and customs. And, of course, they mingled and mated. The ironic outcome was that Indian slavery ended with the eventual absorption of Indian slaves into the black population.

*INDIVIDUAL* relations between Africans and Indians were mediated on the level of the group by concrete ties of solidarity and communal assistance. What perhaps is most astonishing is that in the first "massacres," i.e., the first attempts of the Indians to defend their land, Indian warriors slew every white they could find and spared every black. "While there existed dissimilarities between free Negroes and Indians," John H. Russell wrote, "there was certainly a common bond of union; and it is significant that in the massacre of 1622 [in Virginia] not an African perished at the hands of the Indians, although there were at the time of the massacre more than twenty Negroes scattered throughout the little colony."

From that "massacre" until the end of the nineteenth century, there was active and constant cooperation between Indians and Africans. The most detailed and diverting evidence respecting this is to be found in the advertisements for runaways. On October 1, 1747, the *Pennsylvania Journal* ran the following ad:

> Runaway on the 20th of September last, from Silas Pavin, at Cohansie, in New Jersey, a very lusty Negro fellow named Sampson, aged about 53 years, and had some Indian blood in him. He is hip short and goes lame. He had with him a boy about 12 or 13 years of age named Sam, was born of an Indian woman, and looks like an Indian only his hair. They are both well clothed, only the boy is barefooted. . . . , They both talk Indian very well, and it is likely they have dressed themselves in the Indian dress, and gone to Carolina.

On April 15, 1778, another advertisement appeared in the *New Jersey Gazette:*

> Was stolen from her mother, a negro girl, about 9 or 10 years of age, named Dianah, her mother's name is Cash, was married to an Indian named Lewis Wollis, near six feet high, about 35 years of age. They

have a male child with them, between three and four years of age. Any person who takes up the said Negroes and Indians and secures them shall have the above reward and reasonable charges.

To the continuing flow of African and Indian runaways was added another and more threatening current: violent resistance. One of the earliest instances of this was an uprising of Africans and Indians in Hartford, Connecticut, in 1657. Thirty-three years later, in 1690, there was a panic in Newbury, Massachusetts, after Isaac Morrill was arrested on a charge of inciting insurrections among Africans and Indians. Among the persons implicated in the plot were an unidentified Indian slave and an African slave named James. In Queen's County, New York, in 1708, "an Indian man Slave and a Negro woman" killed their master, his wife, and five children. In 1712 in New York City a band of black warriors, with marginal Indian support, staged a serious insurrection and killed nine whites.

All this had a sharp impact on whites, who feared a united thrust by Africans and Indians. It was also said in some circles that Africans exercised undue influence over the Indians and incited them against the whites. In the 1760s, for instance, a fugitive slave in the Mohawk camp created such a furor that the British Army had to reinforce its frontier garrison. When the fugitive was captured, General Thomas Gage ordered him sold out of the province "so that he may never have an opportunity of getting among the Indians again."

To prevent Africans from "getting among the Indians" and Indians from getting to the Africans, the leaders of the white colonists adopted the old but nonetheless effective policy of divide and conquer. As usual in such cases, the masters told the subordinate groups that they would be much better off if they kept to themselves.

Far more serious than such tactics was the use of force and artifice to involve Africans and Indians in European aggression. One need not be well read in Freudian psychology to understand that the Indian or African who made the first step in that direction would be bound by guilt as well as by self-interest to take the second and third steps. The "recovery clauses" illustrate this technique perfectly. These clauses required Indian tribes to return runaway slaves to Europeans and were considered so important that they were inserted into practically every Indian treaty. As a matter of fact, one of the first foreign treaties negotiated by the United

States required the Creeks to give up blacks on their reservations. Although the Creeks and other tribes signed these treaties under pressure, they generally ignored the provisions regarding runaways. Hardly less revealing in this general context were the material rewards Europeans offered Indians for betraying blacks. In 1676 the Maryland legislature offered "a Matchcoate .... or the value thereof" to any Indian apprehending a fugitive slave.

When these inducements didn't work, whites brought into play the standard mechanisms available to colonizers in dealing with different groups. First of all, systematic attempts were made to indoctrinate Indians with racism. Secondly, systematic attempts were made to give Indians an interest in the system. In some areas, for example, Indians were elevated or favored at the expense of blacks. In other areas, such as South Carolina, Indian tribes were used to suppress and terrorize blacks. In April, 1744, South Carolina accepted an offer of the Notchee Indians "to assist .... in Case of any Insurrection, or rebellion of the Negroes." Three months later the governor wrote to the chief of the Notchee and asked for "the assistance of some Notchee Indians, in order to apprehend some runaway Negroes, who had sheltered themselves in the Woods, and being armed, had committed disorders in the neighborhood."

While the masters were inciting the Indians against the blacks with one hand, they were using the other hand to set the blacks against the Indians. In 1729 and 1730 the governor of Louisiana armed black slaves and used them against the Chonaches. "In the latter year, however," Herbert Aptheker writes, "certain of the Negroes, being armed, becoming aware of the dependence of the white man upon their assistance, and realizing that they and the Indians had a common foe, conspired to unite their forces against the whites." This conspiracy was betrayed and the leaders were executed.

Neither executions nor rewards nor legal enactments separated the Indians and Africans, who continued to reach out to one another across the massed rifles of their common foe. Indian tribes continued to assist and protect runaways, and Indian reservations continued to be places of asylum and refuge for Africans. To be sure, certain tribes, such as the Notchee, hunted blacks and enslaved them. But these tribes were exceptions. Most Indians not only granted runaways asylum but often made them full-fledged members of the tribe. This was not an entirely disinterested gesture, for runaway Africans brought with them needed knowledge and skills. To understand this fact in all its fullness, one must remember that runaway slaves knew the white man at first hand and were privy to some of his secrets. More specifically, they had a superior knowledge of the white man's technology and his ways. Hence, they were highly valued by the Indians as technicians and interpreters.

Some of these runaways intermarried with their hosts and adopted Indian customs. After a generation or two, their descendants became Indians, achieving freedom, as one writer put it, at the price of racial oblivion. No one can state with accuracy how many blacks disappeared into the Indian population, for, as author Edgar J. McManus wrote, "many [Indians] who were visibly Indian were of Negro ancestry." Surveying the New Jersey scene, Robert B. Lee made the same point about the black population, saying that "unions between Indians and Negroes were so commonly frequent, indeed, as to have left a permanent impress upon many families of Negroes of the present day."

As more and more blacks ran away to the Indians, drawn to the reservations as if to a magnet, whole Indian tribes, in the words of Gunnar Mydral, "became untraceably lost in the Negro population of the South." It was during this period, for instance, that the remnants of most of the coastal tribes disappeared into the black population. A report to the secretary of war in 1822 said that "very few of [the Massachusetts Indians] are of unmixed blood, the number of pure Indians is very small, say fifty or sixty, and is rapidly decreasing. The mixture of blood arises far more frequently from connection with Negroes than with whites." Something very similar was widespread in other states. A report to the New York legislature said the Indians of Southampton and Montauk Point had been largely Africanized. "Their social condition," the report said, "is not enviable; during the time the Negroes were held as slaves in this state, these Indians largely intermarried with [them] and their descendants have more of the Negro than of the Indian in their veins; in fact, they are Indian only in name."

It would be a mistake to assume, as this report assumes, that the African-Indian connection only involved slaves and free Indians. There was also extensive contact between Indians and free blacks, many of whom married Indian maidens. This trend was particularly pronounced in New England, where there was a shortage of black women. We learn on the authority of Lorenzo Greene that marriages between free blacks and Indians were common in New England, where a number of well-known blacks, including Paul Cuffee, the product of an African-Indian union, and Salem Poor married Indian maidens. The amalgamative process continued throughout the Colonial period and reached such a level that some states attempted to create an intermediate caste of African-Indians, who were legally identified as mestizos and griffes.

The ultimate consequences of all this were, of course, far-reaching and are visible even today in the black and Indian populations. Some of the immediate consequences however, were equivocal and even curious. One curious consequence was the white movement to appropriate Indian land on the grounds that the Indians were no longer Indians. In 1784 the whites of Northampton County, Virginia, asked the legislature to take the land of the Gingaskins. The petition alleged that "the land is at present an asylum for free Negroes and other disorderly persons who build huts thereon and pillage and destroy the timber without constraint to the great inconvenience of the honest inhabitants of the vicinity, who have ever considered it a den of thieves and a nuisance to the neighborhood." The legislature rejected this request, and the white inhabitants filed a second petition three years later alleging that the Indians "have at length become nearly extinct, there being at this time not more than three or four genuine Indians at most . . . the place is a harbour and convenient asylum for an idle set of free Negroes." This petition was also denied and a third attempt was made in 1812. The petition of that year said: "The place is now inhabited by as many black men as Indians . . . . the Indian women have many of them married black men, and a majority of the inhabitants are black or have black blood in them." This petition was approved and the Gingaskins passed into history and into the mainstream of the African tribe.

Thirty-one years later a similar petition was filed against the Pamunkies of the same state. The petition claimed that "there are two parcels or tracts of land situated within this county, on which a number of persons are now living, all of whom, by the laws of Virginia would be deemed and taken to be free mulattoes, in any court of justice; as it is believed they all have one-fourth or more of Negro blood; and as proof of this they rely on the generally admitted fact that not one individual can be found among them whose grandfathers or grandmothers one or more is of Negro blood, which proportion of Negro blood constitutes a free mulatto." The petition went on to say: "The claim of the Indians no longer exists . . . . his blood has so largely mingled with that of the Negro race as to have obliterated all the striking features of Indian extraction. Your petitioners express the general voice of the free white inhabitants of the county and as slaveholders they protest against this dangerous and anomalous condition, for it has assumed all the feature of legally established body of free Negroes, the general resort of free Negroes from all parts of the country . . . the harbor of runaway slaves. . . ."

Another curious consequence of the relationships between Africans and Indians was the formation of isolated communities, such as the Croatans of North Carolina and the Melungeons of Tennessee. The Melungeons, who lived in the upper counties of eastern Tennessee, were generally regarded as a mixture of African, Indian, and European elements. In 1834 they were disenfranchised as "free persons of color." One year later the Croatans of North Carolina were also declared "free persons of color." But some fifty years later a group of experts declared that the descendants of Sir Walter Raleigh's lost colony of Roanoke were to be found among the Croatans. What happened next was pure farce. In a crude attempt "to preserve the purity" of the long-lost Elizabethan blood, the North Carolina legislature reversed itself, declared the Croatans "Indians" and made it a crime for them to marry Negroes.

*PARTLY* because of the bonds of blood and solidarity between Africans and Indians and partly because Africans knew the ways of both Indians and whites, the lucrative fur trade and other activities requiring skilled linguists and diplomats relied heavily on black mediators. As trappers, traders, and scouts, these black mediators played a pivotal role in the opening of the West. In the process, some of them became wealthy and famous. "The earliest Negroes known to be connected with the fur trade," Professor Porter says, "were among those who occupied the highest functional category—that of independent entrepreneur." One of the leading black entrepreneurs was George Bonga of Duluth, who "became quite a prominent trader and a man of wealth" and served as interpreter for Governor Lewis Cass at the signing of the Chippewa Treaty in 1837. Two other trailblazers were Jacob Dodson, a free black who was a guide on the second expedition of John Charles Fremont, and George William Bush, who led a party through the hazardous Oregon Trail and helped to found the state of Washington.

Certain of these men blended with ease into the Indian landscape and rose to high rank in the tribes. Edward Rose, a trapper and trader, became a chief in the Crow tribe; so did York and James Beckwourth, both of whom were scouts and explorers. Jean Baptiste Pointe DuSable, the founder of Chicago, married an Indian woman and was reputed to have considerable influence over the Indians in the Lake Michigan area.

Of the men cited here, three—York, Beckwourth, and DuSable—should be spotlighted for the record, for in their careers they summed up the spirit and the possibilities of the age. It is best perhaps to begin with York, who came to public attention as the guide of the Lewis and Clark expedition of 1803. Although he was a slave, York was one of the most important men in the expedition. Olin D. Wheeler said, "His color, kinky hair, size, and prodigious strength were a revelation to the Indians and he was looked upon as a very god. He was the greatest kind of great 'medicine' and the tribes from the north of Missouri to the mouth of the Columbia took particular pains to propitiate his sable majesty. And he was so overwhelmed with feminine attention." York served as scout, interpreter, and "medicine man" and was generally the center of attention among the Indians. On one occasion William Clark noted that ". . . . the three great Chiefs [of the Arikaras] and many others came to see us to day . . . . much astonished at my black Servent, who did not lose the opportunity of [displaying] his powers Strength &c. &c. . . ." The next day Clark noted: "Those Indians were much astonished at my Servent, they never Saw a black man before, all flocked around him & examined him from top to toe, he Carried on the joke and made himself more turribal than we wished him to doe." It should not be thought, however, that York was a minstrel. At one meeting a chief ran his fingers across York's face to see if the black would rub off. York whipped out his knife and fixed the offender with his eyes. This incident became a part of the legend of the Nez Perce tribe whose chroniclers said the black man "make big eyes much white in eyes and look fierce at chief."

Along with his other duties, York served as interpreter. Charles Mackenzie, of the North West Company, said that "a mulatto [York], who spoke bad French and worse English, served as interpreter to the Captains, so that a single word to be understood by the party required to pass from the Natives to the woman to the husband, from the husband to the mulatto, from the mulatto to the captains."

Although the evidence is not conclusive, there are some indications that York later cast his lot with the Indians. In 1832 a trapper said he met a black chief of the Crows who said he had accompanied Lewis and Clark on their expedition. The black chief, who was probably York, was "residing in the Crow village at the junction of Bighorn and Stinking rivers .... had .... four Indian wives and possessed much reputation and influence among the Crows."

Another black with "much reputation and influence among the Crows" was James Beckwourth. A former slave, born in Virginia in 1789, Beckwourth became a leading figure in the Westward movement as a trapper, trader, and Indian chief. He later wrote a famous and controversial book in which he detailed his exploits. Skeptical historians have questioned some of his gargantuan claims, but enough remains to sustain his assertion that he founded the best-known trading post of the Old West —the Gant Blackwell Fort at Pueblo, Colorado—and discovered the pass through the Sierra Mountains which still bears his name.

Beckwourth later settled among the Crow Indians and became a chief. According to tradition, he carried a medicine bag which contained a hollow bullet and beads. The Crows, it is said, believed that Beckwourth's medicine brought them luck. Whatever the potency of Beckwourth's medicine, it seems that he was indeed good medicine for the Crows. He led them into battle several times and, according to his account, was always successful. We get a glimpse of Beckwourth in battle from Paul Dorion, a Dacotah Indian who witnessed a confrontation between the Crows and the Blackfeet Indians. The Crows, Dorion said, were reluctant and Beckwourth urged them on, saying:

"You are all fools and old women. Come with me, if any of you are brave enough, and I will show you how to fight."

Dorian added:

"He threw off his trapper's frock of buckskin and stripped himself naked, like the Indians themselves. He left his rifle on the ground, took in his hand a small light hatchet, and ran over the prairie to the right, concealed by a hollow from the eyes of the Blackfeet. Then climbing up the rocks, he gained the top of the precipice behind them. Forty or fifty young Crow warriors followed him. By the cries and whoops that rose from below he knew that the Blackfeet were just beneath him; and running forward he leaped down the rock into the midst of them. As he fell he caught one by the long loose hair, and dragging him down tomahawked him, then grasping another by the belt at his waist, he struck him also a stunning blow, and, gaining his feet, shouted the Crow war-cry. He swung his hatchet so fiercely around him, that the astonished Blackfeet bore back and gave him room. He might, had he chosen, have leaped over the breastwork and escaped; but this was not necessary, for with devilish yells the Crow warriors came dropping in quick succession over the rock among the enemies. The main body of the Crows, too, answered the cry from the front, and rushed up simultaneously. The convulsive struggle within the breastwork was frightful; for an instant the Blackfeet fought and yelled like pent-up tigers; but the butchery was soon complete, and the mangled bodies lay piled together under the precipice. Not a Blackfoot made his escape."

This episode casts light on the temper of the time and establishes beyond doubt that Beckwourth was a good man to have on your side in a fight. This, at any rate, was the opinion of the Crows, who reportedly poisoned the man they called Morning Star when he decided to leave them and return to the ways of the white man. According to tradition, which has been questioned by some authorities, the Crows poisoned Beckwourth because they believed his departure would bring them bad luck.

Although this aspect of the opening of the West is slighted in mass media, there is a great deal of evidence to substantiate the credentials of Beckwourth and his black colleagues. These men, bold, resourceful and, in some cases, unscrupulous, occupied a dangerously ambivalent position. Although most were sympathetic to the Indians, it was very difficult, perhaps impossible, for them not to end up as agents of more powerful and more sinister interests. To this picture, one should add, in all justice, that most black scouts and explorers recognized the ambiguity of their position and did what they could to protect the Indians. This again was not a matter of disinterested humanitarianism. For it quickly became apparent to many, if not all, black scouts and traders that white policy was a threat to blacks as well as Indians. Perhaps the best evidence of this was that white settlers generally appropriated the land opened up by black scouts and instituted Jim Crow regimes. In fact, as soon as a large number of whites poured into the new areas, the social climate became inhospitable to black and Indian settlers.

Nothing attests to this more forcefully than the life and times of Jean Baptiste Pointe DuSable, who was the first non-Indian to settle on the site of Chicago, America's second city. Six feet tall, handsome, of pleasant mien and disposition, he had qualities that recommend him to every American. He was industrious, imaginative, and enterprising. As a trapper, trader, farmer, and entrepreneur, he left an indelible mark on the history of

Chicago. Although he was a Negro and seemed to be proud of it, he was the product of a French environment. And yet he was a man of the world, speaking not only French but also English, Spanish, and several Indian dialects.

It is rather difficult to say where this extraordinary man came from. The Illinois country was controlled first by Frenchmen, who imported a large number of slaves from Haiti to mine lead along the Mississippi River. We know from baptismal records and other documents at Detroit, Mackinac, and other settlements that there were many blacks, slave and free, in the Illinois area before it passed to English control in 1763. It was not unusual in this period for French and English settlers to establish common-law arrangements with Indian and black women. From this fact and others, Milo M. Quaife inferred that DuSable was the illegitimate son of a member of a distinguished French family. Tradition insists, however, that DuSable was a free black who migrated to New Orleans from Haiti and came up the Mississippi River to Illinois. In the absence of concrete evidence to the contrary, there is no good reason for doubting this tradition. Indeed, there are modern Haitians who claim descent from the DuSable family. Scholars believe DuSable was born about 1750.

Whether Chicago's Father came down from Canada, as some scholars contend, or up from Louisiana, as others say, is not of overriding importance. The important thing is that he was in Chicago—and that he was in Chicago first. Contemporary evidence tells us that DuSable had a cabin in Chicago by July, 1779, and that he probably came by way of Peoria, Illinois, where, in the 1770s, he built a home and cultivated thirty acres of land between the old fort and the new settlement. DuSable probably married the Indian maiden Catherine during his sojourn in Peoria. His two children, Jean Baptiste DuSable *fils* and Susanne, were probably born in or near Peoria.

In the late seventies, the elder DuSable made an eventful trip. Leaving Peoria, he traveled north until he reached the shores of the most southwestern of the Great Lakes. The spot entranced DuSable, who saw immediately what others had missed: Chicago was a natural crossroads of travel for both Indians and Europeans. It was, moreover, the gateway to one of the noblest valleys in the world, the Mississippi. A merchant established at that point would have easy access to the furs of the Indians and the markets of entrepreneurs in Detroit and Mackinac, the fort and trading center at the tip of the Michigan bulge. At that time there were few, if any, signs of the future greatness of the area. The scenery was bare and monotonous and the ground was damp and marshy. Despite these disadvantages, DuSable persevered. On the north bank of the river, he built a large cabin and established a trading post. Soon Indians were bringing him pelt and other items. Within a short time he had established trading connections with merchants in St. Joseph, Mackinac, and Detroit.

Illinois, at that point, was a teakettle of simmering emotions. The American Revolutionary War was raging, and Spaniards, Frenchmen, and Indians were pursuing their own private vendettas. In order to remain alive in this volatile situation, a man, especially a black man, had to think quickly and sleep with one eye open. DuSable apparently sided with the Americans, a decision which did not endear him to the Indians who were suspicious of the intentions of the colonists. Charles de Langlade, a pioneer Wisconsin resident, organized Wisconsin Indians for a strike against the Americans. His first act apparently was an attempt to capture DuSable, who fled Chicago and settled on the River du Chemin at the mouth of modern Michigan City, Indiana.

The first official reference to DuSable stems from this episode. Colonel Arent Schuyler de Peyster, a New York Tory who commanded Mackinac and Detroit for Britain during the Revolutionary War, was an amateur poet with a fondness for puns. On July 4, 1779, he told a group of Indians that if they did not join the British he would send them to the devil ("*tout au diable*") "as he did Baptiste Pointe de Saible." It was a dreadful pun, but De Peyster could not resist the temptation to record it for posterity in his book, *Miscellanies*, which was published later in Scotland. In a footnote, the British officer explained that DuSable was a "handsome Negro (well educated and settled in Checagou) but much in the French interest." This proves rather conclusively that DuSable had established a home in Chicago by 1779.

DuSable was arrested in the summer of 1779 in Michigan City by the British on suspicion of treasonable intercourse with the enemy. But his credentials were so impressive that he was released and employed as a factor by Lieutenant Governor Patrick Sinclair, who succeeded De Peyster as commandant of Mackinac. In July, 1780, a band of Indians traveled to Mackinac and demanded that Sinclair fire the French manager of his trading establishment at modern Port Huron, Michigan, and employ DuSable in his stead. Sinclair immediately appointed DuSable manager and ordered one Mr. Guthrie to convey him by boat to the Pine River.

For the next three years, DuSable spent most of his time at "The Pinery," Sinclair's establishment on the St. Clair River, south of present-day Port Huron. During this period, however, he maintained his Chicago address and his Peoria connections.

In the spring of 1784, DuSable returned to Chicago and was joined by his wife, son, and daughter. He refurbished the original cabin and added barns and stables. Soon there was a large family home of squared logs surrounded by nine substantial outbuildings. The home of Chicago's First Family was a long, low building of five rooms. A broad green space stood between the house, which faced south, and the river. To the east at a distance of about fifty feet was the lake; to the west were patches of scrub timber and open prairie.

Although Chicago's founder lived one hundred or more miles from the nearest settlement, his house contained every convenience, including a large fireplace and a stove. The furnishings included a large French walnut cabinet with four glass doors, a couch, four tables, a bureau, seven chairs, a pair of candlesticks, a churn, an iron coffee mill, a pair of scales and weights, a large feather bed, two mirrors, and two oil paintings. The last item deserves comment. At one time DuSable owned twenty-three European paintings, including several religious works and one with the interesting title of *Love and Desire* or *The Struggle*. The tools, the livestock, and the furnishings bespeak a man of culture and wealth. Other sources underline this impression. On Sunday, May 9, 1790, Henry Heward, a Detroit trader, stopped at DuSable's and picked up forty-one pounds of flour, twenty-nine pounds of pork, and a large quantity of baked bread. He gave DuSable in exchange thirteen yards of fine cotton.

DuSable's business flourished in the period after the Revolutionary War. The Chicago portage became a key feature in a small boom. Spanish traders in the Mississippi Valley sent furs and other items over the portage to northern factories. Detroit and Mackinac merchants sent merchandise and hard goods over the same route. As a middleman and wholesaler, Chicago's first citizen received furs from the Indians and trappers and sent them on to Detroit and Canada. He also grew wheat, baked bread, and sold meat. Within a short period his establishment became the nucleus of a small group of fur traders and Indian trappers.

For at least sixteen years, the wealthy merchant lived on the banks of the Chicago. He shot duck, stalked deer, piled his furs, and tilled his land. In the winter, when the white desolation was broken only by the footprints of wild animals, he sat before the fire, no doubt, and drank brandy and dreamed dreams. He would have dined on roast pig, wild turkey, rabbits, raccoons, and a pioneer delicacy, opossum. And from time to time his routine of trading, traveling, and farming would be broken by a visitor from Detroit, St. Joseph, or Green Bay.

One event in this period opens a window on DuSable's soul. He had married Catherine according to frontier rites. This fact apparently disturbed DuSable, who was a devout Roman Catholic. So, in October, 1788, he and Catherine went some three hundred miles to Cahokia and stood before a priest. Perhaps, as has been suggested, their two grown children stood with them. Two years later Susanne, the daughter, was married to one Jean Baptiste Pelletier. And DuSable's granddaughter, Eulalia, was born on October 8, 1796, the first immigrant—black or white—born in Chicago.

Throughout this decade DuSable maintained excellent connections with the Potawatomi Indians. To the Indians, he was a brother, counselor, and leader. Tradition says that he sought, unsuccessfully, the chieftainship of the Potawatomi Indians.

Surrounded by his children and grandchildren and his houses and fields, DuSable, the wealthy merchant, passed over into the autumn of life. Leaves fell from the trees, the wind whistled and howled on the lake, winters and summers passed—and DuSable's wealth and, for all we know, his contentment grew. Then a very strange thing happened. On May 18, 1800, he sold his holdings (which would be worth a thousand million dollars today) for about $1,200 and moved on. Why? Some historians say he moved on to new adventure or that he was piqued by his failure to be elected an Indian chief. Others say he was in ill health. Still others say he moved or was forced to move because Dixie had come to the Midwest. There is an interesting item in the inventory of sale: "One horse stable—all the wood for a barn." This can only mean that DuSable, before selling his holdings, had planned to erect another barn and had already manufactured lumber for it. We are entitled to conclude from this that DuSable was planning to expand his holdings. Why did he change his mind?

There can be no definite answer, of course. But social developments in the Northwest at this juncture offer much food for thought. This was an era of great ferment and change. New people and new ideas, some of them hostile to Negro advancement, were pouring into the area. With the defeat of the Indians at the Battle of Fallen Timbers in 1794, America established effective control over the Northwest. And colonists, most of them Southerners, began to pour into the Midwest.

The DuSable sale must be considered within the context of these converging pressures and desires. The circumstances surrounding the sale were rather unusual. On May 7, 1800, an inventory of sale was made of his Chicago property. Ten days later the sale was consummated, not at Chicago but in St. Joseph, Michigan. Joseph La Lime, the Frenchman who bought the property, was a trader employed by William Burnet, who witnessed the sale, as did John Kinzie, another St. Joseph trader who also bought and sold slaves. Six months later La Lime's title was recorded in Detroit by John Kinzie, who bought the property from La Lime in 1804.

These facts add to the mystery of DuSable's sudden departure. Was he forced to sell? Or did he see the handwriting on the wall? At this point we can only guess. All we know is that he moved on, first to Peoria and then to St. Charles, Missouri, where he died in poverty on August 28, 1819.

Nothing more clearly shows the perversity of white policy and its obvious threat to black and Indian interests as this story of the rise and fall of Jean Baptiste Pointe DuSable, who is neither remembered nor honored today in the city he founded.

*As* the Africans and Indians were sucked into the vortex of the white man's politics, with some supporting England, others supporting the French, and still others supporting white Americans, the relations between Indians and Africans became more complicated, especially in the South, where some tribes adopted the racist attitudes and the racist institutions of their conquerors. The Chocktaws, Chickasaws, and Cherokees became substantial slaveholders and articulators of their own brand of racial purity. The Creeks and the Seminoles also owned slaves or vassals but mingled freely with them and eventually became largely Africanized.

Estimates of the number of slaves held by these tribes vary. On the eve of the Civil War, it was said that "the Seminoles had a thousand slaves; the Cherokees and Chickasaws had each about fifteen hundred slaves; the Creeks and Choctaws had each about three thousand slaves. In these Red nations there were less than fourteen thousand full-blooded Indians to ten thousand Negro slaves." Some of the descendants of these slaves played an important role in African-Indian life. Edmonia Lewis, the sculptress, was born into the Choctaw tribe.

The racial attitudes of the "Southern-White-Slaveholding-Indian," to use James Hugo Johnston's phrase, were determined largely by their relations with whites. "The entire southwestern territory," Johnston says, "was very much infested by settlers from the slaveholding States. Many of these white settlers intermarried with the Indians and became leading men in the tribes." He concluded that the racial attitudes of these tribes were the result of the "artificial influence" of whites, adding: "The white settlers who came into the Indian country brought with them the antipathies of the slave South; and from them the tribes learned to regard the Negro as he was regarded in the slave country."

Two points should be made about this general situation. The first is that African slavery among the Indians was vastly different from African slavery among the whites. The second point is that the institution of slavery assumed different forms in different tribes. Ethan Allen Hitchcock, who observed slavery among the Indians, said that "the full-blooded Indian rarely works for himself and but few of them make their slaves work. A slave among wild [sic] Indians is almost as free as his owner, who scarcely exercises the authority of a master beyond requiring something like a tax paid in corn or other product of labor." Among the Creeks and their offshoots, the Seminoles, slavery approximated a condition of vassalage. Slaves and Indians mingled and mated on a plane of practical equality. A slave could become a leading councilor or even chief. Writing in 1834, an observer said: "[The Seminole slaves] live in villages separate, and, in many cases, remote from their owners, and enjoying equal liberty with their owners, with the single exception that the slave supplies his owner annually, from the product of his little field, with corn, in proportion to the amount of the crop; and in no case that has come to my knowledge, exceeding ten bushels; the residue is considered the property of the slave. Many of these slaves have stocks of horses, cows, and hogs, with which the Indian owner never assumes the right to intermeddle." Analyzing this same situation some years later, Kenneth W. Porter said: "Not only were the Seminole slaves not slaves in the usual sense of the word; they might even lay claim to being the true rulers of the nation. Some had been purchased from the Spanish; others had originally belonged to the English. They thus had a better knowledge of the white man and of his customs than did their masters, and were indispensable as go-betweens between their old masters and their new. The greater freedom they were given among the Seminoles stimulated their intelligence so that it was noted as being distinctly superior to that of the slaves among the whites, and they lost no opportunity to advance the interest of their masters, which they rightly recognized as being identical with their own. Their agricultural skill gave them an economic advantage over the Seminoles, and as a consequence of their importance in all these relations they were accepted as the equals of their masters both in war and in council. . . ." The Seminoles also allied themselves with a large number of runaway blacks who established *independent* maroon camps in and around the principal Seminole settlements.

The relations between the Seminoles and the African-Americans led to the longest and most expensive of all Indian wars, a fact which opens a fascinating lode of speculation. By and large, Africans and Indians dealt with one another on an individual basis. And, in retrospect, it seems that one of the greatest tragedies of African and Indian history was the failure of these two groups to create a common front on a group basis. With the benefit of hindsight, one can say that there was probably only one way for the Indians and Africans to save themselves and that was a total and sustained alliance on the basis of total resistance.

One need only refer to the two African-Seminole wars of 1817–1818 and 1835–1842 to see the pertinence of these observations. The two wars were a direct outgrowth of the peculiar relations between the Seminoles and African-American slaves and assumed such an African orientation that they are properly considered as African wars with Indian support. The Seminole settlements, situated in the dense forests of Florida, then under the control of Spain, were a magnet for runaway slaves and occasioned frequent outcries from Georgia slaveowners and their allies in Congress. The Seminoles were constantly harassed by slaveholders seeking runaway slaves, and from time to time U.S. soldiers were pressed into service as slavecatchers. The pace of events accelerated drastically during the War of 1812. At the end of that war, the British abandoned a fort on the eastern side of the Appalachicola River. The fort was promptly taken over by a band of about three hundred blacks and a group of Choctaw Indians. This group, under the command of a redoubtable black man named Garcon, became the dominant force in the area. By the summer of 1816, it was said that "the Negro Fort" commanded ground extending fifty miles up the river and that it was used as a base for military expeditions into American territory.

The business came to a head in July, 1816, when Garcon's guerrillas ambushed a United States gunboat and killed or captured all of the crew except one sailor. United States forces, aided by the Creeks, immediately laid siege to the fort. But the blacks and their Indian allies refused to surrender, hoisting "the English Jack, accompanied with the red or bloody flag." After several inconclusive skirmishes, the white Americans opened artillery fire, scoring a direct hit on the fort's magazine and killing most of the guerrillas. Garcon and the Choctaw Indian leader were captured and executed.

Of minor importance in itself, the Battle of the Negro Fort was yet an event of far-reaching implications, and one which enraged the Seminoles and their black allies, who mobilized for war. By 1817 United States military intelligence reported that some six hundred blacks were drilling with arms in Seminole towns *under their own officers*. The report said that the blacks were boasting that if they met the whites "they would let them know they had something more to do than they had at Appalachicola." From this report and other evidence, it is evident that the Africans considered themselves the equals and not the subordinates of the Seminoles. They did not, it was said, "act together [with the Seminoles] in the performance of military duty . . . but they always said they would fight together." The independence of the blacks puzzled one observer who asked a friend: "Did not Nero command the blacks, and did not Bowlegs [the Seminole chief] own Nero; and was not the latter under the immediate command of Bowlegs?" The friend replied that it was indeed true that "Nero commanded the blacks, and was owned and commanded by Bowlegs; but there were some Negro captains who obeyed none but Nero."

During the summer of 1817, the Seminoles and blacks mounted a number of attacks on white settlements, slaying the whites and carrying off the blacks for military duty. By November Seminole forces were said to amount to "more than two thousand, besides the blacks, amounting to near four hundred men, and increased by runaways from Georgia."

Faced with this determined and organized force, United States authorities tried first to divide the two groups. General Edmund P. Gaines sent the following letter to the Seminole chiefs: "You harbor a great many of my black people among you at Sahwahnee. If you give me leave to go by you against them I shall not hurt any thing belonging to you." The Indian chiefs contemptuously refused the bait and reaffirmed their commitment to their black allies.

The United States government then sent in additional military forces under the command of Andrew Jackson. On April 16, 1818, Jackson's troops captured the Seminole stronghold on the Suwanee River, killing nine blacks and two Indians and capturing nine Indians and seven blacks. Of the blacks, it was said, "They fought desperately, and did not give way until eighty out of three hundred and forty, were killed." The survivors withdrew in order into the swamps, and the United States forces decided not to pursue them, thus bringing to an end a confrontation Andrew Jackson called "this savage and Negro war." But, as it turned out, nothing had been settled. And when America acquired Florida and mounted a campaign to enforce the Indian Removal Act, which called for the transfer of Indians west of the Mississippi, the Seminoles mobilized for war. In the end, all Indian tribes, except the Seminoles, migrated to concentration camps west of the Mississippi. But it required a seven-year war and the expenditure of $32 million to break the will of the Seminoles and their African allies.

The main factor in this protracted war was the opposition of Seminole blacks to the Indian Removal Act. A United States Army officer said: "The Negroes exercised a wonderful control. They openly refused to follow their masters, if they removed to Arkansas. Many of them would have been reclaimed by the Creeks, to whom some belonged. Others would have been taken possession of by the whites, who for years had been urging their claims through the government and its agents. . . . In preparing for hostilities they were active. . . . It was not until the Negroes capitulated, that the Seminoles ever thought of emigrating."

The immediate cause of the war was the determination of Southern whites to humiliate Seminole blacks. As it happened, Osceola, the fabled Indian chief, was married to a black woman with the entrancing name of Che-Cho-Ter, which, translated, means Morning Dew. While visiting an Indian agency, Morning Dew, the mother of Osceola's four children, was captured by whites and carried into slavery in Georgia. Osceola immediately threw down the gage of battle, telling the whites: "You have guns, so have we. You have powder and lead, and so have we. Your men will fight, and so will ours till the last drop of Seminole blood has moistened the dust of his hunting ground."

Nobody could mistake Osceola's meaning, and when he punctuated his words by cutting down a United States Army patrol, killing one hundred soldiers, both sides deployed for war. At the time Osceola had a force of about two thousand warriors, including some three hundred blacks. Among the leading black warriors were John Caesar, who was very successful in raiding plantations for black recruits; Inos, "the commander of the Negro forces on the Withlacoochee, the chief counsellor among the Negroes, and the most important character"; and Abraham, "the principal Negro chief." Abraham, who has been called one of the outstanding black men produced in America, was about forty at the beginning of the war. He was born in slavery in Pensacola but ran away and settled among the Seminoles, becoming the slave of Micanopy, the principal Seminole chief. He received his freedom after serving as interpreter for Micanopy on his trip to Washington and later "married .... the widow of the former chief of the nation."

Several reports on the Seminoles have come down to us, and all agree that Abraham was undisputed leader of the Seminole blacks and had "as much influence in the nation as any other man." A large man, generally pictured in the traditional Seminole turban, Abraham was described by various witnesses as "plausible, pliable, and deceitful," "a sensible shrewd Negro," "the most cunning and intelligent Negro we have seen." A United States Army officer said that "Abraham was the most noted, and for a time an influential man in the nation. He dictated to those of his own color, who to a great degree controlled their masters. They were a most cruel and malignant enemy. For them to surrender would be servitude to the whites; but to retain an open warfare, secured to them plunder, liberty, and importance."

No less intransigent were the rank-and-file black warriors. An official United States report contained the following information on black warriors: "Ben, 22, Jacob, 24, Muredy, 20, Most intrepid and hostile warriors." Also cited were "Prince, 35, Toney, 25, Toby, 32, Hostile, either qualified to take the lead in an insurrection." With these men and others in the forefront of the Seminole forces, the war continued for seven years with frequent changes in the fortunes of the combatants. By almost all accounts, the Seminole-Africans were formidable foes. One report said that "in all the numerous battles and skirmishes that have taken place, not a single first-rate warrior had been captured, and only two Indian men have surrendered. The warriors have fought as long as they had life, and such seems to me to be the determination of those who influence their councils—I mean the leading Negroes."

The nature of the war was very clear to the participants. A United States officer said that "the Negroes, from the commencement of the Florida war, have, for their numbers, been the most formidable foe, more bloodthirsty, active, and revengeful, than the Indian. . . . Ten resolute Negroes, with a knowledge of the country, are sufficient to desolate the frontier, from one extent to the other." The commanding officer, General Thomas Jesup, said, "This, you may be assured is a Negro, not an Indian war; and if it be not speedily put down, the South will feel the effects of it on their slave population before the end of the next season." While the war continued, there was a general panic among Southern slaveowners, who feared that the Seminole-African war would trigger a southwide alliance between the Indians and the slaves.

The war came to an inconclusive end in 1842 after the cowardly capture of Osceola and other Indian chiefs, who were lured to a peace conference under a flag of truce and surrounded by United States soldiers. A treaty was concluded which gave both Indians and Africans the status of prisoners of war. Most of the Seminoles—Indians and Africans—made the long march to Indian Territory, but many remained in Florida. The Seminole agony continued in Indian Territory, where other tribes, particularly the Creeks, attacked them and attempted to enslave their black allies. Finally, in 1850, some Seminole-Africans migrated to Mexico, where slavery was illegal. In return for their services as guardians of the Mexican frontier, the Mexican government awarded them several grants of land. After the death of their chief, Wild Cat, many of the Seminole-Africans returned to the Indian Territory.

After the Civil War, the Indian Territory was reconstructed and the government demanded "the unconditional emancipation of all persons held in bondage, and . . . . their incorporation into the tribes on an equal footing with their original members, or suitably provided for." At the same time there were official demands from Radical Republicans for the opening of the Indian Territory to Negro colonization. Speaking in Congress, U.S. Senator Jim Lane called for the creation of an African-Indian empire, saying: "The finest specimens of manhood I have ever gazed upon in my life are half-breed Indians crossed with Negroes. . . . I should like to see these 80,000 square miles . . . . opened up to the Indian and to the black man, and let them amalgamate and build up a race that will be an improvement upon both." Nothing came of Lane's proposal for an African-Indian empire in the West. In fact, the Indian tribes rejected Negro colonization. Many tribes, however, adopted their black slaves and allies. The Seminoles, for instance, "adopted their former slaves, and made them citizens of their country, with equal rights in the soil and annuities. Their Negroes hold office and sit in the councils." Several tribes, such as the Choctaws, Chickasaws and Cherokees, resisted racial integration. Although the Choctaws and Cherokees eventually granted blacks limited rights, the Chickasaws resisted to the bitter end. In 1888 the Chickasaw National party passed a resolution opposing "the adoption of the Negro in any way, shape, or form." Acting on this premise, the Chickasaws even refused to grant land to their former slaves. But the federal government intervened and gave each freedman forty acres of land.

After emancipation Africans and Indians entered a new and menacing phase, marked by a rising tide of racism and more sophisticated modes of exploitation. The immediate results were not only a marked deterioration in the status of Africans and Indians, but also a rise in the tensions between the two groups. As we have seen, several Indian groups opposed liberal Reconstruction policies. In the meantime there were curious eddies and cross-currents in the black community. The best and worst example of this was the participation of black soldiers in the white man's last campaign against the Indians in the West, a particularly ironic twist to a history shot through with irony and agony. Important as these auguries were, it would be a mistake to exaggerate their meaning. For despite the divisive forces of the age, many Indians and blacks continued the old traditions by helping one another and fighting one another's battles. Behind this, deeper than this, were the memories and the seeds, which continued to grow. By 1907, to quote Professor Porter again, "it was said that there was then not a Seminole family entirely free from Negro blood and only two or three Creek families." Nineteen years later Professor Herskovits reported that one-third of a sample of 1551 blacks examined by him claimed partial Indian ancestry.

Nobody paid much attention to these figures, or the implications of these figures, in the first decades of the twentieth century. With the Indians on the reservations and the blacks on the plantations, it seemed that the Plan had reached a point of perfection from which there could be no appeal. But this was an optical illusion, the fault of a narrow historical perspective, which time would soon correct. The Indians (of America and of the world) refused to stay on the reservations, the blacks (of America and of the world) refused to stay on the plantations, and even the land turned against the new owners, yielding harvests of dust and disaster and sending the harvesters in ever-increasing numbers to the cities. And so, in the end, the planners increasingly became victims of their own Plan, which was swallowed up by other forces, more muffled, less clearly discernible, infinitely more powerful—forces that pushed reds, blacks, and whites, in the last quarter of the twentieth century, toward a settlement of the long-overdue accounts of history.

CAPT. PAUL CUFFEE

REV. RICHARD ALLEN

# The Black Founding Fathers

*O*UT of blood, out of terror, out of pain, out of the Land of No and the Fire of White, out of the negation of the fire and the cold white night of death, out of the death of the dead, out of the death of the ancestors (who were silent), out of the death of the drums (who no longer called the gods), out of the death of the gods (who did not rise on the third day), out of the silence of the third day and a heaviness of heart no one living can imagine—out of all this but also out of a paradoxical Joy and a fierce and irresistible will to life came, in the years preceding and following the American Revolution, a new historical form. At first the new thing was nameless and shapeless. And then, gradually, under the impact of favorable and unfavorable events, the new form crystallized and was named. The new form, which had never been seen before in that environment, was called African-America. This is the story of the birth of that form and of the black pioneers, the black founding fathers, if you will, who named it and laid the foundations for it by creating permanent structures to contain it.

The years of the making and shaping of this new historical form were the pioneer years of black America. Although this period extended from the middle of the eighteenth century to the middle of the nineteenth century, it reached a peak of development in the fifty-year span between 1787 and 1837, a period which was perhaps the most important in the history of black America. It was during this period that black pioneers took the first wavering steps into the unknown by grafting Western political and social forms onto the conscious and unconscious body of the African legacy. It was during this period that black pioneers created the first permanent African-American institutions and articulated the issues which would give a special tone and texture to Africans in America.

Despite its obvious importance as a backdrop and a point of perspective, the Black Pioneer Period is generally ignored or overlooked by historians, who assume that the birth of white America was the birth of black America. But this assumption imposes a white time on black reality and gives black people fathers they never knew.

To understand this properly, we shall have to begin by noting that concrete historical time is not the same thing as the time of clocks. On the contrary, men and groups secrete their own time and that time is *timed*, so to speak, by their situation and their praxes. The same time, in other words, can be long or short or open or closed according to the experiences men are undergoing. So, to cite a simple example, a man in love in the presence of the beloved does not live the same time as a man in prison in the hands of the torturer.

What, then, is the real meaning of historical time? Time, real time, the time men live, is a structured unity of a lived *no longer* and a lived *not yet* in the explosion of a project that gathers the *now* and the *no longer* and the *not yet* into a lived synthesis. And from that standpoint, it is easy to see that the lived synthesis of the black founding fathers was different from the lived synthesis of the white founding fathers. Although this idea sounds radical and complicated, it is really quite simple. It means simply that Thomas Jefferson and Thomas Jefferson's slaves lived a different Declaration of Independence, a different Revolution, and a different America.

The idea is simple, but the implications are profound and require a rethinking of the time-line of black America, which began with the black pioneers and not the white founding fathers. The white founding fathers were not the black founding fathers; the white constitutional convention was not the black constitutional convention; the white beginning was not the black beginning. For, as everybody knows, the white fathers defined the white beginning as a black negation. To them, and to many who came after them, America was a white place defined negatively by the absence of blackness. The Puritans' celebrated dream of a City on the Hill was a dream of a white city. The vision of Patrick Henry, Thomas Jefferson, and George Washington, slaveholders all, was a vision of white. "I could wish," Benjamin Franklin wrote, "their [white] Numbers were increased. And while we are, as I may call it, *Scouring* our Planet, by clearing America of Woods, and so making this Side of our Globe reflect a brighter Light to the Eyes of Inhabitants in Mars or Venus, why should we in the Sight of Superior Beings, darken its People? Why increase the Sons of Africa, by Planting them in America, where we have so fair an Opportunity, by excluding all Blacks and Tawneys, of increasing the Lovely White and Red?"

One could wish that, and many did, most notably Franklin, Washington, and Jefferson. Not everyone, however, shared their *public* tastes, and it is worth emphasizing that certain men, such as James Otis and Thomas Paine, openly denounced the hypocrisy of patriots who wrote liberty and lived slavery. But the protests of these men were only straws in the winds, and they had little effect on white American leaders, who told themselves and others that they were creating a white paradise. This, of course, was an open contradiction of the multinational fact of America, and it committed the white fathers to a struggle against reality and the representatives (red and black) of reality.

Among the many manifestations of this will to whiteness were the slave codes and the discriminatory provisons against free blacks. And it was partly in response to these provisions that pioneer blacks began early in the eighteenth century to develop a sense of themselves as Africans separated from Africa and from the Europeans, who excluded them and mocked their aspirations. This dawning sense of peoplehood was stimulated by external exigencies, by segregation on the plantations and in the towns; but it was stimulated also by internal exigencies, by the need to be together, by the need to express a different worldview, by the need to see beyond the blocked horizon. Working together in the fields, playing together on holidays, and suffering together on good days and bad days, the pioneer African-Americans began to think of themselves as a common people with common aspirations and a common enemy. And out of it all there finally emerged the first shoots of a new synthesis, neither European nor African. The emergence of this synthesis was not a matter of a cool and leisurely selection of different options presented by the shopping lists of two cultures. On the contrary, the new synthesis was forced by the violent wrenching of African minds out of African sockets, by the killing of African gods and the banning of the drums, by the forced learning of new words and new concepts, by the adoption, at gunpoint, of new gods, new heroes, new habits. But this was by no means the whole story. For the black American was present at his creation. He was not only present, he was present and acting—he helped to make himself. We must never lose sight of that fact. Nor must it be forgotten that the black American was the product of tenacious traditions and that the traditions worked in him and through him as he blended the old and new.

As one would expect, the new synthesis, at its first appearance, was a hodgepodge of various doctrines, methods, and styles. Composed for the most part of bits and pieces of the African worldview, the Bible and the European natural rights philosophy, the synthesis was a practical philosophy, forged in the heat of battle as a tool of survival.

Neither the bits and pieces nor the synthesis was entirely accidental. The religious strain, for instance, was a telling and ironic commentary on the work of white missionaries. Of pivotal importance in this regard were the missionaries who taught blacks to read and write so they could understand the Bible. In 1704 in New York City, Elias Neau, a Frenchman acting on behalf of the Society for the Propagation of the Gospel, opened one of the first American schools for blacks. Thirteen years later Cotton Mather opened a school for Indians and blacks in Boston. In other areas in the same period, the Quakers and other religious organizations provided formal and informal instructions for selected blacks. One of the most important of these institutions was the school founded by Anthony Benezet and other Quakers in Philadelphia. By 1813 this school had more than four hundred pupils. In addition to the mission schools, certain blacks also attended secular schools, some of which were integrated.

There is some evidence to indicate that these institutions, particularly the mission schools, helped to create a black American vanguard. But the heightened consciousness of black Americans cannot be attributed solely to the influence of missionaries. In the first place, the missionary effort touched the lives of only a handful of blacks. Almost all authorities are agreed that only a small minority of blacks were affiliated with white Christian churches at the end of the Colonial period. In the second place, the missionary effort was tainted by the universal vice of white missions, which were designed not to free non-Europeans but to pacify them and to accommodate them to their misery. Many blacks saw this clearly. Certain blacks, such as Lancaster Hill, Prince Hall, and Nero Brewster, appropriated the missionaries' messages and turned them against their teachers. Still others, perhaps the majority, created their own church, the fabled "invisible church of slavery." This church was not, as some people suggest, a simple imitation of European forms. As DuBois said in 1903 and as a great many scholars are belatedly learning, the Negro Church was as much an African as an American invention.

In one of his books, DuBois describes the central figures of this invisible institution in terms that communicate perfectly the creative ferment that lay behind the deceptive appearances of Slave Row. "The Negro priest," DuBois wrote, ". . . early became an important figure on the plantation and found his function as the interpreter of the supernatural, the comforter of the sorrowing, and as the one who expressed, rudely, but picturesquely, the longing and disappointment and resentment of a stolen people. From such beginnings arose and spread with marvelous rapidity the Negro Church, the first distinctively Negro American social institution. It was not at first by any means a Christian Church, but a mere adaptation of those heathen rites which were roughly designated by the term Obi Worship, or 'Voodooism.' Association and missionary effort soon gave these rites a veneer of Christianity, and gradually, after two centuries, the Church became Christian, with a simple Calvinistic creed, but with many of the old customs still clinging to the services. It is this historic fact that the Negro Church of today bases itself upon the sole surviving social institution of the African fatherland, that accounts for its extraordinary growth and vitality. . . ." Future consequences apart, the Negro Church had immediate consequences. Because of the centrality of the spiritual in the African worldview and because religion was the only politics possible in the slave regime, the Negro Church became the platform from which the whole panorama of Negro life in America was launched. But the launching was a complex process, with various interwoven strands, of which one, the natural rights philosophy, should be exposed and simplified. This philosophy, of course, was the cornerstone of the white American Revolution, which was based on the idea that all men have a natural and inalienable right to life and liberty. For some reason, probably because they did not think of blacks as human beings, it did not occur to the leaders of the unfolding American Revolution that this was a persuasive argument against white Americans. If the Jeffersons and Washingtons did not immediately recognize the implications of their ideas, the leaders of the black community did, and they were soon hard at work, demanding the natural and inalienable rights of the servants and slaves of the white colonists.

Thus, the famous American Dilemma, which was not a dilemma at all, certainly not to the Jeffersons and Washingtons, who never intended to commit suicide socially by freeing their slaves, who constituted the foundation of their existence. The fact that hypocrisy was etched into their situation, the fact that the economic foundations of the American economy made it impossible to create a democratic revolution for blacks or whites, does not make the men or the situations less tragic or less sad. To be fair, one should add that this situation disturbed some whites, notably the Quakers, who adopted a less compromising posture on slavery in the pre-Revolutionary epoch. Beginning with the organization of the Pennsylvania Abolition Society in 1775, antislavery organizations spread throughout the North and South.

As the white colonists pressed their suit against England, provocatively championing the right of revolution against tyrants, the climate of the colonies became inflamed, and black consciousness rose sharply. One symptom of this was the sharp increase in the number of runaways and slave conspiracies. A second and more decisive symptom was the Black Protest movement, which appropriated the rights-of-man philosophy and turned it to the advantage of men oppressed by the creators of that philosophy. Moving with a boldness that testified to their new level of consciousness, the blacks of the North, led by men like Prince Hall and Lancaster Hill of Boston, brilliantly exploited the contradictions between Colonial pretension and Colonial practice, filing petitions and legal documents, turning out tracts and pamphlets, and assailing the ears and the consciences of their countrymen.

One can hardly overestimate the importance of this movement, which marked a fundamental turning point in the development of the black community. For the first time anywhere, Africans appropriated the ideas and techniques of Europeans in a sustained movement against Europeans. There had been individual protests before, and the slaves had protested by revolting and running away. But the new movement constituted a pioneer attempt to use the weapons of the system in an attempt to destroy the system from within. In the 1770s, for example, slaves filed several petitions against American tyranny—petitions based, for the most part, on the same ideas the colonists were using against George III. Consider, for example, the petition of many slaves of Massachusetts who demanded freedom and remarked that "they Cannot but express their Astonishment that It have Never Bin Considered that Every Principle from which America has Acted in the Cours of their unhappy Difficulties with Great Britain Pleads Stronger than A thousand arguments in favours of your petitioners...."

Another tactic, extremely effective in that day and of enduring importance for African-Americans, was the filing of test cases. As early as 1701 a Connecticut slave, Abda, filed a suit for trespass against his master. Although Abda lost the case on appeal, many of his fellow slaves were successful in later years. The reasons for their success lay in the changing climate of the age and the weight of collective action. In the Revolutionary War period, which served as a sort of dress rehearsal for the Black Pioneer Period, slaves in Boston and other Northern centers pooled their money and hired lawyers, who filed suits challenging the legality of the system. In some cases slaves carried appeals to the highest courts and won.

In this same period of renewal and rehearsal, blacks made long strides toward groupness by forming or attempting to form organizations. As early as the 1730s blacks attempted to form a Masonic organization in New York City and were denounced for having "the Impudence to assume the Stile and Title of FREE MASONS, in imitation of a Society here; which was looked upon to be a gross Affront to the Provincial Grand Master and Gentlemen of the Fraternity.... and was very ill ACCEPTED."

More ambiguous in its immediate effect was the organizational efforts surrounding the election of Negro governors in the New England states. The Negro governors, who were installed at elaborate balls which dragged on, we are told, for days, administered Negro governments, which included judges, magistrates, and courts. The Negro officials were empowered, it seems, to arrest, try, and punish some offenders. Lorenzo Greene, an authority on the Negro in New England, says the institution contained negative and positive factors. On the one hand, he says, it was "a subtle form of slave control, for, by inducing the slaves to inform on and to punish their fellows, the threat to the masters' security was minimized." On the other hand, it served "as a sort of political school wherein the slaves received the rudiments of a political education which could be drawn upon once they were enfranchised."

Still another indication of the rising level of group consciousness was the emergence of black artists like Jupiter Hammon, who was perhaps the first black poet; and Phillis Wheatley, who was the first major black poet and the second American woman to write a book. Neither Hammon nor Wheatley dealt in depth with the African-American situation, but both were symptoms of what was still gestating in the depths of the people. Wheatley, a poet of more than topical interest, was the best-known black artist until the emergence of Paul Laurence Dunbar more than one hundred years later.

*F*OR both black and white Americans, the American Revolution marked a crucial turning of the road. But, as usual, the two groups did not experience the same time or the same event. For most white Americans the American Revolution was the first link in a chain of hope. For most black Americans the American Revolution was the last link in a chain of betrayal.

Significantly, the first black institutions were organized in the middle of this struggle. Perhaps the first such institution was an African Baptist church founded around 1776 at Williamsburg, Virginia. At about the same time, George Liele, the servant of a British officer, founded another Baptist church in the Augusta, Georgia, area. When the war ended, Liele left America with his master, and his work in America was continued by his disciple, Andrew Bryan.

It would be wrong to interpret all this as the unfolding of the democratic possibilities of the American Revolution. A great deal of the activity of this period evolved not because of the American Revolution but in spite of it and against it. By and large, the main preoccupation of blacks during this period was freedom from the British *and* the white colonists. Tens of thousands of slaves, including some belonging to George Washington, Thomas Jefferson, and other white founding fathers, escaped during the war. And when the white fathers repudiated the principles of the Declaration and barred blacks from the army, thousands more flocked to the lines of the British, who proclaimed freedom to all male slaves who were willing and able to bear arms.

Although both sides made encouraging noises, it soon became clear that neither side was irrevocably committed to black freedom. And black Americans, caught between the fire of enemies and unreliable allies, bided their time and maneuvered for advantage between the contending white forces. The British promise, the militant mood of slaves, the protests of free blacks, and the lagging enlistment campaign among whites finally forced George Washington and his aides to reverse their policy and admit blacks to the army. At least five thousand black patriots served in the American army, including black leaders like Prince Hall, Lemuel Haynes, Salem Poor, and Peter Salem. An even larger number of blacks served the British as soldiers, laborers, and spies. One of the outstanding British soldiers was Thomas Peters, an African-American pioneer who later helped found the colony of Sierra Leone. When the British left America, they were accompanied by at least twenty thousand black Americans.

At the end of the war, there were 687,000 slaves and 59,000 free blacks in the former British colonies. The black population constituted 19.3 percent of the total population, the highest black percentage in history.

The postwar years, which were the truly critical years in the formation of the African-American personality, marked the beginning of the Black Pioneer Period proper. This period unfolded in two great waves from 1787 to 1816 and from 1817 to 1837. During the first wave, the free blacks of the North laid the institutional infrastructure of the black community. In the second wave, they completed the infrastructure and moved to a new level of protest and affirmation.

The period as a whole was characterized by both negative and positive trends. On the positive side, there was the beginning (as a result of the Revolutionary ideology, the nature of the economy, and the protests of blacks and whites) of the gradual emancipation of Northern slaves. The Northern emancipation movement, which continued until 1827, had immediate and far-reaching consequences. Not the least among these was a sharp and dramatic rise in the number of free Negroes. In the last twenty years of the eighteenth century, many of the emancipated blacks migrated to the cities and created the urban foundations of the Black Pioneer Period. Between 1780 and 1790 the black population of Philadelphia increased by 176 percent. By the end of the century, Philadelphia and New York were the two Northern cities with the largest concentrations of blacks. In Philadelphia and New York, as well as in other Northern centers, black colonies developed along the wharves and alleys. In Philadelphia blacks lived around Sixth and Lombard streets. In Boston they lived on the North Side of Beacon Hill in "New Guinea." In Cincinnati they lived in the "Little Africa" of the First and Fourth wards. In New York they lived in the notorious integrated slum of Five Points and in the area which is known today as Greenwich Village.

No less immediate and dramatic was the emergence of an urban artisan and small business class. Interestingly enough, this class, which produced most of the black pioneer leaders, was based on the white economy and consisted of merchants and artisans. Between 1790 and 1820, according to DuBois, "a very large portion, and perhaps most" of the artisans of Philadelphia were black, and the same situation obtained in other cities.

The existence of this class at this early period is significant. For one thing, as we shall see in Chapter X, it contradicts the oft-repeated statement about the limitations of the black business experience. What is even more important is that this class was the first seed of a black business stratum that would sprout up again and again in forthcoming years only to be cut down by the scythe of racism. In this respect, as in others, the history of the black people in America is a spiral which passes repeatedly by the same point.

The emancipation of Northern slaves, the creation of a black urban base, and the development of a business stratum were among the positive factors in the trends of the period. On the debit side, the period was characterized by a conservative reaction, which reversed the liberal impulses of the Revolution. As soon as the Revolution was won, the upper classes were gripped by a consuming fear of what John Adams and other white founders called "the swinish multitudes."

This fear was accentuated by Shays's Rebellion, the French Revolution, and the Haitian Revolution. And to the immense weight of these events must be added the desire to protect property and to pave the way for exploitation of the riches of the colonial West. The immediate result was a concerted movement among the upper classes to keep the lower orders, both black and white, in their places. On the political level, the conservative reaction expressed itself in the generally conservative biases of the Constitution, which was designed, in part, to erect unassailable ramparts against the populist thrust of the governed. The explicit recognition of human slavery in the United States Constitution was the most blatant example of a general anti-democratic thrust, which included the checks and balances system. Governor Morris recognized this fact, saying: "Domestic slavery is the most prominent feature in the aristocratic countenance" of the Constitution.

The Compromise of 1787, as the bargaining which led to the Constitution has been called, was a compromise not only over power but also over the basic principles of human rights. "The bargain between freedom and slavery contained in the Constitution of the U.S.," John Quincy Adams said later, "is morally and politically vicious, inconsistent with the principles upon which our Revolution can be justified."

Adams's analysis was echoed by a modern critic, Staughton Lynd, who said: "Unable to summon the moral imagination required to transcend race prejudice, unwilling to contemplate social experiments which impinged on private property, the Fathers, unhappily, ambivalently, confusedly, passed by on the other side. Their much praised domestic coolness of temper could not help them here. The Compromise of 1787 was a critical, albeit characteristic, failure of the American pragmatic intelligence."

Other signs of the same characteristic failure were the enactment by Congress of a national fugitive slave law, the limiting of naturalization to white aliens, and the barring of blacks from the militia and the postal service. This period also witnessed the invention of the cotton gin, the expansion of the slave regime, and the intensification of the war against the Indians. Nor was this all. On the local level, there was acute economic strain, which led to bitter conflict between white and black workers. By the end of the century, white workers, with the open or tacit support of the white fathers, were organizing pogroms and massacres in bloody attempts to eliminate black competition.

Yet another matter was involved: the default of Christian churches. Following the Revolution, there was a brief but interesting period in which it seemed that the Church would take an uncompromising position on racism. In 1784 the Methodists denounced slavery and gave traveling ministers twelve months to liberate their slaves. Five years later the Baptists called slavery a "violent depredation of the rights of nature and inconsistent with a Republican government." It is sad to have to add that the Baptists and Methodists later retracted these statements and joined other Christians in a policy of spiritual segregation.

Then what happened? More repression, naturally. Blacks were insulted and assaulted on the streets, their homes were burned, their children were stigmatized. Blacks were barred from public celebrations, they were shunted to the back seats and back doors, to the alleys and the margins of society. Doors that had been open to them in the honeymoon period of the Revolution were slammed in their faces.

The effect of all this on black Americans was explosive. Blacks had expected to share in the fruits of victory, they had expected the white founders to honor the explicit promises of the Declaration and the implicit contract between the soldier and the land fought for, between the worker and the land cleared and harvested. But the dream, not for the last time, was deferred. And under the impact of this deeply searing experience, something snapped within the developing African-American psyche. There was an internal convulsion, an internal explosion. And flowing with and out of this explosion was a new sensibility and a realization, nebulous at first but always waxing clearer, that another way had to be found.

The way was found.

Denied space and dignity in white institutions, the black fathers went out into the deserted places and created their own institutions. Placed beyond the pale, they became a pale.

It was a critical moment.

Institutions are mirrors, sounding boards, communication channels, and deposits of energy. They are mediations between man and man, between man and things, between man and the past, between man and the unknown. Without institutions, men cannot see themselves or be themselves. Without institutions, without rituals, without structures of relationship and meaning, men cannot communicate with their dead or pass on their experiences to the unborn. In order to be and in order to become, men must have institutions. It was in obedience to that primal law that the white founding fathers gathered in Independence Hall to create a structure and an order. And it was in obedience to that same law that the excluded came together in the same year to create an order of another kind. Perhaps the key move in the second ingathering was made in Philadelphia in the same year of the Constitutional Convention. In that year

Richard Allen and Absalom Jones, two former slaves, withdrew from the St. George's Methodist Episcopal Church and created a germinal black institution. The immediate cause of the withdrawal was the rising tide of racism in the church. But there were other and deeper causes. Richard Allen and Absalom Jones and their followers already had a new sense of themselves and of what they wanted and of what they would accept. In their minds, in a larval state, was the idea of an African-American personality. They felt, they said, *cramped* in the exclusionist and whitened atmosphere of white institutions. They did not want, they said, to be *under* the government of whites but an integral part of that government. An admirable formulation, as you can see, and one which would form the dominant thrust of the African-American personality for years to come.

When whites transgressed the line Allen and his colleagues had defined as inviolable, they marched out of St. George's Methodist Episcopal Church in the first mass demonstration in black American history. Richard Allen was there. Let him speak:

"A number of us usually attended St. George's church in Fourth street; and when the colored people began to get numerous in attending the church, they moved us from the seats we usually sat on, and placed us around the wall, and on Sabbath morning we went to church and the sexton stood at the door, and told us to go in the gallery.... We expected to take the seats over the ones we formerly occupied below, not knowing any better.... Meeting had begun and they were nearly done singing and just as we got to the seats, the elder said, 'Let us pray.' We had not been long upon our knees before I heard considerable scuffling and low talking. I raised my head up and saw one of the trustees ... having hold of the Rev. Absalom Jones, pulling him up off his knees, and saying, 'You must get up—you must not kneel here.' Mr. Jones replied, 'Wait until the prayer is over.' [The trustee] said, 'No, you must get up now, or I will call for aid and force you away.' Mr. Jones said, 'Wait until prayer is over, and I will get up and trouble you no more.' With that [the trustee] beckoned to one of the other trustees .... to come to his assistance. He came, and went to William White to pull him up. By this time prayer was over, and we all went out of the church in a body, and they were no more plagued with us in the church."

There were no more plagued with black people in a great many places. The Philadelphia demonstration was the focal point of a spontaneous movement that erupted in city after city. Without premeditation or plan or design, blacks in Boston, New York, and other Northern centers walked out of white institutions and created counter-institutions. Here again the key move was made in Philadelphia, where, on April 12, 1787, Richard Allen and Absalom Jones created the Free African Society, which DuBois called "the first wavering step of a people toward a more organized social life." The society was a mutual aid society, an embryonic church, and a political structure. It also contained the germ of a major black business, the insurance company.

Similar societies were formed in New York City, Boston, and Newport, Rhode Island. In the formation and rapid spread of these societies we have irrefutable proof of the growth of an independent black consciousness. The product of a new consciousness, the free African societies engendered an even higher level of consciousness, creating links between the isolated free Northern colonies. Through the medium of these societies, free blacks exchanged information, ideas, and programs.

The formation of the African societies was a crucial and formative educational experience for the pioneer leaders. In these organizations pioneer leaders learned how to resolve and how to bring collective pressure to bear. They learned to see their lives in a time-line which extended from Africa to the Day of Judgment they believed would vindicate them.

From this fount concentric circles of commitment spread to all of the communities of the North, leading to the creation of a second level of organization, the independent Black Church. Out of the Free African Society of Philadelphia came two of the first black churches; the First African Church of St. Thomas, the first black Episcopal church, and Bethel AME Church, the mother church of the African Methodist Episcopal Church. In 1796 the first congregation of the AME Zion Church was organized in New York City. Around 1809 black Baptist churches were organized in Boston, Philadelphia, and New York. By the War of 1812, there were black churches of every conceivable description, including a black Dutch Reformed church in New York City.

A further development of these organizational acts was the founding of national church bodies. In 1816, sixteen ministers met in Philadelphia and formed the African Methodist Episcopal Church. Five years later nineteen ministers representing six churches formed the African Methodist Episcopal Zion Church. A third level of organization consisted of lodges and fraternal orders. In 1787 Prince Hall, the Revolutionary War veteran and Methodist minister, organized African [Masonic] Lodge No. 459 in Boston. Five years later a Grand Lodge, the first black interstate organization, was launched with Hall as the Grand Master.

Less dramatic but no less relevant was the fourth level of educational and cultural institutions. In 1787 Boston leaders, led by Prince Hall, sounded one of the dominant themes of black concern by petitioning the state legislature for equal educational facilities. The plea was denied; and in 1798 the black parents of Boston opened a school in Prince Hall's home. The school was transferred later to the African Meeting House and was operated for some twenty-nine years. A similar course of development was roughly characteristic of other Northern centers, including Philadelphia, where Richard Allen opened a day school for black children and a night school for black adults.

Substantial help came from white organizations, in particular the New York Manumission Society, which was largely responsible for the organization of the famous African Free Schools of New York City. According to some authorities, the opening of the first African Free School in November, 1787, marked the beginning of free secular education in New York. James Weldon Johnson called the school, which received aid from the city and state, the "precursor of the New York Public School System."

The Free African Schools were run with dispatch and efficacy. Males were taught "reading, writing, arithmetic, English grammar, composition, geography, astronomy, use of the globe, and map and linear drawing." Females were taught reading, writing, arithmetic, grammar, geography, sewing, and knitting.

According to contemporary accounts, the black students were models of industriousness and seriousness. In its issue of May 12, 1824, the *Commercial Advertiser* commented:

> We had the pleasure on Friday of attending the annual examination of the scholars of the New York African Free School, and we are free to confess that we never derived more satisfaction, or felt a deeper interest, in any school exhibition in our life. The male and female schools.... were united on this occasion, and the whole number present was about six hundred.... The whole scene was highly interesting and gratifying. We never beheld a white school of the same age (of and under the age of fifteen) in which, without exception, there was more order, and neatness of dress, and cleanliness of person. And the

exercises were performed with a degree of promptness and accuracy which was surprising. . . . We were particularly struck with the appearance of the female school. . . . There was a neatness of dress and person, a propriety of manner, and an ease of carriage, which reflected great credit upon themselves and their teacher.

The work of the schools for children and adults was supplemented by study circles, reading groups, and benevolent organizations. By 1831 there were more than forty-three benevolent organizations in Philadelphia alone. Among the groups listed were the African Friendly Society of St. Thomas, Sons of Africa, United Brethren, Humane Mechanics, African Female Band Benevolent Society of Bethel, Female African Benevolent, and the Daughters of Ethiopia.

Perhaps the best known of the black cultural institutions was the African Theater of New York City, which presented performances of *Othello, Richard III,* and other European fare. One observes with interest that the theater, at the African Grove, corner of Bleecker and Mercer streets, had a partitioned section in the back for white patrons. The managers said whites were segregated because they "do not know how to conduct themselves at entertainments for ladies and gentlemen of color."

With the organization of the first newspapers and magazines, the different organizations and colonies of black America began to coexist in the same time zone. The first edition of the first black newspaper, *Freedom's Journal,* was published on Friday, March 16, 1827, under the editorship of Samuel E. Cornish, a minister and writer, and John B. Russwurm, the first black college graduate (Bowdoin). Russwurm later withdrew from the editorship and settled in Liberia, where he edited the *Liberia Herald*, a pioneer newspaper, and served as governor of the colony of Maryland. Cornish continued to edit the paper under a new name, *Rights for All.* He later edited another newspaper, the *Colored American.* David Ruggles, another pioneer New York leader and one of the most radical men of his times, was editor of the first black magazine, *Mirror of Liberty*, which appeared in August, 1838, one month before the publication of William Whipper's *National Reformer.*

The appearance of the first newspapers and magazines brought the black community closer together and focused its thinking. "It is our earnest wish," Cornish and Russwurm said in the first issue of *Freedom's Journal,* "to make our Journal a medium of intercourse between our brethren in the different states of this great confederacy; that through its columns an expression of our sentiments, on many interesting subjects which concern us, may be offered to the publick: that plans which apparently are beneficial may be candidly discussed and properly weighed; if worth, receive our cordial approbation; if not, our marked disapprobation."

Continuing, the editors went on to develop a theme all too familiar to contemporary readers.

> We wish to plead our own cause. Too long have others spoken for us. Too long has the publick been deceived by misrepresentations, in things which concern us dearly, though in the estimation of some mere trifles; for though there are many in society who exercise towards us benevolent feelings; still (with sorrow we confess it) there are others who make it their business to enlarge upon the least trifle, which tends to the discredit of any person or colour! and pronounce anathemas and denounce our whole body for the misconduct of this guilty one. . . .
>
> Our vices and our degradation are ever arrayed against us, but our virtues are passed by unnoticed. And what is still more lamentable, our friends, to whom we concede all the principles of humanity and religion, from these very causes seem to have fallen into the current of popular feeling and are imperceptibly floating on the stream—actually living in the practice of prejudice, while they abjure it in theory, and feel it not in their hearts. Is it not very desirable that such should know more of our actual conditions; and of our efforts and feelings, that in forming or advocating plans for our amelioration, they may do it more understandingly?

Speaking thus to friends and foes, *Freedom's Journal* defined and articulated six issues of enduring concern to the black community: 1) Black Assertion, 2) Defense of the Black Image, 3) Equal Education, 4) Economic Development, 5) Civil and Political Rights, 6) African Renaissance. Among the contributors to this pioneer black periodical were black leaders like Richard Allen, James Varick, Peter Williams, and David Walker.

*I*N the second great wave of the pioneer period, a period extending roughly from 1817 to 1837, the plowmen of the black experience pioneered in the art of protest, using petitions, ballots, pamphlets, the sword, and fire. Although these men worked on narrow ground, with little support in the white community and no avenue of escape, they etched the outlines of the fundamental issues of black America. Should blacks separate or integrate, should they call themselves Africans or coloreds, should they use violence or nonviolence, should they return to Africa or struggle here: all these issues were defined and spoken to by the men who organized Africa *in* America. In the process pioneer leaders experimented with and refined a whole arsenal of techniques. They staged mass meetings and held mass marches. They filed petitions against slavery, discrimination, and taxation without representation in America. They filed court suits and maneuvered between the Federalists and the Jeffersonians in balance-of-power politics.

There were differences, in some cases bitter differences, within black leadership circles over the location of the Promised Land and the road to it; but there was agreement on the need for collective action and persistent, manly assertion. And against the background of that agreement, the differing programs and actions of the pioneer leaders blended into a single chorus of resistance. Black leaders like David Walker, David Ruggles, and Richard Allen hacked away at the system from within, and from without their blows were answered by the acts of slave rebels like Denmark Vesey, Gabriel Prosser, and Nat Turner.

One of the pioneer protests from within the system came from a group of free blacks of Philadelphia, who filed an antislavery petition in the House of Representatives on the second day of the nineteenth century. The petition, which was organized by Absalom Jones, the minister and protest leader, sought legislative relief from the slave trade, the fugitive slave law, and the institution of slavery. Congressional response to the petition was instantaneous and explosive. John Rutledge, Jr., of South Carolina denounced the petition and associated it with "this new-fangled French philosophy of liberty and equality. . . ." Harrison Gray Otis of Massachusetts thought the matter was more serious. "To encourage a measure of this kind," he said, "would have an irritating tendency, and must be mischievous to America very soon. It would teach them [blacks] the art of assembling together, debating, and the like, and would so soon, if encouraged, extend from one end of the Union to the other." The measure died in committee after the House expressed the opinion that it had a "tendency to create disquiet and jealousy."

Even more disquieting was the rising tide of extra-parliamentary protest. In 1788 a free black, identified only as Othello, published a mordantly antislavery essay, which questioned the good faith and the good sense of white Americans. "When the united colonies revolted from Great Britain," he wrote, "they did it upon this principle, 'that all men are by nature and of right ought to be free.'—After a long, successful, and glorious struggle for liberty, during which they manifested the finest attachment to the rights of mankind, can they so soon forget the principles that then governed their determinations? Can Americans, after the noble contempt they expressed for tyrants, meanly descend to take up the scourge? Blush, ye revolted colonies, for having apostatized from your own principles."

Othello called white Americans to repentance, warning: "So flagitious a violation can never escape the notice of a just Creator, whose vengeance may be now on the wing, to disseminate and hurl the arrows of destruction."

He added:

"Beware, America!"

This was clear enough, and ominous enough, and it was underlined by the emergence of the militant phase of the antislavery movement. In the general literature, this movement is depicted as a white man's uplift movement with marginal black support. This was not the case. The militant phase of the antislavery movement was inaugurated by black pioneers, who did more to help themselves than their more celebrated allies. Of at least equal consequence is the fact that blacks were instrumental in focusing the demands of the new movement. Most of the pioneer white abolitionists were in the orbit of innocuous and sentimental paternalism until they were educated and transformed by the black pioneers. It is established beyond doubt, for instance, that Samuel E. Cornish and other black leaders were primarily responsible for turning William Lloyd Garrison and Gerrit Smith against the deportation ideas of the American Colonization Society.

What was more important than the missionary work of the black pioneers was the development of the first militant antislavery organizations. According to author John Daniels, blacks initiated the antislavery struggle in Massachusetts by organizing around 1826 the General Coloured Association of Massachusetts, "which had for its purpose promoting the welfare of the race, principally by working for the destruction of slavery." Other antislavery organizations in that state and New York and Pennsylvania were the African Abolition Freehold Society, the African Female Anti-Slavery Society, and the New York Committee of

Vigilance. The vigilance committee, which was headed by David Ruggles, advocated a militant program of self-defense. Ruggles, who has been called "the Father of the Underground Railroad," was a pioneer advocate of self-reliance. "Know ye not," he said, "who would be free, themselves must strike the first blow."

In addition to the formation of the first militant antislavery societies, black leaders, such as Prince Hall, Samuel E. Cornish, and Paul Cuffee, laid the cornerstone of the perennial struggle for equal rights. On February 10, 1780, Cuffee and six other blacks sent a petition to the General Court of Massachusetts, charging taxation without representation and asking voting rights for blacks. The petitioners told the court that "we apprehand ourselves to be Aggreeved, in that while we are not allowed the Privilage of freemen of the State having no vote or Influence in the Election of those that Tax us yet many of our Colour (as is well known) have cheerfully Entered the field of Battle in the defence of the Common Cause and that (as we conceive) against a similar Exertion of Power (in Regard to taxation) too well Known to need a recital in this place."

In the first phase of the protest movement, black leaders relied primarily on petitions and muted pressure-group tactics. But as the crisis deepened, with no sign of relief, blacks shifted to mass pressure and militant assertion.

Gabriel Prosser, a twenty-four-year-old slave rebel, sounded the dominant note of the new age with an abortive slave revolt in Southampton, Virginia. Twenty-two years later, in 1822, Denmark Vesey, a militant free black, organized another slave conspiracy in Charleston, South Carolina.

The shock waves from these two underground depth charges reverberated throughout the white and black communities and had repercussions above ground. One result was a general movement to contain the free black population. The spearhead of the movement was the American Colonization Society, which denounced free blacks as "a dangerous and useless element" and organized a national campaign to send them back to Africa.

Faced with this unexpected development, free blacks moved to a new level of expression, taking their first tentative steps in the field of mass protest. In January, 1817, some three thousand blacks, including delegates from major Northern centers, met at Philadelphia's Bethel Church in one of the first black mass meetings in America. James Forten presided at the meeting, which denounced the American Colonization Society and resolved:

> Whereas our ancestors (not of choice) were the first successful cultivators of the wilds of America, we their descendants feel ourselves entitled to participate in the blessings of her luxuriant soil, which their blood and sweat manured; and that any measure or system of measures, having a tendency to banish us from her bosom, would not only be cruel, but in direct violation of those principles, which have been the boast of the republic.
>
> Resolved, That we view with deep abhorrence the unmerited stigma attempted to be cast upon the reputation of the free people of color, by the promoters of this measure, "that they are a dangerous and useless part of the community," when in the state of disenfranchisement in which they live, in the hour of danger they ceased to remember their wrongs, and rallied around the standard of their country.
>
> Resolved, That we never will separate ourselves voluntarily from the slave population in this country; they are our brethren by the ties of consanguinity, of suffering, and of wrong; and we feel that there is more virtue in suffering privations with them, than fancied advantages for a season.

The issue of African colonization triggered the first major debate in black America. Most black leaders were bitterly opposed to the pro-slavery and anti-free black orientation of the American Colonization Society, but a minority cooperated with the organization in the founding of the state of Liberia. As early as 1787 the Negro Union of Newport, Rhode Island, had suggested a mass exodus to Africa. But the suggestion was vetoed by the powerful Free African Society of Philadelphia which replied: "With regard to the emigration to Africa you mention we have at present but little to communicate on that head, apprehending every . . . man is a good citizen of the . . . world."

Paul Cuffee, the black ship captain, revived the idea in 1815 by carrying thirty-eight blacks to Sierra Leone in one of his own ships. But Cuffee and other black colonizationists dissociated themselves from the racist orientation of the American Colonization Society. In later years Daniel Coker and John B. Russwurm sailed to Africa under the auspices of the society. Russwurm said: "We consider it a waste of words to talk of ever enjoying citizenship in this country." Russwurm, in turn, was called a "traitor" by some black leaders, who said: "This is our home and this is our country. Beneath its sod lies the bones of our fathers; for it some of them fought, bled, and died. Here we were born; and here we will die."

Another controversial issue in the emerging black community was nonviolence. Most pioneers were advocates of nonviolence, particularly in the first phase of the pioneer period. But as forces matured and issues ripened, a number of black leaders adopted a policy of militant self-defense. Perhaps the leading critic of this posture was William Whipper, a leader of the Philadelphia-based Moral Reform Society. In an 1837 address Whipper said that "the practice of non-resistance to physical aggression is not only consistent with reason, but the surest method of obtaining a speedy triumph of the principles of universal peace." Samuel E. Cornish opposed Whipper's argument, saying, "We honestly confess that we have yet to learn what virtue there would be in using moral weapons, in defense against kidnappers or a midnight incendiary with a torch in his hand."

The Age of Andrew Jackson and the Common (white) Man accentuated the fissiparous tendencies in the emerging black community and made the search for a way out more desperate. In general, Jacksonian democracy tended to destroy the conditions for democracy for reds and blacks. In several states, for instance, the adoption of universal white male suffrage led directly to the disenfranchisement of black males who had voted since the Colonial period. In the 1820s and 1830s, as Jacksonian democracy unfolded, racism in America reached levels never before known to man. To make matters worse, industrialization and the influx of millions of poor white immigrants compounded the problems of black workers. The net result of all this was that antagonism between black and white workers rose to a dangerously high level. One indication of this was a flurry of petitions urging forcible deportation of free blacks and additional laws to protect the livelihood of white workers. Another and more ominous manifestation was the practice of expelling blacks from American cities. In 1827 the blacks of Cincinnati, Ohio, were given sixty days to get out of town. In 1830 all blacks of Portsmouth, Ohio, were driven out of town by order of local officials.

More sinister yet were the open calls for genocide. The Indiana state constitutional convention was told that "it would be better to kill [blacks] off at once, if there is no other way to get rid of them." The speaker added: "We know how the Puritans did with the Indians who were infinitely more magnanimous and less impudent than the colored race." The result of all this was as predictable as it was unfortunate—a wave of white riots that began in Cincinnati in 1827 and leaped from city to city.

As the white menace crystallized under the banner of democracy for the common man, the ideological physiognomy of the black community changed dramatically with new voices demanding a deeper level of commitment and different forms of struggle. In 1829 David Walker, a Boston merchant and professional revolutionary, announced a new theme in a pamphlet that called for a slave uprising and total war. Walker's *Appeal,* which anticipated Fanon's ideas on the value of violence in a colonial context, cited four reasons for the subordination of blacks: 1) Slavery, 2) Lack of Education, 3) Christian Ministers, 4) the American Colonization Society. He called for a violent revolt against racism, saying: "O Americans! Americans!!! I call God—I call angels—I call men, to witness, that your DESTRUCTION is at hand, and will be speedily consummated unless you REPENT."

In a situation maintained by the violence of the oppressor, Walker said, the only solution was violence by the oppressed. Unlike modern theoreticians, Walker did not offer long arguments in defense of the violence of the oppressed. To him, it was self-evident, like the principles of the Declaration of Independence. It was as natural, he said, as taking a drink of water. "Now," he wrote, "I ask you, had you not rather be killed than to be a slave to a tyrant, who takes the life of your mother, wife, and dear little children, and answer God Almighty: and believe this, that it is no more harm for you to kill a man, who is trying to kill you, than it is for you to take a drink of water when thirsty. . . ."

Walker issued a clarion call for resistance, saying: "Never make an attempt to gain our freedom or *natural right* from under our cruel oppressors and murderers, until you see your way clear—when that hour arrives and you move, be not afraid or dismayed; for be you assured that Jesus Christ the King of heaven and of earth who is the God of justice and of armies, will surely go before." He added: "[If] you commence, make sure work—do not trifle, for they will not trifle with you—they want us for their slaves, and think nothing of murdering us in order to subject us to that wretched condition—therefore, if there is an *attempt* made by us, kill or be killed." Two years later, in August, 1831, Nat Turner, a thirty-one-year-old preacher-revolutionary, organized a slave rebellion in Southampton County, Virginia. Fifty-seven whites were killed.

With this, the climate of both black and white America changed, and action and reaction occurred with increasing speed. The reaction from the white community was swift and heavy-handed, culminating in a wave of terror that claimed the lives of many blacks. This, in turn, deepened the consciousness of blacks, triggering a new round of organization that peaked with the convening of the first national convention of black Americans. This convention opened in Philadelphia on September 15, 1830, with Richard Allen in the chair. There were twenty-seven elected delegates from seven states and thirteen honorary delegates. Among the leading delegates were William S. Whipper, Junius C. Morel, Austin Steward, Hezekiah Grice, and Abraham Shad.

The Forty Immortals, as John W. Cromwell called the delegates to the first black convention, denounced slavery and discrimination and urged blacks to take up "agricultural and mechanical arts." They criticized the return-to-Africa program of the American Colonization Society and urged hard-pressed blacks to settle in Canada. Major emphasis, however, was placed on "raising the moral and political standing of blacks in the United States." To this end, the delegates requested "our brethren throughout the United States, to cooperate with us, by forming societies auxiliary" to the national convention. From this time until the Civil War, national black leaders held periodic conventions to "investigate the political standing of our brethren wherever dispersed."

*O*UT of the ferment created by the pioneer convention holders and institution-makers came a people, an orientation, and a culture. The culture, in its first blooming, was characterized by an "ethos of mutuality," to borrow E. P. Thompson's phrase. More concretely, the culture was based on mutual aid, stressing communal values and the responsibility of each to all and of all to each. Although most blacks were desperately poor, the community ideal required sharing, and, to a great extent, this ideal was lived. In many cases blacks handled their own welfare cases and provided structures for the care of the sick and the lame and the unfortunate. At a somewhat later date, a New England commentator said blacks were "seldom seen in the almhouses, for they have many benevolent societies—some of them on the mutual principle—and in case of need are ready to help each other." Nor was this sort of thing confined to the black community. When the town of Westport, Massachusetts, refused to meet its responsibilities, Captain Paul Cuffee built a school on his property and opened its doors to all children in the township. Cuffee also helped build a meeting house for the Quakers.

The spirit of self-discipline and communal action was manifested in other developments that vitally concerned black Americans. The surviving rules of the benevolent societies show a definite institutional etiquette and strong community sanctions. Alcoholics and disorderly persons were not eligible for membership. Plural mating was frowned on. "No man," according to the rules of the organization, "shall live with any woman as man and wife without she is lawfully his wife, and his certificate must be delivered to the clerk to be put on record."

Needless to say, this culture was not embraced unreservedly by all. Many blacks were compelled by circumstances to live in misery and wretchedness, and some free blacks found the emerging culture of the societies and churches too Puritan, too white, and too otherworldly. There was a strong secular component, even then, and that component added its own blues counterpoint to the spiritual theme to create the overall melody of black life. (Since the blues and the spirituals were complementary facets of the same reality and since there was as much of the blues in the spirituals as there was of the spirituals in the blues, the emerging black melody was a subtle and complex fusion of both realities.)

Such, in broad outline, was the synthesis called into life by the external pressures of white Americans and the internal exigencies of black Americans. Nowhere in black America was the product quite the same and often the contrasts were many and vivid. All in all, however, the new synthesis indicated a level of consciousness and an effort at self-determination of a truly impressive order.

Who were the leaders of this movement for renewal and self-determination? Who were the fathers of black America?

They were men of different temperaments, different persuasions, different visions. But they were also men molded by the same crucial experiences and forged in the fire of the same hopes and disillusionments. Most were former slaves and second- or third-generation Americans. Most were ministers, and most defined themselves as Africans *and* Americans. Most were self-taught, and all were strong-willed and self-reliant. Some had white mothers (Daniel Coker, Lemuel Haynes), some had Indian mothers (Paul Cuffee), some had white fathers (Prince Hall, John B.

Russwurm), but most had black fathers and black mothers. Some were born in Africa (Phillis Wheatley), some were born in the West Indies (Prince Hall), but most were of old African-American stock and were identified as "full-blooded Negroes." Some, in contemporary terms, were nationalists, some were integrationists, some were pluralists.

It is obviously impossible to list all the men and women who made germinal contributions in this period. But at least twenty-six men and women can be identified as pioneers in the founding of black institutions and the definition of issues and boundaries: Richard Allen, cofounder of the Free African Society, founder of Bethel African Methodist Episcopal Church, pioneer bishop of the AME Church, and first president of a national Negro convention; Absalom Jones, cofounder of the Free African Society, protest leader, and founder of the first black Episcopal church; Prince Hall, founder of the first black Masonic lodge and protest leader; George Liele, pastor of one of the first black Baptist churches; Andrew Bryan, pioneer Baptist pastor; Phillis Wheatley, poet; James Forten, protest leader and entrepreneur; Benjamin Banneker, astronomer, mathematician, protest leader, and a member of the Presidential commission to lay out the city of Washington, D.C.; Jean Baptiste Pointe DuSable, a leader in the Westward movement and a founder of Chicago, Illinois; Gabriel Prosser, leader of a slave conspiracy; Denmark Vesey, leader of a slave conspiracy; Nat Turner, leader of a slave revolt; Peter Williams, Sr., one of the founders of the African Methodist Episcopal Zion Church; Paul Cuffee, ship captain and colonizationist; William Whipper, protest leader and magazine editor; Dr. James Derham, one of the first black doctors; James Varick, first bishop, AME Zion church; Crispus Attucks, leader of the Boston Massacre and the first martyr of the American Revolution; Samuel E. Cornish, Presbyterian minister and cofounder of the black press; John B. Russwurm, cofounder of the black press; Lemuel Haynes, Revolutionary War veteran and a pastor of white churches; Daniel Coker, one of the founders of the AME church and one of the founders of Liberia; David Ruggles, protest leader, and founder of the first black magazine; David Walker, author and protest leader; Charles Lenox Remond, first black to lecture for white antislavery organization; and Nathaniel Paul, pioneer black Baptist pastor.

Most of these leaders were relatively young when they came into prominence. Allen was only twenty-seven when he helped found the Free African Society; Prince Hall was thirty-nine when he founded the

African Lodge; Russwurm was twenty-six when he founded the black press; Turner was thirty-one when he attacked the state of Virginia, and Wheatley was only thirty-one when she died. With few exceptions, the pioneers were artisans, small businessmen, or professionals. Most were, as we have seen, ministers; but even the ministers had one foot solidly planted in the business world. Prince Hall was a soapmaker, Richard Allen was a shoemaker, Absalom Jones was a real estate operator, and David Walker operated a clothing store. The outstanding professional in the group was Dr. James Derham, a former slave who learned his trade as an assistant to his master, who was a physician. Dr. Derham was freed after the war and became one of the leading physicians of New Orleans. Dr. Benjamin Rush, writing in 1789, said: "I have conversed with him upon most of the acute and epidemic diseases of the country where he lives. I expected to have suggested some new medicines to him, but he suggested many more to me. He is very modest and engaging in his manners. He speaks French fluently, and has some knowledge of Spanish."

Most of the pioneers were men of moderate means, but some were well-to-do. Paul Cuffee left an estate valued at $20,000. In 1832 James Forten was worth $100,000. At about the same time, Richard Allen's widow was worth $25,000.

Richard Allen was in some respects the prototypical figure in this group. Born a slave, he helped convert his master, bought his freedom, and played a pivotal role in defining the black posture in America. In fact, he was so closely identified with the birth of black America that author Vernon Logain called him "the Father of the Negro." John W. Cromwell was of like mind, saying Allen "had a greater influence upon the colored people of the North than any other man of his times." An artisan and a believer in sobriety, hard work, and thrift, Allen was a pioneer black abolitionist, the founder of one of the first black churches, and the organizer and first president of the first national Negro convention in the Western world. In these different roles he came to personify the dominant values of the Black Pioneer movement: 1) the assertion, backed up by practical work, that black people would not accept a subordinate role in any white institution; 2) the importance of sustained assertion; 3) the importance of collective action. Allen's fundamental thesis—and it is still relevant—was a thesis of power. As I have said elsewhere (*Confrontation: Black and White*) he demanded not only the right to participate in American institutions but also the right to share in the governing of those institutions.

By modern standards Allen was somewhat moderate and conciliatory. But it is significant that David Walker, one of the most radical leaders in the history of black America, considered Allen the major leader of his day. "Richard Allen," Walker wrote, "O my God! The bare recollections of the labors of this man and his ministrations among his deplorably wretched brethren (rendered so by the whites) to bring them to a knowledge of the God of Heaven, fills my soul with all those high emotions which would take the pen of an Addision to portray. It is impossible, my brethren, for me to say much in this work respecting that man of God. When the Lord shall raise up coloured historians in succeeding generations, to present the crimes of this nation to the then gazing world, the Holy Ghost will make them do justice to the name of Richard Allen of Philadelphia."

Richard Allen and other black pioneers defined themselves in African terms. This orientation was expressed concretely in the names of the first black institutions (the Free *African* Society, the *African* Methodist Episcopal Zion Church, the *African* Baptist Church, *African* Lodge No. 459, the Free *African* Theater). One can find additional evidence of this same orientation in the documents and newspapers of the day. The preamble of the Free African Society of Philadelphia began: "We, the free Africans and their descendants, of the City of Philadelphia. . . ." The pioneer blacks defined themselves as Africans but as Africans of a special sort. They were, they said, Africans *in* America. Most, as we have seen, rejected the idea of a return to Africa, saying they were African-American. For all that, the black pioneers had a cosmopolitan orientation, a fact emphasized by David Walker in his *Appeal,* which was addressed "To the COLOURED CITIZENS OF THE WORLD; but in particular and very expressly, to those of THE UNITED STATES OF AMERICA." In this pamphlet Walker told African-Americans that it was an "unshaken and for ever immovable fact, that your full glory and happiness as well as all other coloured people under Heaven, shall never be fully consummated, but with the entire emancipation of your enslaved brethren all over the world." Since many, perhaps most, black pioneers believed this, they were deeply involved in African affairs all over the world. George Liele carried the independent black Baptist idea to Jamaica, founding one of the first African churches there. Lott Carey, John B. Russwurm, and Daniel

Coker were among the founders of Liberia. Joseph Jenkins Roberts, a free black man from Virginia, was the first president of Liberia. Thomas Peters and other black American veterans of the British struggle in America were among the founders of Sierra Leone. At the same time, black Americans of all ranks and persuasions were deeply influenced by the example of Touissant L'Ouverture and the Haitian revolutionaries.

Almost all pioneer leaders were motivated by the equal rights philosophy, the prudence, thrift, and sobriety maxims of Benjamin Franklin, and the spiritual egalitarianism of primitive Christianity. They believed that blacks had a providential mission. They believed, in general, that God had chosen black people to come to America and that their coming had a meaning and would have an issue. They believed that racism was a symptom of a deeper sickness, and they raised their voices in support of world peace, temperance, and equal rights for women. On the debit side, it should be said that some of the pioneer leaders were unduly influenced by white-oriented ideas which were designed, in part, to keep them from seeing.

What was the relationship between the black pioneers and the great mass of slaves? The free black pioneers, most of whom were former slaves, saw themselves as the vanguard and representatives of the slaves. Beyond all that, they were linked to the mass of slaves by bonds of interests and aspirations. What the pioneers accomplished grew out of and reflected a body of experience that was grounded in the slave community.

The relationship between the black pioneers and the white pioneers was more complex. In general, it can be said that the pioneer black leaders were teachers and way-showers. It is a fact of more than symbolic significance that Richard Allen began his career by arranging the conversion of his white master. Because of the white default, Allen and other black pioneers became the inheritors and guarantors of the American Dream. Benjamin Banneker underscored that point in a famous 1791 letter to Thomas Jefferson. "Sir," he wrote, "suffer me to recall to your mind that time, in which the arms and tyranny of the British crown were exerted, with very powerful effort, in order to reduce you to a state of servitude; look back, I entreat you, on the variety of dangers to which you were then exposed; reflect on that time, in which every human aid appeared unavailable. . . .

"This, sir, was a time when you clearly saw into the justice of a state of slavery and in which you had just apprehensions of the horror of its condition. It was now that your abhorrence thereof was so excited, that you publicly held forth this true and invaluable doctrine, which is worthy to be recorded and remembered in succeeding ages: 'We hold these truths to be self-evident; that all men are created equal . . . .' you were then impressed with proper ideas of the great violation of liberty, and the free possession of those blessings, to which you were then entitled by nature; but, sir, how pitiable it is to reflect, that although you were so fully convinced of the benevolence of the Father of Mankind, and of his equal and impartial distribution of these rights and privileges, which He hath conferred upon them that you should at the same time counteract his mercies in detaining by fraud and violence, so numerous a part of my brethren under groaning captivity, and cruel oppression, that you should at the same time be found guilty of that most criminal act, which you professedly detested in others, with respect to yourselves."

Banneker and the black fathers also transcended the white fathers by raising new issues. In his *Almanac* of 1793, Banneker proposed the establishment of a new cabinet office, a Secretary of Peace, "who shall be perfectly free from all the Present absurd and vulgar prejudices of Europeans upon the subject of government. . . ."

As a result of the pioneering work of the black fathers, the boundaries and dimensions of America were extended and a structure was created for a new historical form. By 1837, largely as a result of their work, it was plain that black people were in America to stay and that room had to be made for them. By that time the piles of the black foundation had been driven so deep into the land that the mark of blackness could never be uprooted or effaced.

HARRIET
TUBMAN

# The World of the Slave

*T*HE crucible for the values institutionalized by the black pioneers was Slave Row, the prototype of all the Harlems of America. In that unpromising setting, the slave, tempered and toughened by the annealing heat of adversity, remade himself as he remade America, creating a new synthesis, in part European, in part African, in part X.

The creation of this synthesis was one of the great flights of the human spirit. For in the doing and the making, the slave endured, *abided* and said many marvelous things about the limits of oppression and the depths of man. Out of the world the slave made, out of his creative responses to a total attempt to destroy him and dehumanize him, came some of the deepest vibrations born this side of the seas. And these vibrations, expressed in folklore, song and dance, expressed in flights of the spirit and the soul, changed the culture and the social terrain of America. This is only another way of saying that the mark of the slave is deep in the flesh of every American. It is another way of saying that America is, in large part, what it is because of what it tried to do to the slave and what the slave did to what was done to him. It is another way of saying that the institution of slavery, as David B. Davis noted, is a key to the meaning of America.

It was slavery and the slave trade that provided the initial thrust to the American economy. It was slavery that built Monticello and Mount Vernon and Boston and Charleston and New Orleans. Slavery shaped the white founding fathers. It shaped and molded the fundamental compromises of the U.S. Constitution. It shaped and molded the Westward movement and the Civil War.

Slavery, in sum, was a major formative influence in the development of America, and it is impossible to understand the black man or the white man or America without a prior understanding of that institution. It is becoming increasingly clear, moreover, that slavery must be understood from the inside out, that is to say, from the standpoint of the slave. And to do that one must deal at a depth level with slave narratives, slave culture, and the slave praxis—one must deal, in other words, with the practical language of the slave. Quite a few scholars have made valuable contributions by reinterpreting slavery from the perspective of the slave. And the purpose of this chapter is to outline the boundaries of the slave world and to indicate the possibilities of viewing the slave community as a distinctive culture complex with its own rules and socially-sanctioned ends. What concerns us here is the shared understandings and shared sensibilities of that world, its modes of perception and expression, its channels of communications, its heroes, symbols, and myths.

But before plunging into that world, let us pause for a moment to sense the atmosphere of the institution that shaped it and distorted it. A precursor of modern totalitarianism, the institution of slavery in America was a total system of social, economic, political, and sexual exploitation based on force and violence and an ideology of racism.

At its peak, in the antebellum period, this system of forced labor claimed the energies of some four million slaves, most of whom raised staple crops on plantation-sized units in the Black Belt areas of the Southern states. For these individuals (and for the parasitic whites who fed off their transcendence), slavery had ominous political and psychological implications. Slavery not only stole the labor of the slaves; it also stole the meaning of their lives and subtly distorted the lives of their tormentors. To put the matter simply, and rather bluntly, slavery was designed to turn human beings into human machines. The infamous slave codes, which were enacted by the legislatures of all slave states, proscribed the humanity of the slave by investing slavemasters with absolute power. The Louisiana slave code said: "[The slave] can do nothing, possess nothing, nor acquire anything, but what must belong to his master." Under the provisions of the slave codes of Louisiana and other states, slaves were sold on the open market, bred like cattle, wagered at poker tables, deeded in wills, and presented as presents at social events.

It was a crime under these provisions for a slave to read and write. It was a crime, punishable by a summary lashing, for an African to stand up straight and look a white man in the eye. It was a crime for slaves to hold meetings or religious services without a white witness. Slaves could not congregate in groups of more than two or three away from the home plantations. They could not beat drums, wear fine clothes, or carry sticks or weapons. They could not marry, they could not protect their children or their mates.

The power of the state, the power of the United States government and of all the presidents from Washington to Lincoln, stood behind these onerous provisions. An immense police apparatus was created by every Southern state to awe the slaves and to beat them into submission. Slave patrols, authorized by state laws, policed plantation areas and made periodic searches of slave cabins. Guards and special patrols stood in readiness at key installations. We get a glimpse of this police state from the writings of Frederick L. Olmstead, who remarked on "police machinery such as you never find in towns under free government: citadels, sentries, passports, grapeshooted cannon, and daily public whippings of the subjects for accidental infractions of police ceremonies. . . ."

Olmstead's observations are extemely interesting for the light they throw on the organic violence of the system. It is fashionable nowadays to speak disapprovingly of the atrocities of the slave system. But to single out isolated atrocities for condemnation is to miss the meaning of the system, which was an atrocity in itself. Violence was not an accidental by-product of that system: the system itself was violent. No one understood this better than the slaves. James W. C. Pennington, who escaped from slavery in Maryland and became one of the outstanding men of the nineteenth century, said: "The being of slavery, its soul and body, lives and moves in the chattel principle, the property principle, the bill of sale principle; the cart-whip, starvation, and nakedness, are its inevitable consequences to a greater or less extent, warring with the dispositions of men." Pennington and other slave annalists said that whippings were common on all plantations and that few slaves made it through life without at least one lashing. "It is the literal, unvarnished truth," slave annalist Solomon Northup said, "that the crack of the lash, and the shrieking of the slaves, can be heard from dark till bedtime . . . any day almost during the entire period of the cotton-picking season." There is furthermore the testimony of Austin Steward who, like Northup, escaped from slavery and made his way to the North. Said he: "No slave could possibly escape being punished—I care not how attentive they might be, nor how industrious—punished they must be, and punished they were."

At least two additional considerations must be taken into account in explaining this system. The first is that slavery was characterized by systematic brainwashing. Slaves were taught to hate themselves and to stand in fear of every white man. Every medium was used to detach them from prior sanctions and to flatten their perceptions and instincts. There is an extremely perceptive remark on this point in Alexis de Tocqueville's study of America. Said he: "The only means by which the ancients maintained slavery were fetters and death; the Americans of the South of the Union have discovered more intellectual securities for the duration of their power. They have employed their despotism and their violence against the human mind."

The second decisive aspect of the slave situation was fascist regimentation. Military discipline prevailed on most plantations, which had a chain of command ranging downwards from the plantation owner to the white overseer and the black driver. Slaves were generally marched to and from their tasks in military formations and housed and fed in collective settings.

In apportioning tasks, slavemasters ignored distinctions of age and sex. The very young and the very old, males and females, worked in the fields. Females dug ditches, cut down trees, cleared wild land, and worked on highways. Some plantations were manned entirely by a work force of women.

For males and females, for young and old, life was a round of toil, whips, bells, and military formations. Looking back on this period many years later, Charley Williams, who was a slave in Louisiana, said: "When the day begin to crack, the whole plantation break out with all kinds of noises, and you could tell what was going on by the kind of noise you hear.

"Come the daybreak you hear the guinea fowls start potracking down at the edge of the woods lot, and then the roosters all start up round the barn, and the ducks finally wake up and jine in. You can smell the sow-belly frying down at the cabins in the Row, to go with the hoecake and the buttermilk.

"Then pretty soon the wind rise a little, and you can hear a old bell donging way on some plantation a mile or two off, and then more bells at other places and maybe a horn, and pretty soon yonder go Old Master's old ram horn with a long toot and then some short toots, and here come the overseer down the row of cabins, hollering right and left, and picking the ham outen his teeth with a long shiny goose-quill pick.

"Bells and horns! Bells for this and horns for that! All we knowed was go and come by the bells and horns!"

Despite the terror of the bells, despite the regimentation and brainwashing, despite the whips and guns and chains, the slaves maintained a sense of expectancy and an incredible optimism. And this expectancy, this leap of the spirit, sustained them in two centuries of struggle against the slave principle. To be sure, some slaves succumbed to the assault on their bodies and minds; and an even larger number, seeing no way out and facing the certainty of death without martyrdom or monuments, masked their feelings and went through the motions of obeisance. Apart from this, it is important to recognize that all slaves were marked, in one way or another, by the inferno that engulfed them. All this is true and a truism. The same thing has happened and will perhaps continue to happen to men of all races and creeds in totalitarian situations. What is astonishing really and worthy of remembrance is that so many slaves transcended the brutality of the system, leaving numerous spiritual artifacts to the quality of their hope. "The record of slave resistance," Kenneth Stampp has written, "forms a chapter in the story of the endless struggle to give dignity to human life. Though the history of southern bondage reveals that men *can* be enslaved under certain conditions, it also demonstrates that their love of freedom is hard to crush. The subtle expressions of this spirit, no less than the daring thrusts for liberty, comprise one of the richest gifts the slaves have left to posterity."

This is the real meaning of the legacy of the slave. Confronted by what one historian called "a social system as coercive as any yet known," the slaves fell back but they fell back by steps, resisting with every weapon they could lay their hands on. They slew masters in hand-to-hand combat. They poisoned whole families. They staged more than two hundred revolts and conspiracies. They burned down barns and cities. They ran away in droves. So many slaves ran away that Dr. Samuel Cartwright of the University of Louisiana discovered a new disease, "Draptomania, or the Disease Causing Negroes to Run Away."

Concurrently, with the elaboration of the more dramatic modes of rebellion, the slaves pushed their suit in ingenious day-to-day resistance, feigning illness or ignorance, accidentally breaking implements or destroying crops. Contrary to common impressions, slavery was a long red ribbon of resistance. Slavery, James Redpath sagely observed, was a "state of perpetual war."

*IT* was in this atmosphere, and against this background, that the world of the slave evolved. It was an elemental world, the world of the slave, a world with no frills, a world of humiliation and dirt and fatigue, a world that placed a premium on creativity and the ethics of survival. This world was dominated by nature and natural needs, but it was populated by spirits and spiritual forces. The world was somewhere between Africa and a place that did not exist, that is to say, it was a world in transition, a world of changing forms and patterns, a world with no guideposts and few firm spots on which to stand. The spatio-temporal dimensions of this world were compressed. It was a world bounded by the fields and fences and the seasons of the year. As a mechanism of control, the slavemasters kept the slaves ignorant. And so the average slave literally did not know where he was. Somewhere on the margins of his mind was a place called Africa. And he would have heard of a place called the North and another place called Canada. But the precise location of these places and their relation to the spot he occupied were secrets the slavemasters closely guarded. As a consequence, the world of the slave was spaceless and timeless. It was a world of repetition, a world of doing the same thing over and over again, day in and day out, of watching the sun go up and the sun come down, of summers turning into falls and winters turning into summers, over and over again, without rhyme or reason. Few slaves knew the days of the month or the months of the year. Frederick Douglass, who slaved for eighteen years on a Maryland plantation, said: "I never met a slave who could tell me how old he was."

The physical infrastructure of this world was Slave Row. From every standpoint Slave Row was a singularly unattractive place, consisting of a single or double row of cabins and shacks located at some distance from the planter's house. The cabins were usually one-room shacks made of logs, without floors or windows. Slave commentators said the windows were unnecessary since the cracks between the walls admitted sufficient light, as well as rain, wind, and dust. Whole families and unattached individuals were housed within the walls of the one-room cabins. "Everything," one slave said, "happened in that one-room—birth, sickness, death—everything...."

A good deal of light is thrown on the parameters of this world by the classic description of Solomon Northup, who spent twelve years in slavery in Louisiana. Let us consider his testimony; he is describing the day-to-day routine of Slave Row. "The hands are required to be in the cottonfields as soon as it is light in the morning, and, with the exception of ten or fifteen minutes, which is given them at noon to swallow their allowance of cold bacon, they are not permitted to be a moment idle until it is too dark to see, and when the moon is full, they often times labor till the middle of the night. They do not dare to stop even at dinner time, nor return to the quarters, however late it be, until the order to halt is given by the driver." But this, Northup said, was not the end of the slave's toil. "Each one must then attend to his respective chores. One feeds the mules, another the swine—another cuts the wood, and so forth.... Finally, at a late hour, they reach the quarters, sleepy and overcome with the long day's toil. Then a fire must be kindled in the cabin, the corn ground in the small handmill, and supper, and dinner for the next day in the field, prepared." The manner of preparing supper, Northup said, was a parable of the life of the slave. "When the corn is ground, and fire is made, the bacon is taken down from the nail on which it hangs, a slice is cut off and thrown upon the coals to broil. The majority of slaves have no knife, much less a fork. They cut their bacon with the axe at the woodpile. The corn meal is mixed with a little water, placed in the fire, and baked. When it is 'done brown,' the ashes are scraped off, and being placed upon a chip, which answers for a table, the tenant of the slave hut is ready to sit down upon the ground to supper. By this time it is usually midnight. The same fear of punishment with which they approach the gin-house, possesses them again on lying down to get a snatch of rest. It is the fear of oversleeping in the morning. Such an offense would certainly be attended with not less than twenty lashes. With a prayer that he may be on his feet and wide awake at the first sound of the horn, he sinks to his slumbers nightly."

A terrifying and a demeaning world, as you can see; and yet it was in the depths of this world that the slave created a new community with its own values, traditions, codes of behavior, aesthetic forms, and even institutions or proto-institutions. On one level, this community was a response to the negative influence of white oppression. It appears from available evidence that slaves adopted white cultural patterns that were necessary for survival and institutions that complemented African customs. Yet, in assessing this development, we must keep in mind the totalitarian system to which it was a response. We must never forget, in short, that we are dealing with the adaptation of human impulses to a pattern of behavior coercively imposed. A second point to bear in mind is that slavery was not imposed on undifferentiated raw material. On the contrary, it was imposed on the African, a man with a past and a point of view. And from this standpoint, it becomes clear that the African made African demands on his new environment and resisted European patterns that did not meet vital needs of his situation and heritage. What we have to deal with, therefore, is a dialectical process: the push of oppression and the pull of men responding, consciously or unconsciously, to the gravitational orbit of African culture. It may be at once observed—though we shall return to this point later in greater detail—that African culture influenced the slave community and the African-American community in many subtle ways. There is, for example, the whole hair-dressing complex, the habit, on one level, of plaiting the hair in braided designs. Nor should we forget the whole area of motor responses, the mode of holding children with legs straddling the mother's body, or the pattern of punctuating conversation and ceremonies with verbal responses like "Amen!" and "Yes, brother!" It would seem that the currently fashionable verbal response, "Right On!" has a provenance and a meaning that extend beyond the twentieth century or continental America.

The language of the slave was a product of the same forces. What men called Negro dialect stemmed from creativity, not stupidity. Lorenzo

Turner and Melville Herskovits, among others, have detailed the process by which Africans transformed the English language. And it will suffice here for us to mention that the language of the slave was rich, poetic, fertile in allusion and metaphor. Turner has pointed out that several African words and names, such as Coffee, gumbo, and tote, passed into common usage and that contemporary African-Americans are still using proper names and other words with an African provenance.

Beyond the creative blendings of different strains, one must stress the overall power of the word in the slave community. The slave reveled in the magical power of words. Language gave him delight and pleasure. The slave was essentially a poet and his language was poetic. Rapping is an old and honorable art in African and African-Americn communities.

At the same time, we should remember, if only for the purpose of perspective, that there was a constant infusion of African influences into the slave community. Men from Africa were brought to America until the nineteenth century, and slave annalists tell us that in some places they were revered and sought out as oracles and priests. One of the leaders of the Denmark Vesey conspiracy, for example, was Gullah Jack, an African-born priest, who was considered invulnerable. There were men made in Gullah Jack's image on many plantations, and some slaves considered it a mark of honor that their parents were African-born. A slave commentator recalled the beauteous Patsey who "glories in the fact that she is an offspring of a 'Guinea nigger.'" Jacob Stroyer, who was a slave in South Carolina, remembered with pride that his father was born in Sierra Leone and that "some [slaves] who were born in Africa, would sing some of their songs, or tell different stories of the customs of Africa."

Although a number of white authorities question the existence of an African-influenced slave community, the authority of the evidence is more imposing. The evidence comes from three sources: the testimony of slaves, the testimony of slaveowners, and the testimony of slave behavior as objectified in events, folklore, and art. Most of the evidence, even the evidence of hostile witnesses, enables us to see that the slaves had a community of feeling, a recognition of special obligations, and an *us* perspective.

It would seem at first blush that the fact that individual slaves betrayed their brothers and identified with the masters contradicts this theory. But the contradiction is more apparent than real. In the first place, traitors are an unavoidable consequence of every situation of oppression.

They were common in the Irish rebellion, they were common in German concentration camps, they were common in occupied France. What is crucial is not the existence of traitors but the attitude of the group toward traitors and the consensus of the group on the primary obligations of its members. Bearing these things in mind, we can readily see that the slaves belonged to a common community. We are told that it was necessary to move black traitors to new environments to protect them from the fury of their betrayed brothers. We are also told that slaves generally did not feel that they had unqualified moral obligations to whites. It was a positive good to take valuables from whites and to deceive them. A former slave, Josiah Henson, left a record of his feelings after the liberation of a pig. He shared the pig, he said, with a "black fair one" and added that the adventure made him feel "good, moral [and] heroic."

As Henson felt, so felt most of the other slaves, including Frederick Douglass. In his autobiography, Douglass emphasized the different bases of the moralities of the community of masters and the community of slaves. He was, he said, a "slave of society which has, in fact, in form and substance, bound itself to assist the white man in robbing me of my rightful liberty and the just rewards of my labor." As a result, Douglass said, "whatever rights I have against the master, I have equally against those confederated with him in robbing me of my liberty. Since society has marked me out as privileged plunder, on the principle of self-preservation, I am justified in plundering in return."

There is corroborating testimony from the other side of the line. Charles C. Jones, writing in 1842, said: "The Negroes are scrupulous on one point: *they make common cause,* as servants, in concealing their faults from their owners. Inquiry elicits no information; no one feels at liberty to disclose the transgressor; all are profoundly ignorant; the matter assumes *the sacredness of a 'professional secret'*; for they remember that they may hereafter require the same concealment of their own transgressions from their fellow servants, and if they tell upon them now, they may have the like favor returned them: besides, in the meantime, *having their names cast out as evil from among their brethren; and being subjected to scorn, and perhaps personal violence or pecuniary injury.*" [My emphasis]

The literature is filled with similar complaints. One master said there was an absence of what he called moral principle among slaves. And by that he meant that "to steal [from white people] and not to be detected is a merit among them." No slave, he added, would betray another slave, for an informer was held "in greater detestation than the most notorious thief."

There is a court case which in a brief illuminating flash seems to describe perfectly the solidarity of the slaves. A Tennessee slave, identified only as Jim, killed a slave named Isaac for betraying him after his escape. At the trial the judge observed that "Isaac seems to have lost caste. . . . He had combined with the white folks . . . . no slight offense in their eyes: that one of their own color, subject to a like servitude, should abandon the interests of his caste, and betray black folks to the white people, rendered him an object of general aversion."

This case is more than a curiosity, for it serves to show that the slave community existed and that it had peculiar interests and characteristics. One of these characteristics was a collective orientation stemming partly from the African past and partly from the exigencies of the situation. Indeed, it is doubtful whether the slaves could have survived without strong traditions of mutual aid and mutual support. The imposed pattern of slavery reinforced the communal orientation of the slave community. On some plantations the food was prepared by one cook and served in a communal kitchen. Children were usually reared in communal nurseries. And, of course, the religion of private property was at a strong discount, partly because the slaves themselves were private property.

A second and equally important characteristic of the slave community was lack of autonomy. The slave community was a deprived community, a put-upon community, a humiliated community. The community lacked autonomy, but it was not completely powerless. Men and women who violated community standards were singled out for scorn, ridicule, and abuse. A rich battery of sayings and songs of derision and condemnation was available for this purpose and was elaborated throughout the slave period. No less important were community sanctions. Violators of community standards were isolated and denied fellowship. The ultimate sanction, physical punishment and even execution, was reserved for flagrant offenders.

There was also an informal judicial system with examining committees and rituals of trial. Stroyer has left an interesting description of the deliberations of the judicial system of one community. "The slaves," he said, "had three ways of detecting thieves, one with a Bible, one with a sieve, and another with graveyeard dust. The first way was this: —four men were selected, one of whom had a Bible with a string attached, and each man had his own part to perform. Of course this was done in the night as it was the only time they could attend to such matters as concerning themselves."

The tragedy of the slave community was that the power available to it was not sufficient to offset the divisive forces of slavery. The pattern of mating, a pattern controlled ultimately by forces hostile to the fundamental interests of blacks, illustrates the point perfectly. Slave marriages had no standing in law, the slave father could not protect his wife and children, and the planter could separate slave families at his convenience. This had at least three devastating results. First of all, the imposed pattern of mating limited the effectiveness of the slave family and had a sharp impact on slave morale. Second, it isolated the black woman and exposed her to the scorn of her peers and the violence of white women. Third, it sowed the seeds of sexual discord in the black community.

This was the most obvious and dramatic aspect of the powerlessness of the slave community, and it is interesting to note that, even in this field, the slave community exercised a small but nonetheless significant degree of power. There is a need for more research in this area, but even at this early stage of research it is obvious that love blossomed in the quarters and that the success of lovers was determined largely by internal forces. Equally obvious is the fact that the proto-blues and love lyrics of the quarters were written in honor of black and not white models. Several decades after the end of slavery, an old black woman cast her mind back to the quarters and said she could still hear the men going to the cotton patch "way 'fore day a-singing 'Peggy, does you love me now?'

> Saturday night and Sunday too
> Young gals on my mind.
> Monday morning 'way 'for day
> Old Master got me gwine.
> Peggy, does you love me now?

This little scene is instructive, for it enables us to see that love in the quarters was more than a simple matter of mating. Slave women had minds of their own, and it seems that it was more important to win their consent than the consent of the slavemaster. We read in the slave narratives that some men went to a great deal of trouble and expense to capture the love of slave maidens. Occasionally, things reached such a pass that it was necessary to consult conjurers who claimed to know the secrets of the heart. "One of these conjurers," Henry Bibb writes, "for a small sum agreed to teach me to make any girl love me that I wished." The conjurer told Bibb to take a certain bone out of the frog and scratch his beloved "somewhere on her naked skin" and she would be certain "to love me, and would follow me in spite of herself; no matter who she might be engaged to, nor who she might be walking with." Bibb said he got the bone "for a certain girl, whom I knew to be under the influence of another young man. I happened to meet her in the company of her lover, one Sunday evening, walking out; so when I got a chance, I fetched her a tremendous rasp across her neck with his bone, which made her jump. But in place of making her love me, it only made her angry with me."

Bones and locks of hair did not always succeed, but this, of course, did not keep others from playing the game of love. There is, in the narrative of Solomon Northup, a delightful description of the wooing of Miss Lively who, it seems, was well-named. At the Christmas dance, Miss Lively, Northup says, was pursued by several young men. She decided, he adds, to grant the first dance to Sam Roberts, adding: "It was well-known that Sam cherished an ardent passion for Lively, as also did one of Marshall's and another of Carey's boys; for Lively was *lively* indeed, and a heart-breaking coquette withal." But Miss Lively, "whirling like a top," soon danced not only Roberts but his chief rival, Peter Marshall, into exhaustion. Marshall's place was taken by Harry Carey "but Lively also soon out-winded him, amidst hurrahs and shouts, fully sustaining her well-earned reputation as being the 'fastest gal' on the bayou."

Political significance apart, in the case of Miss Lively and the perplexed young lovers of the slave quarters one is brought face to face with the human dimensions of slavery and the attempt of the slaves to wrest some peace and joy from an inhospitable climate.

Because of the disruptive influence of the slavemaster, the course of true love did not run smooth in Slave Row. Slavemasters encouraged promiscuity, and there were men and women who were willing to exploit the opportunities. Some slaves had two or more wives, and some women were contemptuous of black males. But, according to slave commentators, there were many stable unions in the quarters. And their testimony is corroborated by the numerous stories of protest and tears on the occasion of forced separations. It was not at all unusual for husbands or wives to escape from the plantations and wander across the South in vain attempts to find lost mates. The behavior of husbands and wives at the end of slavery is also significant. After emancipation the roads of the South were clogged with freedmen searching for wives, children, brothers, and sisters. This is hardly the picture of a non-community without a sense of family involvement. In fact, researchers have turned up new evidence indicating that the reverse was true. Recent studies of official records of the Freedmen's Bureau suggest that an extraordinary large number of slaves remained faithful to one mate for years and even decades.

In marital relations, as in other relations, the slaves survived by imposing their own values on European institutions and by inventing their own rituals and customs. It was fairly common, for example, for slave couples to get married by jumping over a broomstick, arm in arm. And we are told that it was customary for slave patriarchs and matriarchs to preside at slave wedding ceremonies.

It is also important to note that the slaves brought pressure to bear to maintain their own marital standards. There are indications that there was widespread disapproval of alliances between black women and slavemasters. In some cases the children of such unions bore the brunt of community disapproval. Candis Goodwin, the daughter of a slave woman and an overseer, recalled that the "children used to laugh at me an' yell, 'Who's yo' pappy? Who's yo' pappy?' But my mamma tole me how to answer dem children. I jus' yell right back at 'em: 'Turkey buzzard laid me, an' de sun hatch me.'"

THE foregoing would seem to indicate that the slaves had their own values and orientations. In other words, there were shared understandings about what was good and what was bad.

Survival was good. Outwitting the master was good. Helping others to survive was good.

Stealing from black people was bad. Informing on black people was bad. Putting on airs was bad. Interfering with somebody else's mate was *very* bad.

The community also valued mother wit, physical strength, age, and the ability to rap.

The community had special heroes. The bold rebel who challenged the system and survived was admired by almost everyone. The slave the overseer was afraid to whip, the slave who ran away and made it to the North, the woman who talked back and got away with it: these were ideal types embodying the value orientation of the slave community.

Even then, the put-on was a highly-developed art in the black community. It was considered right and proper to hide oneself and one's truth from the slavemasters, and many slaves seemed determined that no white man would ever know what they were thinking and what they felt.

The status hierarchy of this community was complex. There was an imposed hierarchy of house slaves and artisans, whose status was defined by their relations to the slaveholders rather than their functions in the internal economy of the slaves. The house slaves, who constituted, according to some authorities, the slave aristocracy, have been universally condemned as parasitic hangers-on who betrayed their brothers for the hand-me-down clothes of the masters. There is some truth in this, but it is not the whole truth. In fact, the whole subject of the house slaves needs to be restudied in the light of considerable evidence which indicates that there was constant dialogue between house and field slaves. It also appears that house slaves, with significant and obvious exceptions, played an active role in the slave underground by "stealing" food and passing on information overheard in the house. House slaves also ran away and engaged in individual acts of resistance. They were particularly adept at seasoning the food of slavemasters with arsenic, ground glass, and "spiders beaten up in buttermilk."

For the house slave, as well as for the field slave, the locus of community was the Slave Row and not the big house. "House servant and field hand might meet there," the authors of *The Negro in Virginia* wrote, "and the testimony of the living ex-slave does not support the tradition of animosity between the two. House servants would regale other members of the 'row,' some of whom had never set foot in the 'big house,' with tales of 'master' and 'missus,' would 'take them off' in speech and gesture so faithful that the less privileged would shake with laughter."

In reading the documents which have come down to us, one gets the impression that slavemasters doubted the loyalty of the house slaves. The most telling evidence on this point is the widespread existence of "spelling-out stories." It seems that slavemasters were accustomed to spelling out words and sentences they did not want the house slaves to understand and pass on to their fellows in the quarters.

An additional and perhaps even more important point in this connection is that slaves did not place the same valuation on work in the house as whites. Olmstead said that slaves "accustomed to the comparatively unconstrained life of the Negro-settlement, detest the close control and careful movement required of the house-servants. It is a punishment for a lazy field-hand to employ him in menial duties at the house...."

In the conventional sense, this was a community without political institutions. But the driver, the leading black authority figure, was an embryonic political figure, roughly similar to the straw boss of the Jim Crow regime and the political mediator of the modern period. The driver was appointed by the slavemaster, who charged him with the responsibility of supervising the work of the slaves in the field and policing the quarters at night. "The head driver," James H. Hammond, a South Carolina slavemaster said, "is the most important Negro on the plantation, and is not required to work like other hands. He is to be treated with more respect than any other Negro by both master and overseer.... He is to be required to maintain proper discipline at all times; to see that no Negro idles or does bad work in the field, and to punish it with discretion.... He is a confidential servant, and may be a guard against any excesses or omissions of the overseer."

For these services, the driver received special food and other perquisites. Daniel, a driver on a Mississippi plantation, was granted the privilege of two wives. But when he displeased the slavemaster, one of his wives, his favorite, was taken away.

Caught in the crossfire between the slavemaster and the slaves, the driver inhabited a twilight world between warring camps. There was, in fact, no solution to the built-in ambiguity of the role, and many drivers succumbed to the corruptions of derived power. Such men were loathed by the slaves. It was not uncommon for slaves to harass and assault drivers. The case of Ely, a driver on a Mississippi plantation, is instructive. He drove his charges so hard that they ambushed him one day and killed him.

There were other drivers who did what they could to soften the impact of slavery. Solomon Northup and other drivers say they conspired with their fellow slaves to outwit the masters by faking whippings and institutionalizing other practices which made the tasks of the slaves easier.

Although the driver was the leading figure on the plantation, he was not necessarily the leading black figure in the slave community. On almost every plantation there were two or three slaves who wielded authority not because of their relations with the slavemaster, but because of their relations with their fellow slaves. One slavemaster said it was a "notorious fact" that "on almost every large plantation of Negroes, there is one among them who holds a kind of magical sway over the minds and opinions of the rest; to him they look as their oracle.... The influence of such a Negro, often a preacher, on a quarter is incalculable."

On one plantation the leading black patriarch was "Old Abram," who was said to be "deeply versed in such philosophy as is taught in the cabin of the slave." An old woman named Juba, who wore charms around her neck and regaled her followers with details of her many visions of the devil, occupied roughly the same position on a Mississippi plantation. And a Louisiana planter noted that Big Lucy was an indigenous leader of the slave community who "corrupts every young Negro in her power."

The slaves also had their own specialists in matters of decorum, dress, and worship. Significantly, the slave community seems to have been totally democratic in the sense that the highest roles were open to female talent.

The roles in the slave community were organized into institutions or proto-institutions. There were institutions, i.e., organized patterns of behavior, for maintaining community standards, for dealing with the white man, for inducting new members into the group, and for expressing the soul and the style of the people. Some of these institutions were more or less direct translations of African institutions in the light of the new realities. Others were creative blendings of African and European forms. Still others were free improvisations on European themes.

A good example of a slave practice in the first category was the John Canoe celebration, which was popular on the East Coast. The participants in this celebration donned masks and paraded along the roads, singing, dancing, and soliciting presents. Another example was the practice of wearing handkerchiefs on the head to indicate rank and status. In Charleston, South Carolina, in this period, William Ferguson, a white visitor, was struck by the fact that married women wore distinctive handkerchiefs, knotted in a peculiar manner, to indicate their status.

Slaves also retained and reinterpreted African codes of polite behavior. Nearly all contemporary descriptions mention the rule of respect for elders. Young men and women were required to address elders with the title of Aunty or Uncle. The whole institution, as described by Frederick Douglass, was reminiscent of the rituals of West Africa. Douglass wrote: "These mechanics were called 'Uncles' by all the younger slaves, not because they really sustained that relationship to any, but according to plantation etiquette, as a mark of respect, due from the younger to the older slaves. Strange, and even ridiculous as it may seem among a people so uncultivated, and with so many stern trials to look in the face, there is not to be found, among any people, a more rigid enforcement of the law of respect to elders. . . . I set this down as partly constitutional with my race, and partly conventional. There is no better material in the world for making a gentleman than is furnished in the African. He shows to others, and exacts for himself, all the tokens of respect which he is compelled to manifest toward his master. A young slave must approach the company of the elder with hat in hand, and woe betide him if he fails to acknowledge a favor, of any sort, with the accustomed 'tankee' etc. So uniformly are good manners enforced among slaves, that I can easily detect a bogus fugitive by his manners."

The slave was equally inventive in the field of religion, creating a whole constellation of patterns and forms that gave a new dimension and a new meaning to Christianity. It has been assumed generally that slaves adopted the religion of their masters. But the slave did not adopt; he adapted. In other words, he transformed Christianity by adapting it to his needs and circumstances. One result of this transformation was that the slave's God was not the white man's God. Nor was his devil the white man's devil. Nora Zeale Hurston very wisely observed: "The devil is not the terror that he is in European folklore. He is a powerful trickster who often competes successfully with God." Another commentator who caught the real meaning of the slave's maneuver was ethnologist Paul Radin, who said that the slave's religion was an expression of a thrust toward liberation. He added: "The ante-bellum Negro was not converted to God; he converted God to himself."

Unquestionably: and it is important to view this conversion in context. Most commentators have managed to suggest that the conversion of the slave was a free choice. But this view is contradicted by two facts. First, slavemasters used force and violence to prevent slaves from practicing their own rites. Secondly, the evidence seems to suggest that the adoption of some religious form was necessary, not only because religion is a focal point of African culture but also because it is generally a focal point of survival in a situation of oppression. Since the slaves could not continue their own mode of spiritual behavior, they had to find an outlet for their spiritual passions or die.

As we know, they found that outlet by transforming Christianity, by infusing it with African-oriented melodies and rhythms and by adding new features, such as the ring shout, ecstatic seizure, and communal, call-

and-response participation. The difference between the hand-me-down patterns and the transformed patterns was striking and obvious, even to the slaves. Nancy Williams, who was a slave in Virginia, said: "Dat old white preachin' wasn't nothin'." Henrietta Perry, another Virginia slave, said: "White folks can't pray to the black man's God."

So saying and so believing, slaves created what authorities have called a vast invisible structure of worship, which differed materially from the visible and oppressive services ("Slaves be obedient to your masters") of the whites. They often slipped away to the fields and praised God in "hush-harbors." A detailed description of a "hush-harbor" was given by Peter Randolph in his book, *From Slave Cabin to Pulpit*. "Not being allowed to hold meetings on the plantation," he wrote, "the slaves assemble in the swamps, out of reach of the patrols. They have an understanding among themselves as to the time and place of getting together. This is often done by the first one arriving breaking boughs from the trees and bending them in the direction of the selected spot. Arrangements are then made for conducting the exercises. They first ask each other how they feel, the state of their minds, etc. The male members then select a certain space, in separate groups, for their division of the meeting. Preaching in order, by the brethren; then praying and singing all around, until they generally feel quite happy. The speaker usually commences by calling himself unworthy, and talks very slowly, until, feeling the spirit, he grows excited, and in a short time, there fall to the ground twenty or thirty men and women under its influence."

Another distinctive element in the religious syndrome of the slaves was a belief in a world of spirits who could be manipulated and persuaded to serve the living. Hence, the widespread beliefs in "hants," charms, and taboos.

Closely linked to the religious syndrome, closely linked, in fact, to the entire life of the slave was the world of music. In a sense, slave music represented the ultimate distillation of the experiences of the slaves. Amiri Baraka has observed that the slave's music—his spirituals, work songs, devil songs, and blues—represented the solidarity, the identity, the social consciousness of the slaves. This music was characterized by the so-called "blues tonality" and a rhythmic, collective, and emotional orientation. It was a collective product, but it was shaped by creative geniuses, by men and women of large vision and even larger voices, men and women immortalized by James Weldon Johnson in the phrase "black and unknown bards." There is no need really to debate here whether the slave songs were songs of protests or songs of adaptation. Let us say simply that they were songs of transcendence and that they are shot through with a cosmic discontent.

Slaves also used music as a medium of communication. The cries and hollers and field calls contained secret messages and code words. In truth, double meanings permeated the whole fabric of this music. There are images of release ("de walls come tumblin' down") and battle ("He said, and if I had'n my way, I'd tear the buildin' down!"). A former slave said: "[slaves] had field calls and other kinds of hollers that had a meaning to them."

One song, for example, used Jesus' name to mask an open and obvious invitation to the slaves to steal away to freedom.

> Steal away, steal away to Jesus,
> Steal away, steal away home.
> I aint got long to stay here.
> My Lord calls me, he calls me by thunder,
> The trumpet sounds within my soul.
> I aint got long to stay here.

Another evoked battle and destruction:

> Joshua fit the battle of Jericho,
> Jericho, Jericho!
> Joshua fit the battle of Jericho,
> And the walls came tumblin' down.

Still another warned the slavemaster:

> When Israel was in Egypt's Land
>   Let my people go.
> Oppressed so hard they could not stand,
>   Let my people go.
> Go down, Moses, way down in Egypt's Land,
> Tell old Pharaoh, let my people go.

Finally, there was the deep and brooding anthem:

> Oh, freedom; oh freedom;
> Oh, Lord, freedom over me,
> And before I'd be a slave
> I'd be buried in my grave
> An' go home to my Lord and be free.

Dancing represented another rhythmic element in the slave ethos. The slaves did the hoedown, the cakewalk, and other prototypes of modern dances. As in other cases, the dances were translations of African movements, a fact verified by an investigator who later photographed an African tribe dancing what was perhaps the original of the Charleston.

Almost all observers were impressed by the skill of the slave dancers. We are told that the slaves danced with the whole body, that they danced "all over," a fact which astonished one white auditor who believed apparently that it was possible to dance some other way.

The way of life embodied in the dances, songs, and social practices was passed on from generation to generation by informal educational institutions. Mothers and fathers and community elders passed on to the young the accumulated vision of the group and its particular perspectives on the realities of power and the shape and contour of the natural and spiritual worlds. They taught the young how to survive and how to outwit the white man. They did this consciously and unconsciously, by the power of the word, as well as by the power of example. Viewed from the vantage point of the twentieth century, some elements of slave lore were negative. But these elements were part of a total process that enabled a besieged group to survive until the balance of forces changed.

Folklore was one of the educational devices of the slave community. Stories about Brer Rabbit and Brer Fox and Old John the trickster transformed the slave world symbolically and created an arena, as one author said, where vindications denied on the plantations were realized on the level of art. Brer Fox, for example, as Bernard Wolfe has pointed out, was a synonym for white people who were portrayed as powerful but stupid bumblers outwitted by clever and resourceful antagonists.

The slave's philosophy of life—and philosophy is not too strong a word—was embodied in his folklore, music, religion, and art. In these products and in his daily life, he created a worldview that contradicted the white worldview at several critical points. To mention only one point: the slave was not cursed by the European sin of dichotomizing. For the slave, good and bad, the flesh and the spirit were different sides of the same coin. There was a balance, a wholeness and a complexity to this worldview that contrasted strongly with Puritan Manichaesm.

There was last of all, and most importantly of all, a stubbornly incandescent optimism. Many men have commented on this fact with wonder and incomprehension. But the truth of the matter is that the slave expected somehow, someway to come out on the other side. That is to say, he believed that his suffering had a meaning and that someday it would have an issue. This was the larger meaning of the world the slave created to contain his spirit. And the creation of this world was, by any standard, an impressive achievement, a fact noted by Ralph Ellison who said: "Any people who could endure all of that brutalization and keep together, who could undergo such dismemberment and resuscitate itself, and endure until it could take the initiative in achieving its own freedom is obviously more than the sum of its brutalization. Seen in this perspective, theirs has been one of the great human experiences and one of the great triumphs of the human spirit in modern times, in fact, in the history of the world."

1865

*Jubilee*

To Felix Haywood, who was there, it was the Time of Glory when men and women walked "on golden clouds."

To Booker T. Washington, a nine-year-old slave on a Virginia plantation, it was a time of "great rejoicing" and "wild scenes of ecstasy."

To Frederick Douglass, a former slave, now forty-eight and the best-known black leader, it was one of the major events of the nineteenth century and a down payment on the redemption of the American soul.

To Sister Winny in Virginia, to Jane Montgomery in Louisiana, to Mary Jane Hardridge in Arkansas, to Ed Bluff in Mississippi and Felix Haywood in Texas, it was the Time of Jubilee, the wild, happy, sad, mocking, tearful, fearful time of the unchaining of the bodies if not of the spirits of the blacks of the land. And across that whole sweep of land the air was sweet with song.

> Free at last.
> Free at last.
> Thank God Almighty
> We're free at last.

W. E. B. DuBois was not there, but he had an eye and a feel for realities, and he summed the whole thing up one day in phrases worthy of the time and of the ages. It was all, he said, "foolish, bizarre, and tawdry. Gangs of dirty Negroes howling and dancing; poverty-stricken ignorant laborers mistaking war, destruction, and revolution for the mystery of the free human soul; and yet to these black folk it was the Apocalypse." And he added: "All that was Beauty, all that was Love, all that was Truth, stood on the top of these mad mornings and sang with the stars. A great human sob shrieked in the wind, and tossed its tears upon the sea—free, free, free."

This was one side of the coin, and it was real. But the coin of "freedom" had another side, equally real, a side that gave Jubilee a desperate undertone of anxiety. Stated simply but bluntly, the other side of the coin was that the fabled "Golden Dawn, after chains of a thousand years" was a false dawn, the first of many illusions and deceptions. Partly because of the default of the federal government and partly because of the bungling and bad faith of state and local officials, the slaves were hurled into "freedom" under the worst possible circumstances. Although they had worked from sunup to sundown for two hundred years without pay, although they had created the wealth of the South and much of the wealth of the North, the slaves were turned loose without clothes to hide their nakedness or shelter to protect them from the storms. Unlike the bondsmen of Russia, the bondsmen of America received no interest in the soil they had tilled for centuries. "They were," as Frederick Douglass said, "free! free to hunger; free to the winds and rains of heaven; free to the pitiless wrath of enraged masters, who, since they could no longer control them, were willing to see them starve. They were free, without roofs to cover them, or bread to eat, or land to cultivate, and as a consequence died in such numbers as to awaken the hope of their enemies that they would soon disappear."

This, then, was the underside of Jubilee. And if we are to assess the meaning of that event, not in terms of contemporary ideas, but in the terms of the men and women who experienced it, then we must see it not only as a time of shouting and dancing, but also as a time of suffering and deprivation. We must see it, in other words, as a time of extravagant expectations and heartbreaking disappointments, a time when perhaps the greatest hope this world has known rose like dew from the unpromising soil of a cataclysmic social upheaval that brought in its wake blood, tears, separation, smallpox, dysentery, cholera, hunger, and mass destitution.

To this analysis we must add two other factors. The first is that Jubilee was a process and not a cut-and-dried event. Emancipation came to different slaves at different times in different ways, and the Emancipation Proclamation was only one step in a protracted process. Some slaves escaped and celebrated Jubilee for the first time in 1861 and 1862. Others were freed, for all practical purposes, by invading Union armies in 1862 and 1863. By 1865, according to some estimates, at least a half-million slaves had escaped to Union lines. By that time, according to historian Vernon Wharton, at least one-third and possibly one-half of all the slaves in Mississippi had tasted some of the fruits of freedom.

The second factor is that the defeat of the Confederate army in the spring of 1865 did not free all slaves. Some slavemasters managed by fraud and violence to keep their workers in bondage until June—hence the "Juneteenth celebrations"—July and even August. The essential point here—and it is a point that cannot be made too often—is that the emancipation of the black slave was a long, slow, painful process that extended over four years—and it has never been completed.

For our purposes, this process can be divided into three main phases: 1) the twilight period of 1861–1862 when the federal government tried to wage war without touching slavery; 2) the post–Emancipation Proclamation period of 1863–1864; 3) the Year of Jubilee following the defeat of the Confederate armies in 1865.

The process began, if social movements of this magnitude can be said to have a beginning, with the firing of the first gun at Fort Sumter on April 12, 1861. When Pierre Gustave Toutant Beauregard gave the signal for the bombardment of this federal fort in the harbor of Charleston, South Carolina, he initiated the process that led to the freeing of the slaves. It was the precise opposite of what he intended to do. But the ideas men form about their acts neither modify their internal logic nor their consequences. And it was clear, at least to those with eyes to see, that the objective consequence of the Southern attack on Sumter was the shattering of the foundations of the slave regime. For abolitionists, who perceived this almost immediately, the war was a godsend. When news of the bombardment flashed across the North, Frederick Douglass shouted, "God be praised." Others, more cynical perhaps, praised the madness of the slaveholders, who had ignited a conflagration that was destined to consume them. Perhaps the most lucid exponent of this point of view was Wendell Phillips, who went up and down the North, telling large and applauding audiences: "I never did believe in the capacity of Abraham Lincoln, but I do believe in the pride of [Jefferson] Davis, in the vanity of the South, in the desperate determination of those fourteen states; and I believe in a sunny future, because God has driven them mad; and in their madness is our hope...."

As the fighting continued, more and more people recognized the relevance of Phillips's remarks. Specifically, there was the case of Secretary of State William H. Seward, who heaped scorn on the Emancipation Proclamation, telling his friend Donn Piatt that "we have let off a puff of wind over an accomplished fact."

"What do you mean, Mr. Seward?" Piatt asked.

"I mean," he said, "that the Emancipation Proclamation was uttered in the first gun fired at Fort Sumter, and we have been the last to hear it."

Seward and his friend were not the only Northerners who failed to hear the message of events. For eighteen months after Fort Sumter, Abraham Lincoln based his policy on the convenient fiction that the war was an argument between white men, an argument, he maintained, that could be pursued and resolved without touching the institution of slavery. And Congress, following Lincoln's lead, declared after Bull Run that the war was not being waged to disturb "the established institutions of the States." During this period the Lincoln Administration refused to accept black volunteers, Union army commanders vied with one another in returning fugitive slaves to their masters, and some Union officers were court-martialed and cashiered out of the service for opposing the proslavery policies of the government. Nor was this all. In one celebrated case, a Union general announced that if slaves rebelled behind Confederate lines he would stop fighting the Confederates and fight the slaves. This was a unique contribution to the strategy and tactics of war, but it drew no rebuke from Lincoln, who later countermanded two emancipation proclamations issued by Union generals. This policy was changed finally not because of the largeness of heart or keenness of insight of Union leaders, but because of the intransigence of Southerners, who forced the North into a protracted struggle, and the passion of the slaves, who flocked to Union lines in such numbers that the North was forced to redefine the nature of the war.

The last point—the passion of the slaves—is worth dwelling on for a moment, for it affected the entire war and marked the first act of the Jubilee drama. To the dismay of some and the delight of others, the slaves pushed to center stage at the opening of the drama. Some slaves—a definite minority—moved immediately, striking out for the nearest Union outpost. Others, more skeptical perhaps, went into a holding pattern, nervously and expectantly surveying the scene of battle, trying to identify the outline of their true interests. We may see them through the eyes of Mary Boykin Chestnut, the wife of a South Carolina slaveholder, who put down the following words during the bombardment of Fort Sumter. "Not by one word or look," she wrote, "can we detect any change in the demeanor of these Negro servants. Lawrence sits at our door, as sleepy and as respectful and as profoundly indifferent. So are they all." But—she added in a telling and chilling phrase—"they carry it too far."

Not everyone was as perceptive as Mary Chestnut. And shortly after the fall of Fort Sumter, a black newspaper, the *Anglo-American*, underlined the meaning of the heavy and expectant presence of the four million slaves. "No adjustment of the nation's difficulty is possible," the paper said, "until the claims of the black man are first met and satisfied. . . . His prostrate body forms an impediment over which liberty cannot advance. . . . His title to life, to liberty, and the pursuit of happiness must be acknowledged, or the nation will be forsworn; and being so, incur the dreadful penalty of permanent disunion, unending anarchy, and perpetual strife. . . ."

Understandably—in view of the record we have cited here—some slaves were skeptical of the claims of both Southerners and Northerners. A characteristic story of the time exemplifies this position. One slave rebuked another slave, who believed the Union was fighting for freedom, saying: "Ain't you never seen two dogs fighting over a bone before now. . . . Well, then, you ain't never seen the bone fight none, is you." There was some point to the skeptic's remarks, but in riddles of this kind a great deal depends on the immediate interests of the two dogs. And it quickly became apparent to many slaves that their immediate interests were linked with the immediate interests of the hostile and always ambiguous Yankees. Proceeding perhaps on the assumption that the enemy of their enemy was their friend, these slaves recognized early that the Yankees, though bitterly anti-Negro for the most part, had embarked on a course that would force them to deal with slavery.

Wholly apart from the question of interest, it is plain that the slaves had definite ideas about the nature and meaning of the war. For most slaves the "Freedom War," as it was called in Slave Row, was associated with the Time of Jubilee and the Coming of the Kingdom. This does not mean that the slaves expected an ethereal triumph of the Lord of History beyond history. On the contrary, the concept of Jubilee was grounded in a concrete expectation of the damnation and destruction of the oppressors in history and the general deliverance of the oppressed. Over and above this, it was clearly understood that Jubilee required blood, sacrifice, and struggle. Specifically, there was a case cited by Susie King, a young slave woman who ran away from Savannah, Georgia, with her uncle and made it to the Union lines at Fort Pulaski. "Oh!" she reported later, "how these people prayed for freedom! I remember, one night, my grandmother went out into the suburbs of the city [Savannah] to a church meeting, and they were fervently singing this old hymn,—

> 'Yes, we all shall be free,
> Yes, we all shall be free
> Yes, we all shall be free,
> When the Lord shall appear'—

when the police came in and arrested all who were there, saying they were planning freedom, and sang 'the Lord' in place of 'Yankee,' to blind any one who might be listening." Another case showing still more clearly the concrete content of the Jubilee concept was the slave cook who heard the cannons roaring at Bull Run and greeted each salvo with a fervent, "Ride on, Massa Jesus."

Because most slaves believed that a force was involved in the war that would ultimately turn it to their advantage, they followed the progress of events with consuming interest. From Fort Wagner forward, an amazingly effective communications network operated behind Confederate lines. Joseph Finegan, a Confederate general, said slave messages were "conducted through swamps and under cover of night, and could not be prevented." This statement is confirmed by another contemporary,

Booker T. Washington, who said that "though I was a mere child during the preparation for the Civil War and during the war itself, I now recall the many late-at-night whispered discussions that I heard my mother and other slaves on the plantation indulge in. These discussions showed that they understood the situation, and that they kept themselves informed of events by what was termed the 'grapevine telegraph.'"

At the hub of the grapevine telegraph were house slaves, who passed on information picked up in and around the house. Washington tells us, for instance, that he monitored conversations while fanning flies from the table. Other slaves obtained valuable information by listening at keyholes, and hiding in closets. The slavemasters, who never really believed the propaganda they organized for external consumption, tried to confuse the slaves by spelling out sensitive words and phrases. Not a few slaves turned this method to their advantage by performing the extraordinary mental feat of remembering the spelled-out letters, which were decodified later by literate slaves. The information received at these listening posts was supplemented by messages from literate slaves, who read the headlines of papers left on restaurant and parlor tables, and illiterate slaves, who picked up information while working or lingering at the post office and other official buildings.

The slaves apparently used code words and songs that enabled them to discuss the war in the presence of slavemasters. Robert Russa Moton, who later became president of Tuskegee Institute, said the word "grease" was a code word in some sections of Virginia. "If a slave coming back from town," he said, "greeted a fellow-servant with the declaration, 'Good morning, Sam, you look mighty greasy this morning,' this meant he had picked up some fresh information about the prospects of freedom which would be divulged later on."

Based on the information received from these disparate sources, the slaves evaluated their situation and formulated tentative strategies, of which three can be noted. Some slaves opted for inaction, doing nothing and committing themselves to nothing until the outlines of their interests were clear. Other slaves continued the holding pattern, watching and waiting for a Union advance that would enable them to move into the Union lines. Still others decided to move immediately, relying on their ability to outwit the sentinels and slave patrols of the Southerners.

From the ranks of the slaves who adopted the third strategy—immediate action by any means necessary—came the slave vanguard, the heroes who pitted their strength and cunning against the armed and organized might of the Confederacy. Slowly at first and then in ever-increasing numbers, these slaves fled the plantations and sought asylum within Union lines. Many were refused admittance, many were returned to their masters, and many were insulted and abused. But nothing—neither insults, nor rejection, nor betrayal—stopped the subterranean migration. Nearly all contemporary descriptions of this migration mention the ingenuity of the slave rebels. Some slaves, we are told, made rafts of grass and pieces of wood and floated down the rivers and bayous to the federal forts. Some escaped by writing false passes, and some stole the slavemasters' carriages and rode away from the plantations in style. There were also men who walked away dressed as women, and women who escaped masquerading as men. Charles Nordhoff, a contemporary witness, said these slaves were "nerved to face every danger, to suffer every loss, to sacrifice every feeling." Benjamin Quarles, a modern investigator, observed: "To the securing of their liberty they brought skill, forecast, and courage. It was a common mistake to assume that slavery was no climate for heroes. Having lived under the pressure of stress and tension since their cradle days, blacks had become immunized to danger." By way of illustration, we can cite the remarkable case of Robert Smalls, who commandeered a Confederate steamer and sailed it out of the Charleston harbor under the guns of Confederate batteries. Less spectacular but no less pertinent was the case of the slave who walked five hundred miles to freedom.

These, then, were the men and women—dauntless, determined, endlessly resourceful—who changed the tone of the war and forced the first breach in the line of slavery.

By singular circumstance, this breach occurred at Fortress Monroe on the same peninsula and within a few miles of Jamestown, where the first Africans landed. It was here on May 23, 1861, a month after the beginning of the war and 242 years after the Jamestown Landing, that three black men—Shepard Mallory, Frank Baker, and James Townsend—presented themselves to the ingenious Union general, Benjamin Franklin Butler. When Virginia slaveholders demanded the return of the three fugitives, Butler refused, stating that they were "contraband of war." Acting on this novel theory, Butler told his subordinates to give the men rations and to put them to work. This information was disseminated by the grapevine telegraph and additional fugitives, accompanied by wives and children, flocked to "the freedom fort." By July, 1861, some nine hundred liberated slaves were living and working in and around Fortress Monroe.

The word *contraband* was pure windfall to the North, which had been looking for a way to deal with slavery without really dealing with slavery. Before long the word was enshrined in Union folklore, and thousands of "contrabands" were working and receiving army rations at Union camps. Butler's military aide, Theodore Winthrop, said, with some truth, that "an epigram abolished slavery in the United States."

One of the immediate by-products of the incident of the epigram was the beginning of the Jubilee celebrations. Perhaps the first celebrations were held in May and June, 1861, at Fortress Monroe. "In the protective shelter of Fortress Monroe," according to the authors of *The Negro in Virginia*, "the tents and barracks assigned [blacks] echoed night and day with 'Freedom's cry of joy.' On Sundays the contrabands would gather beneath Emancipation Oak, a six-hundred-year-old tree on the grounds where Hampton Institute now stands, to sing the 'Freedom Song.' Here exhorters would lead in prayer, many of them elderly preachers who had not been allowed to 'talk to God out loud' since Nat Turner's strike for freedom thirty years before."

Not long thereafter a second round of Jubilee celebrations began in South Carolina. In November, 1861, a scant seven months after the attack on Fort Sumter, Union forces captured Port Royal and other Sea Islands some fifty miles southwest of Charleston. The rebels fled, leaving the plantations and some eight thousand slaves. In the weeks and months that followed, the liberated islands became a magnet for slaves in the interior. By the summer of 1862 there were more than ten thousand slaves on the Sea Islands. By 1865 there were at least thirty thousand. Here, as at Fortress Monroe, Jubilee came early. By 1862 slaves in this area were singing:

> No more driver's lash for me
> No more, no more:
> No more driver's lash for me
> Many thousand gone.

As the war turned the corner of 1862 and as Union troops occupied additional Confederate territory, the number of liberated blacks increased appreciably. In April Union forces captured New Orleans, and the tremors set in motion by that event traveled swiftly through Louisiana and far beyond. In the same month the slaves of Washington, D. C., were emancipated by an act of Congress, and an old slave woman went to her knees, shouting, "Glory to God, the jubilee has come at last."

M*ANY* thousands were gone, many thousands were going, but many thousands were still in the fields. What of these slaves? What were they doing all this time? Most were pursuing the second strategy of waiting and watching, eyes and ears alert for targets of opportunity. While waiting, most of these slaves apparently did everything they could to impede the Southern war effort and to hasten the day of liberation. There is a great deal of evidence, some of it based on the private letters of slavemasters and overseers, to indicate that the slaves were constantly probing for weak spots in the slaveholders' line of defense. After an exhaustive survey of the evidence, Professor Bell Irwin Wiley said that "disorder and unfaithfulness on the part of Negroes were far more common than postwar commentators have usually admitted." Wiley also pointed out that "the tenor of statements [made by slaveowners] during the war is generally in marked contrast to those made afterwards."

During the war there were repeated complaints from slaveowners, who said their slaves refused to answer the old slave bells and staged slow-downs and sit-downs in the cottonfields. A South Carolina slaveowner complained in August, 1862, that "we have had hard work to get along this season, the Negroes are unwilling to do any work, no matter what it is." In some instances the more or less unorganized idleness assumed the precise and organized form of the strike. A Louisiana overseer reported in 1862 that the slaves "would not work eny moore unles they got pay for their work."

Nor would some slaves accept the rituals and sanctions of slavery. One manifestation of this, widely reported, was the refusal of slaves to accept punishment. A Texas slaveowner who tried to whip a slave in 1863 was, according to a report of his neighbor, "cursed . . . all to pieces" by the slave who "walked off into the wood, and then sent back word that he would return to his work if a pledge were given that he would not be whipped. The terms were accepted and he came back."

Yet another manifestation of slave discontent was that bugbear of the Southern disciplinarian: "insolence and insubordination." In August, 1863, the Selma, Alabama, *Morning Reporter* said "the Negroes . . . are becoming so saucy and abusive that a police force has become positively necessary as a check to this continued insolence." Of like spirit and quality were the complaints in the Georgia house of representatives, where a bill was introduced "to punish slaves and free persons of color for abusive and insulting language to white persons."

If there was widespread resistance to slavery behind Confederate lines, there was something approaching open rebellion in invaded areas. We have the testimony of both Yankees and Confederates on this point, and there is general agreement that the slaves were creatively subversive in giving aid and comfort to the enemies of their enemies. After a Union raid in South Carolina, a planter wrote that "the people about here would not have suffered near as much if it not been for these Negroes; in every case they have told where things have been hidden and they did most of the stealing." There is similar testimony from Union sources. A Union soldier, foraging in Louisiana in 1863, said slaves stood at the gates with unerringly accurate information on the location of saddles, horses, and other valuables. He added that in most cases "it was the favorite servants who pointed out the hiding places and said, 'you give us free, and we helps you all we can.'"

Slaves also assisted the Union war effort by aiding Union soldiers who escaped from Confederate prisons. Junius Henri Brown, who was held in prisons in North Carolina and Virginia, said that "during our entire captivity, and after our escape, they were our firm, brave, unflinching friends. We never made an appeal to them they did not answer."

Many masters who boasted of the loyalty of their slaves were forced to face reality by the arrival of federal troops. "Many a man who has boasted that all his slaves could be trusted," wrote Yankee George H. Hepworth, "... had his eyes opened on those days of our advance." Writing from Selma, Alabama, in 1863, John F. Andrews said that "the 'faithful slave' is about played out. They are the most treacherous, brutal, and ungrateful race on the globe."

As the slave resistance movement widened, slaveholders launched a counteroffensive, tightening slave patrols and the pass system and organizing a reign of terror. In some areas slaveowners adopted a policy of punishing slave rebels summarily, oftentimes by death sentences on the spot.

Buckling under the massive pressure, many slaveowners adopted a policy of "refugeeing," moving slaves from invaded or threatened areas to the interior or to Texas. We learn from contemporary witnesses that

Southern roads in those days were choked with caravans of slaves en route to the Southwest. "About that time," according to Allen V. Manning, "it looks like everybody in the world was going to Texas."

While executing these maneuvers with one hand, the slaveholder extended the olive branch of pacification with the other, organizing barbecues and dances for the slaves and lightening their work loads. At the same time that they offered the olive branch they began with skill and duplicity to insert the wedge of dissension, telling slaves that the Yankees were human devils who raped slave women and sold slave men into slavery in Cuba.

Why did the slaves put up with this?

Why didn't they stage a massive rebellion?

After all—the critics say—most of the white men were away in the army.

In dealing with these questions and accusations, we have to notice first that the slaves organized revolts and conspiracies in every slave state and were repeatedly and brutally suppressed. A few examples will illustrate this point. In April, 1861, seven blacks were hanged for attempting a rebellion near Charleston. In July, 1862, there was a conspiracy in Adams County, Mississippi, and the Confederate provost marshal informed the governor that "there is a great disposition among the Negroes to be insubordinate, and to run away and go to the federals. Within the last 12 months we have had to hang some 40 for plotting an insurrection, and there has been about that number put in irons." The next month slaves revolted up the river from New Orleans, forcing "the women of that neighborhood," Union General B. F. Butler said, "to apply to an armed boat, belonging to us, passing down, for aid; and the incipient revolt was stopped by informing the negroes that we should repel an attack by them upon the women and children."

Meanwhile, there were other evidences of slave unrest, including joint action by marauding bands of fugitive slaves and deserters from the Confederate army. On April 11, 1862, Confederate General R. F. Floyd asked Governor John Milton of Florida to impose martial law on Nassau, Clay, Putnam, Duval, Volusia, and St. John's counties "as a measure of absolute necessity, as they contain a nest of traitors and lawless negroes." In January, 1863, Governor John Gill Shorter asked the Confederate government to send troops to southeastern Alabama which was, he said, "the common retreat of deserters from our armies, tories, and runaways."

The point that emerges clearly from all this, a point clearly understood by the slaves, who were not as simple as some people think, is that the climate was scarcely propitious for large-scale insurrections. The South at that juncture was an armed camp with sentinels standing guard at vital installations and armies deployed at strategic points. Moreover, Union generals—as the Butler communication above testifies—were opposed to slave rebellions and some of them had vowed to put down slave insurrections "with an iron hand." To all this must be added lastly that the totalitarian climate—constant surveillance, the pass system, etc.—hampered communications and made concerted action difficult.

For all these reasons and for others as well, most slaves either adopted a strategy of individual escape or waited until the vibrating earth or the sound of cannons told them that marching Union soldiers were nearby. And then, whatever the dangers, whatever the obstacles, they moved, packing a few pieces of bread and all their worldly goods in sacks and striking for freedom in ones, twos, and thousands. A contemporary writer said the advance of Union troops into a slave area was like "thrusting a walking stick into an anthill." Some of the slaves set into motion by the advancing sticks of marching Yankees moved en masse to the nearest federal camp or outpost. Others, more venturesome perhaps, attached themselves to the moving columns of Yankee soldiers and wandered across the South.

As the Union armies advanced, freeing additional thousands, the Jubilees that began in Fortress Monroe continued and assumed new and more political dimensions. Certain slaves, believing apparently that the last would finally be first, initiated the celebrations by demanding and receiving reparations for unpaid labor. When the Union army marched into Culpepper, Virginia, a coachman "went straightly to his master's chamber, dressed himself in his best clothes, put on his best watch and chain, took his stick, and returning to the parlor where his master was, insolently [sic] informed him that he might for the future drive his own coach."

In Louisiana, as in Virginia, Jubilee assumed the form of celebrations and the seizure and destruction of property. An interesting case of this sort was reported in Rapides Parish, where slaves seized the furniture in Governor Thomas Moore's house. In a letter to the governor, a neighbor said the "Yanks coming directly afterwards and telling them everything was theirs and that they were free to do as they pleased, they turned out and

I assure you that for the space of a week they had a perfect jubilee—Every morning I could see beeves being driven up from the woods to the quarters—and the number they killed of them . . . . it is impossible to tell."

An instance similar to the Moore plantation Jubilee was reported by the overseer of the Allston plantation in South Carolina, who told his employer that the slaves had "Puld down the mantle Pieces taken off all the doors and windows Cut the banisters and sawed out all such as they wanted and have taken away the fenceing a Round the yeard brok down the old Stabel and Carpenter Shop." In this area there was a revolution in social relations. The overseer informed his employer that "it looks verry hard to pull ones hat to a negro."

An unusually graphic description of the Jubilees of the transition period was reported in the *Chronicles of Chicora Wood*. According to the report in this book, the slavemistress narrowly escaped violence when she marched into the middle of a celebrating crowd and demanded the keys to the barn. An old black man was about to give up the keys when a large slave came forward and shouted, " 'If you give up de key, blood'll flow,' emphasizing his threat by shaking his fist in the old slave's face. The shout rose up among the pressing, clamoring, gesticulating crowd, 'Yes, blood'll flow for true.' " The report added:

"The crowd continued to clamor and yell first one thing and then another but the predominant cry was 'Go for de officer, fetch de Yankee.' . . . They sang, sometimes in unison, sometimes in parts, strange words, which we did not understand, followed by a much repeated chorus:

> I free, I free,
> I free as a frog
> I free till I fool,
> Glory Alleluia!

"They revolved around us holding [the report continued] out their skirts and dancing now with slow swinging movements, now with rapid jig motions, but always with weird chants and wild gestures. When the men sent for the officer reached the gathering, they turned and shouted, 'Don't let no white man e'en dat gate,' which was answered by many voices, 'no, no, we don't let no white pusson e'en—we'll chop um down wid hoe—we'll chop um to pieces sho' '—and they brandished their large sharp gleaming rice field hoes. . . . Those who had not hoes were armed with pitchforks and hickory sticks and some had guns."

After celebrating for a spell, many slaves marched to Union camps. All this was witnessed by a number of contemporary witnesses, who left several felicitous descriptions. Susie Melton, a young Virginia slave, said it "was winter time and mighty cold that night, but ev'body commence gittin' ready to leave. Didn't care nothin' bout Missus—was goin' to the Union lines. An' all that night the niggers danced an' sang right out in the cold. Nex' mornin' at day-break we all started out with blankets an' clothes an' pots an' pans an' chickens piled on our backs.... An' as the sun comes up over the trees the niggers all started to singin':

> Sun, you be here an' I'll be gone
> Sun, you be here an' I'll be gone
> Sun, you be here an' I'll be gone
> Bye, bye, don't grieve after me

So it went everywhere, and by the fall of 1862, the flow of black humanity on Southern roads had reached flood proportions.

"There was no plan in this exodus," John Eaton, a contemporary witness, said, "no Moses to lead it. Unlettered reason or the mere inarticulate decisions of instinct brought them to us. Often the slaves met prejudices against their color more bitter than any they had left behind. But their own interests were identical, they felt, with the objects of our armies: a blind terror stung them, an equally blind hope allured them, and to us they came." They came by the thousands and tens of thousands, some of them diseased, some of them decrepit, some of them naked, in the largest mass movement of its kind in American history. "Imagine, if you will," Eaton added, "a slave population ... rising up and leaving its ancient bondage, forsaking its local traditions and all the associations and attractions of the old plantation life, coming garbed in rags or in silks, with feet shod or bleeding, individually or in families and larger groups,—an army of slaves and fugitives, pushing its way irresistibly toward an army of fighting men, perpetually on the defensive and perpetually ready to attack. The arrival among us of these hordes was like the oncoming of cities."

There had never been anything quite like it. It was a fire storm of emotions. It was a mass movement unprecedented in scope and intensity. It was the biggest coming-out party in history.

*THERE* is a bias deeply engrained in the institutional fiber of America against comprehensive government planning for the poor. And when this bias links up with the pervasive prejudice against black, brown, and red people, public men are smitten with palsy, and they develop a curious inability to feel and see. In the light of this syndrome, which has marked the social history of America, it is scarcely surprising that the Lincoln Administration remained lamentably inactive in the face of the massive problems accompanying the oncoming of these cities. The problems—and the needs—were obvious to almost everyone. Hundreds of thousands of slaves had thrown off the shackles of slavery and were living in a twilight land between slavery and freedom. It was necessary to provide food, shelter, and medicine for these refugees. Of equal and perhaps even greater importance was the question of definition. Who were these people? What was their legal status? What was to be done for them and with them?

There were no clear answers to these questions in Washington, D.C., in the first two years of the war. And in the absence of a coherent government policy, field commanders coped with the flood of black humanity as best they could. Most adopted variants of the Fortress Monroe model, issuing army rations and surplus tents to the refugees and employing them at minimal wages in and around the camps as teamsters, road builders, orderlies, nurses, cooks, and woodcutters.

This was not a program of charity. The refugees not only paid their own way, but they also generated capital for the Union war effort. Almost from the first, the refugees were put to work harvesting crops of cotton and sugar cane, which were sold in the North. Some of the profits were returned to the slaves, who were paid modest wages, and some of the profits were used to finance the refugee program. In addition to the money value of laborers attached to the Union army and the money received from the sale of products grown and harvested by the refugees, the government required every able-bodied refugee to pay a tax for social welfare. It was thought at first that the slaves would object to the special tax. But John Eaton, an army chaplain attached to the refugee program, said the slaves "freely acknowledged that they ought to assist in bearing the burden of the poor."

Meanwhile, other forces were at work, most notably Northern churches and philanthropic organizations. Responding to the pleas of abolitionists and black leaders, these organizations collected "contraband boxes" and "bundles for blacks" and dispatched teachers, missionaries, and social workers to the liberated areas. Among the leading organizations in this work were the American Missionary Association, the Western Freedmen's Aid Commission, the United Brethren in Christ, the Northwestern Freedmen's Aid Society of Cincinnati, the Assembly of the Presbyterian Church, the Freedmen's Aid Society of Chicago, and the Western Sanitary Commission.

Of all the groups and individuals associated with this missionary movement, none were more important than the churches and societies of the free blacks of the North. In practically every large Northern city, black churches and mutual aid societies sponsored benefits, collected clothes, and sent social workers and teachers to the South. The African Methodist Episcopal Church, for example, sent the Reverend James Lynch and the Reverend James D. Hall to South Carolina in 1863. The Reverend Henry McNeal Turner expressed the sentiments of most black Northerners when he said that "every man of us now, who has a speck of grace or a bit of sympathy, for the race that we are inseparably identified with, is called upon by force of surrounding circumstances, to extend a hand of mercy to *bone of our bone and flesh of our flesh...*."

Moved by like sentiments, free blacks were in the front ranks of the movement that blanketed the South with freedmen's schools. It was Mary Chase, a freedwoman of Alexandria, Virginia, who established the first freedmen's school in the South on September 1, 1861. Sixteen days later Mary Peake, a free black woman of Hampton, started the first school for freedmen at Fortress Monroe. Meanwhile, other blacks—slaves, freedmen, and free men—were active on other fronts. On the Sea Islands, a number of blacks, including Harriet Tubman, Charlotte Forten, and Susie King Taylor, worked side by side with the celebrated New England schoolmarms. In Arkansas blacks formed a Freedmen's School Society and organized the first free schools in Little Rock. "To the best of my belief," Eaton said, "these were the first free schools in Arkansas—whether for whites or blacks—to subscribe and pay in full the compensation of the teachers."

These missionaries and others—black and white—contributed immeasurably to the well-being of the refugees, but the need for a more comprehensive government program was recognized early by some commanders, notably Ulysses S. Grant in the Mississippi Valley and Rufus Saxton on the Sea Islands. In November, 1862, General Grant appointed

John Eaton superintendent of Negro affairs and gave him sweeping powers in smoothing the transition of the refugees. Eaton was appalled by the enormity of the task before him. "The scenes," he said later, "were appalling: the refugees were crowded together, sickly, disheartened, dying on the streets, not a family of them all either well sheltered, clad, or fed; no physicians, no medicines, no hospitals; many of the persons who had been charged with feeding them either sick or dead." Realizing that the situation was rapidly worsening, Eaton organized a comprehensive government program of relief and revitalization. As steps necessary to accomplish this purpose, he established contraband camps for the refugees and put able-bodied men to work harvesting crops on abandoned plantations.

Not content with these stopgap measures, Eaton and his aides probed for ways to come to grips with the root causes of black destitution. One response was the leasing of abandoned plantations to black entrepreneurs. A second and more decisive response was the organization of semi-autonomous black governments. At Davis Bend, Mississippi—to cite the most impressive example—the abandoned plantations of Jefferson Davis were divided into districts and black families were settled on the land. Each district had a black judge and a black sheriff, and the officers of the courts were black. Under the provisions establishing the settlement, white speculators were banned. By the winter of 1863, some six hundred freedmen were producing crops in the area.

The results of all this were encouraging, as we can see from Eaton's report of July 5, 1864: "These freedmen are now disposed of as follows: In military service as soldiers, laundresses, cooks, officers' servants, and laborers in the various staff departments, 41,150; in cities, on plantations, and in freedmen's villages and cared for, 72,500. Of these, 62,300 are entirely self-supporting—the same as any industrial class anywhere else—as planters, mechanics, barbers, hackmen, draymen, etc., conducting enterprises on their own responsibility or working as hired laborers. The remaining 10,200 receive subsistence from the government; 3,000 of them are members of families whose heads are carrying on plantations and have under cultivation 4,000 acres of cotton. They are to pay the government for their sustenance from the first income of the crop. The other 7,200 include the paupers, that is to say, all Negroes over and under the self-supporting age, the crippled and sick in hospital. . . . Instead of being unproductive, this class has now under cultivation 500 acres of corn, 790 acres of vegetables, and 1,500 acres of cotton, besides working at woodchopping and other industries. There are reported in the aggregate over 100,000 acres of cotton under cultivation. Of these about 7,000 are leased and cultivated by blacks. Some Negroes are managing as high as 300 or 400 acres."

On grounds of both policy and necessity, the same experiments were pressed in South Carolina, where General Rufus Saxton articulated a far-reaching program of land and self-determination for blacks. Under Saxton the South Carolina refugees accumulated capital, organized cooperatives, and bought plantations that were sold for non-payment of taxes. At one sale, Saxton reported, "six out of forty-seven plantations sold were bought by them, comprising two thousand five hundred and ninety-five acres, sold for twenty-one hundred and forty-five dollars. In other cases, the Negroes had authorized the superintendent to bid for them, but the land was reserved by the United States." One of the plantations was bought by a resourceful black identified only as Henry. "The other five were made by the Negroes on the plantations, combining the funds they had saved from the sale of their pigs, chickens, and eggs, and from the payment made to them for work,—they then dividing off the tract peaceably among themselves."

These facts have an interest that is distinct from the small events they recount. In them, as in the reports of other field commanders, we find most conclusive proof of the latent strengths of the freedmen and the plastic possibilities of the situation. This did not escape the eye of Saxton, who added: "To test the question of their forethought and prove that some of the race at least thought of the future, I established in October, 1864, a savings bank for the freedmen of Beaufort district and vicinity. More than $240,000 had been deposited in this bank by freedmen since its establishment. I consider that the industrial problem has been satisfactorily solved at Port Royal, and that, in common with other races, the Negro has industry, prudence, forethought, and ability to calculate results. Many of them have managed plantations for themselves, and show an industry and sagacity that will compare favorably in their results—making due allowances—with those of white men."

The South Carolina experiment was given impetus by General William Tecumseh Sherman's epochal Special Field Order Number 15. This order, which is of paramount importance for an understanding of the possibilities and the failures of Jubilee, was a direct outgrowth of the swarming of the slaves, who abandoned plantations and attached themselves to Sherman's columns as they cut a swath of fire and destruction on the famous March to the Sea. The passion and the determination of the slaves moved Sherman, and when he reached Savannah he sent for the leaders of the black community and asked them what the slaves wanted. The answers —to condense a long dialogue—were land, education, and self-determination. Sherman thought about the thing for a while, conferred with "slave experts" like General Saxton, and then issued, on January 15, 1865, Special Field Order Number 15. Here are some excerpts:

I. The islands from Charleston, south, the abandoned rice fields along the rivers for thirty miles back from the sea, and the country bordering the St. John's river, Florida, are reserved and set apart for the settlement of the negroes now made free by the acts of war and the proclamation of the President of the United States.

II. At Beaufort, Hilton Head, Savannah, Fernandina, St. Augustine, and Jacksonville, the blacks may remain in their chosen or accustomed vocations, but on the islands, and in the settlements hereafter to be established, no white person whatever, unless military officers and soldiers, detailed for duty, will be permitted to reside; and the sole and exclusive management of affairs will be left to the freed people themselves, subject only to the United States military authority and the acts of Congress....

III. Whenever three respectable negroes, heads of families, shall desire to settle on lands, and shall have selected for that purpose an island or a locality clearly defined, within the limits above designated, the inspector of settlements and plantations will himself, or by such subordinate officers as he may appoint, give them a license to settle such island or district, and afford them such assistance as he can to enable them to establish a peaceable agricultural settlement. The three parties named will subdivide the land, under the supervision of the inspector, among themselves and such others as may choose to settle near them, so that each family shall have a plot or not more than forty (40) acres of tillable ground, and when it borders on some water channel, with not more than 800 feet water front, in the possession of which land the military authorities will afford them protection until such time as they can protect themselves, or until Congress shall regulate their title....

IV. Whenever a negro has enlisted in the military service of the United States he may locate his family in any one of the settlements at pleasure, and acquire a homestead and all other rights and privileges of a settler, as though present in person.... But no one, unless an actual settler as above defined, or unless absent on government service, will be entitled to claim any right to land or property in any settlement by virtue of these orders.

V. In order to carry out this system of settlement, a general officer will be detailed as inspector of settlements and plantations, whose duty it shall be to visit the settlement, to regulate their police and general management, and who will furnish personally to each head of a family, subject to the approval of the President of the United States, a possessory title in writing, giving as near as possible the description of boundaries, and who shall adjust all claims or conflicts that may arise under the same, subject to the like approval, treating such titles altogether as possessory....

In accordance with these provisions, some forty thousand blacks were settled on forty-acre tracts on the Sea Islands. "Public meetings were held," Saxton said, "and every exertion used by those whose duty it was to execute this order to encourage emigration to the Sea Islands, and the faith of the government was solemnly pledged to maintain them in possession. The greatest success attended the experiment, and although the planting was very far advanced before the transportation to carry the colonists to the Sea Islands could be obtained, and the people were destitute of animals and had but few agricultural implements and the greatest difficulty in procuring seeds, yet they went out, worked with energy and diligence to clear up the ground run to waste by three years' neglect; and thousands of acres were planted and provisions enough were raised for those who were located in season to plant, besides a large amount of sea island cotton for market...."

Here, as in Mississippi, semi-autonomous black governments were organized. A typical instance of this occurred in Mitchelville, where the following order was issued:

1. All lands now set apart for the colored population, near Hilton Head, are declared to constitute a village, to be known as the village of Mitchelville. Only freedmen and colored persons residing or sojourning within the territorial of said village, shall be deemed and considered inhabitants thereof.

2. The village of Mitchelville shall be organized and governed as

follows: Said village shall be divided into districts, as nearly equal in population as practicable, for the election of councilmen, sanitary and police regulations, and the general government of the people residing therein.

. . . . . . . . . . . . .

5. The Council of Administration shall have power:

To pass such ordinances as it shall deem best, in relation to the following subjects: To establish schools for the education of children and other persons. To prevent and punish vagrancy, idleness and crime. To punish licentiousness, drunkenness, offences against public decency and good order, and petty violation of the rights of property and person. To require due observance of the Lord's Day. To collect fines and penalties. To punish offences against village ordinances. To settle and determine disputes concerning claims for wages, personal property, and controversies between debtor and creditor. To levy and collect taxes to defray the expenses of the village government, and for the support of schools. To lay out, regulate, and clean the streets. To establish wholesale sanitary regulations for the prevention of disease. To appoint officers, places and times for the holding of elections. To Compensate municipal officers, and to regulate all other matters affecting the well-being of the citizens and good order of society. . . .

8. Hilton Head Island will be divided into school districts, to conform, as nearly as practicable, to the schools as established by the Freedmen's Association. . . . And the parents and guardians will be held responsible that said children so attend school, under the penalty of being punished, at the discretion of the Council of Administration.

To the dismay of the black settlers and the delight of white speculators, these social experiments were later abandoned in favor of "free enterprise." Pursuant to the directions of the Lincoln Administration, many of the captured and abandoned plantations were later leased to private entrepreneurs, who employed the refugees at scandalously low wages and abused them almost as much as the slavemasters. The final blow came in 1865 when Lincoln's successor, Andrew Johnson, issued pardons and restoration of property to the owners of most of the plantations occupied by blacks.

What all this meant in simple and not inexact terms was that most of the possessory titles, authorized by Sherman and other commanders, were not worth the paper they were written on. This became clear, shortly after the beginning of the experiment, when agents of the U.S. government, backed by Yankee soldiers, began to drive blacks from the land granted them by other agents of the U.S. government. It was all very confusing and productive of much mischief and pain. And it is worthy of note and much thought that the black settlers did not go gently. They armed themselves and posted notices, warning government agents to stay off their land. They banded together, posted sentinels, and fought pitched battles with U.S. soldiers. The forces in this struggle were terribly imbalanced, and there was never any doubt about the outcome. All the same, the black settlers pursued the struggle with tenacity and imagination, fighting at least one battle with sticks and stones.

The struggle continued for several months, inflaming the climate in South Carolina and other states, giving rise to a great deal of concern in Washington, where President Johnson bestirred himself, sending General Oliver O. Howard, a particular favorite of the slaves, to South Carolina to calm the storm. Howard, who was a man of some sensitivity and social consciousness, had no enthusiasm for the new policy or the assignment, but he went through the motions, crisscrossing the state, explaining the new policy in halting and contradictory statements. After a particularly embarrassing colloquy at a mass meeting of freedmen on Edisto Island, Howard, who headed the Freedmen's Bureau, asked if someone would sing him one of those good old Negro spirituals. The freedmen complied, singing *Nobody Knows the Trouble I've Seen*, and General Howard broke down and wept.

This was a political as well as a musical statement—and if it was not the beginning of emancipation, it was at least the beginning of wisdom, which is a prerequisite of emancipation.

*As* usual in such matters, the word followed the fact. Thousands of slaves were celebrating freedom, thousands were working for wages and managing farms and plantations, before the federal government got around to saying the word. The word came first from the U.S. Congress, which initiated, in the spring of 1862, the tortuous legal process, which continues today. Prodded by Radical Republicans like Representative Thaddeus Stevens of Pennsylvania and Senator Charles Sumner of Massachusetts, Congress seized the initiative from the hesitant and vacillating Lincoln and passed a series of acts, notably the District of Columbia Emancipation Act (April 16, 1862), and the Second Confiscation Act

(July 17, 1862), which declared "forever free" the slaves of all rebels. This act, which has received insufficient attention in general media, was actually more sweeping than the Emancipation Proclamation, which Abraham Lincoln signed on Thursday, January 1, 1863. Lincoln signed this document with hesitation and forebodings, saying with great honesty that he had been driven to it by political and military exigencies, including military reversals and Northern war weariness. Although he did not say so explicitly, another and possibly more urgent motivating factor was the danger of foreign intervention—a danger effectively foreclosed by the proclamation, which turned a vague civil war into a war for freedom.

For all the confusion and problems surrounding it, the proclamation seems to have been inevitable, and it unleashed a chain reaction, whose three major links were a hurricane of emotion in the black community, an intensification of the black exodus, and the recruitment of more than 180,000 black soldiers.

The hurricane of emotion began before the document was signed. On Wednesday night, December 31, 1862, freedmen held a watch meeting at the Washington, D.C., contraband camp and were addressed by a former slave, who said: "Onst the time was, dat I cried all night. What's de matter? What's de matter? Matter enough. De nex mornin my child was to be sold, an she was sold, and I neber spec to see her no more till de day ob judgment. Now, no more dat! no more dat! no more dat! Wid my hands agin my breast I was gwine to my work, when de overseer used to whip me along. Now, no more dat! no more dat! no more dat! When I tink what de Lord's done for us, an brot us thro' de trubbles, I feel dat I ought go inter His service. We'se free now, bress de Lord! (Amens! were shouted all over the building.) Dey can't sell my wife and child any more, bress de Lord (Glory! glory! from the audience.) No more dat! no more dat! no more dat, now!"

The next day a larger group gathered at Washington's Israel Bethel AME church. "Seeing such a multitude of people in and around my church," the pastor, Henry McNeal Turner, said, "I hurriedly went up to the office of the first paper in which the proclamation of freedom could be printed, known as the 'Evening Star,' and squeezed myself through the dense crowd that was waiting for the paper. The first sheet run off with the proclamation in it was grabbed for by three of us, but some active young man got possession of it and fled. The next sheet was grabbed for by several, and was torn into tatters. The third sheet from the press was grabbed for by several, but I succeeded in procuring so much of it as contained the proclamation, and off I went for life and death. Down Pennsylvania I ran as for my life, and when the people saw me coming with the paper in my hand raised a shouting cheer that was almost deafening. As many as could get around me lifted me to a great platform, and I started to read the proclamation. I had run the best end of a mile, I was out of breath, and could not read. Mr. Hinton, to whom I handed the paper, read it with great force and clearness. While he was reading every kind of demonstration and gesticulation was going on. Men squealed, women fainted, dogs barked, white and colored people shook hands, songs were sung, and by this time cannons began to fire at the navy-yard, and follow in the wake of the roar that had for some time been going on behind the White House. . . . It was indeed a time of times, and a half time, nothing like it will ever be seen again in this life."

We may set beside Turner's picture of the Washington celebration Frederick Douglass's reminiscence of the historic meeting that night in Tremont Temple in Boston. It was not at all certain at that time that Lincoln would issue the proclamation, and the crowd, knowing Lincoln's painful ambiguity on the subject, awaited word from Washington with some anxiety. "Eight, nine, ten o'clock came and went, and still no word," Douglass wrote. "A visible shadow seemed falling on the expecting throng, which the confident utterances of the speakers sought in vain to dispel. At last, when patience was well-nigh exhausted, and suspense was becoming agony, a man . . . with hasty step advanced through the crowd, with a face fairly illumined with the news he bore, exclaimed in tones that thrilled all hearts, 'It is coming!' 'It is on the wires!'

"The effect of this announcement was startling beyond description, and the scene was wild and grand. Joy and gladness exhausted all forms of expression, from shouts of praise to sobs and tears. My old friend Rue, a Negro preacher, a man of wonderful vocal power, expressed the heartfelt emotion of the hour, when he led all voices in the anthem, 'Sound the loud timbrel o'er Egypt's dark sea, Jehovah hath triumphed, his people are free.' "

On the morning after freedom and the mornings after that, Douglass and other leaders had sober second thoughts. The proclamation—it was noticed—declared slaves "forever free," but it did not apply to slaves in the Border States and liberated areas in the South. The meaning of all this was plain and not a little ominous: Lincoln had freed slaves where he had no power on January 1, 1863, to free them, and had left them in slavery in areas where he had the power on January 1, 1863, to free them. And so, in the end, what the proclamation boiled down to was this: It offered freedom to slaves behind Confederate lines who were quick enough and bold enough to free themselves by abandoning plantations and fleeing to Union lines. It is only fair to add that the proclamation changed the meaning of the war, not only for blacks but also for whites. The word or at least *a* word had finally been said, and in its wake came an ever-increasing stream of refugees, laborers, and soldiers.

The proclamation was one word. Another word, less dramatic but nonetheless significant, was the act establishing the Freedmen's Bureau, an omnibus social agency that was granted virtually unlimited judicial, executive, and legislative authority and a mandate to organize the transition from slavery to freedom. As I have said elsewhere (*Black Power U.S.A.*), the bureau combined the governmental functions of the WPA, the Office of Economic Opportunity, and Medicare with the defensive functions of the NAACP and the National Urban League. It made laws and executed them; it established courts, schools, asylums, hospitals; and it assumed full jurisdiction in the economic field, instituting a system of written contracts, transporting freedmen to jobs and supervising the terms of their employment. Despite its vast powers, the bureau was never adequately funded, and it was legislated out of existence before its mission was completed.

The two final and most important acts in this legal sequence were passage of the Thirteenth Amendment by Congress on January 31, 1865, and the defeat of the Southern armies in the spring of 1865—a defeat which would not have been possible without the help of the 180,000 black soldiers and the 200,000 black laborers attached to the Union Army.

*I*T had begun with a word, the word *slavery*, spoken softly and furtively at first and then openly and defiantly, a word that became a white tumor, proliferating without rhyme or reason, racing through the blood stream, touching everything and poisoning everything, a carcinoma of social malignancy. And now, 250 years or 13,000 weeks later, it was going to end with a word, the word *freedom*, spoken in different tones in different places by different men with different results.

The word was a government man—"a freedom man"—riding up to

the big house on "a big white horse" and the cow horn blowing and all the slaves "coming running 'cause that horn mean, 'Come to the big house quick,'" and the government man standing up before an assembly, reading from a paper, telling the slaves they were free.

The word was one Captain Barkus, a Union soldier with one arm cut off at the elbow, getting up on a platform and declaring peace and freedom, and pointing to a black man yelling, "You're free as I am."

The word was a master saying, "Go if you wants and stay if you wants."

The word was the master of Pauline Howell saying, "Go on away, you don't belong to us no more, you been freed."

The word was the master of Anna Miller saying, "All that wants to go, git now. You has nothing."

However it came, whether by way of the government man or the slavemaster, the word blessed, cursed, annealed, cauterized.

To the owner of Anderson Edwards, a young slave in Texas, the word was a curse. "'Fore war," Edwards said later, "Massa didn't never say much 'bout slavery, but when he heared us free he cusses and say, 'God never did 'tend to free niggers,' and he cussed till he died."

For a slaveholder named Jim and a slavemistress named Lucy the word was terminal. Mahalia Shores said that "Massa Jim got sick that day and vomited and vomited" until he died. James Reeves said "Miss Lucy" had been sick "for quite a bit, and she was just able to come to the door and deliver that message. Three weeks after that time, they brought her out of the house feet foremost and took her to the cemetery. The news killed her dead."

Not all masters, by any means, were as obstinate as "Miss Lucy." Some gave the slaves small pieces of land to work. "But the mostest of them," said Tines Kendrick, who lived on a plantation near Macon, Georgia, "never give 'em nothing, and they sure despise them niggers what left 'em." We learn from the same reporter that "a heap of the marses got raging mad and just tore up truck. They say they gwine kill every nigger they find. . . . They shot niggers down by the hundreds. They just wasn't gwine let 'em enjoy the freedom." Quite typical of the lot was Mary Adams, who was recalled later by William Mathews of Texas. "It was 'way after freedom that the freedom man come and read the paper," Mathews said, "and tell us not to work no more 'less us git pay for it. When he gone, Old Mary Adams, she come out. I'lect what she say as if I just hear her say it. She say, 'Ten years from today I'll have you all back 'gain.'"

Regardless of the hostility, regardless of the developing political situation, regardless of everything, the slaves received the word with praise and thanksgivings. Some slaves took off before the slavemaster or government man was through reading the document, but most stayed around long enough to participate in the chain of emotional bombs that exploded one after another, shattering the silence of centuries, breaking the earth for a new growth.

"Hallelujah broke out," said Felix Haywood, a nineteen-year-old slave in Texas. "Soldiers, all of a sudden, was everywhere—coming in bunches, crossing and walking and riding. Everyone was a-singing. We was all walking on golden clouds. Hallelujah!" Everybody, Haywood continued, "went wild. We all felt like heroes, and nobody had made us that way but ourselves. We was free. Just like that, we was free."

Just like that, the slaves moved into the center of their own history, ringing farm bells, blowing cow horns, dancing, weeping, shouting for joy.

In the village of Pamplin, Virginia, near Appomattox, the word was glory. "Glory! Glory!" shouted Fannie Berry. "Yes, child, the Negroes are free, and when they knew that they were free they, oh! baby! began to sing:

> Mammy, don't you cook no more,
> You are free, you are free!
> Rooster, don't you crow no more,
> You are free, you are free!
> Old hen, don't you lay no more eggs,
> You free, you free!"

"Such rejoicing and shouting," she added, "you never heard in your life."

In the fervor of the moment, there were seizures and miraculous cures. Lucretia Alexander, who was there, said that "old colored folks" in Arkansas "that was on sticks, throwed them sticks away and shouted." One Reverend Mr. Hammock of Virginia recalled that "Ole Ant Sissy done been par'lyzed for years." But when the good news came "slaves shout and sing so loud that Ant Sissy got out of the bed, hobbled on out the door, and stood there praying to God for his mercy. Wouldn't let nobody touch her, wouldn't set down. Stood there swaying from side to side and singing over and over her favorite hymn:

> Oh, Father of Mercy
> We give thanks to Thee
> We give thanks to Thee
> For thy great glory."

As the hot weeks passed, in this summer of summers, the freedmen were swept with gales of emotional fervor. Something unendurable, something unimaginable had ended. And in celebrating that ending, and the hope of a new beginning, the people began to move, going from one plantation to another, from one county to another. Some were looking for long-lost brothers, sisters, mothers, and fathers; some were looking for land and decent wages; some were just looking. "Right off," Felix Haywood said, "colored folks started on the move. They seemed to want to get closer to freedom, so they'd know what it was—like it was a place or a city."

The movement generated its own intensity, racing across the land, gathering momentum as it moved, setting into motion four million people, galvanizing them, churning them up inside, sending them in long black lines down the dusty roads, weeping, laughing, shouting, releasing the accumulated emotions of the centuries.

After moving around a bit, stretching their legs and testing the limits of freedom, most freedmen settled down within a few miles of the "home plantations." Some returned to the "home plantation" because, Pauline Powell said, "they didn't have no place to go and nothing to eat.... Seemed like it was four or five years before they got to places they could live."

Perfectly well aware that they had won no more than a chance to fight for freedom, most of the slaves set about with fierce energy and determination to reknit the bonds of community severed by slavery. In the first few months of freedom, most of the adult freedmen were married legally for the first time in mass ceremonies. This presented some unique and delicate problems. Some men and women, separated from their families by slavery, traveled hundreds of miles only to find that their mates had remarried. Some men with two or three wives were given several weeks or several months to choose one for the long haul. There were, of course, spirited discussions on how this should be done. Some elders suggested that men with several wives should marry the oldest wife or the one with the most children.

While all this was going on, the freedmen were organizing themselves and defining themselves. The first step in this process was choosing the surname denied blacks by the slave system. Some slaves chose the surname of their former masters. But most agreed with the old slave who said he "had had enough of old master." The naming process was complicated and extended over a period of several months. A freedman would sit for a spell and pick a surname. If he changed his mind the next day or the next month, he simply changed his name. This process went on until the man or woman was satisfied. Some freedmen chose names based on their occupation, appearance, personality, or locale. A tailor named Sam, for example, chose the name Sam Tailor which later became Samuel Taylor.

As the people moved from place to place, trying out new roles and new names, they grew in consciousness and pride. We are told that the freedmen refused to yield the sidewalks to whites and that they refused to bow and scrape. We are told also that almost all slaves shunned the badges of slavery—"the fo day horn," and working in gangs under the supervision of white overseers.

There were other concerns as well. Males began to assume patriarchal roles, and women left the fields and busied themselves with their homes and their children. "The Negro women," Robert Somers wrote from South Carolina, "are now almost wholly withdrawn from field labor [and the] children who were made available under slavery for industrial purposes are being more and more absorbed by the schools." As this happened, the institutional infrastructure of the black community was completed and extended. Black churches and black fraternal organizations sprang up, and the bonds of community were strengthened and defined in mass celebrations and mass meetings.

What did the freedmen want?

What did freedmen mean to them?

Beyond any question, the freedmen wanted land and education. From Jubilee onwards the freedmen demonstrated a passion for education that has never perhaps been equalled in the history of the world. The whole race, eyewitnesses reported, wanted to go to school, and it was said that black "children love the school as white children love a holiday." Charlotte Forten, the granddaughter of James Forten, the pioneer black leader and sail manufacturer, was teaching then on the Sea Islands, and she said she "never before saw children so eager to learn, although I had had several years' experience in New England schools. Coming to school is a constant delight and recreation to them. They come here as other children go to play."

The same phenomena were observed in Louisiana. "Go out in any direction," said the Reverend Thomas Calahan, a missionary of the United Presbyterian Church, "and you meet negroes on horses, negroes on mules, negroes with oxen, negroes by the wagon, cart and buggy load, negroes on foot, men, women, and children; negroes in uniform, negroes in rags, negroes in frame houses, negroes living in tents, negroes living in rail pens covered with brush, and negroes living under brush piles without any rails, negroes living on the bare ground with the sky for their covering; all hopeful, almost all cheerful, everyone pleading to be taught, willing to do anything for learning. They are never out of our rooms, and their cry is for 'Books! Books! and 'when will school begin?' "

This unprecedented burst of enthusiasm for books changed the social climate of the South and led to the founding of the first public school systems in the South. The first advance on this road was made by black and white missionaries like Charlotte Forten and Thomas Calahan. The second step was made by the Freedmen's Bureau, which created a network of day, night, and adult schools. Between 1865 and 1871 the bureau spent more than five million dollars on public education in the South and founded or helped to found most of the best-known black colleges, including Howard, Fisk, Talladega, and Atlanta University.

The contributions of the Freedmen's Bureau and the white missionaries have been extensively documented. What is less often noted is that blacks were among the leaders of this movement. Black ministers, notably Frank Quarles, Alonzo Cardozo, and James Lynch, provided leadership and organizing ability, and black ministers and black laymen organized several of the first black colleges, including Wilberforce, founded before the Civil War by the AME Church, and Jackson College, and Morehouse College.

As one examines the records of this period, one is struck not only by the leading role of black ministers and black missionaries but also by the contributions of the freedmen, who were among the major financial supporters of the first black educational institutions. Individual blacks contributed nickels and dimes and carpentry skills, and black communities organized suppers, excursions, and entertainments to raise money for schools. Of the 236 black schools in Georgia in 1867, 152 were entirely or partly supported by freedmen, who owned 39 of the buildings. By 1870 the freedmen of Virginia were supporting 215 schools and owned 111 school buildings.

No less important, though far less successful, was the black thrust for land. It was inconceivable to the slaves that the government would free them without providing the means of livelihood. Thus was born the mystical idea that the government was going to give every adult slave forty acres of land and a mule. It was believed in the summer of Jubilee that the land would be distributed on January 1, 1866. And as that date approached, many freedmen left the plantations and began another round of celebration in anticipation of the land distribution. But there were neither mules nor acres on January 1, and most slaves were driven back to the plantations by hunger and force. The same thing happened in the Christmas seasons of 1866 and 1867.

Despite warnings from friends and foes, the great mass of slaves continued to believe that land distribution was around the next turning. So deeply held was this idea that thousands were defrauded by cynical and unscrupulous operators who sold them colored pegs to mark off their land. T. H. Ball, who was witness to one of these frauds, said in 1873 "there passed through [Clarke County, Alabama] a *white* man, supposed to be from the North, with a large bundle of little colored stakes, who called upon the freed-men and told them that the President had authorized him to distribute among them those stakes in order that they might become owners of land, and that wherever they stuck one of those stakes the land should be theirs, no matter who had owned or claimed it. They could make their own selections for their farms. The price of a stake was three dollars, but when the freed-men could not raise that amount the stake-man would sell even for one dollar. And many of the credulous and trusting colored people . . . bought these little stakes, stuck them on the lands of their white neighbors, and some began to work their newly acquired plantations, with what results need not be told."

Such were the snares and delusions of the false dawn of freedom.

"We knowed freedom was on us," Felix Haywood said, "but we didn't know what was to come with it. We thought we was going to get rich like the white folks. We thought we was going to be richer than the white folks, 'cause we was stronger and knowed how to work, and the whites didn't, and they didn't have us to work for them any more. But it didn't turn out that way...."

Another freedman, Allen V. Manning, echoed Haywood's plaint.

"It seems like the white people can't git over us being free, and they do everything to hold us down all the time.... They had us down and they kept us down."

This was the heart and center of the trouble, a fact noted by General Carl Schurz in his classic report to President Johnson on postwar conditions in the South. "In some localities," he wrote, "... where our troops had not yet penetrated and where no military post was within reach, planters endeavored and partially succeeded in maintaining between themselves and the Negroes the relation of master and slave partly by concealing from them the great changes that had taken place, and partly by terrorizing them into submission to their behests...."

In summation, Schurz said:

> Wherever I go—the street, the shop, the house, the hotel, or the steamboat—I hear the people talk in such a way as to indicate that they are yet unable to conceive of the Negro possessing any rights at all. Men who are honorable in their dealings with their white neighbors, will cheat a Negro without feeling a single twinge of their honor. To kill a Negro, they do not deem murder; to debauch a Negro woman, they do not think fornication; to take the property away from a Negro, they do not consider robbery. The people boast that when they get freedmen's affairs in their own hands, to use their own expression, 'the niggers will catch hell.'
>
> The reason of all this is simple and manifest. The whites esteem the blacks their property by natural right, and however much they admit that the individual regulations of masters and slaves have been destroyed by the war and by the President's emancipation proclamation, they still have an ingrained feeling that the blacks at large belong to the whites at large.

One could see evidence of this all over the South in the waning days of the Jubilee—in the shooting down of blacks in public highways, in the bombing and burning of black churches and homes. Indeed, we are told that the roads of the South were littered with the broken and mangled bodies of the celebrants of Jubilee.

Perhaps the most arresting picture of the rationale and methods of this reign of terror is contained in a contemporary story in the *New York Herald*: "Springing naturally out of this disordered state of affairs is an organization of 'regulators,' so called. Their numbers include many ex-Confederate cavaliers of the country, and their mission is to visit summary justice upon any offenders against the public peace. It is needless to say that their attention is largely directed to maintaining quiet and submission among the blacks. *The shooting or stringing up of some obstreperous 'nigger' by the 'regulators' is so common an occurrence as to excite little remark. Nor is the work of proscription confined to the freedmen only.* The 'regulators' go to the bottom of the matter, and strive to make it uncomfortably warm for any new settler with demoralizing innovations of wages for 'niggers.' "

To all this must be added lastly the effects of destitution and epidemics of smallpox and cholera. In some of the freedmen communities, one out of every two persons died, giving rise to the Southern myth that the black was destined to die out, like the Indian. A South Carolina planter said: "They perish by hunger and disease and melt away as the snow before the rising sun." The *Meridian [Miss.] Clarion* said: "A hundred years is a long time to one man; but to a nation or to a race, it is but a limited period. Well, in that time the Negro will be dead. Slavery is abolished now, but in a hundred years the Negro himself will be abolished...."

It was in this milieu, under these conditions, and in the harsh light of these expectations, that the African-American embarked on the road of freedom. As the road twisted and turned, doubling back on itself, his enemies and his problems multiplied. But he endured, and endures.

Part Two

**DIRECTIONS**

FREDERICK DOUGLASS

DR. W. E. B. DU. BOIS

# *System*

*Slavery has been fruitful in giving itself names. It has been called "the peculiar institution," "the social system," and the "impediment. . . ." It has been called by a great many names, and it will call itself by yet another name; and you and I and all of us had better wait and see what new form this old monster will assume, in what new skin this old snake will come forth next.*

—Frederick Douglass, May 9, 1865

*THE* history of black America is an act in the larger drama of the worldwide colonization of peoples of color by Europeans and the progeny of Europeans.

In America, as in the countries of Asia, Africa, and South America, Europeans created a colonial system that perpetuated the political, economic, and cultural exploitation of non-Europeans. And although the system created in America has its own weight and density, it is clearly a variation on the universal theme of (European) domination and (non-European) subordination. In America, as elsewhere, the colonial system elaborated the same mechanisms to attain the same end: the exploitation of the labor power and the resources of the colonized. And the American system of colonialism, like its counterparts in other areas, followed the traditional pattern, changing its skin at crucial junctures in order to protect its essential content. In America, then, as in the West Indies and some African areas, the formal phase of slavery was succeeded by another system, which reproduced the old relationships of dominance and subordination under new names and new formulae.

Since the system created to contain American blacks is structurally and phylogenetically related to the colonial systems of Asia, Africa, and South America, and since the American colonial system and other colonial systems are products of the same soil and use the same methods to achieve the same goal, an increasingly large number of scholars believe that the history of black Americans cannot be understood without recourse to a conceptual formulation of internal colonialism. There are, to be sure, minor problems in the use of the colonial analogy as a conceptual envelope for the African fragment of America. But used with due regard for specific contexts the colonial analogy illuminates many corridors of the African-American experience.

The methodological implications of this approach are immense. First, and perhaps above all, the new approach focuses on the system rather than on individuals and isolated events. Second, it stresses the colonial relationship between the white sector and the black sub-sector. Third, the new approach makes it possible to use Third World methodologies in deciphering the black experience and formulating developmental strategies.

The concept of internal colonialism releases these and other resonances and enables us to see how the colonial situation produces archetypal responses in both the colonized and colonizer communities. And so we can note in passing that it is virtually certain that a colonial group will produce a Booker T. Washington. It is a fact of more than topical interest that South Africa, for instance, has produced several men cast in the accommodating Washingtonian mold.

Before developing these notions in some detail, let us pause for a moment to anchor concepts and definitions. It is customary today to think of colonialism as an external-internal relationship between a metropolitan government and transplanted or indigenous people beyond its borders. But there can also be internal colonialism, a process by which an alien group subjugates and exploits an indigenous or transplanted people within the borders of a single country. In fact, all colonialism is internal in the sense that control is exercised by people on the scene, whether they represent a distant metropolitan power, or a metropolitan center within the country. Beyond doubt this is the case in South Africa and Zimbabwe (Southern Rhodesia). Beyond doubt, this is the case in the United States of America, not only for black people, but also for red people and some brown people. What Britain was to Ghana, what France was to Senegal, white America was (and is) to the black colony of America.

The traditional definition of colonialism ignores this fact and emphasizes the internal-external relationship between a metropole and a distant colony. But the decisive factor in colonialism is not geography but the sociopolitical relationship between a colonial center and the indigenous or transplanted people forcibly brought within the orbit of the colonizers' influence. For our purpose here, this means that colonialism is that relationship of domination and violence established by Europeans as a result of the slave trade and military conquest and extended by a process of mystification, administration, and coercion. Stated in somewhat different terms, colonialism is a mass relationship of economic exploitation based on inequality and contempt and perpetuated by force, cultural repression, and the political ideology of racism. It follows from this—and this is what I want to stress—that internal colonialism is the establishment of a colonial relationship between a developing center and an underdeveloped circumference within the borders of the same country.

In assessing the colonial relationship, one must always be careful to remember that it appears in many guises and changes form according to the concrete needs and interests of the colonizers or white settlers. Hence, it can be direct or indirect, paternalistic or nakedly brutal, internal or external. The fundamental distinction between colonial systems, of course, is the distinction between settler colonies (South Africa, Kenya,

America) established by a relatively large group of permanent white settlers, and transient colonies (Ghana, India) established by a relatively small number of sojourners seeking short-term economic advantages.

Within these parameters, the relationship between the colonizer and the colonized can assume different forms, as Oliver Cromwell Cox noted twenty-six years ago in his standard work, *Caste, Class, and Race*. Speaking specifically of majority-minority racial situations, he listed seven archetypal modes:

> 1. Situations in which the colored person is a stranger in a white society, such as a Hindu in the United States or a Negro in many parts of Canada and in Argentina—we shall call this the stranger situation.
>
> 2. Situations of original white contract where the culture of the colored group is very simple, such as the conquistadors and Indians in the West Indies, and the Dutch and Hottentots in South Africa—the original-contact situation.
>
> 3. Situations of colored enslavement in which a small aristocracy of whites exploits large quantities of natural resources, mainly agricultural, with forced colored labor, raised or purchased like capital in a slave market, such as that in the pre-Civil War South and in Jamaica before 1834—the slavery situation.
>
> 4. Situations in which a small minority of whites in a colored society is bent upon maintaining a ruling-class status, such as the British in the West Indies or the Dutch in the East Indies—the ruling-class situation.
>
> 5. Situations in which there are large proportions of both colored and white persons seeking to live in the same area, and whites insisting that the society is a "white man's country," as in the United States and South Africa—the bipartite situation.
>
> 6. Situations in which colored-and-white amalgamation is far advanced and in which a white ruling class is not established, as in Brazil —the amalgamative situation.
>
> 7. Situations in which a minority of whites has been subdued by a dominantly colored population, as that which occurred in Haiti during the turn of the eighteenth century, or the expulsion of whites from Japan in 1638—the nationalistic situation.

This admirably lucid text was written before the political liberation of the Third World, but it still has value as a heuristic model which reminds us to look not only for recurring patterns but also for structural differences.

The differences can be explained, as Cox suggested, by many variables, such as the population ratio of the dominating and dominated groups, the material configurations of the area, the nature of the original contact, and the needs, intentions, ideologies, and political exigencies of the colonizers.

Variables apart, the system is characterized almost everywhere by the same institutional roots (the quest for cheap land, cheap labor, and cheap resources), the same agents (the mandatory, the missionary, the merchant, and the money-lender), the same mechanisms of subordination: slavery (North America, South America, Asia, Africa, and the Caribbean), peonage (North America, South America, Asia, Africa, and the Caribbean), disenfranchisement and political manipulations (North America, South America, Asia, Africa, and the Caribbean), dual labor and housing markets, and dual educational systems (North America, South America, Asia, Africa, and the Caribbean). Since separation of groups is one of the oldest devices for subordination and stratification, we also find segregation in various forms (Indian reservations, "native" reserves, compounds, *kampongs*, ghettos) in all or almost all colonial areas.

Whatever the demographic situation, whatever the ideologies and intentions of the colonizers, the system is also characterized by five constants: political control, economic exploitation, cultural repression, racism, and force based on superior scientific technology. Of all these constants, the most important and the most pervasive is force. No one understood this better than the prominent white citizen who defined the black situation in America—and the white situation in America—in a frank talk with Robert R. Moton, Booker T. Washington's successor as president of Tuskegee Institute.

"You understand," the prominent white citizen said in 1923, "that we have the legislature, we make the laws, we have the judges, the sheriffs, the jails. We have the hardware store and the arms."

Force.

The colonial situation is a situation established by force, institutionalized by force, and maintained by force or the threat of force.

But force alone is not enough. In order to create a system, the colonizer must use force to penetrate into the secret zones of the minds and bodies of his victims. And to do that he relies on several mechanisms, foremost among which is cultural repression, which permeates the whole system, especially the educational system, which is used to make the oppressed ashamed of themselves and their values and their history. A point of critical importance here is that the oppressor can use diametrically opposed methods to accomplish the same end. He can forcibly deny the oppressed education, thereby limiting their social and economic possibilities, or he can forcibly "educate" the oppressed, thereby giving them his values and making them instruments of his purposes. Whether he educates or miseducates, whether he uses missionary institutions or mass media, the aim is the same: the planned cultural retardation of a whole people and the systematic repression of their values, insights, and expressions. Hence, French colonial administrators could say without apology or shame that their policy was based on a systematic destruction of the cultural infrastructure of African peoples—the tribe, collective property, and the polygamous family.

In addition to cultural repression and force, colonialism is inevitably accompanied by racism, which should not be confused with individual prejudice or ethnocentrism. In marked contrast to individual prejudice or the justifiable or nonjustifiable pride in one's own ethnic group, racism is a political ideology of racial supremacy supported by or even mandated by the focal institutions of a society. In other words, racism is not a personal attitude; it is a group structure. It is not simply personal dislike of physical appearances or cultural differences; it rests basically, as Cox pointed out, on the concerted determination of a white ruling class to keep some people and their resources exploitable.

Like other structures in the colonial syndrome, racism is a functional requirement of the system, and it serves three specific needs. First, it appeases the consciences of the oppressors and enables them to sleep without bad dreams. Secondly, it mystifies the oppressed and makes it extremely difficult for them to think well of themselves. Thirdly, it defends and justifies the social order and past, present, and future aggressions against the oppressed.

Almost without exception, colonizers based their enterprises on the claim that the colonized were biological and cultural inferiors. And the corollary of this claim was the assertion of the biological superiority of the colonizers, who were said to have a divine right to appropriate the services and resources of the colonized. "Who can deny the right of the hungry people of Europe to utilise the wasted bounties of nature . . . ?" asked Lord (Frederick) Lugard, the architect of English colonial policy in Africa. He added: "We hold these countries because it is the genius of our race to colonise, to trade, to govern. The task in which England is engaged in the tropics—alike in Africa and in the East—has become part of her tradition, and she has ever given of her best in the cause of liberty and civilisation."

Similar words in defense of liberty and plundering were spoken by French colonialists, who said they had a *mission civilistre* (a civilizing mission); South African colonialists, who said apartheid—separateness—was based on their "divine calling and . . . privilege"; and American colonizers like U.S. Senator Albert Beveridge, who said that "God has made us adept in government that we may administer government among savage and servile people."

This was a shortcut way of saying that God had given the colonizers the right to steal the land and appropriate the resources of non-Europeans. Whether the colonizers actually believed this or not is irrelevant. The essential fact is that the idea was soothing to the conscience and a powerful stimulus to theft on a scale unparalleled in human history.

However the matter was justified, whether as a civilizing mission or a divine calling, the colonial system was established throughout the world after the military conquest and subjugation of non-Europeans, some of whom were exterminated or forcibly expelled, some of whom were transplanted to new areas, some of whom were undermined and ultimately destroyed by the treaty system and forced trading agreements.

By way of explanation, we can cite one of the most shameful episodes of colonial history, the forced agreement by which Cecil Rhodes received from King Moselekatse all metal and mineral rights in a 75,000 square mile area of Zimbabwe (Rhodesia) for a payment of one hundred pounds a month, a thousand rifles, and the *promise* (later forgotten) of a gunboat. "Not since Manhattan island was bought from the Indians," wrote John Gunther with truth, "has any piece of real estate so valuable been had so cheaply." Cecil Rhodes and his cohorts later added injury to insult by deliberately instigating massacres and appropriating everything King Moselekatse and the Bantus owned.

The destruction of the Bantus of Zimbabwe was a classic example of the first phase of the colonial process, which was usually followed by a protracted process of "pacification" and appropriation of the land, minerals, and labor power of the colonized. This was done almost everywhere under a system of open or disguised slavery. During the first stage of colonization, the Spaniards instituted slavery or extended servitude under the *repartimientos* or allotments of Caribbean and South American Indians to public bodies and individuals for forced work on plantations and in mines. The English, French, Dutch, and other European groups used similar techniques in North and South America, decimating whole populations before instituting systems of legal slavery. This system reached a cruel pinnacle in the Caribbean and North America and spread to Africa and Asia, where tens of thousands were enslaved and millions more were marched to work at gunpoint in subtler but equally repressive systems of forced labor. In Java, for instance, the Dutch developed a system of part-time slavery under which Asian workers were forced to give the colonizers a part of their production.

When the contradictions of slavery reached explosive proportions, endangering the whole, the system changed in order to remain the same, emancipating its victim in name but continuing forced labor under new names. The usual procedure in most areas was the creation of a system of legal debt slavery based on peonage, vagrancy, tenancy, and apprenticeship laws. The Jamaica Emancipation Act of 1833, for instance, freed the slaves but permitted white slavemasters to hold them for seven additional years as compulsory apprentices. Within a few months after the emancipation of Portuguese slaves in the late nineteenth century, a new system of indentured labor emerged. From that point until the middle of the twentieth century, colonial masters elaborated a bewildering variety of mechanisms to continue slavery and servitude under different names. One technique, widely used in English colonies, was the imposition of a hut or poll tax, which the African had to pay in cash. Since Africans could only earn cash by leaving the villages and working on the plantations and in the mines of Europeans, the hut and poll tax laws were, in effect, forced drafts of labor. Another mechanism, equally effective, was colonial legislation requiring Africans to spend twenty, forty, or even sixty days a year on forced labor details, building roads and bridges and clearing the forests. Still another mechanism was contract labor, which compelled Africans and Asians to live in compounds and rendered them liable to imprisonment for desertion.

As events unfolded, the mechanisms of exploitation changed with changing conditions. The industrial revolution eliminated some of the more brutal manifestations of colonialism; and after about 1870, according to Stephen H. Roberts, the colonized "had to play their part in providing markets for the cheap products of European factories and in working to supply the necessary raw materials, especially when industry became increasingly dependent on those originating in the tropics, such as the oleaginous products." With the changes in economic reality the colonial climate changed again, culminating in the Berlin Conference of 1884 and the partitioning of Africa among the European powers.

*C*ERTAIN mechanisms, as the preceding implies, are common to all colonial systems, but each colonial system is characterized by specific realities. This is a point of exceptional importance for our analysis, for colonial mechanisms have different meanings and enter into different combinations in different situations. It is even possible, as we said before, for colonizers to use different mechanisms to achieve the same purpose. They can dominate the colonized by advocating either separation (the white supporters of Booker T. Washington and the advocates of parallel societies in South Africa) or integration-assimilation (the white liberal establishments of America and French colonial Africa). They can dominate the colonized by granting or withholding formal civil and political rights. "Equal rights," for example, were extended to some French blacks, who sent delegates to the French National Assembly and watched with pride as certain of their brothers were elected to the French cabinet and highly visible posts in the French government. A very different approach was championed by the English, who said they were preparing *their* colonials for freedom by gradual and indirect methods. The curious and interesting fact is that the announced rhetoric, whether of French *assimilation*, Portuguese *assimilado*, or English Indirect Rule, made little or no difference in the daily lives of the French, English, and Portuguese subjects, all of whom were equally exploited.

The meaning of this is plain. Colonialism is a matter of social structures, not rhetoric or good intentions. More to the point, colonialism is a coherent whole, and the different parts of that whole assume their true importance as structures of a total system that maintains the domination of one group and the subordination of another group.

Two factors obscure the relevance of this analysis to the American situation: the length of white overlordship, and the size of the white population vis-à-vis the oppressed. These factors should be taken into consideration in assessing the specificity of American internal colonialism, but they do not affect the form or the substance of the relationship. Neither longevity nor arithmetic defines colonialism, which is, to repeat, an organic structural relationship between a dynamic, developing, dominating center and a stagnant, underdeveloped, dominated circumference. The center-circumference relationship is pivotal. The underdevelopment of the circumference is a function of the development of the center. The dynamic center expands at the expense of the stagnation and underdevelopment of the colonized periphery.

It is instructive in this regard to recall the history of the white settlers of South Africa, who left Holland and settled on the Cape of Good Hope in 1652, twenty-six years after other Dutch settlers founded New York. Most of these settlers, like most of the white settlers of America, were poor indentured servants, and most professed a Calvinist religion as stern and intolerant as the Puritanism of the New England settlers. In South Africa, as in Virginia and other American colonies, the white settlement was followed by a period of ambiguity in which there was widespread mating between the Dutch Boers and the Hottentots, some of whom were baptized and accepted as free men. This situation changed in the last part of the seventeenth century (in South Africa and Virginia) with the extermination of the Bushmen, the displacement of the Hottentots, and the importation of slaves from West Africa, Malaya, and Madagascar. And it is significant that the Dutch Boers adopted the same expedient used in Virginia and other American colonies, declaring that baptism did not alter the earthly status of the slaves.

As time went on, there was considerable in-migration from England, which assumed political control and imposed some of the same racial restrictions used in North America. In South Africa, as in North America, the oppressed population was divided into different classes, some of whom were identified as "free men of color."

When, in 1834, Britain abolished slavery in South Africa, the Boers launched a vigorous counteroffensive, demanding—in phrases strangely reminiscent of the Declaration of Independence—freedom from "the yoke of oppression." The immediate result was the Great Trek, which is usually compared with the Westward movement of the white settlers of America. Abandoning the niceties, the Boers said frankly that they initiated the Great Trek because of the emancipation of their slaves. According to Anna Elizabeth Steenkamp, the niece of one of the leaders of the Trek, the Boers were motivated primarily by "the shameful and unjust proceedings with reference to the freedom of our slaves. . . ." And yet, she added, it was not so much "their freedom that drove us to such lengths, as their being placed on an equal footing with the Christians, contrary to the laws of God and the natural distinction of race and religion, so that it was intolerable for any decent Christian to bow down beneath such a yoke...."

Like the white settlers of North America, the white settlers of South Africa moved north in wagons, and, like the North Americans, they initiated a genocidal war against the owners of the land—in this case the Zulus, under the leadership of the great kings, Shaka and Dingane.

Overwhelmed finally by the rifles of the Boers and the muskets of the British, the Zulus were herded into reservations called "tribal reserves." There then occurred an intramural struggle between the Dutch Boers and the English, a struggle which ended with the formation of Boer republics and the writing of Boer constitutions modelled on the U.S. Constitution. One of the inalienable rights demanded by the Boers was the right to oppress non-Europeans; and when the two sides were once again reunited in a new Union, South Africa and the American South became the most racist areas in the world. In South Africa, as in America, blacks and whites were separated by Jim Crow laws. In South Africa, as in America, blacks were excluded from skilled trades and were bound to white employers by peonage, vagrancy provisions, and convict labor laws.

A complicating factor in the South African situation—and in the American situation—was the presence of a relatively large number of poor whites, who demanded differential pay scales for black and white workers and quotas "progressively favorable to the white race." These demands were pressed by organized white labor, which barred black workers and organized strikes against the employment of non-Europeans. The most serious of these strikes was the Witwatersrand uprising of 1921, which led to the death of more than two hundred blacks.

The resulting course of events followed the familiar pattern, culminating in *baasskap* (white supremacy) and a philosophy of apartheid based on the idea of splitting South Africa into white and black areas—a Bantustan for blacks comprising 13 percent of the land, with the remaining 87 percent reserved for the whites.

In this abbreviated history of South Africa, we have a classic case of an internal colonialism. The parallels between this system and the American system are clear and obvious and are recognized by South Africans, who usually tell visitors that their country is "like the American South at its best." This should not be taken to mean that the South African and North American situations are identical, for there are equally clear and equally obvious differences, most notably the number of colonizers, who constitute a definite majority in America and a definite minority in South Africa. This is an important factor, but here again we must emphasize that differences in detail do not alter the nature or the results of colonial systems.

In this light, we can better understand the ambiguities of black America, which is essentially a colony—an internal colony—of white America. It is obvious, for example, that the white settlers of America broke with Great Britain seventy-nine years before the Boers founded the Orange Free State of South Africa. It is equally obvious, however, that the white settlers of America created a colonial situation in America by making the reds and blacks their colonials. And despite surface differences relating to the number of white settlers and their ideological postures, the colonial situation created in America is characterized by the same constants we have noticed in other colonial situations.

Although this system was established initially by laws and conscious acts of institutional subordination, it soon became an autonomous entity propelled by its own internal dynamic. For this reason, among others, changes in the name and the form of the system did not affect its content.

The foundations of this system were constructed during the slave regime, which was a paradigm of a colonial situation. After the brief interval of Black Reconstruction, the power brokers of America sacrificed the Constitution and legalized the subordination of blacks. The key elements in this development were the Compromise of 1877, the nullification of the civil rights and voting rights laws of the Reconstruction period, the *Plessy* v. *Ferguson* decision (which gave legal sanction to the Jim Crow or American apartheid system), and the creation of a system of peonage.

The Jim Crow system and other inventions of the post-Reconstruction period were functional elements in a new system, which continued slavery under a new name. And the elements of the new system, like the elements of the old, meshed and intermeshed in an interlocking network of political, economic, and cultural barriers, all of which presupposed a unity of intentions and the unity of a policy.

While the white leaders of the North and South were building the new system, they were at the same time digging pits for the new stratum of black merchants, teachers, and preachers spawned by the burgeoning network of black schools, churches, businesses, and fraternal institutions. The point at issue here was, at bottom, simple enough: how to use these emerging leaders in a classically colonial campaign of indirect rule. This stratagem was strenuously opposed by black leaders like Frederick Douglass, W. E. B. DuBois and others; but social structures (including the violence of the social structure) and social attitudes (which are products of social structures) pushed many, though by no means all, in the direction of accommodation and worse.

In general, the situation of black leaders then (and now) was similar to the situation in other colonial areas, where institutions forced leaders into debilitating dependence on political, economic, and cultural interests hostile to the fundamental interests of their primary constituency. The unfortunate but perhaps inevitable result was that many men who started out with good intention moved from small compromises to big compromises and ended up finally in the tight white embrace of the system. But this must be viewed in proper perspective, for the objective contradictions of the behaviour of black leaders and followers were, in large measure, prestructured by the objective contradictions of a colonial situation masked by the formal rhetoric of equality. And, as Jean-Paul Sartre has said, "institutions that pretend to be founded on freedom are necessarily degraded when their real truth is servitude."

This much was clear to a number of black men and women, who launched certain organizational initiatives that created the superstructure of black America. Foremost among these initiatives were the continuation of the Black Church movement and the organization of new fraternal organizations; the Protest movement, beginning with the Niagara movement and taking organizational form with the founding of the National Association for the Advancement of Colored People and the National Urban League; the Black Culture movement, beginning with the American Negro Academy and flowing with and out of the Negro History movement led by Carter G. Woodson, and the Harlem Renaissance led by black artists from the four corners of the colony.

Like other colonial phenomena, the superstructure of the black colony was at once relative and specific. That is to say, it was a typical elaboration of typical colonial themes (protest, accommodation, assimilation, separation), and yet it was distinctly American, reflecting American realities fully as much as the superstructures of the French African and English African colonies reflected French and English realities. Partly because of the massiveness of the white presence and partly because of the peculiar American economic and political realities, certain themes (African renaissance, the importance and priority of black culture, Black Power, Pan-Africanism, etc.) surfaced first in the American milieu and had reverberations in Africa and elsewhere.

As in other colonial areas, these organizational initiatives were led initially by the new stratum of educated blacks, who appropriated the words of their adversaries and made weapons out of them. But the truly decisive step in the making of modern black America was the Great Migration of the black masses to the North, a leaderless movement that changed the infrastructure of the black community, loosing explosive forces that are still rippling through American society.

Neither the new forces nor the organizational initiatives changed the colonial system. After the Great Migration, the form of this system changed, but the domination and dependency continued. In the twenties and thirties, black laborers were consigned to the bottom of the labor pool, and the cities were divided racially by restrictive covenants and the discriminatory practices of federal, state, and municipal agencies. This made an immense difference to blacks, who, by World War II, were caught, as it were, in a web that imprisoned every faculty and sense, a web as soft as cotton, yet unbreakable as steel.

Assessing this situation in 1945, Richard Wright deplored the "processes that [made] the majority of Negroes on Chicago's South Side sixth-graders, processes that [made] 65 percent of all Negroes on Chicago's South Side earn their living by manual labor." He added: "The imposed conditions under which Negroes live detail the structure of their lives like an engineer outlining the blueprints for the production of machines."

There was another change in form in the wake of the Supreme Court decision of 1954 and the Freedom movement led by Martin Luther King, Jr. But the reforms of the fifties and sixties, important as they were, did not go to the heart of the colonial relationship. By that time, moreover, the colonial idea had become so deeply embedded in institutional practices not directly linked to race that the abolition of legal segregation and discrimination had little immediate impact on the functioning of the system. As a consequence, the black colony of American presented, at the end of this period, the paradoxical picture of a rapidly growing urban middle sector and a rapidly growing reserve army of unemployed and underemployed workers. In succeeding chapters we will deal with the implications of these developments in the fields of labor and economic development. For the moment, however, we are concerned simply to establish the existence and the parameters of a system that became increasingly visible after the Freedom movement destroyed the legal incrustrations that masked its true meaning.

Writing in 1965 after the passage of the civil rights legislation of the fifties and sixties, Kenneth Clark said that "the dark ghettos [of America] are social, political, educational, and—above all—economic colonies. Their inhabitants are subject peoples, victims of the greed, cruelty, insensitivity, guilt, and fear of their masters."

The essential point here, a point Clark and other students have made, is that the black colonies of America are controlled politically, economically, and culturally from the outside. Ultimate policy-making power is in the hands of outsiders who have their own representatives on the spot, some of them black intermediaries, to see that the will of the white center is obeyed in the black circumference. Another point of importance in establishing the existence of the American colonial situation is that the inhabitants of the black circumference and the white center do not deal with each other directly. They deal with each other, as Gunnar Myrdal noted, like two foreign countries, "through the medium of plenipotentiaries."

Viewing the same data from a slightly different angle, William K. Tabb said that the colonial relationship between the black and white groups is fundamental to an understanding of American reality. "The economic relations of the ghetto to white America," he added, "closely parallel those between third-world nations and the industrially advanced countries. The ghetto also has a relatively low per capita income and a high birth rate. Its residents are for the most part unskilled. Businesses lack capital and managerial know-how. Local markets are limited." Pointing out that the ghetto is dependent "on one basic export—its unskilled labor," he said that "local businesses are owned, in large numbers, by nonresidents, many of whom are white. Important jobs in the local public economy (teachers, policemen, and postmen) are held by white outsiders. The black ghetto, then, is in many ways in a position similar to that of the typical underdeveloped country."

*From* the preceding analysis, it is unmistakably clear that black Americans are victims of a system which prestructures events and colonial relationships. Every structure of power in America—capital, labor, the intelligentsia, the church—had a hand in the creation of this system, and every structure of power in America profits in one way or another from it.

The system is a synthesis of individual acts and institutionalized practices. Programmed by socioeconomic arrangements and propelled by the feedback of past and present exploitation, the system produces racist results from actions that may not be consciously racist.

Equally important in the working of the system are dual labor and housing markets linked to dual educational structures. "The manpower problems of the urban ghetto," Michael Piore observes, "appear best defined in terms of a dual labor market: a *primary* market offering relatively high-paying, stable employment, with good working conditions, chances of advancement and equitable administration of work rules; and a *secondary* market, to which the urban poor are confined, decidedly less attractive in all of these respects and in direct competition with welfare and crime for the attachment of the potential labor force."

The same general situation obtains in the total American market. William Tabb has said that black Americans have always inhabited a twilight area "somewhere between Marx's reserve army and Cairnes's noncompeting group. That is, they are an available source of labor when needed by the economy and at the same time a group set apart which can be confined to certain types of work (low-paying, hard, and unpleasant jobs). They have been given the worst jobs the society had to offer. When labor is scarce they are given the lower rungs of better jobs; when economic conditions decline, whites move in to take even the jobs previously set aside as 'Negro work.' The blacks act as a buffer pool, keeping labor costs from rising. In this way the entire white society benefits by receiving goods and services more cheaply and white employment is cushioned."

There are white primary and black secondary sectors in every institutional area of American life. But the crucial fact is not the existence of individual sectors but the interlocking of the sectors within an overarching system. In a fine phrase, Harold Baron said the institutions of the system "have been woven together into a web of urban racism that entraps Negroes much as the spider's net holds flies—they can wiggle but they cannot move very far. There is a carefully articulated interrelation of the barriers created by each institution. Whereas the single institutional strand standing alone might not be so strong, together the many strands form a powerful web." What this means on the concrete level is that political and economic domination leads to cultural domination which, in turn, reinforces political and economic domination. In Baron's words, the "inferior education in ghetto schools handicaps the Negro workers in the labor market. Employment discrimination causes low wages and frequent unemployment. Low incomes limit the market choices of Negro families in housing. Lack of education, low level occupations, and exclusion from ownership or control of large enterprises inhibit the development of political power. The lack of political power prevents black people from changing basic housing, planning, and educational programs. Each sector strengthens the racial subordination in the rest of the urban institutions."

By all this we must understand that racism in America is not merely the irrational and sporadic acts of eccentric bigots but a system with an overall logic—a system that institutionally excludes certain groups from full consumption and forces on some men and women a disproportionate share of the hazards of life, a system that daily, secretly, hands down death sentences, condemning twice as many black babies as white babies to death and insuring that white men live on the average seven years longer than black men.

This does not mean that the system operates automatically over the heads of individuals. Systems do not operate that way; they are created by individuals and groups of individuals with common purposes and common intentions, and they are retreaded at critical moments by individuals and groups of individuals who reassume and reanimate the purposes and intentions of the creators. In the years between the creation and the critical turning points, individuals maintain and sustain the system by acting as individuals, group-individuals and institution-individuals on four levels.

The first level is the level of individual action, the level of overt acts of subordination and exclusion by men and women acting in their own names. For lack of a better terminology, we shall call this *oppression*, using the word *exploitation* for institutionalized acts of subordination and exclusion.

Individual men and women (and children) also oppress blacks by tacit acceptance of institutional practices and by passive support and identification with their group and the systematic processes of their group, systematic processes that bring them certain benefits and make them beneficiaries of past, present, and future acts of aggression against blacks.

On the second level, the level of the collectivity, individuals improvise themselves into group-individuals and participate in the oppression of black people by supporting or taking part in the praxis of the pressure groups that have a vested interest in black subordination. Of overriding importance in this connection are "the exclusionary interests," to use Alvin L. Schorr's apt phrase, "that establish and maintain vast sanctuaries from Negroes and poor people." Among the leading exclusionary interests are real estate boards, suburban governments, financial institutions, unions, and property owners associations.

At a still deeper level, the level of institutions, individuals acting as institution-individuals participate in the process of exploitation by manipulating the levers of objectively racist institutions. This happens, according to the United States Civil Rights Commission report, *Racism in America*, when acts are:

> a. Directly linked to other actions that are overtly racist (such as basing employment policies on acceptance of unions that deliberately exclude Negro members).
>
> b. Heavily reliant upon personal qualifications or skills which minority group members have not been permitted to achieve because of past overt racism (such as requiring passage of academically oriented tests for getting a job, or basing early ability groupings of children in public schools on tests administered only in English in areas where many children have been reared in Spanish-speaking homes).
>
> c. Dependent upon institutional arrangements which embody the residual results of past overt racism (such as policies—like the neighborhood school policy—which mainly benefit persons living near facilities in all-white neighborhoods).
>
> d. Likely to perpetuate any of the three causal factors cited above—that is, overt racism, low achievement among minority groups of key skills or traits, or residual institutional arrangements from past overt racism (as distortions of reality in mass media and textbooks do).

These observations make clear that the fabric of the system is woven out of millions of individual acts of oppression and indirect institutional exploitation. And since the system would crumble if it were not continually reinvented by the acts of individuals, the system protects itself by continually producing and reproducing colonizers. This, however, does not absolve the colonizer of responsibility for maintaining the system. For although he was born into the system with a certain skin-uniform that committed him from birth, and although he lives and breathes in the ambience of racist institutions, it is still up to him to give meaning to himself and the system by deciding how he is going to live his life within a system which makes him an illegitimately privileged person and an oppressor, no matter what he does or says.

If the system commits the white colonizer totally, it makes even more drastic demands on the colonized black, whose life course is predetermined in general and who lives under the constant menace of violence, unemployment, and repression. Exiled in an unlivable present, excluded from the general good and kept in a state of political, economic, and cultural dependence on men and institutions hostile to his fundamental interests, the colonized black is imprisoned in a space that imposes on him its path and its perspectives. The system molds his character, determines his conduct, and narrows his horizons. It charges him more for less (housing, food, commodities) and yields fewer returns for proportionately greater efforts. The end result is that the colonized finds himself in pawn psychologically and sociologically to a system that feeds on his transcendence and mocks his efforts to overcome.

The system is equally overwhelming on the level of the colonized group, taking the form of a great spastic octopus which stretches its tentacles relentlessly, indefatigably, in every direction, pushing into strange and distorted shapes all institutions and organizations. The confinement of black workers and black merchants to secondary and marginal markets, the systematic cultural repression of black children, and the structural steel surrounding black leaders: all are the rigorous results of a dependent colonial relationship.

If we look at this matter more closely, several generalizations become obvious. First, the situation of the colonized is defined not by his personal qualities but by his membership in a group. He is oppressed, in other words, not because of what he has or has not done but because he is a member of a group institutionally subordinated by social structures. Secondly, the system is affected by the action or lack of action of the colonized, who is secretly tempted—historical experience has shown—by the sirens of imitation, accommodation, adventurism, and escapism. This is not the place for a phenomenology of the colonized, or a discussion of strategy, and it is enough for our purposes here to indicate that historical experience has also shown that the authentic colonized person, that is to say the colonizer who accepts himself and his situation in order to change both, realizes that collective dramas cannot be resolved by individual acts and that the only viable solution for him and the persons who share his destiny is a change in the colonial relationship, i.e., decolonization. But here again we must stress, as Memmi has stressed, that every colonial situation is relative and specific at the same time. This means simply that decolonization in America must grow out of and reflect the specific features of internal colonialism in America.

It is easy enough to say this; it is another and quite different thing to say how this can be done or even whether it can be done. What makes the question of decolonization in America so difficult is the black situation, which is quite possibly the most urgent and difficult in the whole colonized world. One element in that situation, of course, is the fact that black Americans are exiled, so to speak, in the midst of a hostile and/or indifferent white population with overwhelming numerical and strategic superiority. (Two countervailing factors, however, are the black birth rate and the fact that blacks occupy strategic ground across the urban lifelines of the nation.)

The second complicating factor in the black situation is that the American colonial situation is perpetuated because it gives or seems to give millions of whites concrete psychological, economic, and political advantages. This explanation is politically and ideologically of exceptional importance, and we ought to dwell on it for a moment, focusing again on the official report of the United States Commission on Civil Rights. According to that report, oppression and exploitation provide the following economic benefits to "a significant number of whites:"

    1. Reduction of competition by excluding members of certain groups from access to benefits, privileges, jobs, or other opportunities or markets....

    2. Exploitation of members of the subordinated groups through lower wages, higher prices, higher rents, less desirable credit terms, or poorer working or living conditions than those received by whites. Where racial or color discrimination *per se* is illegal, such exploitation probably cannot be effectively carried out unless the subordinated groups are

spatially segregated from the white majority. Then differentials in wages, prices, credit terms, and other policies actually based upon color can be more easily concealed and even rationalized as based upon geographic differences.

3. Avoidance of certain undesirable or "dead-end" jobs (like garbage collection) by creating economically depressed racial or ethnic groups which will be compelled by necessity to carry out those jobs, even though their potential skill levels are equal to those of other groups.

On the political level, according to the commission, whites benefit from racism by receiving a "disproportionate share of the advantages which arise from political control over government"—political power that enables whites to control "government actions and policies as well as jobs." Political racism, according to the report, occurs in the following ways:

1. Manipulation of potential nonwhite voters in order to maintain exclusive white control over an entire governmental structure (such as a county government in the South), or some portion of such a structure (such as a ward in a northern city), which would be controlled by nonwhites if all citizens enjoyed equal voting rights, since nonwhites are a majority of the potential electorate in that area.

2. Manipulation of political district boundaries or governmental structures by whites so as to minimize the ability of nonwhite voters to elect representatives sensitive to their needs....

3. Exclusion of nonwhites from a proportionate share—or any share—of government jobs, contracts, and other disbursements through the decisions of white administrative officials.

4. Maintenance of the support of nonwhite voters by either white or nonwhite politicians who fail to provide reciprocal government policy benefits and other advantages to the same degree as for white groups in the electorate....

5. Voter refusal to support a politician who is clearly superior to his opponent merely because he is not a member of the same racial or color group as the voters themselves and his opponent is....

As in all colonial situations, political and economic control yields psychological advantages, including:

1. Creation of feelings of superiority in comparison to nonwhites.

These feelings are extremely widespread among whites, though not always openly expressed or even consciously recognized. . . .

2. Suppression in oneself or one's group of certain normal traits which are regarded as undesirable. This is accomplished by projecting an exaggerated image of those traits and "legitimizing" attacks upon them. For example, many American whites unjustly accuse Negroes of laziness, sexual promiscuity, and general irresponsibility. These are exaggerated versions of normal human impulses. But they happen to be the very impulses which the Puritan ethic, long dominant in America, seeks to suppress in favor of extreme industry, sexual purity, and individual self-reliance.

3. Promotion of solidarity and reduced tension among white nationality and social class groups. Racism enables them to focus the inevitable hostilities and antagonisms which arise in modern life upon the subordinated colored groups, and to identify themselves together in contrast to those groups.

4. Avoiding the necessity of adopting difficult or costly policies to solve key social problems by falsely blaming those problems upon "immoral behavior" by members of the subordinated groups. For example, many whites erroneously blame unemployment and high welfare costs upon laziness and sexual promiscuity among Negroes. In reality, more than three-fourths of all unemployed persons are white, most persons on welfare are white, and more than 90 percent of all persons on welfare are incapable of supporting themselves because they are either too old, disabled, children, or mothers who must care for children. By falsely converting these problems into "the results of sin," such scapegoating provides a moral excuse for relatively affluent whites to reduce their economic support for the unemployed and the dependent poor without feeling guilty about doing so.

5. Diverting one's own energies from maximum self-improvement efforts by claiming that white racism makes any significant self-help attempts by colored people ineffective and useless. . . .

This record is quoted at length because it supports a number of important propositions, including the fact that the system is a two-edge sword that maims the colonized *and* the colonizer, who pays a disproportionately high price in terms of his own personal and social interests for the alleged advantages of the system. Over and above this, the record makes clear that the subjugation and exploitation of black people as a group is an integral part of the institutional infrastructure of the American brand of internal colonialism. In sum, black subordination is not an aberration of individuals or an institutional anomaly but the essence of the American system.

This system, which has assumed so many forms, which has changed skin and colors and names so many times, was/is the central factor in the making of black America. Every aspect of black life and culture has been marked by it and by the struggle against it.

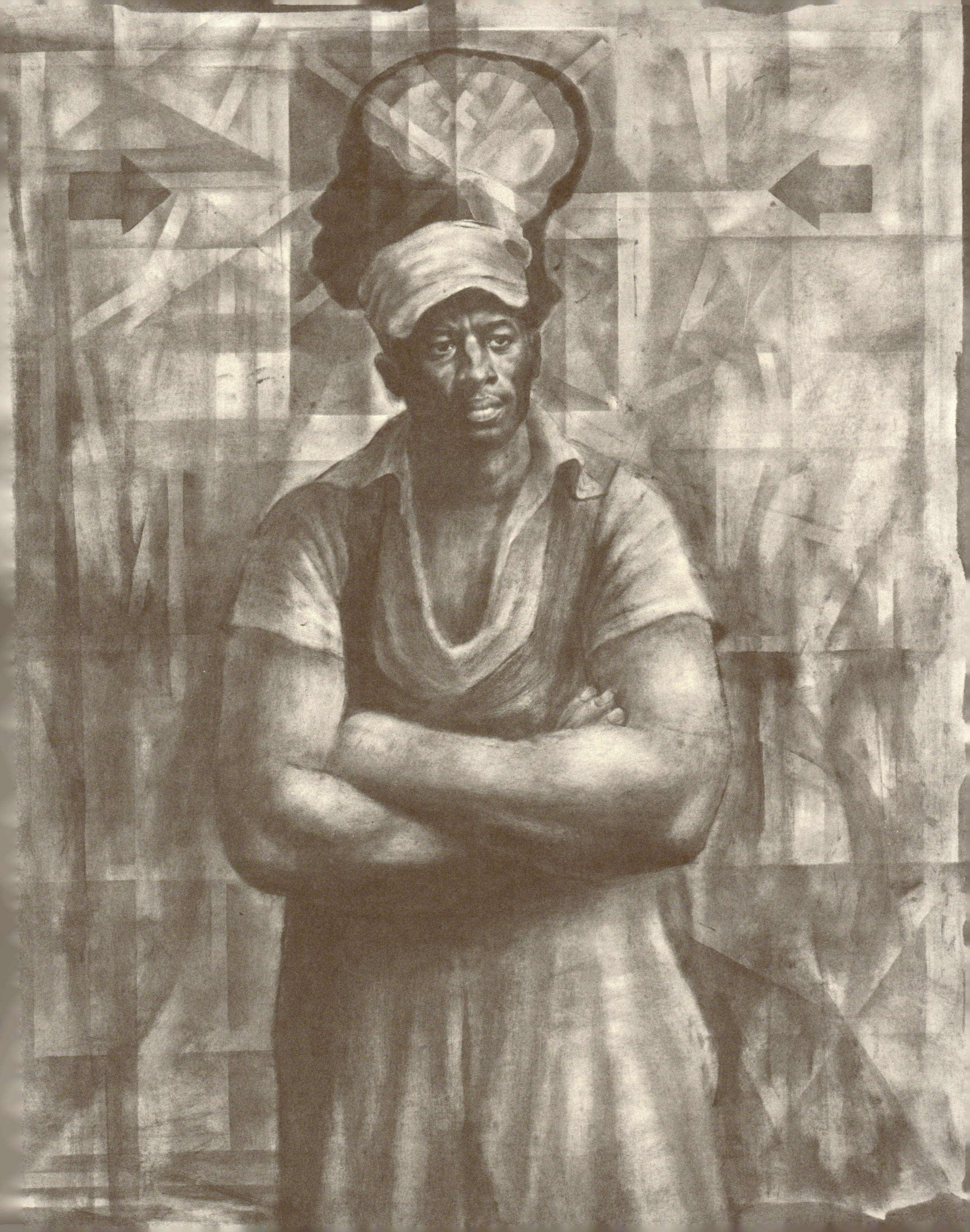

# The Black Worker

*Labor has built this great metropolis of the new world, built it as coral insects build the foundations of islands—build and die; build from the fathomless depth of the ocean until the mountain billows are dashed into spray as they beat against the fortifications beneath which the builders are forever entombed and forgotten.*

—Eugene V. Debs

*To* understand black is to understand work—and the denial of work.

It was work or, to be more precise, it was the European demand for cheap and exploitable labor that brought black people to these shores. And it was in and through the work relationship that the fundamental structures of the black community were formed. The same thing can be said about the impact of black labor on the structures of the white community. It was the work of black workers, it was the unpaid and underpaid work of black men, women, and children that changed the flora and fauna of large sections of the New World and created the initial pool of capital that made possible the economic growth from which they were excluded by fraud and violence.

To understand the black experience is to understand this. It is also to understand that leap of the spirit which enabled embattled black workers to endure slavery, peonage, and internal colonialism.

> Take this hammer and carry it to the captain,
> Tell him I'm gone,
> Tell him I'm gone,
> Tell him I'm gone.
>
> This is the hammer that killed John Henry,
> But it won't kill me,
> But it won't kill me,
> But it won't kill me.

This image, at once aural and visual, reverberates through all the reaches of the black experience and underlines the fact that the history of black people is, among other things, a history of work.

To assess the meaning of that history, and to situate it in the dynamics of the declining phases of capitalism, it is necessary to trace the arc of black labor from legal slavery to economic slavery. More than that: it is necessary to follow that arc with the guidance of four conceptual formulations that release the reality which isolated statistics oftentimes conceal.

The first point to be stressed is that white Americans have deliberately and systematically used black workers for white economic purposes. In the slave epoch, for instance, black workers were forced to play the role of pump primers in the development of the capital that assured the growth of America. When, after the Civil War, legal slavery gave way to economic slavery, black workers were assigned the role of an industrial labor reserve which could be called into play in times of emergency and acute national need.

Flowing out of this conceptual envelope is a second point which is less obvious but equally important: and that is that the relationship of black workers to the American economic structure is a mass relationship. Black workers, in other words, are oppressed as a group. This means, on one level, that the role of black workers is a result not of chance or individual characteristics but of white national decisions on the use of black workers. It means, at a still deeper level, that black workers as a group have been confined to marginal economic roles by fraud, violence, and a system of institutionalized exploitation. As was shown in the last chapter, the primary mechanisms of this system are dual labor markets: a white primary market of relatively well-paid occupations and a black secondary market of marginal low-paying occupations.

The third item in this equation is that white Americans have deliberately manipulated the educational system and cultural media in order to assure a dependable supply of uneducated and mystified black laborers.

The fourth and final point is that black workers have been forced to fight a rearguard action against a pincer movement of both white capital and white labor. Since the eighteenth century, white capital has repeatedly used black labor to depress wages and to divide and mystify the labor force. For almost as long a period, white labor has used every weapon at its command to restrict black labor to menial occupations.

The implications of these points are clear and extensive, as Dan Lacy pointed out in a recent book on *The White Use of Blacks in America*. "Most studies of white actions and attitudes towards blacks in America," he wrote, "have treated them as the product of irrational racist emotion and as problems in social psychopathology. Though there has been a marked paranoid component in white racial attitudes, white actions with regard to blacks have not in fact been an aggregation of irrationalities. In their totality they have constituted a deliberate and carefully interlinked set of policies intended to assure the presence and the exploitability of a large semiskilled labor force, primarily in agriculture, whose labor could be commanded at subsistence wages. Changes in the economy that increased or diminished the need for such a labor force have been the principal determinants of racial policy. Indeed, the paranoid elements in America, and especially in Southern, racial attitudes have been in no small part deliberately cultivated as a means of sustaining racial policies having primarily economic objectives."

This testimony and the testimony of W. E. B. DuBois, Eric Williams, C. L. R. James and others prove that the work relationship is central to an understanding of black and white America. As is well known, the founding of America was inextricably intertwined with the capturing, transporting, and colonizing of African workers. In the seventeenth century, as was shown in the first two chapters, attempts were made to colonize Indian and European workers. But it quickly became apparent that the mastering of the vast stretches of the New World required more laborers than Indian America and Europe could supply. And this perception, dim at first but growing ever clearer, led to a national white decision to base the economy on the use of workers forcibly transported from Africa. The key word here is *national*. Slavery and the slave trade were foundation stones of the entire American economy. This development was analyzed with great subtlety and perception by W. E. B. Du Bois in his standard work, *Black Reconstruction*. "First of all," he wrote, [the work of black workers] called for widening stretches of new, rich black soil—in Florida, in Louisiana, in Mexico; even in Kansas. This land, added to cheap labor, and labor easily regulated and distributed, made profits so high that a whole system of culture arose in the South, with a new leisure and social philosophy. Black labor became the foundation stone not only of the Southern social structure, but of Northern manufacture and commerce, of the English factory system, of European commerce, of buying and selling on a world-wide scale; new cities were built on the results of black labor, and a new labor problem, involving all white labor, arose both in Europe and America."

Bent, as DuBois said, "at the bottom of a growing pyramid of commerce and industry," the black workers of America were indispensable sources of primary capital accumulation. It is established by a great deal of evidence that the capital that financed the growth of America in the nineteenth century came largely from foreign exchanges earned from the export of slave-grown cotton. In a recent and important study, Douglass North pointed out that "it was the growth of the cotton textile industry and the demand for cotton which was decisive" in the crucial years of primary capital accumulation in America. It was cotton, he said, which paid for American imports "and the demand for western foodstuffs and northeastern services and manufactures was basically dependent upon the income received from the cotton trade." In the final analysis, therefore, it was the power of black bodies that financed the building of American railroads and factories and the settlement of the West.

To this formative influence must be added the contributions of slave laborers who worked on docks and in factories and were largely responsible for the construction of Southern railroads. Nor can we forget the contributions of black artisans, who were the master craftsmen of the South, plying their trade not only on plantations but in all of the major cities. These carpenters, blacksmiths, masons, and millwrights were uncommonly talented. Some of their work, notably the iron grills of New Orleans, evokes praise, even today. Looking back on this period many years later, an engineer who learned his trade from a slave artisan said that "one only needs to go down South and examine hundreds of old Southern mansions, and splendid old church edifices, still intact, to be convinced of the fact of the cleverness of the Negro artisan, who constructed nine-tenths of them. . . ." He continued: "There are few, if any, of the carpenters of today who, if they had the hand tools, could get out the 'stuff' and make one of those old style massive panel doors—who could work out by hand the mouldings, the stiles, the mullions, etc., and build one of those windows, which are to be found today in many of the churches and public buildings of the South. . . . For the carpenter in those days was also the 'cabinet maker,' the wood turner, coffin maker, generally the pattern maker, and the maker of most things made of wood. The Negro blacksmith held almost complete sway in his line, which included the many branches of forgery, and other trades which are now classified under different heads from that of the regular blacksmith. The blacksmith in the days of slavery was expected to make any and everything wrought of iron. He was to all intents and purposes the 'machine blacksmith,' 'horseshoer,' 'carriage and wagon ironer and trimmer,' 'gunsmith,' 'wheelwright'; and often whittled out and ironed the hames, the plowstocks, and the 'single trees' for the farmers, and did a hundred other things too numerous to mention. They were experts at tempering edge tools, by what is generally known as the water process. But many of them had secret processes of their own for tempering tools which they guarded with zealous care."

One can scarcely overemphasize the contributions of these artisans. According to M. W. Jernegan, an authority on labor in the South, "the weight of evidence shows that there was a great increase in numbers [of slave artisans]; that they were more valuable than untrained slaves, and much sought after; that they competed with free white labor especially in the towns; and *they were the most important agency in the commercial development of the South.*" [My emphasis]

Indisputably; and yet it must be noted that neither the artisans nor the laborers profited from their contributions, which were soon forgotten and are seldom mentioned in general media today. Since slave workers were not paid and since they could not use their energies and skills for the advancement of the black community, their contributions enriched the white community at the expense of the black community. To make things even more vexing, slavemasters and the managers of the social structure used black labor—free and slave—to impoverish all workers, thereby making black workers political footballs who were kicked from one end of the field to the other in the never-ending struggle between white capital and white labor.

This last point is of crucial importance, for it played a role in sowing the seeds of disunity in the working class. White capital, which divided black and white workers, the better to control both, unhesitatingly used black workers to undermine the positions of white workers and to remind them of their precarious position. At the same time, and at first sight somewhat paradoxically, white capital encouraged the emerging demonology of white labor, which tended to blame its troubles not on the system or on white capital but on black workers, who were victims of white capital, white labor, and the system. By paying white workers in the coin of racism, which gave them a false sense of self-esteem, and by reserving for whites, when economic conditions permitted and social peace dictated, privileged white sanctuaries, white capital cemented white labor into the system and channelled hatred of the system into hostility and violence against black scapegoats. Thus, black workers became victims of the whole society, a fact unwittingly admitted by certain whites who opposed the African Colonization movement on the ground that the system needed blacks to perform the necessary roles of scavengers and psychological safety valves. In 1828, for example, the Senate Foreign Relations Committee expressed opposition to the Colonization movement because black workers were needed, it said, to perform "various necessary menial duties." Four years later the *New England Magazine* deplored the Colonization movement, warning that if blacks returned to Africa white men would have to "hew our wood, draw our water, and perform our menial offices." Black workers, the magazine said, "supply the place of so many whites, who may be spared for higher purposes."

These quotations are very instructive, for they tell us in unmistakable language that the confinement of blacks to "menial offices" was deliberate and systematic. What is equally clear is that these and similar phrases were used to mystify whites who were spared for different purposes when economic conditions dictated. In slave states and not infrequently in free states, white masters and white employers used slave artisans and slave laborers to undermine the position of white workers, who were driven to the margins of society, where they lived at a subsistence level and nursed their passionate hatred of black workers. The results were as unfortunate as they were predictable. Instead of attacking slavery, the white workers attacked the slave. Instead of attacking the oppressors of black labor, the white workers attacked black labor, organizing a campaign against the employment and training of black artisans. As early as 1708 there were complaints from the white mechanics of Pennsylvania against the hiring out of black mechanics. In 1722 the white mechanics renewed their campaign and the Pennsylvania legislative assembly declared that the hiring of black mechanics was "dangerous and injurious to the republic and not to be sanctioned."

From Maryland, from Georgia, from Massachusetts, from practically every colony came similar complaints and similar resolutions, none of which altered the economic realities that favored the employment of slave artisans. Speaking to the Virginia General Assembly in January, 1832, Thomas Marshall said the continued preference for black artisans "sufficed to deprive the white mechanics of their chief encouragement to perfect themselves in their trades, and generally [has] the effect of expelling them from one neighborhood to another until they finally expatriate themselves."

Most of the expatriate artisans settled in the North and West, where they formed white-only unions and petitioned legislative bodies for strict measures against the training and employment of black artisans. Not content with those methods, white workers physically attacked black workers, organizing and leading the series of anti-Negro riots that periodically wracked the big cities of the North. The effect of all this was not long in making itself felt in the North, as the Pennsylvania Abolition Society reported in 1795. "Some of the [black] men follow Mechanick trades," the society reported, "and a number of them are mariners, but the greatest part are employed as Day labourers. The Women generally, both married and single, wash clothes for a livelihood." The situation was much the same in New York City, where a brilliant black high school graduate lamented the black situation in a valedictory address of 1819. "Why should I strive hard and acquire all the constituents of a man," he asked, "if the prevailing genius of the land admit me not as such, or but in an inferior degree! Pardon me if I feel insignificant and weak. . . . What are my prospects? To what shall I turn my hand? Shall I be a mechanic? No one will employ me; white boys won't work with me. Shall I be a merchant? No one will have me in his office; white clerks won't associate with me. Drudgery and servitude, then, are my prospective portion. Can you be surprised at my discouragement?"

Bad as the situation was, it soon became immeasurably worse as waves of white immigrants slammed against American shores. Between 1830 and 1860 some five million white immigrants came to America. Most of these immigrants, poor, illiterate, and willing to accept almost any job at almost any wage, settled in the cities, depressing wages and driving blacks out of traditional black preserves. The struggle continued for three decades, but the immigrants were white, and the outcome was preordained. The struggle between the Irish workers and black workers was particularly acrimonious. At that time and for several decades thereafter, the Irish were considered "white niggers" and were subject to the same disabilities as blacks. "To be called an 'Irishman,' " an English traveler noted, "is almost as great an insult as to be stigmatized as a 'nigger feller,' and in a street-row, both appellations are flung off among the combatants with great zest and vigour." In some circles the Irish were regarded as inferior to blacks, a fact emphasized by a *New York Herald* advertisement, which read: "WANTED: A Cook, Washer, and Ironer, who perfectly understands her business; any color or country except Irish."

The results of all this were curious and tragic. Instead of linking up with black workers, Irish workers became the most vociferous champions of white supremacy, driving blacks from neighborhoods and occupations, flocking to the polls on election day, shouting, "Down with the Nagurs! Let them go back to Africa, where they belong."

The grand outcome of the Irish campaign and the campaigns of the Germans, Scandinavians, and Italians was not only the disappearance of traditional black jobs but the strengthening of white workers at the expense of black workers. Year by year, decade by decade, black workers were forced out of occupation after occupation. The traditional image of wave after wave of white immigrants rolling to relative security over the bruised and battered backs of blacks is rooted in fact and history. Writing in the *Colored American* in 1838, a black man said that "these impoverished and destitute beings—transported from the trans-Atlantic shores are crowding themselves into every place of business and of labor, and driving the poor colored American citizen out. Along the wharves, where the colored man once [commanded] the whole business of shipping and unshipping—in stores where his services were once rendered, and in families where the chief places were filled by him, in all these situations there are substituted foreigners or white Americans."

Faced with this growing threat, the black community was far from idle. Some black leaders, such as Martin R. Delany, advocated emigration to Central America or Africa; others called for nonviolent and violent protest; still others called for intensified political pressure or the formation of Tuskegee-type trade schools.

For the most part, these calls were confined to the arena of resolutions and had little effect on the situation. Much more important in an organizational sense, though hardly more effective in the crushing climate of reaction, were the first black trade unions, which were formed in the 1850s. Perhaps the first black trade union was the short-lived American League of Colored Laborers, which was organized in New York City in July, 1850.

These organizational initiatives were of pivotal importance in the making of black America, but they did not immediately improve the position of black workers, which was perhaps beyond the possibility of improvement by black agencies alone. At any rate, the situation of black workers became more difficult, and a tone of desperation crept into the black dialogue.

This was expressed very clearly in the general alarm sounded by Frederick Douglass in the March 4, 1853, edition of *Frederick Douglass' Paper*. "LEARN TRADES OR STARVE!" the headline said. Douglass supported this grim alternative with the following argument: "The old avocations, by which colored men obtained a livelihood, are rapidly, unceasingly and inevitably passing into other hands; every hour sees the black man elbowed out of employment by some newly arrived emigrant, whose hunger and whose color are thought to give him a better title to the place; and so we believe it will continue to be until the last prop is levelled beneath us." To make the meaning clearer, Douglass explained:

"White men are becoming house-servants, cooks, and stewards on vessels—at hotels. —They are becoming porters, stevedores, wood-sawyers, hod carriers, brick-makers, white-washers, and barbers, so that the blacks can scarcely find the means of subsistence—a few years ago, and a *white* barber would have been a curiosity—now their poles stand on every street. Formerly blacks were almost the exclusive coachmen in wealthy families: this is so no longer; white men are now employed, and for aught we see, they fill their servile station with an obsequiousness as profound as that of the blacks. The readiness and ease with which they adapt themselves to these conditions ought not be lost sight of by the colored people. The meaning is very important, and we should learn it. We are taught our insecurity by it. Without the means of living, life is a curse, and leaves us at the mercy of the oppressor to become his debased slaves. Now, colored men, what do you mean to do, for you must do something? The American Colonization Society tells you to go to Liberia. Mr. [Henry] Bibbs tells you to go to Canada. Others tell you to go to school. We tell you to go to work; and to work you must go or die. . . ."

This was true enough, but it didn't help. For the crisis, as the editorial so eloquently pointed out, was bound up with the fact that white Americans refused to give black Americans work precisely because they were black. Even white abolitionists refused to hire blacks.

This, then, was the situation of free black workers, who, by 1850, had been confined to the subcellars of American industry. In 1855 roughly nine out of every ten black workers in New York City held menial or unskilled jobs. Not only in New York City but in every major metropolitan center most black men were laborers, waiters, servants, porters, bootblacks, and hod carriers. A considerable number of black male workers were also employed on the docks and on ships. It has been estimated that one-half of all American seamen in 1850 were black.

For most blacks in the North, as well as for most blacks in the South, work was a family affair, which involved not only black women but also black children. Most black women workers were maids and laundresses. Because of the pervasive discrimination against black men, many black women were also the main supporters of their families. A few statistics will help us to see this more clearly. In 1849 there were 7,607 gainfully employed blacks in Philadelphia—4,249 black females and 3,348 males. Of the 4,249 black female workers, 1,970, or almost 50 percent, were working as laundresses or day workers. "Without a doubt," Lorenzo J. Greene and Carter G. Woodson concluded, "many a Negro family in the free states would have been reduced to utter destitution had it not been for the labor of the mother as washerwoman."

Under these circumstances, with white workers openly organizing to exclude black workers and white capitalists openly cooperating with white workers to limit the opportunities of black workers, it is no wonder that blacks willingly accepted the only role left to them, that of strikebreaker. From the 1840s onward, black workers repeatedly pre-empted the jobs of striking white workers, precipitating violent clashes and riots. In the 1840s black and Irish workers skirmished in the coal mines of Pennsylvania. In the 1850s black workers battled Irish workers on the Erie Railroad and on the docks of Cincinnati and New York City. The strategy of black workers was generally supported by black leaders. "Of course," *Frederick Douglass' Paper* said, "colored men can feel under no obligation to hold out in a 'strike' with the whites, as the latter have never recognized them."

This internecine urban warfare continued during the Civil War and culminated in the New York Draft Riot of 1863. The immediate cause of this riot, which was perhaps the largest in American history, was friction between black and white workers and a feeling on the part of some workers, most notably the Irish, that the Civil War was a war for "rich white folks and poor naygurs." The riot continued uninterruptedly for three days in July, 1863. Before federal troops restored order, thirty-four blacks and two whites had been killed, and more than two hundred had been wounded. "At least nine-tenths of the casualties," General Philip Sheridan said later, "were perpetrated by the police and citizens by stabbing and smashing in the heads of many who had already been wounded or killed by policemen.... [It] was not just a riot but an 'absolute massacre by the police'...."

WHEN President Andrew Johnson said the Emancipation Proclamation freed more white people than black people, he put his finger on a sensitive but important point. For the destruction of planter power freed white capital (which began organizing the industrial state) and white labor (which inherited Western homesteads and began organizing national unions). This had two immediate and curious effects in the black community, one of them being an intensification of the competition between white and black workers, the other being the unveiling of the latent antagonisms between black workers and white capital. The second factor did not immediately become apparent, for the last phase of the triumph of Northern capital was the Reconstruction period, which was based on a very complicated scheme in which Northern capital used black labor in the South to forestall a threatened resurgence of planter capital—a tactic strongly and paradoxically opposed by white labor in the North and West.

If all this sounds confusing to the contemporary reader, consider the freedmen, who embarked on the road of freedom under the sponsorship of the Republican party, the voice of Northern capital, which granted the franchise but withheld the economic wherewithal to make the franchise effective. As so many scholars have observed, the central failure of this program was the failure to free black workers and to provide an economic infrastructure for the paper freedom of the Thirteenth, Fourteenth, and Fifteenth amendments. Certain public leaders, notably Frederick Douglass, Thaddeus Stevens, and Charles Sumner, perceived this almost immediately and made numerous attempts to provide the necessary economic thrust. Senator Sumner, for instance, demanded homes for the freedmen and a permanent policy of federal aid to education. When the Senate refused to sanction this policy, Sumner fled the Senate in tears.

Thaddeus Stevens, the representative from Pennsylvania, was no more successful in the House, where he introduced one of the most radical measures ever presented to that body. In a move designed to free American institutions of "every vestige of human oppression, of inequality of rights, of recognized degradation of the poor, and the superior caste of the rich," Stevens introduced resolutions providing for the immediate enforcement of the Confiscation Act of July, 1862. Specifically, he called for the seizure of the land of Southern rebels with the understanding that "the land so seized and condemned should be distributed among the slaves who had been made free by the war and constitutional amendments, and who were residing on said land on the 4th of March, 1861, or since; to each head of a family 40 acres; to each adult male whether head of a family or not, 40 acres; to each widow, head of a family, 40 acres; to be held by them in fee simple, but to be inalienable for ten years after they should become so seized thereof. . . ."

This proposal and others of similar depth were rejected, primarily because Northern capital had no intention of endangering the exploitability of the vast black labor reserve. As I have said elsewhere, the managers of the political economy of the North had never admitted the full logic of the democratic idea for poor whites; it was unthinkable that they would countenance it for poor blacks, especially since wholesale confiscation of property in the South would have set an ominous precedent for the restless white workers in the North and West.

When the federal government reneged on the issues of land reform and economic reconstruction, the freedmen turned to the Reconstruction governments in the South, with interesting and often-overlooked results. During the ten-year span of Radical Reconstruction, roughly from 1867 to 1877, black workers wielded considerable and, in some cases, overwhelming political influence in the Southern states. And although the white Southerners and Northerners in the Radical Republican coalitions were generally conservative and biased, they were compelled by self-interest to make at least minimal gestures in the directions of the passionately expressed desires of their largest constituency. The end result was a corpus of social legislation—stay-laws, homestead provisions, crop lien laws, etc.—that anticipated the more progressive measures of the New Deal. In general, these measures reversed the political economy of slavery and tilted the balance for the first time—and the last time—in America in favor of debtors, renters, and workers.

Far more decisive was the creative use of the taxing power of the state for frankly social purposes, such as land reform and large-scale social and educational programs. Some Radical Republicans said candidly that the tax policy of the new governments was designed to redistribute the income. It was designed, as a black delegate to the South Carolina Constitutional Convention said, "to force owners of large tracts of waste land to sell and give us a chance." Another delegate, who later became treasurer of South Carolina, was more specific:

"Taxes are always (at least in hard times) a burden, will be assessed yearly upon all lands, and they must be paid. The expenses of the State (constantly increasing, will be a continual drag upon those who attempt to carry on large landed estates with a small amount of money,) will alone force sufficient lands upon the market at all times to meet the wants of all the landless. This Convention will cost the State quite a large sum of money. A legislature will soon assemble, and that will cost money. Education, once limited, is to be general, and that will be expensive; and, to keep up with the age, it is fair to presume that the State tax will be greater next year than this, and increase yearly; this will be felt, and will be the stimulus to many for owning less land, and cause them to see the necessity for disposing of their surplus."

Acting on these or similar premises, the black and white legislators of South Carolina created a Land Commission and authorized the purchase of improved and unimproved land, which was to be resold to settlers at purchase price and on easy terms. This project was almost destroyed by a corrupt and inept white administrator, but his successor, a black man, did excellent work in retrieving a vitally important venture.

Additional pressure in favor of black workers was generated by the black workers and former black workers who held administrative and judicial posts in the new regimes. In South Carolina and other states, most of the cases involving sharecroppers and planters were heard in lower magistrate courts, some of which were presided over by black magistrates. It was the opinion of most planters and employers that the black magistrates and their white Republican colleagues bent over backward to rule in favor of sharecroppers, debtors, and renters. In this case, as in others, however, the planters and employers probably interpreted equity for black workers as injustice for whites. At any rate, they were very vocal in deploring the alleged abuses of the "radical" courts. After an arbitration proceeding in Spartanburg County Court, one David Golighty Harris denounced the whole system. "To Day," he wrote, "Warren & I had an arbitration at the mill concerning the rent & fencing he was to pay & to do. The arbitrators (as usual) divided the claim & gave me about ½ that I should have had." He added: "This is the consequence of dealing with negroes, one can not get justice of a negro."

In addition to the direct economic impact of favorable administrative, legislative, and judicial decisions, black workers also benefitted from the social welfare and educational (liberal scholarship programs, free textbooks, etc.) programs of the Reconstruction regimes. The effect was immediate and obvious on both the social and economic levels. In the 1870s a white writer reported from Louisiana that "the colored people are generally better supplied than the whites with free schools."

All of this—the progressive social legislation, the administrative and judicial decisions, and the liberal social and educational programs—strengthened the hands of black workers, who reached a peak of unparalleled militancy in the postwar period. Even before the Radical Republican governments were installed, black workers sprang into action, staging sit-down demonstrations and strikes. In 1865 black washwomen organized a union in Jackson, Mississippi, and demanded what a Southern newspaper called "exorbitant" prices for laundry. The next year, in August, black Union veterans employed at the iron factories in Elyton (later renamed Birmingham) struck for higher wages and were driven out of town. Three months later a *New York Times* correspondent reported from South Carolina that the freedmen were organizing unions to force concessions from the employers. "There is a large general movement," he wrote, "in the interior districts to change the conditions of labor, especially to increase the compensation for labor." He said the movement "is entirely spontaneous on the part of the freedmen" and has the "symptoms of something very like a Northern 'strike.'"

This spontaneous movement spread throughout the South. In Mobile, Alabama, in 1867, black levee workers went out on strike when their demands for an additional twenty-five cents an hour were refused. In the same year, the black longshoremen of Savannah, Georgia, carried out a successful strike against the city government, leading the *National Workman* to observe that "this is not the first time since their Emancipation that they have resolutely asserted and vindicated their rights. The fact is that the black man likes to be paid for his work just as well as the white man, and are [sic] rapidly learning how to secure their demands."

In many cases militant black workers were seconded by militant black legislators, who were particularly prominent in the Southwide movement of sharecroppers who demanded one-half of the crop. In November, 1869, a South Carolina planter complained that "Senator [Lucius] Wimbush [a black South Carolinian] & some new Scalawag Converts are going about making speeches, & advising the freedmen to demand the Half &c. The consequence is that every thing is in Confusion, & will remain so until the New Year." For Senator Wimbush and for the black legislators and workers who shared his sentiments, the central issues in Reconstruction were economic, a fact that was not lost on Southern planters who continued to believe, as Carl Schurz noted, that the black worker existed "for the special object of raising cotton, rice, and sugar for the whites, and that it [was] illegitimate for him to indulge, like other people, in the pursuit of his own happiness in his own way."

When the planters and employers organized the Klan and other white terrorist organizations, they said frankly that their central concern was not race but property and labor. They claimed that the new state governments were being used to favor the interests of laborers at the expense of employers. In a memorial to President Ulysses S. Grant, the white taxpayers of South Carolina protested against "the unprecedented spectacle of a State in which the government is arrayed against property." Lewis E. Parsons, a former governor of Alabama, later told a Congressional investigating committee that the fundamental purpose of the terrorist campaign was to control the black man and his labor. It came to be understood, he said, "that in this way Negroes might be made to toe the mark again, to do the bidding of the employer, to come up to time a little more promptly, and do more work than they would otherwise do."

With these purposes foremost in their minds, and with the tacit consent of Northern industrialists, the emerging class of Southern bankers, railroad men, industrialists, and planters organized a Southwide revolution, crushed the Reconstruction regimes, and created conditions that made it possible for white men to exploit black men socially, politically, and economically.

*A* new system of repression—more subtle, more diffuse, but equally effective—rose on the ruins of Reconstruction. The slavery of debt replaced the slavery of the statutes, and the discipline of hunger, to quote Eric Williams, replaced the discipline of the whip.

Four major subsystems—peonage, disenfranchisement, segregation, and cultural domination—constituted the cutting edge of the new system, which relegated most black workers to a condition not markedly different from slavery. The proof of this—if proof is needed—is that in 1890, a generation after slavery, seven out of every eight black workers were still harvesting the crops of slavery in the old plantation settings or performing domestic work in demeaning urban settings.

The new system, like the old system, was solidly grounded on economic exploitation backed up by violence and political intimidation. And the new system, like the old, was a construct of interacting subsystems that meshed and intermeshed in an overarching framework that forced black workers to live at a subsistence level while the fruits of their labor were appropriated by others. Different students considering different aspects of this system in isolation have called it the Jim Crow or segregation system. The name is irrelevant really if we only remember that Jim Crow was only one of several subsystems, each of which served a particular function and contributed to the overall stability of the whole.

The first subsystem—a system of forced labor based on tenancy and peonage laws—bound most black workers to the plantation almost as effectively as slavery. Under this system, which formed the material base of black life until World War I, the black worker entered into an agreement with a planter to work a section of the plantation. The planter provided the land and oftentimes the seed and equipment. He also advanced credit at exorbitant rates of interest for food and other necessities purchased at the plantation store. The sharecropper provided the only thing he had, his labor power, and the labor power of his wife and children. At the end of the year, the planter and tenant settled accounts by dividing the profits. This meant, in practice, that the planter—who kept the books—subtracted from the tenant's share (generally one-third) the amount allegedly advanced for goods, equipment, etc. Somehow the subtracting almost always worked to the disadvantage of the tenant, who almost always ended up owing the planter for the privilege of working. Since peonage laws required tenants to remain on the plantation until all debts were cleared, tenants were de facto slaves. As late as 1912, according to some estimates, at least 250,000 black workers were being held to service on Southern plantations by force. Although peonage laws were finally declared unconstitutional by the U.S. Supreme Court in 1911, the system continued to operate; and as late as the 1920s one could find advertisements reminiscent of slavery in Southern newspapers:

### NEGRO BOY RUNAWAY

A small colored boy about 14 years old ran away from his home near Stapleton Jan. 4th [1927]. Anyone seeing him will please notify me and hold him untill I arrive. I will pay reward. I object to anyone useing him.—Roy Haines, Stapleton, Ga., Rt. 1 Box 16

The essence of this system was captured by John Carlson, who related a story of a white landlord settling accounts with a tenant and saying, "George, you've worked hard this year, and even though prices have been low, you made out very well. All you owe me is $12."

Another story, illustrative of the same point, appeared in the *American Mercury* in 1932:

The old Negro farmer took off his battered hat and scratched his head meditatively. He was in the throes of achieving his annual settling up with the country storekeeper, who advanced him what he needed in the way of food, clothing, and supplies during the year.

"Then, we's all square?" he repeated.

"Yes, J. C., all square," said the white man.

"And I don't owe you nothin'?"

"No."

"And you don't owe me nothin'?"

"That's right."

"And yit. . . ." J. C. shook his head dubiously. "And yit I still got two bales o' cotton on my hands."

The storekeeper took out his quid and tossed it into the sawdust box.

"Well, goddam it, J. C. Why'n you say so before? Now I've got to do some more figurin'."

This little incident is illuminating, for it makes clear that the essence of the new system was legalized robbery, the direct and open fleecing of a whole people and the appropriation of their surplus for alien purposes. What makes this all the more appalling is that most white plantation owners admitted that they were stealing from their illiterate and terrorized tenants. In 1868 Mrs. Ambrusio Gonzales, a leader of white South Carolina society, explained to her mother how she fleeced blacks at the plantation store she operated. ". . . I determine the prices of the last [cloth]—the Gen. [her husband] thinks I am too exorbitant but I tell him I am sure the nigs do not do 'full work'—A piece of nice blue check which costs 88 cts by the piece, your Jewess' of a daughter gets 60 cts for—& the freedmen get 12 yds at a time. I have now a box of assorted candy to tempt them—but as these articles are paid for in work of course my satisfaction at getting high prices is greatly diminished."

Mrs. Gonzales was hardly alone. From the 1860s to the 1940s, white Southerners repeatedly and openly admitted duplicity. Writing in 1944, Gunnar Myrdal said that in "several conversations with white planters—as also with employers of Negro labor in cities, particularly of domestics—the writer has noticed the display of a sort of moral double standard. White people of the landowning class who give the impression of being upright and honest in all their other dealings take it for granted and sometimes brag about the fact that they cheat their Negroes. . . ." Black tenants, who had a clear appreciation of the white double standard, usually greeted the settlin' up time with a satirical song:

> Naught's a naught, and five's a figger,
> All for the white man and none for the nigger.

It quickly became apparent to some Southerners that the exploitation of free men was more profitable and more efficient than the exploitation of slaves. "On the eve of World War I," Dan Lacy wrote, "the new system of white control had reached its peak of effectiveness, and it provided a much more efficient and profitable method of exploiting black labor in commercial agriculture than had slavery. Output per man-hour of black labor in cotton production was substantially higher than before emancipation. Sharecropping made the Negro's own meager income dependent on his productivity and got more work out of him than could any form of discipline under slavery. . . . At the same time, the cost of black labor was probably less. Only an unusual worker in an unusual year could hope to gain more than the subsistence that had formerly been given all slaves. And the freedom of the planter from the burden of support of the elderly and invalid and from the necessity of tying up capital in the purchase of slaves probably actually significantly lowered his man-hour labor cost in constant dollars."

The importance of black labor to the South was admitted by most Southerners, some of whom said that the development of the white South was dependent on the underdevelopment of the black South. "The negroes of the South are its wealth . . . ," the Jackson *Weekly Clarion* said in April, 1886. "The South, without the negro, for a generation at least, would be a wilderness and a waste. . . ."

While developing the white South, black workers paradoxically impoverished the black South, which usually ended up with a net annual deficit, unable to make enough money from its only export—black labor—to cover the cost of imports. The fate of the black workers of Daugherty County, Georgia, was characteristic. In 1898, 175 of the 300 tenant families of that county ended the year with a total debt of $14,000. Of the remaining 125 families, fifty cleared nothing and seventy-five made a total profit of $1,600. This meant that the net deficit of the black families of Daugherty County for 1898 was $12,400. At that point it was said that the accumulated net deficit of the black tenant families of Daugherty County was at least $60,000. The implications of this were extensive, not only in Daugherty County, but also in other Black Belt counties. The paradoxical result was that the longer and harder blacks worked the deeper they sank in debt.

All this was enormously profitable not only to the white South but also to the white North and the white West. Between 1870 and 1910 cotton production tripled, and the appropriated black surplus helped pay for the physical reconstruction of the South and provided foreign exchange values for the industrialization of the North, and the Western settlement.

What we have to deal with here, therefore, is not a regional but a *national* system of subordination. The system was created in the South by Southerners, but it could not have survived without a national white consensus on the role and status of Southern black workers. It was this consensus that prepared the way for and sanctioned the Southwide revolution that overturned the legal governments of the Reconstruction period. And, in the aftermath of that revolution, President Rutherford B. Hayes, the U.S. Congress, and the U.S. Supreme Court formally ratified the white consensus in the Compromise of 1877, which granted white Southerners the right to reduce blacks to a state of subordination. This agreement, in turn, was buttressed by two explicit or implicit agreements between Northern and Southern men of power. The first agreement was that the national consensus would not be "disturbed" by national agitation on the Negro question. The second agreement was that Northern and Southern industrialists would not bid for the services of black workers, who would therefore be confined to agricultural work and menial offices. This was a period, it should be remembered, of feverish industrial growth; and yet, curiously, Northern industrialists made little direct use of black labor, relying almost completely on white immigrants from Europe. At the same time, Southern industrialists refused to use blacks in the developing textile industry, citing racial reasons and the alleged fact that the "hum of machinery would put [the Negro] to sleep." Thus, in the 1880s and 1890s, in the peak years of the American Industrial Revolution, black labor formed an industrial reserve upon which employers could draw in times of extreme labor shortages or strikes.

The implications of this national consensus were shrewdly weighed by Paul H. Buck in *The Road to Reunion*. "Cotton brokers of New York and Philadelphia, and cotton manufacturers of New England . . . ," he said, "knew full well the importance of bringing discipline to the Southern labor force. When theories of Negro equality resulted in race conflict, and conflict in higher prices of raw cotton, manufacturers were inclined to accept the point of view of the Southern planter rather than that of the New England zealot."

Against this background, we can better understand the national white consensus of the 1890s, a consensus expressed in Supreme Court decisions sanctioning peonage and segregation (*Plessy* v. *Ferguson*), Presidential politics, philanthropic activity, and Sunday morning sermons.

The propulsive forces behind this consensus, as we have indicated repeatedly, were primarily economic. But these forces unfolded in a political context that made everything economic and everything political. They unfolded, in fine, in a political system of neo-colonialism in which political and economic domination gave rise to cultural domination and cultural domination, in turn, gave rise to political and economic domination. Thus, economic and non-economic phenomena were so closely intertwined that it is difficult, even today, to say where economics ended and politics and culture began.

This process was clearly understood by the power brokers of the North and South, who went to extraordinary lengths to limit the economic development of black America. The evidence on this point is overwhelming, and is crucial to an understanding of the underdevelopment of the black community and the marginal position of the black worker. The manipulation of the educational structures of the black community was a prime example of the process. In the 1880s and 1890s there were repeated attempts to destroy or limit the effectiveness of black schools. It was clear to almost everyone that these attempts were motivated primarily by a desire to keep blacks ignorant so they would accept the least desirable occupations. Time and time again Southern orators and statesmen said that education would "spoil" black workers, keep black children from the cottonfields, and undo the intricate literacy arrangements upon which black disenfranchisement was based.

Moved by these and similar arguments, Southern whites systematically withheld funds from black schools. In 1915, for example, South Carolina spent $13.98 per white child and $2.57 per black child. The upshot of this was that there were only a handful of black elementary schools in South Carolina and other Southern states until well into the twentieth century—and these schools were usually one-room shacks which operated only three or four months a year.

The use of education as an instrument of economic underdevelopment was even more apparent on the secondary level. In 1916 there were only nineteen black high school students in the whole state of North Carolina. In 1917 there was not a single high school for black students in Atlanta. As late as 1933 there was not a state-supported high school in Alabama or South Carolina offering a four-year course for blacks.

Throughout this period and on into the twenties and thirties, there was a similar use of economic weapons on black college campuses. The black and white founders of most of the black colleges were men of their time and place, but some had a vision of education as an instrument of social, political, and economic transformation. With the passing of time and the triumph of the industrial state, this vision receded into the background and a new vision of black colleges as instruments of racial subordination became dominant. As David M. Reimers (*White Protestantism and the Negro*) noted, "The attacks on racial injustice, which in the 1860s had assumed the proportions of a crusade to redeem the South, gave way to new attitudes by the 1880's and 1890's. Education, the vehicle for Negro mobility and equal participation in American society, began to change its emphasis by 1880; industrial education and manual training, fitting the Negro for a subordinate role in society, became the policy of the *northern-run* church schools in the South." [My emphasis]

The new hero of the men pursuing this policy was Booker T. Washington, the Tuskegee Institute president, who had a clear understanding of the economic and political dimensions of black education. In his famous Southern Exposition speech of 1895 and in other addresses, he called for a compromise on political and educational matters. "We are trying," he said on one occasion, "to instill into the Negro's mind that if education does not make the Negro humble, simple, and of service to the community, then it will not be encouraged." It is not clear, even today, whether Washington believed this or whether he was dissembling in order to save the few remaining black educational outposts. Whatever the case, the hard fact is that the Washington stratagem did not work. Educational discrimination continued and reached something of a peak in the halcyon days of Washington's power.

Besides educational discrimination and peonage, the new system relied on three other subsystems: 1) political disenfranchisement, which deprived blacks of the political power they needed to defend their economic interests; 2) segregation, which isolated black workers and made it easier for their enemies to deprive them of vital services; 3) negative cultural conditioning in an apartheid system which reminded every black every hour that he was a pariah and outcast.

And behind and over all was terror. The most obvious manifestation of this was lynching, which reached murderous heights in the 1890s, when a black was lynched somewhere every two or three days. Bad as these lynchings were, they were simply dramatic expressions of the truth of a system founded on violence and sustained by violence. The court system, the police apparatus, the county courthouse ring, the legislature, the mayor, the police chief, the sheriff: all were fingers pointing to the organic violence of a system dedicated to the subordination of blacks by whatever means necessary. Perhaps the worst injustice, in this systematized round of wrongs, was embodied in the fact that black criminals were deliberately manufactured by the criminal justice system, which was an adjunct of the notorious prison convict system. On the slightest pretext, and oftentimes with no pretext at all, young men were sentenced to long prison terms and leased out to plantation owners, railroad builders, and other businessmen. After an exhaustive study of the Southern convict lease system, Fletcher M. Green said the only parallels he could find were in "the persecutions of the Middle Ages or in the prison camps of Nazi Germany."

Such, then, was the system which rose on the ruins of the hopes of Jubilee.

Before passing on to the responses of black workers, we should make at least three obvious but important points about this system. First, black workers were impoverished and suffered a deterioration in all their social relations. Second, black impoverishment was systematically induced by all American institutions. Third, the systematic impoverishment of black workers set cruel and narrow limits to the development of the black community.

Let it be said also that black workers resisted the encroachments of their adversaries with every weapon at their command. But these weapons were sadly inadequate, and the force of circumstances had driven their potential allies from the field. By this time most Northerners, including most of the old abolitionists, were tired, they said, of "the eternal nigger question." White labor was hostile to the whole Radical Reconstruction position, and white Northern capital was busy cementing a new alliance with Southern white capital. Because of this, the outnumbered and largely powerless black workers were confronted with a situation in which all of their options were bad.

For all the limitations of the period, there were loud voices of outrage and militancy. Quite typical of the lot were the militant black farmers, now largely forgotten, who formed a tentative but highly significant entente with poor whites in the Populist movement of the 1890s. In the first great wave of that movement, white Populist leaders told black and white tenants and farmers that it was in their interests to forget race and coalesce on economic issues. Perhaps the most eloquent exponent of this point of view was Tom Watson of Georgia, who told blacks and whites: "You are kept apart that you may be separately fleeced of your earnings." By the thousands and tens of thousands blacks heeded this and other cries. And by 1890 more than one million black farmers were members of the Colored Farmers Alliance which cooperated with the Populist movement.

Faced with this unexpected alliance of blacks and whites, the white masters of the South fell back to their first line of defense—racism—using the racial fears of poor whites (intermarriage, black domination, etc.) to drive a wedge in the movement. Following up their advantage, the masters crushed the movement and institutionalized the use of racism as a political weapon to arrest the forces pulling blacks and whites together. It is a curious fact, worthy of some thought, that Tom Watson, the eloquent apostle of the first wave of the movement, became the virulent racist apostle of the forces that destroyed the movement.

The collapse of the Populist movement eliminated the political alternatives, and most black workers fell back on traditional modes of protest. Some sought escape in millenarian movements; others organized abortive exodus movements to the Midwest and to Liberia; still others dropped out, gave up hope, and wandered across the land.

*I*F, as Frederick Douglass has suggested, the new system was the same old snake in a new skin, it does not follow, as some have argued, that the false freedom of the new system was the same as the real slavery of the old system. "Freedom" was not freedom, as almost all blacks discovered; but "freedom" was better than slavery, as almost all blacks testified. Despite the confusions and disappointments of the transition, there were new possibilities, which some black workers exploited with brilliance and passion. In the 1870s and 1880s many black workers fled the plantations and found work in the cities as longshoremen and draymen. Others, more venturesome perhaps, migrated to the West and played key and generally unrecognized roles in the development of the cattle industry. It has been conservatively estimated that at least one-third of the cowboys who drove herds up from Texas in the years between 1865 and 1895 were blacks and Mexicans. Professor Kenneth Porter said that "without the services of the eight or nine thousand Negroes—a quarter of the total number of trail drivers—who during the generation after the Civil War helped to move herds up the cattle trails to shipping points, Indian reservations, and fattening grounds and who, between drives, worked on the ranches of Texas and the Indian Territory, the cattle industry would have been seriously handicapped." What the black cowboys were to the cattle industry the freed black workers were to the Southern lumbering and mining industries. Also important were the prototypical John Henrys, who built and maintained most of the Southern railroads. In addition to these new and expanding outlets, the freed black workers were employed in increasing numbers in the old antebellum preserves of domestic service and skilled trades.

But "progress"—not for the first or the last time—raised new and formidable obstacles for black workers. Toward the end of the nineteenth century, racism and the new forces unleashed by the Industrial Revolution eliminated most of the black sanctuaries, intensifying the black worker's quest for security and survival. To add to the confusion, nine million white immigrants from Europe invaded Northern cities in the 1880s and 1890s and widened their assaults on the traditional preserves of black laborers and domestic servants. The immediate result was that the style and the color of domestic service changed, and black workers were displaced in several occupations. By 1900 black waiters and service employees had been displaced in most leading hotels in the North. By 1910, Carter Woodson noted, "the Italians and Germans had virtually displaced the Negro barbers who had been catering exclusively to whites in the North." Writing in 1905, Samuel Scrotton said black workers had lost most of their occupations to white foreigners. The newcomers, he said, occupy "every industry that was confessedly the Negroes forty years ago. They have the bootblack stands, the news stands, barbering, waiters, victualers, restaurants, janitorships, and the catering business . . . . and furthermore occupy the very homes of Negroes, and the Negro pays [them] rent."

By singular circumstance, the displacement of Northern black workers coincided with an ominous assault on the precincts of black artisans, who had dominated the economy of the South for more than two centuries. In 1865, according to a census of occupations cited by Charles Wesley in his standard work, *Negro Labor in the United States*, 100,000 of the 120,000 artisans in the South were black. "It was said," Wesley wrote, "that there were at least two Negro craftsmen of most kinds to one of the white craftsmen in Mississippi, and in North Carolina more than one-third of the colored population was engaged in mechanical occupations. They were about six to one when compared with the white mechanics. . . ."

All this changed drastically in the postwar period, partly because of unfair labor practices by white artisans, partly because of a deliberate decision by white men of power to favor free white artisans at the expense of free black artisans. As a result of these and other factors, the black monopoly in the artisan field was broken between 1865 and 1890, and the proportion of black artisans dropped alarmingly. Although blacks continued to play a major role in some occupations, notably masonry and carpentry, whites moved to a position of dominance in the twentieth century and used their considerable resources to isolate and rout their black competitors.

Impersonal factors—technological change, large-scale production and financing—played a role in the displacement of the black artisans; but here, as elsewhere, the dominant forces were racial. In some cases whites —laborers and capitalists—combined to deny black artisans access to capital and new technology. In other cases white laborers and capitalists, aided and abetted by white legislators, administrators, jurists, and consumers conspired to limit the jurisdiction and advancement of black artisans.

It is important to establish these points, for the destruction of the black artisan class was a central event in the history of black Americans. The precipitous decline in the number of black engineers, blacksmiths, gunsmiths, cabinetmakers, plasterers, painters, masons, and bricklayers changed the tone and texture of the black community. It diminished the options of black workers, depressed the level of aspirations of black youths, and deprived the community of resources and leadership potential. All this snowballed in a disastrous manner with cumulative effects that have not been reversed, even today.

To understand the central importance of the decline of black artisans, one must back up a little and explore the rise of the labor movement, which was, paradoxically, a major instrument in the destruction of the artisan class and the narrowing of the economic alternatives of black workers.

From the seventeenth century on, as we have already indicated, white men combined as white men to limit the employment opportunities of blacks, whom they feared as real or potential competitors. This movement assumed a new dimension with the formal organization of national white labor unions in the postwar period. To be sure, some pioneer white union leaders recognized the dangers of a divided working class and attempted to organize racially inclusive unions. But these were small hopes, tender shoots pushing their way through the hard crust of parochial craft unionism. Something of this can be traced in the history of the National Labor Union, organized in 1866, and the Knights of Labor, organized in 1869. In its first address, issued in July, 1867, the National Labor Union pointed out that the problem of black labor was an important question "in the successful solution of which the working classes have an abiding interest." The black workers of America, the Address said, "must necessarily become in their new relationship an element of strength or an element of weakness, and it is for the workingmen of America to decide which that shall be." The question of the hour, therefore, the Address said, was: "Shall we make them our friends, or shall capital be allowed to turn them as an engine against us?" Coming to close grips with this question, the Address added:

"Can we afford to reject their proffered cooperation and make them enemies? By committing such an act of folly we would inflict greater injury upon the cause of Labor Reform than the combined efforts of capital could accomplish. Their cherished idea of an antagonism between white and black labor would be realized and . . . capitalists, north and south, would foment discord between the whites and blacks, and hurl the one against the other . . . . to maintain their ascendancy and continue the reign of oppression."

"Taking this view of the question," the Address concluded, "we are of the opinion that the interests of the labor cause demand that all workingmen be included within its ranks, without regard to race or nationality; and that the interests of the workingmen of America especially require that the formation of trade unions, eight-hour leagues, and other labor organizations, should be encouraged among the colored race; that they be instructed in the true principles of labor reform, and that they be invited to cooperate with us in the general labor undertaking."

Although the vagueness of the conclusion did not reflect the precision and passion of the premises, this was a significant statement, which adequately summarized the tasks of the hour. But the problem then—as now—was not analysis but action, and the National Labor Union approached that question with caution and timidity. At its next congress in Chicago, in

August, 1867, one faction argued for immediate admission of blacks into existing unions, and another faction, including the delegates from the Eight-Hour League of Michigan, took the position that black workers should be organized into separate unions. In the end, the Committee on Negro Labor decided "after due deliberation [that] the Constitution already adopted by the labor Congress precludes the necessity of any action of this body in behalf of any particular class of the laboring masses." This, of course, was an evasion of the issue, an evasion repeated by the 1868 Congress, which expressed approval of black emancipation and issued an invitation to the "working classes of the South" to join the labor movement.

Despite the vagueness of this appeal and the vacillation of white labor leaders on craft union bias, black workers joined the Union and participated in organizing campaigns. In fact, black workers were the cutting edge of the movement in some areas. In the fall of 1871, for example, some two thousand workers staged an organizing march for the Union in Nashville, Tennessee, and, according to the *Workingman's Advocate*, all except four or five were black. "Strange as it may seem," the paper said, "our colored citizens are more active in the cause than the whites, and exhibit far more independence of capital and party influence."

The enthusiastic black response did not immediately change the vision of national white labor leaders, who continued to procrastinate. More important in its final effect, however, was the action of local white labor leaders, who continued to build walls of exclusion. There were other questions, too, questions of political interpretation and posture. By and large, most white labor leaders were hostile to the Radical Republican program, which most black workers considered essential to their survival and safety. Oblivious to the real needs of black workers in the South and the radical implications of the Reconstruction governments, white labor leaders like William H. Sylvis denounced the entire Reconstruction program and called the Freedmen's Bureau "a huge swindle upon the honest workingmen of the country."

Partly because of the hostility of white labor to the Radical Republican Reconstruction program, and partly because of the continuation of craft union bias, black workers started hedging their bets by organizing independent black unions. By 1868 there were several black unions in New York City, including the Saloon Men's Protective and Benevolent Union, the Colored Waiters' Association, and the American Seamen's Protective

Union Association. There were unions of caulkers, hod carriers, engineers, bricklayers, butchers, and draymen in Baltimore, which was the center of black union militancy. Perhaps the most powerful unions of this period were the longshoremen's unions of New Orleans and Charleston.

Beginning in 1869, black workers organized state and national unions. On January 13, 1869, the first black national convention with significant labor representatives met in Union League Hall in Washington, D.C. The 161 delegates demanded equal rights and free land but divided over the question of whether blacks should fight for admission into white unions or create independent black unions. In the weeks and months that followed, this question was debated at a series of black state labor conventions. The first of the black statewide labor conventions was held in Baltimore, Maryland, in July. The guiding spirit behind this convention was Isaac Myers, who has been called "the great pioneer of organized Negro labor." A Baltimore caulker and the leader of the radical black unionists of Maryland, Myers was an early supporter of the National Labor Union and an advocate of black and white labor solidarity. He believed, however, that it was necessary for black workers to organize independent black unions to defend their interests and to force white labor to the high ground of integration. Acting on these premises, he urged the Maryland unionists to adopt a two-pronged strategy: independent black unionism *and* cooperation with progressive white unions. Myer's strategy was adopted by the Maryland convention, which elected delegates to the next convention of the National Labor Union and issued a call for a national black labor convention. The purpose of the convention, Myers said in his convention address, was to "consolidate the colored workingmen of the several states to act in cooperation with our white fellow workingmen in every state and territory of the Union, who are opposed to distinction in the apprenticeship laws on account of color, and to so act cooperatively until the necessity for separate organization shall be deemed unnecessary."

With tenacity and vigilance, Myers and his colleagues pursued this strategy, sending out calls for the national labor convention and establishing links with the leaders of the National Labor Union. When the third annual congress of the National Labor Union opened in Philadelphia in August, Myers and eight other blacks were seated and became the first black delegates to a national labor assembly. Responding to the cordial reception accorded the black representatives of the caulkers, molders, painters, and engineers of Maryland and the United Laborers and Hod Carriers' Association of Philadelphia, Myers told the congress that black workers wanted equality of opportunity and a chance to participate as equals in the common struggle. He said that friction between black and white workers was a direct result of the exclusion of blacks from factories and shops, and added that he and his colleagues were willing to forget the past. "We mean in all sincerity a heart cooperation," he said. "You cannot doubt us. Where we have had the chance, we have always demonstrated it. We carry no prejudice. We are willing to let the dead past bury its dead." In conclusion, Myers asked the National Labor Union to take a strong stand on the question of black and white labor solidarity, adding:

"I speak today for the colored men of the whole country, from the lakes to the Gulf—from the Atlantic to the Pacific—from every hilltop, valley, and plain throughout our vast domain, when I tell you that all they ask for themselves is a fair chance; that you shall be no worse off by giving them that chance; that you and they will dwell in peace and harmony together; that you and they may make one steady and strong pull until the laboring men of this country shall receive such pay for time made as will secure them a comfortable living for their families, educate their children, and leave a dollar for a rainy day and old age. . . ."

This passionate and reasonable request was applauded but not heeded by the delegates, who again straddled the fence in an eloquent but equivocal declaration, which stated that "the National Labor Union knows no North, no South, no East, no West, neither color nor sex on the question of the rights of labor, and urges our colored fellow members to form organizations in all legitimate ways, and send their delegates from every State in the Union to the next Congress."

This was admirably phrased and was no doubt well-intentioned, but it did not speak to the pressing concerns of black workers and leaders, who gathered in Washington, D.C., in December, 1869, for the first annual convention of the Negro National Labor Union. There were 203 delegates from twenty-one states at this meeting, which is generally considered the first national black labor convention.

With J. H. Harris, a militant black legislator from North Carolina, in the chair, the convention deplored "the exclusion of colored men and apprentices from the right to labor in . . . industry or workshops . . . by what is known as Trades' Unions" and announced that its purpose was "to consolidate the colored workingmen of the several states to act in cooperation with our white fellow workingmen . . . who are opposed to distinction in the apprenticeship laws on account of color, and to so act cooperatively until the necessity for separate organizations shall be deemed unnecessary."

Since the overwhelming majority of black workers were then employed as agricultural laborers on Southern plantations, the convention spent a great deal of time deploring the economic inadequacies of the Radical Republican program, noting that "abundant evidence has been laid before this convention showing that the average rate of wages received by the colored agricultural laborer of the South does not exceed sixty dollars ($60) per annum."

To remedy this situation and to redress the other grievances of the black workers of the South, the convention asked Congress to grant freedmen forty-acre tracts on the public lands of the South and requested "a law authorizing the President to appoint a land commission . . . , whose duty it shall be to purchase lands in those southern States in which there are no public lands, and have the same divided into tracts of forty (40) acres each, and sold to freedmen in five (5) years, the whole sum to be thus used in the purchase of homesteads for freedmen not to exceed two million ($2,000,000) of dollars."

Before adjourning, the delegates created a permanent organization —the Negro National Labor Union—elected Isaac Myers president, and authorized the establishment of a National Bureau of Labor "to protect the rights of workingmen" and to assist the president in the "organization of Labor Unions, land, loan, building, and co-operative associations generally. . . ."

Under the leadership of Myers, the Negro National Labor Union organized state and city auxiliaries and agitated for cooperatives, massive federal subsidies for education, and liberal labor legislation. As the white labor movement spread, denying training and employment to black workers, Myers became increasingly militant, telling black artisans that if they did not organize the trades would pass from their hands and they would become "the servants, the sweepers of shavings, the scrapers of pitch, and carriers of mortar."

Myers's cry was echoed by thousands of other black unionists, who organized city and state labor conventions. A South Carolina labor convention, chaired by the powerful black politician, Robert Brown Elliott, called for a radicalization of the Radical Republican program in that state.

Among the immediate demands of the South Carolina workers were one-half of the crop or a minimum daily wage of 70 cents for tenants and sharecroppers, a nine-hour day, the division of land sold by the sheriff into tracts not exceeding fifty acres, and a reconstruction of the legal system "in order that the laboring classes may have a fair representation on the juries."

There were similar demands in Alabama, where the Colored Labor Convention demanded the abolition of sharecropping and expressed the opinion that the interests of "the laboring masses" would be best served by working for a fixed annual wage, payable monthly.

While all this was going on, the National Labor Union and the National Negro Labor Union were disintegrating in factionalism and political controversy. The National Labor Union split in 1870 after an abortive call for a national labor party. The National Negro Labor Union held a second convention in Washington in January, 1871, and a third convention in Columbia, S.C., in October, 1871. By that time, the precise demands of black workers had been submerged in the general demands for a continuation of the Radical Republican Reconstruction program. Most scholars say the organization failed because of its pronounced political orientation. But this view needs rethinking in the light of modern experience which indicates that a labor organization cannot carry out its fundamental purposes without abandoning the artificial distinction between politics and economics.

In the years following the collapse of the National Labor Union and the National Negro Labor Union, the dream of black and white labor solidarity was revived by the Knights of Labor, which adopted an advanced program of industrial unionism and attracted some sixty thousand black workers at the height of its influence in 1886. The black and white members of this seminal organization made some headway, but they were overwhelmed finally by the dominant trend of the age, craft unionism dominated by a spirit of black exclusion and subordination.

The collapse of the independent black labor movement and the failure of the National Labor Union and the Knights of Labor coincided with the emergence of the American Federation of Labor (AFL), a craft-oriented combine that exacerbated the problems of black workers. After an initial period of rhetorical liberalism, the AFL came down hard on the side of white racism. By 1899 the AFL was openly admitting white-only unions like the telegraphers and railroad trackmen. By 1910 the organization was indifferent or hostile to the demands of black workers.

The emergence of a formidable white union structure with a pronounced anti-Negro posture had the most serious consequences. On the national level, AFL policy widened and sealed the existing divisions between black and white workers. On the local level, AFL policy strengthened the hand of biased white union leaders, who launched a national campaign to exclude and subordinate black workers.

In this campaign, which reached a peak in the first two decades of the twentieth century, a number of techniques were used. The usual procedure was to bar blacks from unions and to make union membership, i.e., whiteness, a prerequisite for employment. A widely practiced variant of this procedure was the establishment of union hiring halls from which black workers were excluded. When black artisans were too numerous to exclude by these methods, separate unions were organized. Since the central white unions controlled policy and jurisdiction, it was relatively easy to isolate the subordinate black unions and destroy them.

An additional and equally effective mode of exclusion was the negative quota, which restricted the percentage and advancement of black workers. The transportation brotherhoods—the engineers, conductors, firemen, and trackmen—frequently used this technique in their long and generally successful campaign to exclude and subordinate black workers. The extensive use of quotas to eliminate black skilled tradesmen is particularly interesting in view of the contemporary white view that quotas are alien to the American experience. The precise opposite is true. Although quotas to include people and to insure fair play *are* alien to the American experience, quotas to exclude people on the basis of race are as American as inflated rhetoric on the Fourth of July. We can illustrate this point with a mass of evidence. In January, 1910, the Brotherhood of Railway Trainmen, negotiated the following agreement with Southern railroads:

> No larger percentage of Negro trainmen or yardmen will be employed on any division or in any yard than was employed on January 1, 1910. If on any roads this percentage is now larger than on January 1, 1910, this agreement does not contemplate the discharge of any Negroes to be replaced by whites; but as vacancies are filled or new men employed, whites are to be taken on until the percentage of January first is again reached.
>
> Negroes are not to be employed as baggagemen, flagmen, or yard

foremen, but in any case in which they are now so employed, they are not to be discharged to make places for whites, but when the positions they occupy become vacant, whites shall be employed in their place.

Another case—a 1927 agreement between the Atlanta Joint Terminals and the firemen and helpers—makes the same point even more clearly:

> White firemen will be given preference over Negro firemen in filling all jobs when the following changes in conditions of work are made:
> (1) A change of 30 minutes or more in the starting time of a job.
> (2) Filling vacancies.
> (3) Creation of new jobs.

There were other mechanisms of exclusion, such as white-listing, refusing to recognize travelling cards, and restricting skilled black artisans to menial tasks and to work on structures in specified sections of the city.

When these methods failed, white workers organized strikes or threatened to organize strikes. Between 1880 and 1890 there were at least fifty major strikes by white workers protesting the employment of black workers.

The ultimate sanction, of course, was violence, perpetrated by white laborers and their allies on the police forces of the country. "These tactics," Sterling D. Spero and Abram L. Harris reported, "reached their height on the Illinois Central system where special agents reported a plot to kill Negro trainmen who refused to give up their jobs. A price of three hundred dollars was said to have been placed on the head of every Negro trainman. Negro employees, firemen as well as trainmen, received letters signed 'Zulus' ordering them to leave the service and threatening them with death if they refused. One colored fireman was shot in the face with a shotgun as his train was nearing a station. In several instances trains were stopped by white men armed with clubs and guns. Negro brakemen were beaten up for holding 'white men's jobs' and were threatened with death if they were caught running in the territory again."

All this—the violence, the quotas, the white-listing—was grist for the mills of white employers, who used the divisions in the working class to limit the power and effectiveness of white and black workers. The best indication of this was the widespread use of black workers to break the strikes of white workers. This happened in several widely reported instances, and one discerns in the literature a systematic attempt to overemphasize the importance of black strikebreakers. If, as critics contend, some but not all black workers engaged in strikebreaking, it must be remembered that this was the inevitable and perhaps necessary response to the hostile and short-sighted policy of white labor unions. It is important, too, to remember that the number of black strikebreakers was small in comparison with the number of white strikebreakers.

Wholly apart from the question of numbers, it is plain that strikebreaking was the only way many black workers could find employment. It was largely by strikebreaking that blacks forced their way into some industries, notably meatpacking, mining, steel manufacturing, and lumbering.

It is only fair to add that white unions were not the first or the only barrier to equal employment. In the North and South, white employers were equally resourceful in limiting the training, employment, and advancement of black workers. Nor should it be forgotten that black workers faced the same problems in non-union trades and factories.

One further point: some white labor unions, notably the United Mine Workers, the Industrial Workers of the World, and the Longshoremen, organized black and white workers and staged interracial campaigns. In 1904 more than one-half of the thirteen thousand United Mine Workers members in Alabama were black. In the 1890s a black man, Richard L. Davis, was a member of the executive board of the United Mine Workers. There were also several black vice-presidents of the Alabama United Mine Workers and the Alabama Federation of Labor, and it is the opinion of a modern student, Paul B. Worthman, that they "probably were more influential among the black masses than highly publicized figures like Booker T. Washington and Reverend William McGill."

*THERE* was no marked improvement in the status of black workers from the end of Reconstruction to the beginning of World War I. For a whole generation, millions of blacks worked from sunup to sundown, picking cotton, crushing sugar cane, washing, scrubbing, sweating, making other people rich and impoverishing themselves.

This dynamic, which runs like a black thread through the leprously white fabric of American internal colonialism, was documented by the census of 1890. In that year 87.3 percent of the 3,073,164 black workers were in agriculture or domestic service. More than half of these workers (1,728,325) were in agriculture, and 31 percent were in domestic and personal service. Of the 327,000 black workers in the North and West, 207,000 were in domestic or personal service.

Although the seven million blacks listed by the 1890 census constituted only 11.9 percent of the total population, black workers were 13.5 percent of all workers. It is to be observed too that a larger proportion of black women were in the labor force than white women. Almost 97 pecent of all black women workers were farm laborers, house servants, or laundresses.

Needless to say, black workers lagged behind both American-born and foreign-born white workers. Only 11 percent of black workers were in trade and transportation, manufacturing, and mechanical industries, as compared with 35 percent of the American-born whites and 45 percent of the foreign-born whites. An even smaller proportion of black workers was listed as professionals: 1 percent of the blacks, as contrasted with 2 percent of the foreign-born whites and 6 percent of the American-born whites.

According to the 1890 census, there were twenty-two thousand black carpenters, seventeen thousand barbers, ten thousand masons, four thousand painters, four thousand plasterers. Of the thirty-four thousand black professionals, there were eighteen hundred musicians, fourteen hundred actors, four hundred lawyers, nine hundred physicians, twelve thousand ministers, and fifteen thousand teachers.

Across the years that followed, there was painful progress in several directions. By 1910, 550,000 or 10.6 percent of employed blacks were in manufacturing or mechanical pursuits. Between 1910 and 1920 the number of black farm owners increased from 120,000 to 218,972. In 1910 blacks owned or were buying 12,800,000 acres of land worth $620 million. Ten years later black farm ownership reached a peak of 41,400,000 acres.

It is reasonable to think of the years around World War I as the outset of a major epoch of transition that was to steer blacks by many paths out of the plantation economy into the modern world. Let it be emphasized that this turning point was not due to a change of heart on the part of white Americans. It stemmed rather from more mundane considerations: white people were in trouble, and white people in trouble tend to remember (temporarily) the Declaration of Independence. It happened that way in the Civil War, and it happened that way again in World War I. The hostilities in Europe dried up the flow of poor white immigrants, and hard-pressed Northern industrialists started tapping the black industrial reserve, sending labor agents into the South to entice black workers northwards. This development awakened deep hopes in the black community, which exploded in the Great Migration to the North. Nobody knows for sure how many blacks moved north between 1915 and 1920, but estimates range from 150,000 to 500,000. A second great wave of black workers came between 1920 and 1924. By 1930 more than two million blacks had moved from the plantations of the South to the Harlems of the North.

Out of this hemorrhage of people flowed the circumstances that enabled black workers to get a foothold in industry. The black immigrants poured into major Northern cities and were employed as laborers and semi-skilled operatives in the packing houses, steel mills, and automobile plants. By 1920, 1,506,000 or 31.2 percent of black workers were employed in industrial occupations and the proportion of blacks in agriculture and domestic service had dropped to 67 percent.

This was a development of far-reaching significance, for it marked the first major shift in the role of the black worker since the seventeenth century. The tremors set in motion by this massive shift traveled swiftly through the streets of metropolitan areas, changing the character and structure of black America. Cohesive black communities developed in major Northern cities, and a black professional class emerged to meet new needs and demands. Parallel with this development was the emergence of a new racial spirit, militant and uncompromising, which found expression in literature (the Harlem Renaissance) and nationalism (Garveyism). This spirit was sharpened by the postwar betrayal of black soldiers and increasing conflict between black and white workers. The riot wave of 1919 was caused in part by rising tensions between black and white workers.

With the Great Migration and the transformation of the economic base of the black worker, black America entered a decisively new phase. Still, one should not exaggerate the immediate impact of these developments on the general situation of black workers, most of whom were still laborers, servants, and peasants. Of the more than five million black workers listed in the 1930 census, two out of three were in agriculture and domestic service.

There is another point which is even more important for an understanding of the postwar transformation: The scope and extent of the industrial invasion by black workers were limited by a deepening of the white conspiracy against black labor. The migration of black workers forced white Americans to make a new decision about the role and status of black workers. As more and more black peasants assumed the garb of urban proletarians, a new variation of the old white conspiracy emerged. Blacks were to be granted limited access to industrial pursuits, but they were only to be used in ways that served the interests and conveniences of either white labor or white capital or both.

This decision, a restatement on the economic level of the Compromise of 1787 and the Compromise of 1877, was institutionalized in the two-track labor system. The first track of this system was reserved for white workers, and black workers were relegated to the hot, dirty, low-paying jobs in the second track. By 1931, as Sterling D. Spero and Abram L. Harris noted, the decision had been woven deeply into the institutional fabric of America. "The most distinctive characteristic of the Negro's position in the world of labor," they said, "is his relegation to occupations in which he does not compete with white workers—in short, the perpetuation of the tradition of black men's and white men's jobs. This tradition is not confined to the South, but extends throughout the country. Pullman porters and dining car waiters are almost invariably black while railroad conductors, locomotive engineers, subway guards, motormen, sales persons in stores, clerks, and white-collar employees of every sort are almost without exception white. Certain of the skilled crafts which Negroes have followed in the South for years are practically barred to the Negro in the North by union regulations or craft traditions where there is no union."

In the face of this, what were black workers to do?

One answer came from the NAACP, the National Urban League, and other traditional leadership circles, which set out to change the interests and perceptions of white labor union leaders. This campaign began in the first decades of the century and culminated in the postwar world with a series of pleas and petitions to Samuel Gompers and other white labor leaders. In 1924 the NAACP addressed an open letter "to the American Federation of Labor and other groups of organized labor."

> For many years the American Negro has been demanding admittance to the ranks of union labor.

> For many years your organizations have made public profession of your interest in Negro labor, of your desire to have it unionized, and of your hatred of the black "scab."
>
> Notwithstanding this apparent surface agreement, Negro labor in the main is outside the ranks of organized labor, and the reason is, first, that white union labor does not want black labor, and secondly, black labor has ceased to beg admission to union ranks because of its increasing value and efficiency outside the unions.
>
> We face a crisis in inter-racial labor conditions; the continued and determined race prejudice of white labor, together with the limitation of immigration, is giving black labor tremendous advantage. The Negro is entering the ranks of semi-skilled and skilled labor and he is entering mainly and necessarily as a "scab." He broke the great steel strike. He will soon be in a position to break any strike when he can gain economic advantage for himself.
>
> On the other hand, intelligent Negroes know full well that a blow at organized labor is a blow at all labor, that black labor today profits by the blood and sweat of labor leaders in the past who have fought oppression and monopoly by organization. If there is built up in America a great black bloc of non-union laborers who have a right to hate the unions, all laborers, black and white, eventually must suffer.
>
> Is it not time then that black and white labor get together? Is it not time for white unions to stop bluffing and for black laborers to stop cutting off their noses to spite their faces?

The leaders of organized labor, Samuel Gompers foremost among them, responded to this eminently sensible appeal with verbiage and fast footwork, and the situation of black workers continued to deteriorate, causing some black leaders to call for new departures. Having become convinced that it was useless to count on white labor unions, black nationalists denounced all unions and urged black workers to make the best deal they could with white capitalists. A very different approach was championed by communists who called for radical economic reconstruction and the creation of a black nation in the Black Belt areas of the South. While awaiting this improbable event, the communists worked inside and outside existing unions, and played a major role in the organization of the short-lived American Negro Labor Congress.

As public concern over the problem intensified, the independent black union movement revived, leading to the organization of scores of black unions, including the National Alliance of Postal Employees. If there was one man who symbolized this movement, that man was Asa Philip Randolph, a brilliant young socialist editor who helped organize several national groups, notably the United Negro Trades, a black federation similar to the United Hebrew Trades. When the fires of this organization faded, Randolph turned to grassroots agitation, organizing in 1925 the Brotherhood of Sleeping Car Porters, which was not recognized by the AFL until 1936.

There was no lack of activity on the part of black leaders, as these instances indicate, but the struggle was not coordinated, the cadres and the masses were divided, and the resources were lacking. The mournful consequence was that the Stock Market Crash and the Great Depression found black workers unorganized and bereft of reserve capital and dependable allies. What happened next has been described many times: the mass discharge of black industrial workers who were the last hired and were therefore the first fired, the precipitous dismissal of black domestics and service workers as housekeepers and service outlets frantically cut expenses, the shock waves of despair and demoralization that spread through the black community. Thus, the continuing crisis of black workers entered a decisive phase; and by 1935 almost one out of every four black families in America was on relief.

Here, once again, we may pause to point out that this situation was not a result of the free play of market forces. On the contrary, white workers were systematically given preference over black workers. In an important essay on *The Demand for Black Labor*, Harold M. Baron pointed out that the "rationing out of unemployment operated in such a way as to reinforce the demarcation of 'Negro jobs.' Blacks were dismissed in higher proportions from the better positions. In Chicago they were displaced from professional and managerial occupations at a rate five times that of whites. The displacement rate from clerical, skilled, and semi-skilled jobs was three times larger, while from unskilled and service jobs it was down to twice that of whites. As a result the total percentage of skilled and white-collar workers in the black labor force declined to half its former proportion. . . . Nationally, blacks lost a third of the jobs they had held in industry, declining from 7.3 percent to 5.1 percent of the total manufacturing employment."

A situation already desperately difficult was made immeasurably worse by widespread invasion of traditional black jobs. T. Arnold Hill noted that there "was actual supplanting of Negroes in bulk on particular jobs or in particular factories where they were employed as household employees, bellmen, waiters, elevator operators, railroad track laborers, diggers of ditches, drivers of wagons and carts."

The welfare provisions of the New Deal relieved some of the economic distress in the black community, but it is significant that the New Deal gave least to black people who needed it most. What was even more significant was that many New Deal programs added to the economic burdens of blacks. Thus—to give one striking example—the subsidies for the reduction of cotton acreage in the South worked to the disadvantage of black farmers, who were pushed off the land. More sinister still was the inevitable corollary of New Deal labor legislation, which increased the power of anti-Negro craft unions at the expense of the unorganized and the powerless. By institutionalizing collective bargaining and by legalizing closed shop arrangements, the government made black exclusion easier and more profitable. Writing in *Opportunity* in September, 1934, Jesse O. Thomas, the National Urban League's Southern field secretary, said that "while Section 7a [of the National Industrial Recovery Act] has greatly increased the security of labor in general, insofar as the different labor organizations thus benefitted deny and exclude Negroes from their membership by constitutions or rituals, the position of Negro labor has been made less favorable."

This viewpoint was echoed by most black leaders, who mounted a national campaign for the inclusion of an antidiscrimination clause in the proposed Wagner labor relations act. The AFL opposed the anti-discrimination clause, and the bill, which has been called the Magna Carta of labor, passed. Consequently, as Clark Foreman said, black workers learned once again that the major forces in the economy were "the industrialists and the AFL, both of whom are hostile to Negro labor, the former because they want to keep Negroes as a reserve of cheap labor, and the latter because they want to eliminate Negro competitive labor."

In the meantime, several concurrent developments shifted the center of gravity of the struggle. One development was the emergence of the Congress of Industrial Organizations (CIO), which transcended the narrow craft barriers of the AFL and organized all workers into racially inclusive industrial unions. Black workers were centrally important in the organization drive of the new union. By 1940 some two hundred thousand blacks were members of the CIO.

A second and equally decisive development was the rising tide of color consciousness. One sign of this was the Black Buying Power movement which started in Chicago and spread from city to city under the slogan, "Don't Buy Where You Can't Work." Another and politically more potent sign was the organization of some thirty-one thousand black and white tenant farmers into the Southern Tenant Farmers' Union, the first successful interracial farm organization since the failure of the Populist movement.

Another significant, though more diffuse, source of pressure was the black voter. The migration of black workers had created new political bases in the North, and this potential power was partly responsible for the increasing responsiveness of white leaders to black demands.

Black political power, welfare legislation, the CIO, the new mood of militancy: all these factors combined to change the social geography of black America. Important as these factors were, however, they did not immediately change the marginal position of black workers. On the contrary, black workers lost ground during the thirties. Not only did total black employment decline in this decade, but opportunities for black workers dropped sharply in the service industry. At the end of the decade it was reported that the percentage of blacks in manufacturing was at its lowest ebb in thirty years.

Even more ominous was the drift of public policy in the first years of World War II. The new employment created by war industries went first to unemployed white workers, and some defense plants announced publicly that they would accept all workers, except Germans and Negroes. The black response to this policy was predictably explosive. From all sides, from nationalists, from communists, from civil libertarians and conservatives, came demands for a war against unfreedom in America. These demands were backed up by a crescendo of demonstrations, which continued throughout the decade. The leader of this campaign was labor leader Asa Randolph, who organized a nationwide nonviolent campaign and threatened to lead one hundred thousand black workers in a March on Washington. Faced with this threat, and an implacable black mood, President Franklin Delano Roosevelt yielded to Randolph's demands and issued Executive Order 8802, establishing the first Fair Employment Practices Commission. This order was the first decisive act by the federal government on behalf of black workers in more than sixty years. And although the commission did not accomplish a great deal before it was emasculated by Southern senators and their

Northern collaborators, it was a point of focus which established the principle of government intervention on behalf of equal employment.

It was during this period and largely as a result of sustained militancy in a tight labor market that black workers made their most dramatic gains since slavery. By 1944 black workers constituted 8.3 percent of the war production work force. The census of 1950 showed that black workers also made substantial gains as skilled and unskilled operatives and white-collar workers.

*H*ISTORICALLY, black workers have danced to the tune of the accordion. In a period of rising employment, the accordion expands, opening up new opportunities for blacks. And then, on the downward curve of hard money and rising unemployment, the accordion contracts, pushing blacks once again into the nether world of unemployment. This has happened in America over and over again for more than two hundred years. The gains of free black workers in the first decades of the nineteenth century were wiped out by waves of white immigrants in the 1830s and 1840s. The advances of the Reconstruction period were nullified by the Compromise of 1877 and the waves of white immigrants of the 1880s and 1890s. Similarly, the gains of World War I were nullified by the Great Depression. *A period of advance followed by a period of disaster*: this has been the story and the burden of the black worker in America. And as the fifties began, the same old drama opened once again with the same villains and the same victims. As we have seen, black workers made substantial gains in the forties, and black median income, which had been 40 percent of the white median income in prewar years, rose in 1952 to 57 percent of white median income. Now suddenly the tide turned abruptly. When the Korean War boomlet collapsed, black workers lost out disproportionately. The black unemployment rate, which had been 5.4 percent in 1952, rose to 9.9 percent in 1954 and continued upward to 12.4 percent during the recession of 1961. In the thirteen-year period from 1952 to 1964, black unemployment averaged 10.2 percent, double the white average.

During this period of reaction and retrogression, black workers lost ground relative to white workers. The median family income of blacks dropped from the 1952 high of 57 percent of median white family income to 51 percent in 1958. It was not until 1964 that blacks were able to recapture the ground lost in this disastrous thirteen-year period.

In a speech at Howard University, President Lyndon B. Johnson noted the "impressive" gains of black Americans and added:

> But for the great majority of Negro Americans—the poor, the unemployed, the uprooted, and the dispossessed—there is a much grimmer story. They still are another nation. Despite the court orders and the laws, despite the legislative victories and the speeches, for them the walls are rising and the gulf is widening.
>
> Here are some of the facts of this American failure.
>
> Thirty-five years ago the rate of unemployment for Negroes and whites was about the same. Today the Negro rate is twice as high.
>
> In 1948 the 8 percent unemployment rate for Negro teen-age boys was actually less than that of whites. By last year the rate had grown to 23 percent, as against 13 percent for whites.
>
> Between 1949 and 1959, the income of Negro men relative to white men declined in every section of this country. From 1952 to 1963 the median income of Negro families compared to white actually dropped from 57 percent to 53 percent.
>
> In the years 1955 through 1957, 22 percent of experienced Negro workers were out of work at some time during the year. In 1961 through 1963 that proportion had soared to 29 percent.
>
> Since 1947 the number of white families living in poverty has decreased 27 percent, while the number of poor nonwhite families decreased only 3 percent.
>
> The infant mortality of nonwhites in 1940 was 70 percent greater than whites. Twenty-two years later it was 90 percent greater.

The fundamental cause of this deteriorating situation was racism aggravated by automation and public policies (tight money, etc.) that penalized the poor and the unorganized. An additional factor was the mechanization of Southern agriculture and the continued subsidization of reduction in crop acreage in the South. As a consequence of these policies, millions of black farm workers were displaced and the black migration to Northern cities increased dramatically. Thus, as the national economy continued to contract, and as the new forces released by World War II began to shake the dispossessed of Africa, Asia, and African-America, passions that had simmered for years finally came to a boil. This unforeseen, though hardly unforeseeable, ferment led to the American Freedom movement, which raced across the country, moving from polite demonstrations for equal rights to turbulent and sometimes violent demonstrations for economic justice, the whole swirling pageant culminating in a massive March on Washington for "Freedom and Jobs."

The Freedom movement was only one front in the siege of the sixties. The new AFL-CIO was besieged by black activists, and demonstrations were staged at building construction sites. In 1960 Asa Philip Randolph, the aging warrior of the black labor struggle, helped organize the American Negro Labor Council. Additional pressure was exerted by Adam Clayton Powell, the new chairman of the House Labor and Education Committee, progressive unions like the United Packinghouse Workers, and the NAACP. Toward the end of the sixties, black workers upped the ante, organizing black caucuses in white unions and demanding positive quotas to compensate for the long years of negative quotas. No less significant was the organization of new forms, like DRUM, Operation Breadbasket, and Operation PUSH.

Another by-product of the new black mood was increased government action. By the early sixties antidiscrimination laws had been passed in more than half of the states. Other milestones on this road were the civil rights acts of the sixties; the 1964 National Labor Relations Board's Hughes Tool Company decision, which defined racial discrimination as an unfair labor practice; Presidential executive orders requiring affirmative action by government contractors; and the 1969 Philadelphia Plan, which required government contractors "to commit themselves to specific goals of minority manpower utilization."

All this made a powerful impact on black workers, who recouped some of their losses and opened new furrows in the last five years of the sixties. This comes out most clearly in 1970 census figures, which indicate that black workers made dramatic gains in some categories. Black employment, for example, rose faster than white employment in the sixties. Blacks, who were only 10 percent of the work force in 1960, accounted for 12 percent of the growth in employment in that decade, and the number of blacks in white-collar and skilled blue-collar jobs increased by 69 percent (compared to a white increase of 23 percent)—from about three million in 1960 to about five million in 1971. In the same decade the number of blacks holding clerical jobs doubled, and the number of blacks in professional and technical occupations increased 131 percent. Conversely—and this is a point of great importance—the number of farmers and farm laborers decreased 56 percent.

The nine million black workers listed in the 1971 census reports constituted 10 percent of the work force, 10 percent of the teachers, and about 8 percent of employees in better-paying jobs. There were, according to these figures, 13,700 black engineers, 11,500 physicians and dentists, 214,500 elementary and secondary school teachers, 167,200 sales workers, 1,000,000 clerical workers, 665,000 craftsmen and foremen, 688,000 laborers, 176,000 farm laborers, 1,475,000 service workers, and 610,500 private household workers. Notwithstanding the confusion and setbacks of the early sixties, these workers made some headway in closing the gap between black and white income. Median family income relative to white income rose from 54 percent in 1964 to 60 percent ($6,400 for blacks and $10,670 for whites) in 1971.

But these figures have to be viewed in perspective, for some of them do not mean what they seem to mean. In some categories, for example, the same figures indicate both progress and deepening deprivation. Another way to see the same point is to notice that black workers were 10 percent of employed persons in 1971 but only 1 percent of the engineers, 2 percent of the physicians and dentists, 3 percent of the managers and administrators, 5 percent of the professional workers, and 6 percent of the craftsmen, as contrasted to 17 percent of the service workers, some 20 percent of the laborers, and 50 percent of private household workers.

We can make the same point about the alleged gain in family income. Although the median family income of blacks as a percentage of white family income increased between 1947 and 1971, the dollar gap in favor of whites increased in the same period from $2,671 in 1947 to $3,720 in 1971.

If we look now at the data on persons below the poverty level, we find the same appalling disparity. Although the proportion of blacks and whites below the poverty line decreased between 1959 and 1971, the decline was greater for whites. In 1971 about 10 percent of the whites and 32 percent of the blacks (7.4 million) were below the poverty level, compared with 18 and 55 percent for whites and blacks respectively in 1959. In that twelve-year period, the number of poverty-stricken whites dropped by 37 percent as compared with a 25 percent reduction for blacks.

We might note, before passing on, that more whites (6.9 million) than blacks (6.4 millon) were receiving public assistance in March, 1971, although the black recipients constituted a disproportionately high percentage of the black population. It is also noteworthy that 23.8 million whites were receiving social security income in 1971, as contrasted with only 2.7 million blacks.

In assessing the status of the black worker, it is important to give special attention to the anomalous position of black women workers, who are probably the most oppressed sector of the working population. In 1971 about 44 percent of all black women workers were in service, private household, and laborer occupations. Interestingly enough, however, a relatively large proportion of black women workers were in higher-paying jobs. In 1971 about the same proportion—13 percent—of black men and black women were in professional, technical, and managerial occupations.

Not surprisingly, in view of the total impact of internal colonialism, there is a substantial gap between the income of black women and white women. In 1969 the median income for black women working fifty weeks or more was $4,126, about 80 percent of the $5,182 for white women working the same length of time. It is also true that black women workers make less money on the average than black men. In 1970 the median income of black male workers was $5,370 as compared with $3,200 for black female workers. Despite this fact, the disparity in the incomes of black men and women is less than the gap between the incomes of white men and white women. The female to male median income ratio is 47 percent for whites and 60 percent for blacks.

For both male and female black workers, the unemployment rate is dangerously and unacceptably high. Throughout the sixties, the unemployment rates for black workers were about double those for whites. The black unemployment rate dropped in the late sixties and then rose again in 1970 and 1971, when some 900,000 black workers were unemployed. The unemployment rate for black women was substantially higher than the rate for black men, and the unemployment rate for black teen-agers was 31.7 percent.

Since census statistics do not reflect subemployment and the thousands of blacks who have dropped out of the market because of continued rejection, the official figures do not reveal the full extent of black unemployment. In 1966 the Department of Labor made a special study of ten slum areas and concluded that "one out of every three slum residents who are already workers, or should and could become workers with suitable help, was either jobless or earning only substandard wages."

It is fashionable in scholarly circles to whitewash this situation by referring to the lack of skills of black workers. But this view fails to take into account two ominous facts. First, the unemployment rate for blacks is higher than the white rate in every major occupational category. Secondly, the unemployment rate for blacks is high even in the skilled categories. *In 1971, 3.8 percent of black professionals were unemployed.* So were 9.3 percent of the sales workers, 7.9 percent of the clerical workers, and 7.6 percent of the craftsmen and operators.

No less significant is the fact that the average black worker makes about $1,200 less than the average white worker for the same kind of work. In fact, the U.S. Census Bureau reported in 1970 that "Negro men who have completed four years of high school have a lower median income than white men who have completed only eight years of elementary school." What is equally true and no less distressing is that black men who have completed four years or more of college have a lower median income ($8,669) than white men who have completed high school ($8,829). Analyzing these figures, Professor Otis Dudley Duncan of the University of Michigan said that at least one-third of the gap between black and white income exists "because Negro and white men in the same line of work, with the same amount of formal schooling, with equal ability, from families of the same size and the same socioeconomic level simply do not draw the same wages and salaries."

It is an interesting and ironic fact—in view of the history we have cited here—that in 1971 there were proportionately more black union members (21.8 percent of all black workers) than white union workers (20.2 percent of all white workers).

One final generalization: The nine industries with the largest proportion of black workers in 1970 were tobacco, medical and other health services, local passenger transit, water transportation, eating and drinking places, real estate, hotel and other lodging places, personal services, miscellaneous repair service. In these nine industries, black workers held 18 percent of all jobs but only 5 percent of the professional, technical, and managerial jobs.

The same general situation obtains in the internal hierarchies of liberal unions and the U.S. government. In May, 1971, blacks held 15.1 percent of all full-time federal jobs but only 2 percent of the occupations in the higher grades.

Bad as the situation is today, all signs indicate that things are going to get a great deal worse before they get better. Blacks are disproportionately concentrated in marginal industries. Automation is destroying the market for unskilled and semiskilled jobs. And despite the real and important gains cited above, it is obvious that Andrew Brimmer spoke gospel truth when he said that the black worker, like Alice in Wonderland, is going to have to run "faster and faster" in order to remain in the same place.

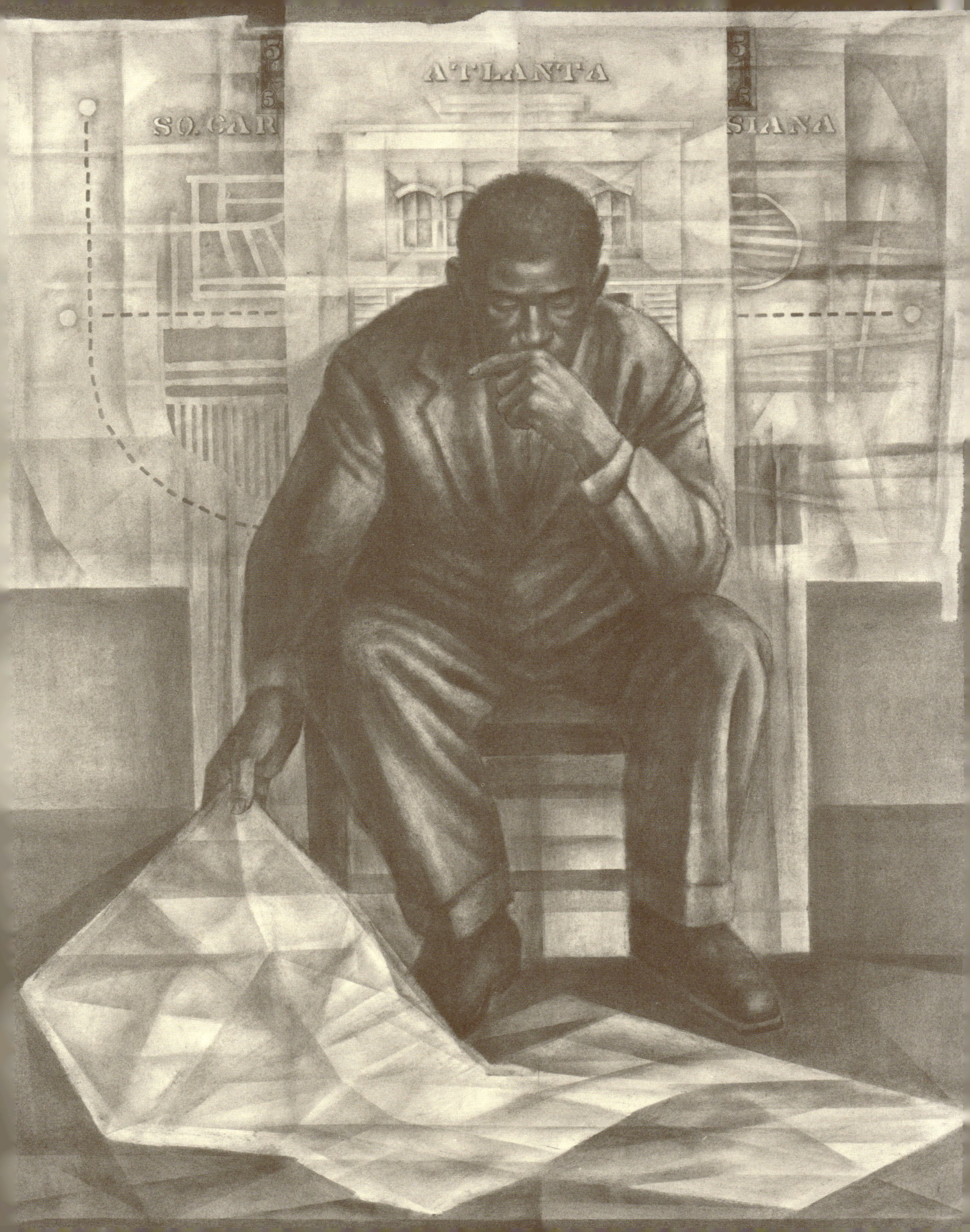

ATLANTA
SO. CAR
SIANA

# Money, Merchants and Markets

*I do not believe that the ultimate contribution of the Negro to the world will be his development of natural forces. It is to be more than that. There is in him emotional, spiritual elements that presage gifts from the Negro more ennobling and enduring than factories and railroads and banks. But without these factories, railroads and banks, he cannot accomplish his highest aim.*

—John Hope

*THE* story of black people in America is, among other things, the story of a quest for the hard rock of economic security. This quest, undergirding all, overshadowing all, gives shape and body to all the strivings of black men and women. Behind the demonstrations, behind the petitions and protests and revolts, behind Jamestown and Montgomery and Watts, lies this deeper and more basic struggle for bread, shelter, clothing, land, raw materials, resources, skills, and space for the heart.

Let there be no misunderstanding: This deeper struggle is not, as some have said, a detour from freedom; it is, on the contrary, the very essence of freedom. For freedom is, above all else, the freedom to do. And a freedom divorced from an economic foundation, a freedom divorced from the wherewithal, cannot guarantee anything except the freedom to talk or the freedom to starve.

This truth, harsh and unyielding, is a fundamental factor in the long and painful struggle of black Americans to create reservoirs of personal and social wealth. On one level, this struggle revolves around the development of private businesses in the white and black communities. On another level, it reflects and amplifies the mutual principle, the development of collective enterprises for social security and sociopolitical emancipation. On both levels, the struggle presents a mottled picture of horribly handicapped men and women blazing trails which have to be endlessly reopened.

The record is gray and white and depressing. But, for all of that, it is immeasurably important and has enormous implications for contemporary public policy. It has been generally assumed by almost all white commentators and not a few black commentators that the economic position of blacks can be explained by "the lateness of their entrance" into the commercial world. Nothing could be further from the the truth. As we shall see, blacks have been operating businesses, some of considerable size, for more than three hundred years. It is to be observed, too, that the first Africans came to this country with a highly developed sense of commerce and industry. The Africans in Africa—as almost all knowledgeable commentators emphasize—were shrewd traders and commercial organizers of considerable ingenuity. Some of these skills and some of this ingenuity survived the brutalities of the Middle Passage and made Africans leading participants in the economic transformation of the New World.

Nothing attests to this more forcefully than the commercial experiences of the first generation of African-Americans. Within a few years after the historic landing at Jamestown in 1619, blacks were hard at work accumulating pounds, plantations, and capital. By 1651 Anthony Johnson, who seems to have worked out his servitude a few years after his arrival in 1621, had accumulated enough capital to import five indentured servants, on whose headrights he received 250 acres on the Pungoteague River in Northampton County, Virginia. In subsequent years, as we have shown, other black Virginians acquired substantial estates in Northampton, Surry, New Kent, York, and other Virginia counties.

The pioneer black landowners apparently made their money on the staple crops of tobacco and rice. They bought and sold in the same markets as their white competitors, and some of them adopted white habits, buying both black and white indentured servants and, in at least one case, a black slave.

In New York and New England, blacks faced similar if somewhat less intensive problems of adaptation. One of the first black landowners in the colonies was Domingo Antony, who owned a parcel of land in New Amsterdam (now New York City) as early as 1634. Ten years later, in 1644, eleven blacks received large grants of land on a swamp on the edge of the New Amsterdam settlement. This area, which is known today as Greenwich Village and Washington Square, was an essentially black settlement for some two centuries. In 1634 Bostonian Ken owned a house and lot in Dorchester, Massachusetts, and had more than four acres planted in wheat. Several decades later Abijah Prince owned one hundred acres in Guilford, Vermont. Prince was one of the founders of Sunderland, Vermont, and received equal shares of land in all six divisions of the township. What happened in Vermont and Massachusetts and Virginia was repeated in one way or another in virtually every colony, and the records indicate that some of the land acquired by the first generation of blacks remained in their possession for several years.

Following this period, the balance of forces shifted to the disadvantage of blacks. Although the "free" black class continued to grow by manumissions and the activities of blacks who purchased spouses and relatives, it became a matter of public policy in this period to limit the economic opportunities of all nonwhites. Beginning in the middle of the seventeenth century and continuing throughout the Colonial period, every colony passed slave codes and other discriminatory laws which limited the options of slaves and "free" men. In 1660, for example, the Boston Town Meeting passed a law forbidding the use of black artisans. In 1670 the Virginia legislative made it illegal for blacks to buy white Christians. In 1712 the Connecticut Assembly decided that no free black could buy land or carry on a business in any town without the permission of the residents.

It was under these conditions and in a climate of massive repression that the foundations of black business enterprise were established. In 1736 Emanuel Manna Bernoon and his wife Mary opened the first oyster and ale house in Providence, Rhode Island; Bernoon's capital reportedly came from his wife, who had prospered, it is said, in the illegal whiskey business. When Bernoon died in 1769, he left an estate of more than 539 pounds. Also operating businesses in the pre-Revoluntary period were "Duchess" Quamino, who became the leading caterer in Newport, Rhode Island, and Jean Baptiste Pointe DuSable, the trader who founded the city of Chicago.

In this period, or shortly afterwards, black Americans were among the founding fathers of several cities, including Los Angeles. Of the forty-four founders of Los Angeles, twenty-six were black. The children and grandchildren of these founding fathers inherited large blocks of land. Maria Rita Valdez, the granddaughter of a founding father, owned Rancho Rodeo de Las Aguas, which is known today as Beverly Hills. Another black, Francisco Reyes, owned the entire San Fernando Valley. Reyes sold his property in the 1790s and became mayor of the city of Los Angeles.

It is scarcely necessary to point out that these businessmen constituted a small minority of the black population. Nor is it necessary to emphasize the weakness of the black business foundation. In that day, as in this one, the pressures were enormous, as Brissot de Warville, a French traveler, observed. "Those Negroes who keep shops," he said, "live moderately, and never augment their business beyond a certain point. The reason is obvious; the whites . . . like not to give them credit to enable them to undertake any extensive commerce nor even to give them the means of a common education by receiving them into their counting houses."

This much was clear early in the game: the deal was stacked. What was equally clear, early in the game, was that there were blacks who could win at least a few rounds, although all the odds were against them. To take one clear example, one Samuel Fraunces came to New York in the pre-Revolutionary period, and became a leading caterer and restaurant owner. In 1762 he paid two thousand pounds for the De Lancey

Mansion on the corner of Broad and Pearl streets and opened a tavern. Before long Fraunces's Tavern was the social center of the city. It was here in 1768 that the New York Chamber of Commerce was organized. It was here in 1774 that the Sons of Liberty planned a New York "Tea Party." It was here finally that George Washington bade farewell to his officers at the end of the Revolutionary War.

With the defeat of the British and the establishment of the American Republic, black Americans entered a new and dangerous period. The first phase of this period was marked by the manumission of thousands of blacks and a sharp rise in the number of free blacks in urban areas. But this period, so promising and yet so deceptive, was followed by a period of reaction and heightened racism stemming from the fear of black competition and the desire to extract capital from the slave population.

To understand the black economic response to this reaction, we must follow two streams, both arising from the same source, both giving mutual expression to the same spirit. The first stream was a continuation and intensification of the private enterprise movement, particularly in the catering industry, which blacks soon dominated. The outstanding caterer of the period was Robert Bogle who was, according to Abram L. Harris, "the first man to advocate the organization of domestic service into a business." In the first decade of the nineteenth century, Bogle opened a restaurant on Eighth Street near Samson in Philadelphia. He attracted the attention of the leading businessmen of the city and was soon the arbiter of palates in Philadelphia. "His taste of hand and eye and palate," W. E. B. DuBois wrote, "set the fashion of the day." Bogle's touch was institutionalized in succeeding decades by Peter Augustin and James Prosser, of whom it was said that "the name of James Prosser, among the merchants of Philadelphia, is inseparable with their daily hours of recreation and pleasure."

There were Bogles and Augustins in major centers in both the North and South. In New York City at that time, as James Weldon Johnson has noted, "the best food that could be procured . . . was that furnished by coloured caterers." From the turn of the century to the 1840s and 1850s, the New York scene was dominated by a number of creative black caterers, including Thomas Downing, who operated a restaurant on Broad Street near Wall Street, and George Bell and George Alexander, who ran a restaurant in nearby Church Street. For many years, according to Johnson, the most exclusive parties and weddings were served by Thomas

Jackson who was "in his day . . . the arbiter of New York in things gustatory."

The black touch was no less compelling in things relating to the hair, for in that decade, as well as in succeeding decades, barbering and hair dressing were black monopolies. By almost all early accounts, the leading black hairdresser in New York City was Pierre Toussaint. A former slave who came to New York with a French planter who went back to Santo Domingo and never returned, Toussaint became a legend in his own lifetime. He was mentioned in several novels and, according to one of his biographers, Hannah F. S. Lee, was unrivalled as a hairdresser for ladies. Author Lee added: "He had all of the custom and patronage of the French families . . . [and] many of the distinguished ladies of the city employed him."

Most of the black enterprises were of modest size and were situated in the more or less traditional areas of the service economy. Two exceptions to this general rule can be noted. James Forten invented and patented a device for handling sails and became one of the major sailmakers in Philadelphia, employing forty men, black and white, in his factory. By 1832 he had earned a fortune of $100,000.

Paul Cuffee was equally successful as a ship captain and ship builder. The seventh of ten children of Cuffee Slocum, a free black, Paul Cuffee was born in 1759 on one of the Elizabeth islands near New Bedford, Massachusetts. At sixteen he went to sea on a whaler. After various misadventures, he settled down to study mathematics and navigation. He later built a vessel and traded along the Connecticut coast, opening up an extensive fishing trade that gave employment to many workers. In 1797 he bought a farm on the Westport River and built a wharf and warehouse. By 1806 he owned one ship, two brigs, and several smaller vessels. For many years he commanded black crews, making voyages to England, Russia, the West Indies, Sweden, and Africa. In 1815 he made a voyage to Africa, carrying thirty-eight black emigrants and a cargo of food, tobacco, soap, candles, naval stores, iron, and agricultural implements. When he died in 1817, he left an estate valued at $20,000.

The individual initiatives of the Cuffees, Fortens, and Bogles were waves in the first stream of black economic development; the second, and possibly more significant, stream flowed from the fount of the mutual aid societies. With the founding of the first of these societies, the famous Free African Society of Philadelphia, in 1787, black economic development entered a new and decisive phase. The Free African Society, like its successors, was a collective business enterprise with ethical, fraternal, welfare, insurance, and burial features. The members of the society agreed "for the benefit of each other to advance one shilling in silver Pennsylvania currency a month; and after one year's subscription, from the dole hereof then to hand forth to the needy of the society if any should require, the sum of three shillings and nine pence per week of said money; provided the necessity is not brought on them by their own imprudence." By 1790 the society had more than forty-two pounds on deposit in the Bank of North America and had applied for a burial ground in Potter's Field.

Similar societies were organized in every major center with a large black population. The Petersburg (Virginia) Beneficial Society of Free Men of Color was organized "to care for the sick, to pay death claims, and to promote the social group spirit." The New York African Society for Mutual Relief was organized "to raise a fund to be appropriated toward the relief of the widows and orphans of the deceased members." The society later constructed a building on Orange Street (now Baxter Street) and invested in rental property on Greenwich Avenue.

The mutual aid idea spread in ever-widening circles, beneficently. By 1821 there were thirty-five or forty mutual aid societies in Baltimore, such as the African Friendship Benevolent Society, the Star in the East Association, and the Daughters of Jerusalem Association. By 1838 there were one hundred such societies in Philadelphia with a membership of 7,448.

In general, the societies operated on the mutual principle with members contributing 25 to 37 cents monthly and receiving sick benefits of from $1.50 to $3.00 weekly and death payments of from $10 to $20. The surplus of the organizations was deposited in banks or invested in real estate.

Out of this promising economic development flowed gains which were reflected at every level of black life. In 1814 Philadelphia blacks owned $250,000 in property. Eighteen years later, in 1832, they owned taxable property of $350,000. In 1836 New Orleans blacks owned property assessed at $2,462,470. In 1840 Cincinnati blacks owned $209,000 in real property. By this time a promising proportion of blacks had become business proprietors. Of the 224 blacks listed in the Boston City Directory of 1829, 32 were hairdressers and most owned their own shops.

Boston blacks also operated fourteen clothing stores, four tailor shops, one junk shop, one provision store, one general store, and four boarding houses. In 1840 New York blacks were publishing a newspaper and operating two restaurants in the Wall Street area. They also owned and operated three tailor shops, two coal yards, six boarding houses, a cleaning and dyeing establishment, two dry goods stores, four pleasure gardens, a confectionary, a hairdressing shop, and a fruit store.

*C*ONSIDERING the time and the circumstances, this was an impressive record; and since it points both to the past and the future, we would be well advised to pause for a moment and draw out the salient implications. What we are describing here is the development of black business colonies during the crucial formative stage of the American economy. At this point capital requirements were small, and it was relatively easy to get a foothold, especially in new industries, with a few dollars and a few workers. Under these circumstances, black businessmen operated primarily in the so-called general (read: white) market, selling goods and services primarily to white customers. For our purposes here this means that some blacks were in on the ground floor of the developing economy and were strategically placed for capitalizing on later developments. To understand why this did not happen, we must probe deeper into the essentially colonial relationships between the black and white communities, relationships which made it impossible for blacks to capitalize on their initial advantages.

There is no secret about the American Way of Making It. One scores, so to speak, in a new and/or expanding industry, capitalizes and then moves out from that base to control other markets. This has worked for entrepreneur after entrepreneur in America. But it has not worked for blacks. Like the black worker, the black entrepreneur is always pioneering in new industries and losing out later to white competitors. Like the black worker, the black entrepreneur is always starting over. His history, like the history of his people, is a history of discontinuity and increasing adversity.

The black entrepreneur has been no more successful in exploiting the social advantages of blackness. As almost everybody knows, the usual pattern in ethnic politics is for an ethnic entrepreneur to score in an industry in which his group has a natural or, to be more precise, a social advantage (Chinese laundries, Italian restaurants, etc.) and then move on to bigger and bigger enterprises. This obviously has not worked for black entrepreneurs. If it had worked, contemporary blacks would control catering, potato chips sales (from crackling), fried chicken outlets, packaged food franchises, office building maintenance, barbering, hair styling, clothes manufacturing, and the sports and entertainment industries.

Why hasn't it worked?

The answer is simple: racism and the colonial relations between a developing pole of growth (the white community) which developed at the expense of the capital and resources of an artificially impoverished pole of stagnation (the black colony). In concrete terms, as Abram Harris pointed out, black business development in this period was limited by eight factors: "1) The Difficulty of Obtaining Capital and Credit; 2) Low Wages, Competition for Jobs, and Immigration; 3) Mob Violence; 4) Occupational Restrictions; 5) Prohibition Against Owning Certain Types of Property; 6) Denial of the Right to Sue; 7) Restrictions Against Settlement in the West; and 8) Civic and Educational Handicaps."

These intertwined factors were orchestrated in the twin experiences of the black workers and black entrepreneurs of the 1830s and 1840s. The first experience, a continuation of the eighteenth century campaign against black artisans and workers, was a tightening of the lines of economic exclusion against "free" blacks. This movement was intensified by the arrival of five million white immigrants, a momentous development that compounded the economic problems of blacks and led to virulent anti-Negroism on at least two levels: increasing antagonism of white trade unionists, and physical violence by whites of all ranks, creeds, and classes. The second experience, which complemented the first, was the cumulative debasement of all blacks as a result of the attempt to preserve slavery and destroy the Indians.

The economic consequences were shattering. As James Weldon Johnson noted in *Black Manhattan*, "The New York Negroes as a class were industrious and thrifty and were making economic gains; then began the wave of foreign immigration, which continued to swell until, economically, it all but submerged them."

During this terrible time of reaction, a time curiously called The Age of Jacksonian Democracy, wall after wall was thrown up in the white mind. Special laws were passed banning black competition. Special laws were passed barring blacks from banks and savings and loan associations. The Maryland law of 1852, for example, not only prohibited blacks from becoming stockholders and depositors in white banks, it also prohibited blacks from organizing black banks.

The ultimate deterrent, of course, was violence. During the peak years of the reaction, in the 1830s and 1840s, there were repeated riots in Northern cities against black workers and black businessmen. The whites of Philadelphia exploded in 1834, 1838, and 1843. There were major race riots in New York City in 1834 and in Pittsburgh in 1839.

The impact of all this on the black community was as predictable as it was unfortunate. In some cases blacks were forced to flee cities, leaving behind all their worldly goods. In other cases the customers and trades of black workers and businessmen were literally stolen at gunpoint. In still other cases black entrepreneurs lost their nerve and yielded the battleground to their adversaries. Consider, for example, the case of the celebrated Robert Boyd, who manufactured furniture in Cincinnati, Ohio, and sold merchandise in the West and South. Boyd's success angered Cincinnati whites who burned his factory. Boyd rebuilt the factory and whites burned it down again. Boyd rebuilt the factory a third and a fourth time and the factory was burned down a third and a fourth time. At this point the insurance company decided that Boyd was a bad risk and he was forced to yield the ground to his competitors.

The risks, as this example shows, were great; but so also were the stakes; and many black businessmen stood their ground, developing, as a counterpoise to the wave of reaction, a black economic development ideology which stressed perseverance, hard work, initiative, and an independent or quasi-independent black economy.

This ideology was propagated by black preachers, black newspapers, and black conventions. Bishop Richard Allen, for instance, told his parishioners not to take literally the biblical injunction against laying up treasures on earth. Bishop Allen apparently accepted his own advice for he left an estate valued at some $25,000, amassed largely in real estate speculation. Other leading advocates of black economic development were Frederick Douglass, the abolitionist and newspaper owner; David Walker, a Boston clothing merchant who authored the fiery *Walker's Appeal*; and Martin Delany, the pioneer black nationalist. Delany's message was blunt and simple: "Let our young men and women prepare themselves for usefulness, trading and other things of importance. . . .

Educate them for the store and the Counting House . . . . to do everyday practical business."

It is customary today to sneer at the "petit-bourgeois pretensions" of Delany and other black leaders of this period. There is some truth in this criticism, but it is the truth of an ahistoricism which refuses to consider historical coordinates and seems to believe that men can do anything at anytime irrespective of material conditions. It is true that some black leaders shared the characteristic illusions of the age. But it is also true that the call for black economic development by any means necessary was historically progressive and indeed unavoidable in that pre-Marxian epoch. Progressive or not, it was the only choice blacks had. History did not offer them a choice between socialism and capitalism. The choice they were offered was economic independence or re-enslavement and/or death.

Considering the alternative, it is scarcely surprising that black businessmen opted for economic development. In the years between 1840 and 1860, they pressed forward, defending their modest gains, turning this way and that, trying to find windbreaks for the black spirit. Many failed and went to the wall of misery. But some succeeded, leaving behind coins of the spirit, if not of the realm. The New York State census of 1850 is important testimony in this regard, for it establishes that a surprisingly large number of blacks were still on the front lines of the economy. According to this evidence, the black business community of that state included two hatters, three jewelers, two confectioners, eleven inkmakers, twenty-one boardinghouse keepers, eight cigarmakers, twenty-three tailors, twenty-three shoemakers, and more than one hundred barbers. Similar progress was reported in Philadelphia, Boston, Cincinnati, and other Northern centers of black business activity.

What perhaps is most astonishing is that free black artisans dominated some sectors of the Southern economy. In cities like Charleston and New Orleans, a disproportionately large number of the leading mechanics, tailors, shoe manufacturers, cigarmakers, barbers, and butchers were black. One of Charleston's leading hotels was owned and operated by Jehu Jones, a free black. Another free black, Anthony Weston, was one of the most celebrated millwrights in the South. Weston also developed a threshing machine.

Of similar tone and texture, though more pointed, was the ferment in New Orleans. Martin Delany, the chronicler of the "free" black business group, said: "There is nothing more common in the city of New Orleans, than Colored Clerks, Salesmen, and Business men. In many stores on Chartier, Camp, and other business streets, there may always be seen colored men and women, as salesmen and saleswomen, behind the counter." In the 1840s there were at least eight black brokers in New Orleans who speculated on cotton futures and performed some of the services of a commercial bank. There were several large cigar manufacturers, including George Alcés, who employed two hundred workers. It was during this period that Norbert Rillieux, a wealthy black engineer, invented and patented a vacuum cup that revolutionized the sugar industry. Rillieux later moved to France.

Perhaps the most important aspect of the changes under discussion was the continued growth of the catering industry, particularly on the East Coast. At the height of the white reaction of the 1830s and 1840s, the black caterers of Philadelphia regrouped and extended their spheres of influence. This development has been admirably documented by W. E. B. DuBois, who said that "it was at this time that there arose to prominence and power as remarkable a trade guild as ever ruled in a medieval city. It took complete leadership of the bewildered group of Negroes, and led them steadily on to a degree of affluence, culture, and respect such as has probably never been surpassed in the history of the Negro in America. This was the guild of the caterers, and its masters include names which have been household words .... for fifty years: Bogle, Augustin, Prosser, Dorsey, Jones, and Minton."

The triumvirate of Thomas J. Dorsey, Henry Jones, and Henry Minton led the catering renaissance and virtually ruled the fashionable world of Philadelphia from 1845 to 1875. At a time, as DuBois notes, "when social circles were very exclusive, and the millionaire and the French cook had not yet arrived," these caterers filled a unique niche in the world of fashion. Looking back on this period some years later, a white Philadelphia reporter said: "Dorsey was one of the triumvirate of colored caterers—the other two being Henry Jones and Henry Minton—who some years ago might have been said to rule the social world of Philadelphia through its stomach. Time was when lobster salad, chicken croquettes, deviled crabs, and terrapin composed the edible display at every Philadelphia gathering, and none of those dishes were thought to be perfectly prepared unless they came from the hands of one of the three men named."

If reliance can be placed on the testimony of contemporary observers, blacks were also the leaders of fashion in other areas. One Mr. Cordovell, a mercer and tailor, reportedly dominated the New Orleans fashion world for more than twenty-five years. To quote Martin Delany again, "The reported fashions of Cordovell are said to have frequently become the leading fashions of Paris; and the writer was informed, by . . . a leading merchant tailor in a populous city that many of the eastern American reports were nothing more than a copy, in some cases modified, of those of Cordovell." Cordovell later moved to France where he created fashions for Paris houses.

Nor was Cordovell unique. John Jones was equally esteemed in Chicago where he accumulated a $100,000 fortune and constructed one of the city's first office buildings. Other leading tailors and clothing merchants were Henry Topp of Albany, New York, and Thomas Dalton, who operated a large Boston clothing store and left property valued at $500,000.

For reasons that are not readily apparent, black businessmen were a force to be reckoned with in the wholesale and retail grocery trade. Most of the black grocers owned businesses in downtown sections, and some operated in interstate commerce. Of these grocers, none attracted more public attention than Samuel T. Wilcox, a former boat steward who opened a wholesale grocery store at Broadway and Fifth in Cincinnati in 1850 and became the largest dealer in provisions in the city with an annual turnover of $140,000. His operations extended southward to New Orleans and eastward to Baltimore, New York, and Boston. Wilcox, like many of the major grocers of the time, owned and operated a pickling and preservative business. Wilcox had no monopoly on the midwest market. The firm of Thompson and Cooley operated on the same scale in Cincinnati, and there were major grocers and provisions merchants in other sections. Edward Hamlin had a grocery store on Main Street in Petersburg, Virginia, and Solomon Humphries of Macon, Georgia, reportedly "had more credit than any other merchant in town."

At that juncture black businessmen also held prominent and, in some cases, preeminent positions in the coal and lumber industry. A striking case in point is Robert Gordon, a Richmond, Virginia, slave, who ran a coal yard for his master, who permitted him to keep the profits from the sale of coal slack. Gordon saved several thousand dollars, bought his freedom and moved to Cincinnati where he invested $15,000 in a coal yard and built a private dock on the waterfront. His success disturbed white competitors who tried to destroy him by price cutting. Gordon's response was ingenious and extremely effective. Carter Woodson said he "sent to the coal yards of his competitors mulattoes who would pass for white, using them to fill his current orders from his foe's supplies that he might save his own for the convenient day. In the course of a few months the river and all the canals by which coal was brought to Cincinnati froze and remained so until spring. Gordon was then able to dispose of his coal at a higher price than it had ever been sold in that city. This so increased his wealth and added to his reputation that no one thereafter thought of opposing him." Gordon later invested heavily in Walnut Hill real estate and Union bonds.

Similarly gifted with the midas touch was Stephen Smith, a lumber merchant and money lender who was one of the wealthiest blacks in America. Smith operated the largest lumber yard in Columbia, Pennsylvania, and was the senior partner of the firm of Smith and Whipper. The size and range of his business can be gauged from an 1849 inventory which indicated that he owned or controlled several thousand bushels of coal, 2,250,000 feet of lumber, 22 cars on the Philadelphia to Baltimore railroad, $9,000 in Columbia Bridge stock, and $18,000 in Columbia Bank stock. In later years Smith spent a great deal of time buying negotiable paper and lending money. He owned fifty-two brick houses in Philadelphia and left property worth $500,000.

Then as now, blacks were negligible factors in the money markets. But even at this early date, there were private bankers and financiers of note. Most of these private bankers lent money accumulated in other occupations. John C. Stanley, a Berne, North Carolina, barber and farmer, amassed property worth $40,000 by barbering, farming, and discounting notes. Peter Van Dyke of New York City accumulated a fortune of $50,000, some of which came from lending money at interest. Perhaps the leading black financier was Thomy Lafon, a New Orleans merchant and money-lender who left an estate of $500,000.

Of the scores of prominent black businessmen in this field and others, the following should at least be noted: William Goodrich, a York, Pennsylvania, financier, who was a major investor in the Baltimore-Lancaster road and owned ten railroad cars; Reuben West, a well-to-do Richmond barber; William H. Riley, a Philadelphia bootmaker; Edward V. Clark, a New York jeweler; George T. Downing, proprietor of one of the main resorts in Newport, Rhode Island; Lunsford Lane, a North Carolina merchant and tobacco manufacturer; Robert Adgar, a Philadelphia hardware and furniture dealer; Henry M. Collins, a Pittsburgh real estate broker; Robert Purvis, a Pennsylvania farmer; J. Pressley and Thomas Ball, Cincinnati photographers; William Wormley, a Washington, D. C., businessman who owned one of the largest stables of riding and driving horses in the South; Henry Knight, who owned the largest livery stable in Chicago in 1852; Robert Clark and Albert Brooks, who owned large livery stables in Petersburg and Richmond, respectively; Dr. James McCune Smith, who operated two drug stores on Broadway in New York City; Henry Scott, a New York pickle manufacturer; and William Alexander Leidesdorff, a millionaire who built the first hotel in San Francisco, organized the first commercial horse race in California, and owned a 35,000-acre ranch.

Black businessmen also operated foundries, made rope, and manufactured hair oil. They were to be found, according to contemporary reports, in practically every industry and occupation. We also learn from contemporary accounts that the spirit of trade and commerce ran deep in the black population. Much of the trading near railroad stations and boat terminals in the North and South, for instance, was controlled by male and female black hucksters.

While the total number of blacks engaged in business appears to have been relatively small, yet this fact, if it is a fact, does not mean that the black community was unaffected by the widespread attempts to realize the black economic potential. In 1853, according to a state convention, New York blacks owned property worth $1 million in thirteen counties and had invested $839,000 in businesses in and around New York City. In 1856 Philadelphia blacks owned $800,000 in real estate. At the outbreak of the Civil War, Washington (D.C.) blacks owned $630,000 in real estate, and New Orleans blacks owned $15,000,000 in taxable property. According to conservative estimates, the total real and personal wealth of free blacks in 1860 was $50,000,000. At that point blacks owned nine thousand homes, fifteen thousand farms, and two thousand businesses.

There is one final point to be noted. With of course remarkable exceptions, the pioneer black businessmen were major supporters of the struggle for black liberation. Almost all of the major black abolitionists —Douglass, Delany, Garnet, Jones, Walker—were involved in one way or another with black economic development and not a few were merchants and/or artisans. James Forten, for example, refused to sell riggings to slaveowners, and Paul Cuffee refused slave-related cargoes. Cuffee, moreover, was a leading advocate of African emigration and used his money to build schools in America and colonies in Sierra Leone. John Jones led the fight against the Illinois Black Codes, gave generously to humanitarian causes and sheltered slaves in his home and office. Most of the Philadelphia caterers were supporters of the abolitionist movement, and some of them, notably Thomas Dorsey, served politics with their food. Dorsey, a white reporter wrote, "had the sway of an imperial dictator. When a Democrat asked his menial service he refused, because 'he could not wait on a party of persons who were disloyal to the government and Lincoln'—pointing to the picture in his reception rooms —'was the government.'" This was not, it should be noted, a matter of rhetoric. Many black businessmen contributed heavily to black causes. As a matter of fact, James Forten, Robert Purvis, and other black businessmen were among the major angels of the Abolitionist movement.

The funds accumulated in the first black businesses were also used to lighten the burden of orphans and widows. Stephen Smith gave $150,000 for the establishment of a home for aged and infirm colored people in Philadelphia. Edward Green, a junk dealer, contributed $73,000 to the same fund, and Henry and Sarah Gordon, caterers, donated $66,000.

There were, of course, men and women who adopted a "business is business" attitude. Some barbers and merchants refused to serve blacks; and big black planters like Cyprian Ricard, who owned a $225,000 Louisiana plantation and ninety-one slaves, were beyond the pale. But Ricard and the men who shared his view were apparently in the minority. For the Fortens and Cuffees and Purvises, and for most of their friends and associates, the real business of black business was liberation.

S*TORIES* in childhood fables to the contrary, it was neither love nor principle which freed the slave. Not New England Puritanism nor Western idealism, not Christianity nor democracy, not one of the big words men use to ennoble their struggles and to hide their real motives—not one of these, for all the books written since in their defense, broke the chain of the slave. That feat was accomplished by money or, to be more precise, the forces of greed massed behind money.

It was the massed power of Northern industrialism; it was the feverish expansion of Northern capital, poised for the kill and stymied by planter arrogance; it was the spirit of the factory; it was the spirit of the railroad and of the telegraph and of what the railroad and factory and telegraph symbolized and promised: these forces *created the situation* which forced the freeing of the slave. The same forces, in uneasy alliance with liberals and abolitionists, many of whom had other dreams, forced the enfranchisement of blacks, the better to perpetuate the defeat of the planters. And when the victory of Northern industrialism was secured beyond the possibility of repeal or recall, when the land was girthed by railroads and parceled out to industrial magnates, when it seemed that men were going to make more money than anyone had ever thought possible, the same forces, anxious now for peace and stability, routed the liberals and abolitionists and helped Southern Bourbons push blacks back towards slavery.

Money gave and money took away.

Does this mean that the leaders of the struggle against slavery were motivated primarily by economic considerations? By no means. The meaning is merely that the forces of industrialization created the climate which made it possible for politicians and abolitionists to rally public sentiment against slavery.

This process has been analyzed with great subtletly and perception by Abram L. Harris (*The Negro as Capitalist*), who said the real factors in the drama of the Civil War were "the rise of big business, the displacement of handicraft production by the factory system, the triumph of industry over agriculture." Continuing, Harris said: "As these forces gathered momentum, the life of the small property owner, independent farmer, and artisan, both black and white, became increasingly precarious. But the same economic forces, culminating in the ascendancy of the capitalist economy after the Civil War, disrupted the slave regime and brought about the liberation of the slave." In other words, the same forces that midwifed the Revolution of Reconstruction dug its grave.

It is scarcely possible to deal with the history of the black businessmen unless we make at least the effort to understand this process. For it was "the ascendancy of the capitalist economy [in a climate of racism]" which thwarted the promising prewar economic developments and shunted blacks to the margins of commerce and industry. As has been shown, black entrepreneurs made small but important gains in the 1840s and 1850s. But these entrepreneurs were left at the starting gate in the crucial Civil War period when the foundations of the great fortunes were laid. This war may have been Hell to Sherman and his soldiers, but to the thousands who made superprofits on war contracts, loans, and the rising price of manufactured goods it was a hustler's paradise. This is not the place to rehearse the appalling scramble for profits in the North, and the point of all this is to stress the fact that the war was a great divide on the economic as well as the political level. The war produced the country's first class of supermagnates (Gould, Vanderbilt, Rockefeller, Armour) and created a wide gulf between the old-fashioned individual entrepreneur and the emerging industrial directorate. Few blacks were in a position to profit from this development and even fewer blacks had a desire to profit from a war which was fought ostensibly to free black people. Place and principle apart, however, the hard economic fact is that black businessmen lost ground by remaining in the same place. They entered the war competing with merchants who had large but not limitless funds; they emerged in the postwar period with the same small enterprises, but their competitors had improved their economic position and had preempted the high ground and most of the resources. The key fact of black economic development—to repeat—is that the war which freed blacks created the economic structures which made black economic development—and hence black freedom—difficult and sometimes impossible.

This paradox dominated black economic life from 1865 to 1873. It explains the curious fact that the triumphant Republicans made blacks the political masters of Southern whites but denied them forty acres of land and a mule. It explains the tacit agreement between Northern and Southern power brokers that the freed blacks would be restricted to marginal and menial occupations. It explains the failure of the missionary campaign to create a black economic system based on hard work, individual initiative, and thrift.

Nothing dramatizes this paradox more ironically than the failure of the Freedmen's Bank, which was the second omen—the failure of land reform was the first—in the economic story of the postwar years. The Freedmen's Savings and Trust Company was founded on the initiative of missionaries and Freedmen's Bureau officials and was chartered in 1865 by the U.S. government. It was generally and erroneously believed that funds deposited in the bank were protected by the government. This misconception was systematically propagated by the managers of the bank. A U.S. Senate committee said later: "The pass book issued to the depositors in the Freedmen's Bank bore on its cover the likeness of President Lincoln, General Grant, also General Howard and others whom the freedmen had learned to revere as the special benefactors of their race. The flag of the United States was draped over the buildings, and designed to assure them that the United States would protect their interest."

The bank was an extension of the military savings banks established during the war to safeguard the funds of black soldiers and workers. At the end of the war there were tens of thousands of dollars of unclaimed deposits ($200,000 in the Beaufort, South Carolina, bank alone) of black soldiers who had disappeared or had died without leaving surviving relatives. The bank was established, in part, as a depository for these unclaimed funds.

A quasi-philanthropic enterprise, "organized and controlled by white friends of the Negro ostensibly for his benefit," the bank was also created to encourage thrift and individual initiative in the black community. No one expressed this approach and philosophy more eloquently than Frederick Douglass, who issued the following statement after he became the last president of the bank.

"The history of civilization shows that no people can well rise to a high degree of mental or even moral excellence without wealth. A people uniformly poor and compelled to struggle for barely a physical existence will be dependent and despised by their neighbors and will finally despise themselves. While it is impossible that every individual of any race shall be rich—and no man may be despised for merely being poor—yet no people can be respected which does not produce a wealthy class. Such a people will only be hewers of wood and drawers of water and will not rise above a mere animal existence. The mission of the Freedmen's Bank is to show our people the road to a share of the wealth and well being of the world. . . ."

As it happened, the road to a share of the wealth of the world was long and hard and mined with booby traps. One of the problems was that the bank which was to show blacks the road to wealth was operated and controlled initially by a curious mélange of missionaries and mercenaries. Far worse was the fact that the affairs of the bank were conducted in secret by a small clique of plunderers who were trying to find *their* road. There was, of course, a reverse side to this coin. Blacks were later appointed to the advisory boards and boards of trustees in some cities. The bank also employed black cashiers and tellers.

The bank began hopefully enough and by the end of the first year there were branches in Louisville, Richmond, Nashville, Wilmington,

Memphis, Mobile, and Vicksburg. By 1871 there were thirty-four branches, thirty-two of them in Southern cities. At its peak the bank had seventy thousand depositors and total deposits of $19,952,647.

For most blacks, the bank was a symbol of black liberation. We catch a glimpse of what the bank meant to blacks of that day in Douglass's poetical description of activities in the $260,000 headquarters in Washington, D.C.

"In passing it on the street I often peeped into its spacious windows, and looked down the row of its gentlemanly and elegantly dressed colored clerks, with their pens behind their ears and button-hole bouquets in the coatfronts, and felt my very eyes enriched. It was a sight I had never expected to see. I was amazed with the facility with which they counted the money. They threw off the thousands with the dexterity, if not the accuracy of the old experienced clerks. The whole thing was beautiful. I had read of this bank when I lived in Rochester, and had indeed been solicited to become one of its trustees, and had reluctantly consented to do so; but when I came to Washington and saw its magnificent brown stone front, its towering height, its perfect appointments and the fine display it made in the transaction of its business, I felt like the Queen of Sheba when she saw the riches of Solomon, that 'the half had not been told me.'"

The half had *not* been told. The view from the gallery was impressive; but behind the scenes things were going from bad to worse. Unbeknown to Douglass and other black leaders, the bank had fallen into the hands of predators, who were making loans to one another and investing in overcapitalized and speculative ventures. According to later investigations, the bank was virtually controlled in its final years by the notorious New York financier, Jay Cooke. By 1872 the bank had been virtually destroyed by mismanagement and fraud.

As economic conditions deteriorated in 1873, the wily white directors threw out a net for a big black name to hide behind. Frederick Douglass, who was unaware of the real state of affairs, was persuaded to accept the honor. Then came the Panic of 1873 and disaster. Douglass ordered drastic economies and even invested $10,000 of his own money in the bankrupt institution. It was all to no avail; and Douglass, sadder but wiser, recommended that the bank close its doors.

The failure of the Freedmen's Bank had repercussions of the gravest sort in the black community. The newly freed blacks lost more than one million of their hard-bought dollars, and the government made no effort to reimburse them. The loss in the realm of the spirit was equally great. "Not even ten additional years of slavery," W. E. B. DuBois said, "could have done so much to throttle the thrift of the freedmen as the mismanagement and bankruptcy of the series of savings banks chartered by the Nation for their special aid."

*MEANWHILE*, all the while, on another plane of existence, that of political expressiveness, blacks were making a desperate attempt to convert their ballots into bread and land. At this juncture black voters outnumbered white voters in several Southern states, and they tried to use their political power for the economic development of the black community.

It quickly became apparent to the first generation of free blacks that political control over lien, land, and tariff policy is economic power of the first order. And as one examines the records of that period one is struck by the repeated attempts of black politicians to use their political power for economic ends. In all or most of the Southern states, as was shown in the last chapter, black politicians passed liberal tenancy, credit, and land legislation.

With this far-reaching change in the political climate, there came a fresh and potent encouragement to black entrepreneurs. Nothing else explains the existence of scores of big black planters with large and flourishing plantations. Typical of these planters were U.S. Senator Blanche Kelso Bruce, who owned a one thousand-acre plantation in the Mississippi Delta; Congressman J. T. Rapier, who owned a large farm in Lauderdale County, Alabama; and Benjamin T. Montgomery, who owned the baronial Jefferson Davis plantation at Davis Bend, Mississippi, and was said to be one of the best planters in Mississippi.

Although the big planters were a distinct minority, the fact that they existed at all a few years after slavery is significant. It is also significant that thousands of blacks slowly and painfully accumulated enough money to buy a mule and a few acres of land. There are no reliable figures on the number of blacks who acquired land in this period, but indirect evidence indicates that the number was considerable. By the mid-seventies, according to Charles Nordhoff, a contemporary reporter, the black people of Georgia owned "nearly 400,000 acres of farming real estate, besides city property."

An even more graphic statement came from Albert T. Morgan, a

Radical Republican politician in Yazoo County, Mississippi. "Several of the colored planters," he wrote, "were in quite independent circumstances. Their wives and daughters no longer worked in the cotton and corn fields. Each one owned a carriage, not always of the best pattern, to be sure, but ample for the family and sufficiently elegant in appointments for country uses. In some instances, it was 'old marstah's' family carriage reconstructed. Many more colored men owned livestock, horses, mules, cows, sheep, hogs, and chicken innumerable. The total value of the property of the colored people of Yazoo at that date [1874] was not less than a million and a half dollars. They were in truth rising. Indeed there was danger that 'our nigros would, before long, own the whole country.' "

Morgan touched the point precisely—the economic threat that the enfranchised blacks posed to the defenders of the status quo. And it was to meet this threat that whites organized a campaign of terror and intimidation. Some planters hired terrorists to assassinate black farmers and to burn down their homes and barns. Other planters banded together in associations which refused to rent or sell farm land to blacks.

Under these circumstances, the farms available to blacks were generally on inferior or indifferent land. It is not surprising, therefore, that many black farmers were wiped out by a series of bad crops and the Depression of 1873. Some of these farmers gave up and made no further effort, but others persisted and made impressive gains. And it was this persistence in the face of adversity which led the Florida African Methodist Episcopal Conference to pass the following resolution: "Whereas labor is the basis of all wealth, and wealth is an absolute necessity of civilized society, and a peaceful condition of society. . . . *Resolved* by the convention of ministers and laymen of the Methodist Episcopal Church of Florida, that we congratulate our people upon the rapid progress they have made in the past six years, and upon the increase of mixed industry, homesteads, and small farms in opposition to the ruinous plantation system, and [we consider] those together with the increase in school houses and churches, and also the deposit of nearly three million dollars in the savings-banks, as a greater pledge of our progress to the friends of freedom throughout the world than can be found in the house of any people who sprang from as lowly a condition as ourselves. . . ."

A further consequence of political power was access to patronage in the larger sense of the word, i.e., control over the granting of lucrative contracts and other modes of enrichment. Richard J. Cain, the South Carolina congressman who later became an AME bishop, was one of the biggest real estate operators in the Charleston area; and James Hill, the Mississippi secretary of state, was deeply involved in railroad and real estate deals.

At the other end of the spectrum were corporate leaders like A. J. Ransier and F. L. Cardozo. Ransier, who was the lieutenant governor of South Carolina, and Cardozo, who was the state treasurer, were among the major stockholders and directors of the Greenville and Columbus Railroad. Cardozo and another black politician, J. H. Rainey, were among the organizers and directors of the Columbia Street Railway Company. C. C. Antoine, the Louisiana politician, was one of the incorporators of the Shreveport Bank and Trust Company which had "the sole and exclusive right" to erect works to supply the city with water and gas and to run a ferry across the Mississippi River. Similar corporate posts were held by other black leaders, who sat on the boards of directors of steamship companies, oil corporations, phosphate factories, and banks.

Parallel with this development there was an expansion of the black merchant class. Slowly at first and then with deeper and deeper commitment, black businessmen developed small businesses (coal and wood yards, restaurants, stores, barber shops) and began to think of larger enterprises.

One of the most striking features of this period, from the point of view of our problem, was the development of black corporations. As an example of this development we might consider the formation of the Chesapeake Marine and Dry Dock Company, which was created by black caulkers, carpenters, and mechanics after they were denied work on the Baltimore docks. The excluded workers banded together and bought a shipyard and marine railway. Before long they were doing more repair work than any of their competitors.

But the Chesapeake Marine and Dry Dock Company is only one case in point. Under the leadership of Tom Lang, a Union veteran, black South Carolinians raised $20,000 in capital and organized the Star Spangled Banner Association. The corporation opened a store in Beaufort and bought a steamer which operated along the South Carolina coast under the direction of Captain Robert Smalls of Civil War fame.

There were analogous examples in virtually every Southern and Border state. Travelling in the South in 1875, Charles Nordhoff saw "men who were slaves but ten years ago, and began life with nothing at that time now driving magnificent horses, seated in stylish equipages, and wearing diamond breastpins." In Georgia, he said, there were "many colored mechanics, and they receive full wages where they are skillful. Near Atlanta and other places they own small 'truck farms,' and supply the market with vegetables. There are fewer black than white beggars in the cities."

We have to be careful about this. Important as these changes were, they did not in themselves constitute economic power. They were rather the first tender shoots of an economic growth which was ripped out by the roots after the destruction of black political power in 1877. With the withdrawal of federal protection and the violent overthrow of the Radical Republican governments in the South, the black economic thrust was halted and in some cases reversed.

Another factor having deep disintegrative effects on black economic development was the steady encroachment on the traditional markets of black merchants, many of whom still serviced black and white customers in downtown locations. In the last decades of the nineteenth century and the first decades of the twentieth, most of these merchants were overwhelmed and destroyed, economically and psychologically, by the rising tides of industrialism and racism. Nowhere was this more clearly visible than in Philadelphia. In his classic study, *The Philadelphia Negro*, DuBois documented the slow and painful retreat of black retail store owners in the late 1890s. "Today," he wrote, ". . . the application of large capital to the retail business, the gathering of workmen into factories, the wonderful success of trained talent in catering to the whims and tastes of customers almost preclude the effective competition of the small store. Thus the economic condition of the day militates largely against the Negro; it requires more skill and experience to run a small store than formerly and the large store and factory are virtually closed to [the black merchant] on any terms."

What DuBois said about retail store owners was true also—though with important modifications—of black barbers, who also were losing ground. There were, in DuBois's opinion, three primary reasons for this. First of all, "the calling was for so long an almost exclusively Negro calling that it came in for a degree of the contempt and ridicule poured on Negroes in general; it therefore grew very unpopular among Negroes, and apprentices became very scarce." Second, "the business became unpopular with Negroes because it compelled them to draw a color line. No first-class Negro barber would dare shave his own brother in his shop in Philadelphia on account of the color prejudice. This was peculiarly galling and has led to much criticism and unpopularity for certain leading barbers among their own people." Third, the competition of German and Italian barbers. "They were skilled workmen," DuBois said, "while skilled Negro barbers were becoming scarce; they cut down the customary prices and some of them found business cooperation and encouragement which Negroes could not hope for. For these reasons the business is slipping from the Negro." Also slipping from the Negro was the catering business, which blacks had virtually invented. At the time of the DuBois study, blacks were still prominent in the catering business, but they no longer dominated the field.

What was the reason for their decline?

"The chief reason for this," DuBois wrote, "is the change that has come over American fashionable society in the last twenty-five years, and the application of large capital to the catering business.... Thus we find a large business built up by talent and tact, meeting with changed social conditions; the business must change too. It is the old development from the small to the large industry, from the house-industry to the concentrated industry, from the private dining room to the palatial hotel. If the Negro caterers of Philadelphia had been white, some of them would have been put in charge of a large hotel, or would have become co-partners in some large restaurant business, for which capitalists furnished funds."

The black caterers of Philadelphia and other urban centers were not white—and so they went to the wall. And DuBois concluded: "It is thus plain that a curious economic revolution in one industry has gone on during thirty-nine years, not unaccompanied by grave social problems. In this case the Negro has emerged in better conditions and has shown more capacity for hand to hand economic encounter than, for instance, in the barbering business. Yet he has not emerged unscathed; in every such battle, when a Negro is fighting for an economic advantage, there is ever a widespread feeling among all his neighbors that it is inexpedient to allow this class to become wealthy or even well-to-do. Consequently the battle always becomes an *Athanasius contra mundum*, where almost unconsciously the whole countenance and aid of the community is thrown against the Negro."

There you have it, then—the system of internal colonialism, cited in the last two chapters, as the major obstacle to black economic development.

As the great octopus of this system grew, spreading its tentacles across the whole landscape of black life, the black business world contracted. White customers started drawing the color line in their dealings with black merchants, and white property owners stopped leasing to black businessmen, who began a one-way migration to the black Main Streets —Auburn Avenue in Atlanta, Beale Street in Memphis, South State in Chicago, Lombard in Philadelphia, Lenox and Seventh in Harlem.

Not content with the white Main Street triumph, white merchants pursued black merchants into the black community and laid claim to the so-called Negro trade. The "freeing" of blacks had created an enormous black market, and white merchants were not slow in recognizing its significance. As early as the 1870s, Charles Nordhoff noted that "the Negro is the principal producer in Mississippi, and since the war he has become a large consumer also. . . . The men who have the Negro trade all get rich."

Most of the men who were getting rich, particularly after the destruction of black political power, were white. Most of the money earned by blacks never touched a black hand: it was appropriated before payday by the plantation owner and the owner of the plantation store, usually the same person. Most of the remaining dollars were appropriated by white peddlers and merchants. Many of these merchants, as M. S. Stuart and other students have noted, were "of Jewish or foreign extraction," but many were also of Anglo-Saxon extraction, and there can be little doubt that Anglo-Saxons ended up with the lion's share. On most of the black Main Streets, to quote Stuart's valuable study (*An Economic Detour*) "the number, the volume of patronage, and the capitalization of business establishments [owned by whites] exceed by far Negro business units . . . Negro merchants offer only feeble competition to them."

SUCH in brief is the story of the varying fortunes of black businessmen in the postwar era. To understand the black response to this situation, it is necessary to go back now and reconstruct the bridges of self-determination that black people built for themselves.

The first bridge was the black church. From 1865 onward most black people were engaged in a frenzy of church organizing and church building. And by 1876 the black South was linked by a network of churches of every denomination and persuasion. Because they were generally the largest buildings in the area, because they were usually the only major buildings owned by blacks and because they touched all of the raw nerves in the black body politic, these churches soon became the social, spiritual, *and* eonomic centers of the community.

The church, then and now, was about the hereafter. But in the first years of freedom it was also an instrument for dealing with the hazards of the here. Whatever the preacher believed, whatever he said, it was necessary for him to speak to the problems of life, particularly the age-old scourges, economic adversity, sickness, and death. Thus it was that the mutual aid or benevolent society became a central part of the theology of the postwar black churches. These societies were in form and in fact embryonic insurance and burial societies, and most of them had their origin, as W. J. Trent Jr., has observed, in the minister's "attempt to hedge against illness and death through his church organization. Practically every church of any size throughout the country had one or more of such benevolent organizations attached to it." These societies were of fundamental importance for four reasons: 1) They provided indispensable emergency services in the crisis-laden days following slavery; 2) They provided business and civic training for ministers and laymen; 3) They were concrete examples of what individuals could do for themselves by pooling their limited resources; 4) They were the cocoons from which emerged several of the major black insurance companies.

Somewhat more worldly but equally relevant to our study were the bridges erected by the fraternal organizations, which were major factors in the black community from 1865 to 1915. During the whole of this period there were lodges of fraternal orders (Masons, Elks, Odd Fellows, True Reformers, etc.) in every city with a sizeable black population, and most of the social and political life of the community revolved around the meetings, conventions, and interminable feuding of lodge members.

These orders collected large amounts of money. (One student estimated that blacks contributed $168 million to fraternal orders between 1870 and 1920.) The money came from an endless variety of dues and assessments. There were local dues, grand lodge dues, supreme grand lodge dues. There were initiation fees, grand lodge fees, supreme lodge fees, and special fees. There were assessments for endowment, education, and the building fund. Most of the fraternal orders also sold paraphernalia and operated insurance or "endowment" departments.

It is not hard, with benefit of hindsight, to see the opportunities, and the dangers, and the temptations of all this. The fraternal orders made available to black leaders more money than they had ever dreamed of. And, not surprisingly, some order leaders soon lost sight of the original purposes of the organizations.

Whatever the motivations of the leaders, the fraternal orders soon became the dominant economic force in the black community. Some orders, as we shall see, created the first black banks, primarily as a depository for order funds. Others loaned mortgage money to their members. Still others started business enterprises. The Grand Lodge of Masons of Mississippi, for example, bought one thousand acres of timber land and went into the lumber business. The True Reformers organized a bank, a chain of retail stores, a hotel, a newspaper, an old folks home, and an all-black community called Browneville. The Independent Order of St. Luke, under the leadership of a dynamic black woman, Maggie L. Walker, operated a printing plant, a bank, an office building, a regalia and supply house, and an emporium.

The major foci of fraternal activity were land and mortar. Largely because of the activities of fraternal orders, this period was characterized by an unprecedented black building boom. The black building boom leaped from community to community, as an electric current leaps across a series of galvanic poles, sweeping the lodge brothers into action and setting them to striving to outdo one another for the good of the order. But many lodge leaders overestimated the economic need for large buildings, and the title of most of the property passed into the hands of whites. Despite the perils, the building frenzy stirred every nerve in the black community, and some fraternal leaders held on to the very end. Perhaps the major building coup of this period was engineered by the Odd Fellows of Georgia, under the leadership of the fiery BenjaminT. Davis. In 1912 the Georgia Odd Fellows bought a whole block of land on Auburn Avenue in Atlanta and constructed a five-story building at a cost of $250,000. The next year the group built an auditorium on the rest of the land at a cost of $180,000. At about the same time, the order exploded in an orgy of recrimination, charges, and counter-charges. It was impossible to resolve the personal disputes, and the order went into receivership in 1916.

Students of the fraternal orders are critical of the mismanagement, financial abuses, squabbling, and conspicuous consumption that characterized some fraternal orders. But there is general agreement that the orders laid the foundation for the first black old-line legal insurance companies. Moreover, as M. S. Stuart pointed out, the orders were "kindergartens in civil government" and high finance. Equally important, in the long sight of history, the orders exposed black leaders to "larger sums of money than, perhaps, would have been otherwise possible, thus causing them to think in greater financial terms, and to organize banks and other financial institutions."

Supported by the bridges of the church, mutual aid societies and the fraternal orders, black businessmen moved in the 1880s to a new ledge of economic activity, organizing the first black banks and the first black insurance companies. The first black-owned banks were organized in 1888, fifteen years after the Freedmen's Bank debacle. The Capital Savings Bank opened in Washington, D.C., in October, 1888. The Savings Bank of the Grand Fountain United Order of True Reformers was chartered in March, 1888, and opened in April, 1889. The Mutual Trust Company opened in that same year in Chattanooga, Tennessee, and the Alabama Penny Savings and Loan Company was organized in Birmingham in 1890. Between 1899 and 1905, twenty-eight banks were organized by blacks. Most of these banks were destroyed by mismanagement and the recurring depressions of the period. But the strongest survived, leaving behind a legacy of homes, businesses, and trained businessmen.

There was a close connection, as we have seen, between the founding of these banks and the fraternal orders and the black church. The True Reformers Bank was an organ of the True Reformers, which was organized in 1881 by a former slave, the Reverend William Washington Browne. The Reverend W. R. Pettiford, pastor of the Sixteenth Street Baptist Church, was the organizer and first president of the Alabama Penny Savings Bank. It is worth noting, at least for perspective, that the vice-president of the bank was a bartender.

The same forces and the same archetypal figures—preachers, fraternal leaders, teachers, and merchants—were instrumental in the organization of the first black insurance companies. John Merrick, a barber and a former agent of the True Reformers, was the central figure in the organization of North Carolina Mutual in 1898. Another barber, Alonzo F. Herndon, created the foundations of Atlanta Life in 1905 by buying two financially pressed church societies.

The founding fathers of North Carolina Mutual and Atlanta Life—

the two largest black insurance companies—were pivotal figures in the history of black business, and it would be well worth our time to spend a few minutes with them.

Both men were former slaves, both were barbers, and both were phenomenally successful in making and holding money. Merrick, who made his financial move first, was born in slavery in Clinton, North Carolina, on September 7, 1859. He taught himself to read and write and went to work at the age of twelve in a Chapel Hill brickyard. From that point onward he made his own breaks, picking up the rudiments of the barbering trade while shining shoes in a Raleigh barber shop and teaching himself the intricacies of high finance. In 1880 he moved to the big city of Durham. Twelve years later he was the owner of five barber shops and the personal barber of tobacco magnate Washington Duke.

Always frugal, always mindful of the value of a dollar, he invested heavily in real estate and branched out into the burgeoning fraternal business, organizing the Royal Knights of King David in 1883. Fifteen years later Merrick and a local physician, Dr. Aaron McDuffie Moore, were the prime movers in the organization of the North Carolina Mutual and Provident Association. The first years of the new organization were difficult, and most of the original incorporators dropped out. In 1900 Merrick and Moore reorganized the company and persuaded a young Durham grocer, C. C. Spaulding, to assume the position of general manager. Under the leadership of this trio, the new company, later named North Carolina Mutual, prospered. In 1918, one year before Merrick's death, the company had $16,096,722 insurance in force. By that time Merrick had played a key role in organizing a network of satellite organizations, including the Bull City Drug Company, the Merrick-Moore-Spaulding Real Estate Company, the Durham Textile Mill, and the Mechanics and Farmers Bank.

Alonzo F. Herndon was cut from the same mold. Born in slavery in Walton County, Georgia, on June 26, 1858, he picked up the skills of a barber at an early age and acquired several barber shops. In 1882, two years after Merrick moved to Durham, Herndon settled in Atlanta. From that time until he entered the insurance business, he was generally considered the finest barber in the city. In 1904 he furnished and opened a plush barber shop on Peachtree Street, which was said to be "the most popular and most successful business of its kind in the country." There then occurred an incident which changed the direction and the tenor of his life. In 1905 the Georgia legislature passed a law which required mutual aid societies to deposit $5,000 with state officials. Most of the mutual aid societies could not meet this requirement and Herndon stepped into the breach, buying several church associations, including two started by the Reverend P. J. Bryant and the Reverend J. A. Hopkins. Herndon bought the assets of the two associations for $160, and Atlanta Mutual (later changed to Atlanta Life) was launched in a one-room office in the Rucker Building on Auburn Avenue. In 1916 capital stock of $25,000 was subscribed and sold, with Herndon purchasing all except a few shares. Six years later, in 1922, the capital stock of the company was increased to $100,000, and again Herndon bought practically all of the shares. When he died in 1927, Atlanta Life was one of the major financial institutions of the black community.

Herndon and Merrick were obviously exceptional men, but the same wind blew, at lesser velocities, on other black Main Streets. In 1898, according to an Atlanta University study, there were 1900 black businesses in America. Most of these businesses were small retail outlets, but some were of substantial size.

There were additionally scores of black inventors, notably Jan E. Matzeliger who created the shoe-lasting machine and later sold the patent to the United Shoe Machine Company; Elijah McCoy, who acquired more than fifty patents relating to the automatic lubrication of moving machinery; Granville T. Woods, the holder of some fifty patents, including an incubator for hatching eggs, and the Synchronous Multiplex Railway Telegraph; and Garrett A. Morgan, who invented the automatic stop-sign and sold the patent to the General Electric Company for $40,000.

It was on these bridges—the bridge of the black church and the fraternal order, the bridge of the black bank and the insurance company, the bridge of the pioneer black entrepreneurs and inventors—that the black business community crossed over into the fateful world of the twentieth century.

*A*LL through the late nineteenth century, as America moved from the frenzy of the post-Reconstruction period into the turbulence of the modern world, the black community was alive with the restless coming and going of men and women. And it was in the coming and going of these men and women, tossed hither and yonder by large and menacing forces they did not understand and could not control, that the new economic world of black America was shaped.

That world was shaped, in part, as we have shown, by the motion of black people who constructed bridges of transit in response to the unrelenting pressures of rampant industrialism. But this response to external challenges triggered, in turn, internal changes, which reoriented large masses of blacks around new axes of interest.

Perhaps the most dramatic internal change, from the point of view of our study, was the development of a relatively small black bourgeoisie which defined itself initially in response to the economic pressures of the age and the impact of these pressures on the structures of the black community. To be sure, there were black bourgeoisie, as we have documented, in the seventeenth and eighteenth centuries. But in the post–Civil War period, largely as a result of the increasingly large number of graduates turned out by black colleges and the cadres trained by the Freedmen's Bank and the churches, lodges and pioneer black businesses, the black bourgeoisie increased in size and became a conscious and more or less organized structure of action and thought. The history of the black bourgeoisie—the history of its failures, its triumphs, its contradictions—cannot detain us here, but two points are crucially relevant to our discussion.

The first point is that the black bourgeoisie was a product of and a causal factor in black economic development in the last decades of the nineteenth century and the first decades of the twentieth. Engendered by the economic processes outlined above, the black bourgeoisie gave further impetus to these processes by leading a campaign of economic development. In fact, after the Compromise of 1877, economic development became an obsession of the black bourgeoisie. (Curiously enough, intense political reaction in the white community seems to trigger a campaign of economic development in the black community, as witness the 1890s, 1920s and the late 1960s.) Within a short time, one wing of the black bourgeoisie was elevating economic solutions above political solutions as offering the only panacea for the ills confronting the black community. The great and ambiguous spokesman for this trend was Booker T. Washington, who preached a gospel of hard work, thrift, business organization, and industrial education. "Here definitely," as Harry Haywood wrote, "was the voice of the embryonic Negro middle class, which, though staggered by the shock of the Hayes-Tilden sellout, was again desperately striving to reform its scattered ranks and break through to a place in the sun. . . ." Continuing, Haywood said: "Considering the times, the program of the sage of Tuskegee was by no means wholly negative. On the contrary, it had its positive features. His was an impressive voice of encouragement in the wilderness of isolation, inspiring some courage, some hope, in the routed ranks of Negro freedom. . . ." But, as most students, including Haywood, observe, these positive features were counterbalanced by a program of accommodation and conciliation on the political and cultural levels. Worse yet, the Washington program was based on a fatal misunderstanding of the connection between politics and economics and an equally fatal misunderstanding of the forces of the age.

The second decisive point here, a point usually overlooked by most commentators, black and white, is that Booker T. Washington was only one of several voices of the embryonic middle class. Washington was preceded in the role of middle class spokesmen by several men, notably Martin Delany and Frederick Douglass, and his position as the preeminent spokesman of black economic development was challenged in his lifetime by several men, notably John Hope and W. E. B. DuBois. As a matter of fact, the theoretical foundations of the black business movement were formulated by DuBois and his colleagues at the Fourth Annual Atlanta University Conference (1898) on "The Negro in Business." It was at this conference that John Hope, the future president of Morehouse College, made his famous speech on the need for a black business class.

> The Negro's status [Hope said] has changed considerably since the Civil War, but he is today to a great extent what he has always been in this country—the laborer, the day hand, the man who works for wages. The great hiring class is the white people. The Negro develops the resources, the white man pays him for his services. To be sure some few Negroes have accumulated a little capital. But the rule has been as I have stated: the white man has converted and reconverted the Negro's labor and the Negro's money into capital until we find an immense section of developed country owned by whites and worked by colored. . . . Let me say here, that while ignorance and incompetency may in some sense explain the mysterious departure of the Negro white-washer, carpenter, newsboy and washer-woman in many quarters, I have seen too many competent Negroes superseded by whites,—at times incompetent whites,—to lay so much stress on ig-

norance and incompetency as a total explanation. This change of affairs in the labor market south, is due to competition between the races in new fields. . . . Industrial education and labor unions for Negroes will not change this condition. They may modify it, but the condition will not be very materially changed. . . . That much we may as well take for granted, calculate the consequences of it, and strive by every means to overcome this falling off in our old-time advantages. . . . We must take in some, if not all, of the wages, turn it into capital, hold it, increase it. . . .

Put that way, the argument for black economic development was apparently irresistible, as the resolutions of this germinal conference indicated. Among the leading topics covered in these resolutions were the following:

1) Negroes ought to enter into business life in increasing numbers. The present disproportion in the distribution of Negroes in the various occupations is unfortunate. It gives the race a one-sided development, unnecessarily increases competition in certain lines of industry, and puts the mass of the Negro people out of sympathy and touch with the industrial and mercantile spirit of the age. Moreover the growth of a class of merchants among us would be a far-sighted measure of self-defense, and would make for wealth and mutual cooperation.

2) Negroes going into business should remember that their customers demand courtesy, honesty, and careful methods, and they should not expect patronage when their manner of conducting business does not justify it.

3) The mass of the Negroes must learn to patronize business enterprises conducted by their own race, even at some slight disadvantage.

4) The most advisable work for the immediate future would seem to be: a) Continued agitation in churches, schools and newspapers, and by all other avenues, of the necessity of business careers for young people. b) Increased effort to encourage saving and habits of thrift among the young that we may have more capital at our disposal. c) The organization in every town and hamlet where colored people dwell, of Negro Business Men's Leagues, and the gradual federation from these of state and national organizations.

This was the script that was followed, consciously or unconsciously, by most of the black spokesmen of that day. And it was this script, tailored to fit his peculiar views, that Booker T. Washington worked from in organizing the National Business League. At the organizational meeting in Boston, in August, 1900, Washington was elected president and an ambitious national program was adopted. Appraising this meeting several years later, Washington said that the mood was "enthusiastic but at the same time practical. Those who were in attendance believed in the timeliness of the organization. They had noticed that almost without exception, whether in the North or in the South, wherever there was a black man who was succeeding in business, who was a taxpayer and who possessed intelligence and high character, that individual was treated with respect by the members of the white race. This fact suggested that, in proportion as we could multiply these examples North and South, our problem would be solved. This was the assumption on which members of the League took up the task it offered them. They recognized that a useless, shiftless, idle class is a menace and a danger to any community, and that when an individual produces what the world wants, whether it is a product of hand, heart or head, the world does not long stop to inquire about the color of the skin of the producer. It was easily seen that if every member of the race should strive to make himself the most indispensable man in his community, and to be successful in business, however humble that business might be, he would contribute much towards smoothing the pathway of his own and future generations."

The launching of the National Business League moved the black business dialogue to a new and more effective level, but it did not unite the black middle class, which continued to revolve around four poles of thought. One group, under the leadership of Washington and his successors, advocated economic development but downgraded and in many cases deprecated political and cultural development. A second group, under the leadership of DuBois and his ideological heirs, advocated simultaneous development on the economic, political and cultural fronts. A third group, organized essentially around Marxian themes, advocated labor organization and a postponement of black capital development until after the socialist revolution. A fourth group, organized around nationalist axes, advocated economic and cultural development in America in the interest of a future political triumph in a black state in Africa or elsewhere. These groups were by no means homogeneous, and there were frequent interchanges of positions and personnel. DuBois, to cite only the most obvious example, seemed to be for economic development by any means necessary, championing at different times—and occasionally at the same time—black business development, black cooperatives, black labor organization, black and white labor organizations, socialism and African nationalism.

It is to be noted also that the four groups were divided over matters of style. The Washington wing, for example, seemed to some critics to champion a program based on an uncritical emulation of the style of white capitalists. The DuBois and radical and nationalist wings, on the other hand, said—practice of course did not always match profession—that the real business of black business was black liberation.

*IT* was against this ideological background and in the context of the forces and pressures outlined above that the black economic development of the first decades of the twentieth century unfolded. Throughout the first decades of the century and on into the twenties and thirties, black entrepreneurs continued to organize banks, insurance companies, and other corporate ventures. In 1900 there were 40,445 blacks in business or business-related occupations. Twenty years later, in 1920, there were 74,424. During this twenty-year span, the first black old-line legal reserve insurance company, Mississippi Life (1909), was organized in Indianola, Mississippi, by Wayne W. Cox. Also organized in this period were the Afro-American Life Insurance Company (1901) and the Mammoth Life Insurance Company (1915).

It was in this same period that publishing became a major focus of black business activity. The changing shape of black America, the restless coming and going of men and women, and the development of a national mass market created new currents which called into being a new breed of business-oriented publishers. Among the leaders of this new development were Carl J. Murphy (*Afro-American*), P. B. Young Sr. (*Journal and Guide*), Robert L. Vann (*Pittsburgh Courier*) and Robert Abbott (*Chicago Defender*). Less spectacular but no less important were the initial successes of the National Baptist Publishing Board and the publications centers of the AME, AMEZ and CME churches.

While all this was going on, black entrepreneurs were pressing forward on the industrial front, organizing factories for the manufacture and processing of mattresses, cotton goods, oil, shoe polish, and hair preparations. By almost all accounts, the first decades of the century were marked by extraordinary initiatives on the part of black businessmen. Of the numerous examples which reflect that spirit we need only cite three. A black corporation was organized in the Indian Territory and started drilling oil wells. A black company was organized in Jacksonville to build and operate a street railway system. A Nashville company was organized to "run a line of automobiles in opposition to the great railroad company of that city."

Among the leading personalities of the period were H. L. Sanders, the white jacket manufacturer of Indianapolis; Junius G. Groves, the Kansas farmer who was known as "the Potato King"; James C. Thomas, the wealthy New York City undertaker; H. C. Haynes, inventor and manufacturer of the Haynes Razor Strop; and A. C. Howard, the Chicago shoe polish manufacturer. The surviving caterers with substantial businesses included John S. Trawer of Germantown, Pennsylvania; Francis J. Moultrie of Westchester County, New York; and Charles H. Smiley of Chicago.

Another significant development of this period was the emergence of black realtors like Phillip A. Payton Jr., president of the Afro-American Realty Company of New York City. Payton and his counterparts in other urban areas played a major role in meeting the housing needs of black migrants. Nothing could better illustrate this than Payton's role in the campaign which saved Harlem for black people. "Some years ago," Booker T. Washington wrote in 1907, "a movement was started by a wealthy white realty company to put the Negroes out of the houses occupied by them on West 135th Street, New York City, with the purpose of filling these buildings with white tenants. . . . It was at this time that the Afro-American Realty Company came into existence. It was formed for the express purpose of meeting this condition. It sought to secure the lease of a number of flat buildings in 135th Street, but without success. Not being able to lease, the company decided to buy two five-story flat buildings in this street. This put an end to the attempt of the white real estate men to drive colored tenants out of this street. . . ."

The culmination and quintessence of the black thrust of this period came with Madame C. J. Walker, who made a fortune manufacturing and selling hair preparations. Like so many of the black business leaders of this period, Madame Walker created her own path. Orphaned at the age of seven and widowed at the age of twenty, she held a number of menial jobs until 1905 when, according to her own version, the formula for a "hair grower" came to her in a dream. She tried the dream-inspired formula on her own hair and the hair of her daughter and decided to organize a business around it. For several years she manufactured and sold the product in Denver, Colorado. Then, after a period of door-to-door selling, she settled in Indianapolis and constructed a laboratory and factory. By 1917 she was considered one of the major business leaders of the black community.

The opportunities for black entrepreneurs expanded appreciably after the Great Migration, which shattered the bonds of the old peasant-based black America and created a new urban-based polity with possibilities and dangers that are still being explored today. Among the immediate consequences of the movement of hundreds of thousands of blacks from the plantations of the South to the urban areas of the North was the creation of huge black colonies with voracious appetites for real estates, goods, and services. This created a marketing vacuum which was speedily filled by a new class of merchants. Some of these merchants were old residents who recognized the marketing possibilities in the new black colonies; others preceded the main migration in the so-called Migration of the Talented Tenth; still others came on the same trains and busses that transported the migrants. Whatever their origin, they were all buoyed up by the new possibilities created by the black cities within the cities of Pittsburgh, Cleveland, Philadelphia and Chicago.

Long before the demographers sensed the new currents stirring in black America, merchants and entrepreneurs were organizing for the new age. One sign of this was the founding of the first black insurance companies in the North. In 1915 William Latham, an attorney from Jackson, Mississippi, organized a Chicago mutual health and accident company that was reorganized in 1918 under the name of the Underwriters Insurance Company. This was the first black insurance company north of the Mason-Dixon line, and it was soon followed by others, including the Supreme Life and Casualty Company (1919) of Ohio.

With the sinking of the first foundations of the black colonies of the North, the stage was set for a business boom which lasted until 1929. During this period the black business community soared to new levels of aspirations.

"It was during this period," Vishnu Oak wrote (*The Negro's Adventure in General Business*), "that Negro businessmen talked about million dollar corporations as if they were playthings and started corporate enterprises for the production of articles of every description, including brooms, dolls, mayonnaise, perfume and toilet goods, hair preparations, soap, hosiery, cotton and woolen goods, mattresses, flour, chemicals, dyes, radios, movies, lumber, burial caskets, tiles, coal, oil, and stoves." Continuing, Oak said: "The 1920's were the years when building and loan associations, banks, insurance companies, real estate agencies, import and export houses, chain stores, steamship lines, stock exchanges for dealing in securities of Negro corporations, and many other wildcat schemes devised to solve the economic problems of the Negro appeared on the scene."

The black business boom was promoted by practically every medium of communication in the black community. There were some skeptics who warned against the dangers of unbridled hucksterism. In September, 1922, W. E. B. DuBois cited some of the opportunities and dangers of the boom.

> Colored folk in larger and larger numbers are investing their savings, and, so far as possible, investing in such ways as will best serve the race. This is a most encouraging symptom, and one has but to visit the Tidewater of Virginia, or Gary, Indiana, or a dozen other centers to see what Negro capital is doing for Negroes.
> At the same time the very eagerness of Negro investors brings the danger of loss and reaction. Scoundrels, both white and black, are hastening to prey upon us, offering large returns in cash and race adjustment for a small amount of money. When failure and bankruptcy follow such schemes, many an honest black man will find himself robbed not simply of money but of faith in leadership. . . . If you are prepared for considerable risk and invest for reasons of race loyalty and hope, then frankly consider how much you can afford to lose before you venture. Do not take desperate chances in flighty dreams and then reach at Negro leadership when you lose every penny invested.

This was good advice, sound as the words of gospel, indisputably—but it did not change the perceptions of the faithful, who continued to invest in wildcat schemes of every imaginable description. It was the Black Gilded Age, it was the age of hope, faith and hucksterism, and tens of thousands believed they would soon be rich.

This faith, which assumed religious dimensions, penetrated practically every segment of the black community, and it is worth emphasizing that black teachers and preachers were the leading missionaries of the movement. Truman K. Gibson, one of the founders of Supreme Life and Casualty Company, was a former teacher. Harry Pace of Northeastern and later Supreme Liberty Life was a former professor of Latin and Greek. Ministers were also active. L. K. Williams, the powerful president of the National Baptist Convention, was a director and later the president of Victory Life. Another director and officer of Victory Life was Bishop R. A. Valentine of the African Orthodox Church.

Heartened presumably by widespread community support, black business leaders went from strength to strength in the twenties. After a somewhat shaky start, marred by the failure of several banks in the Depression of 1920, the black financial community rallied and made substantial gains. By 1926, a peak year, there were thirty black banks with total resources of some $13 million.

The insurance industry also prospered. In 1921 Liberty Life Insurance Company was organized in Chicago by a group headed by Frank L. Gillespie, a former officer in a white insurance company. Four years later another group, headed by Harry H. Pace, organized the Northeastern Life Insurance Company in Newark, New Jersey. In that same year several investors, led by William Nickerson and Norman O. Houston, opened a new front on the West Coast with the organization of the Golden State Guarantee Fund Insurance Company. Other major insurance companies founded in this decade included the Unity Mutual (1920), Universal Life (1923), Victory Life (1924), and Great Lakes Mutual (1928).

Not the least among the things that startle us in this decade is the black thrust in the entertainment field. In these years black businessmen financed and produced major musicals and dramas. They built and bought movie houses. They made repeated attempts to control the management and booking of black acts. Among the major operators in this field were Edward C. Brown and Andrew F. Stevens, two shadowy financiers who controlled two Philadelphia banks that failed in 1925. Subsequent reports indicated that the banks failed primarily because of the speculative dealings of the partners in real estate and the amusement industry. When the banks failed, Brown and/or Stevens controlled the Dunbar Amusement Corporation, which was organized to construct a theater on the corner of Broad and Lombard streets in Philadelphia; the Elite Amusement Corporation, which was created to supply black theaters with entertainment; the Clef Club Singers and Players, which was formed "to supply music and entertainment at dances and balls chiefly in the exclusive and fashionable white circles"; and the Douglass Amusement

Corporation, which operated theaters in Virginia and Maryland and supplied them vaudeville acts. Another sign of the times was the formation of the Pace and Handy Music Company and the Black Swan Phonograph Company. Both companies were organized in 1920 in New York City by W. C. Handy and Harry H. Pace, the young businessman, noted above, who later organized the Northeastern Life Insurance Company.

More effective than these ventures in the entertainment field were the efforts of black businessmen to create viable institutions by mergers and collective buying and selling. One of the most successful developments on this level was the 1929 merger of Northeastern Life Insurance Company of Newark, New Jersey, the Supreme Life and Casualty Company of Columbus, Ohio, and the Liberty Life Insurance Company of Chicago. The end product was the Supreme Liberty Life of Chicago with Harry H. Pace as president.

Another significant, though less dramatic, initiative was the creation of a network of cooperative merchants associations. This network, which was called the CMA (Colored Merchants Association), was created by black merchants and the National Business League to make it possible for black merchants to deal with the challenges of chain stores and mass production outlets. As for strategy, the plan was to reduce operating costs through cooperative buying, the standardization of goods and services and group advertising. Pursuing this strategy, the CMA organized black merchants into cooperative associations in Dallas, New York, Montgomery, Richmond, Brooklyn, Philadelphia, Hampton, Norfolk, Winston-Salem, Tulsa, Nashville, Detroit, and Chicago.

These are but a few of the examples of the hope and faith spawned by the black business boom of the twenties. In a large number of cases, this hope and faith ended in blind alleys of poverty and despair. Worldly success apart, however, these examples are instructive for the light they shed on a period when many black businessmen apparently believed that there were no limits to their aspirations.

We see this most clearly perhaps in the careers of three men who symbolized in different ways the limitations and the possibilities of the twenties. The first man was Marcus Garvey, who organized one of the largest mass movements in the history of black America on the twin themes of African nationalism and economic self determination. In pursuit of the last theme, he organized a chain of cooperative enterprises (grocery stores, laundries, restaurants, hotels and factories) and collected more money (an estimated $10 million in one two-year period) than any black leader before or since. Garvey was severely criticized for the grandiosity of his dreams, but he silenced most of his critics when he incorporated the Black Cross Navigation and Trading Company with a capitalization of $10 million. He sold stock to his followers and admirers under an arrangement which barred white purchasers.

True to his rhetoric, Garvey created the Black Star Line and bought several ships, including the *Booker T. Washington* and the *Yarmouth*. Black Star ships made voyages to Europe and Africa, but the line sustained crushing losses and went into liquidation in April, 1922. At that time it was estimated that the total loss on the venture was $688,515. Garvey was later convicted—unjustly, his defenders say—for using the mail to defraud in the complicated scheme to finance the Black Star Line. After two years of prison, he was deported in 1927 to Jamaica.

In 1924, at the height of the Garvey drama, there was a story in *Forbes Magazine* on the owner of "the largest Negro Commercial Enterprise in the World." According to the story, this man was "the directing genius of a $30,000,000 enterprise, earns $75,000 annually, is insured for $1,000,000 and is said to be worth $8,000,000." Who was this man? His name was Heman E. Perry, and he is almost wholly forgotten today. Born in Houston, Texas, on March 5, 1873, he completed the sixth grade and went out into the world to make his fortune. He went to New York, he said later, "with the idea of getting rich." Failing there, he decided to go to Georgia and start all over again. "I went to a pawn shop," he said, "and disposed of my cuff buttons for $5. I went down to a river boat and gave the purser the $5 to work my way to Savannah. Before the boat got out of the water I made 65 cents in tips." This quote gives the measure of Perry, who was nothing, if not a gambler. As could be expected, he landed on his feet in Georgia, where he became an insurance salesman for a white company. In 1908 he startled the black business world by announcing that he was going to organize an old-line legal reserve insurance company with a capital stock of $100,000. It was widely believed at the time that that was impossible. "Why even Alonzo Herndon couldn't raise that much money," one Atlantan is reported to have said.

The skeptics were right. The money had to be raised in a two-year period, and Perry missed the mark by $30,000. Characteristically, he turned this failure into a great triumph, publicly and dramatically returning every cent of the money he had raised. M. S. Stuart said: "He was adroitly laying the foundation for the appearance of an encore, and right well did it succeed. His second campaign to sell $100,000 of stock made its *debut* dressed up in the colors of a response to a demand on the part of the public. This time he perfected better plans, for actually he had a majority of the authorization already pledged before he again applied for state permission to sell. . . . And yet Perry did not actually sell the entire $100,000 issue this time. However, the cash he lacked was secured on a note endorsed by T. H. Hayes of Memphis, A. L. Lewis of Jacksonville, and Alonzo F. Herndon of Atlanta."

When Standard Life opened for business in March, 1913, it was the first black legal reserve company organized to write only ordinary business. Under Perry's leadership, the company prospered. One of the secrets of his success, according to contemporaries, was that he surrounded himself with the best black talent available.

With Standard Life as his foundation, the restless and daring Perry created a dazzling pyramid of satellite businesses, including the Citizens Trust Company Bank, the Citizens Discount Corporation, the Penny Savings Bank of Augusta, Georgia, Service Engineering & Construction Company, Service Farm Bureau, Service Foundation, Inc., Service Fuel Corporation, Service Holding Company, Service Laundry, Service Pharmacy, Service Printing Company, Service Realty Company, and the Sunset Hills Development Company.

As to one thing, most observers are agreed: Perry was completely consumed by his dreams of financial grandeur. He did not drink or gamble, he shunned the social spotlight and he never married. He had no interests in clothes or conspicuous consumption and had to be persuaded by friends to buy decent suits.

We get a glimpse of Perry from the *Forbes* Magazine interview, which appeared in the February 2, 1924, edition.

> When I entered the $152,000 office building of the Standard Life [Eric D. Walrond wrote] I felt like one in a trance. I could not imagine Negroes owning or operating anything like it (the office equipment alone cost close to $100,000.) I saw dozens and dozens of colored men and women, of the very finest type, employed as clerks, stenographers, bookkeepers, statisticians, accountants, actuaries and executives. . . . Altogether this company and its affiliates have 2,500 people, all colored, on its payroll.
>
> In addition to the Citizens Trust Company, whose total deposits up

to December 5, 1923, amount to $846,998.79, an increase of $550,422.83 over the previous year's, it operates the Service Company which, in its turn, operates twelve other corporations with combined assets of $8,498,217.37.

The Service Company was organized in 1917 with an authorized capital of $100,000; this was increased in 1920 to $500,000, and in 1923 to $1,000,000. Later it grew, in its varied and ramified way, until today it owns $2,000,000 worth of real estate; 300 acres of land within the city limits of Atlanta; seven four-ton trucks; eight box-car loads of building material; 1,000,000 feet of lumber; 1,000 acres of agricultural land in Calhoun County; $50,000 worth of hoisting apparatus, concrete mixers, tools and office equipment; the Verdery Estate, a $138,350 piece of property situated in the business district of Augusta; and a $50,000 printing plant.

Also, the Construction Company is in possession of contracts to the extent of $48,576.00, exclusive of a $212,000 contract recently awarded it by the municipality of Atlanta for the construction of a public school house.

Singularly, the man who founded Standard Life and who is responsible for its gigantic success, while the busiest, brainiest Negro in the South, is modest, brisk-moving, unassuming. . . .

Wherever I went, whether to banker or college president, lawyer or minister, laborer or politician, farmer or millionaire, white or black, I heard in glowing terms of the financial genius of Heman Perry.

This was true enough, but it did not cover all of the essential facts. For, appearances to the contrary, Perry was heavily and dangerously in debt. He had borrowed $300,000 from Will Harris, the president of the white Southern Insurance Company of Nashville. He had also borrowed $200,000 from New York financiers. Always persuasive, always certain of the pot of gold over the next rainbow, Perry later induced Harris to assume the $200,000 New York obligation and to advance him approximately $50,000 more. As security for the $550,000, Perry had pledged the majority stock in Standard Life and a mortgage covering all the assets of Service Company. The due date on the loan was December 15, 1924. On that date Harris could either foreclose on the mortgage or assume full control of Standard Life as the majority stockholder.

As the due date approached, Perry maneuvered frantically in a vain effort to convert some of his frozen assets into cash. Perhaps his most spectacular deal was the purchase of the majority stock in Mississippi

Life. In a complicated maneuver, he used, according to Stuart, "Mississippi Life's own funds to buy the majority of the capital stock of that company and then [sold the industrial business of Mississippi Life] to get money to pay on Standard's great debts."

It looked good on paper, but it didn't work out in practice, and on January 15, 1925, most of Perry's empire passed into the hands of Will Harris and other white men.

Perry later tried to recoup his fortune in the Midwest. But the flame was gone, and one day in 1928 he was found dead in the bathroom of a friend. It is not entirely clear whether it was a heart attack or suicide. But it is clear, as Stuart said, that Perry "lived and died a martyr to his wild zeal to build a combination of Negro financial enterprises of favorable comparison with any in America."

Jesse Binga—the third symbol of the age—had the same dream. Binga was a former barber, Pullman porter and huckster who made his mark in Chicago real estate and branched out into banking. In 1908 he opened a private bank on 36th Place and State Street in Chicago. Twelve years later the bank was reorganized as a state bank with a capital of $100,000; and Binga was boasting, according to the *Afro-American*, that "he could lay claim to more footage on State Street, Chicago's principal thoroughfare, than any other man in the city." He later moved his bank to 35th Street in a specially designed building costing more than $200,000. In 1927 he constructed the 35th Street Arcade at a reported cost of $200,000.

Binga shared the Chicago and national spotlight with Anthony Overton, the cosmetics tycoon, who was also president of the Victory Life Insurance Company and the Douglass National Bank, the second black bank granted a national charter (the first was the First National Bank of Boley, Oklahoma). In 1929 the Binga and Douglass banks were the two largest black banks in the nation with combined resources of almost $4 million.

T*HUS*, the dreamers and symbols, as winds hostile to dreamers and symbols gathered. It seemed to some of these dreamers and symbols that the black business boom would go on forever. In 1929, for intance, Binga was planning a dramatic expansion program. But things were happening over which he had no control, things which would drastically alter his life and the life of all his customers and admirers.

If all this was not clearly seen in 1929, it was beginning to be clearly felt, particularly in the black community, which is always the first to feel the icy blast of new and hostile winds. As economic conditions deteriorated in the late 1920s, black workers, always the first to be fired, were cast out into the cold, and black businessmen, always the first to feel the effect of tightening economic lines, experienced increasing difficulty. With the collapse of the Stock Market and the ensuing Depression, the black business community came apart at the seams. The Depression was a blow, of course, to all businessmen, but, as usual, the repercussions were more severe in the black community. On July 31, 1930, the state examiner closed the House of Binga, and shock waves of fear and dismay spread through the streets of Chicago and other urban black centers. "The closing," the *Chicago Defender* said, "threw the South Side into turmoil. Crowds of depositors gathered in front of the bank. Two uniformed policemen were out on guard for several days. There were no disorders. Instead, there was a deathlike pall that hung over those who had entrusted their life savings to Binga, not so much that they had any love for the head of the bank, but it was pride—that pride of seeing their own race behind the cages, that led them to 35th and State Street to do their banking. For years, the Binga Bank was pointed out to visitors as something accomplished by our group."

*It was pride*: these are the key words. Many white banks in Chicago and elsewhere failed before the Binga Bank, and many failed afterwards. But the Binga Bank, as this quote indicates, was more than a bank, and the closing of its doors was the closing of a wide and airy corridor in the black spirit. As the crisis intensified, other landmarks disappeared, most notably the Douglass Bank, the National Benefit Insurance Company and the CMA stores.

With the collapse of these and other institutions, the infrastructure of the business boom disappeared, and blacks lost ground spiritually and materially. One result was a subtle but profound change in the spirit of the black business community. The old spirit of daring, the old idea that black businessmen could create and manage billion-dollar enterprises, faded and was replaced by a new spirit of caution and even timidity. Black customers began to question the mettle of black businessmen. More importantly, black businessmen began to doubt themselves. And out of this began to emerge the feeling, nebulous at first but always waxing clearer, that another line had to be found. One indication of this was the Black Consumer movement which started in Chicago with the "Don't

Buy Where You Can't Work" campaign and spread rapidly to other urban areas. Using direct action tactics, black activists laid siege to white-owned business in the black community, demanding a fair share of clerical and management positions. There were campaigns against lunch counters, dime stores, movies, newspapers, bakeries, milk companies and public utilities. By the mid-thirties, blacks all over America, in Cleveland, in Los Angeles, in Richmond, were in the streets, marching, demonstrating, demanding. They were led by a number of new organizations such as the New Negro Alliance of Washington, the Citizens League for Fair Play of New York, the Citizens Committee of Baltimore, the Housewives League of Detroit, and the Greater New York Coordinating Committee. The leader of the New York group was a young New York activist named Adam Clayton Powell, Jr. Looking back later, after his election to Congress, Powell evaluated the work of the New York committee: "We set out to blitzkrieg 125th Street. We made it a disgrace for any Negro to cross a picket line. Our picketing was so effective that we could march in front of a corner drug store, such as Liggetts, whose usual traffic was two hundred an hour, and soon clear the store so that only six people would enter of an entire Saturday. We picked the largest five and ten cents stores and picketed them simultaneously. Black phalanxes marched in front with signs crying—'Don't buy where you can't work.' Terror struck the exploiters. On one day we picketed ten stores successfully. Flanking us was the militant nationalistic radical Harlem Labor Union. The Street, as 125th is called, was in a turmoil. We didn't look like a group of Negroes that could be split; nor did we seem to be the kind whose indignation would pass away over night. The exploiters began to bargain. Some attempted to buy us out, but Uncle Tom was dead. . . .

"The Coördinating Committee could pack the largest hall in Harlem in forty-eight hours with 7,000 people and leave 3,000 outside. It was honest because it was poor. The most we ever had in the treasury at one time was $300 for a single week. We never conducted a real membership campaign. We always acted on the assumption that all Harlem belonged. As victories came the bandwagon crowd began to jump on. Cautious but well meaning folks had waited to see how we would make out. They joined and we welcomed them. The committee grew until it represented the mass power of 207 Harlem organizations. . . . One Hundred and Twenty-fifth Street was wide open now, merchants were appealing for so many workers that the Harlem YMCA, the Urban League, and the

African Patriotic League set up classes training men and women as sales clerks."

A very different approach to the potential power of black consumers was suggested by W. E. B. DuBois, who resigned from the NAACP after an explosive internal struggle. The resignation was triggered by DuBois's belief that the economic debacle of the thirties required a new black political economy. To achieve this end, DuBois issued a call for the mobilization of black buying power and the organization of producers and consumers cooperatives. What was his program? "The only thing that we not only can, but must do, is voluntarily and insistently to organize our economic and social power, no matter how much segregation it involves. Learn to associate with ourselves and to train ourselves for effective association. Organize our strength as consumers; learn to cooperate and use machines and power as producers; train ourselves in methods of democratic control within our own group. Run and support our own institutions." To critics who accused him of advocating segregation and an independent black economy, DuBois replied heatedly that the black economy was already partially segregated and the only option black people had was to use that segregation to destroy segregation. "In the first place," he said, "we have already got a partially segregated Negro economy in the United States. . . . We not only build and finance Negro churches, but we furnish a considerable part of the funds for our segregated schools. We furnish most of our own professional services in medicine, pharmacy, dentistry and law. We furnish some part of our food and clothes, our home building and repairing and many retail services. We furnish books and newspapers; we furnish endless personal services like those of barbers, beauty shop-keepers, hotels, restaurants. It may be said that this inner economy of the Negro serves but a small proportion of its total needs; but it is growing and expanding in various ways; and what I propose is to so plan and guide it as to take advantage of certain obvious facts. It is of course impossible that a segregated economy for Negroes in the United States should be complete. It is quite possible that it could never cover more than the smaller part of the economic activities of Negroes. Nevertheless, it is also possible that this smaller part could be so important and wield so much power that its influence upon the total economy of Negroes and the total industrial organization of the United States would be decisive for the great ends toward which the Negro moves."

This controversy, which raged throughout the thirties and continues today, assumed different and yet complementary forms on the level of the masses, who were also in search of a new economic strategy. A particular expression of this quest was the Harlem Riot of 1935. In a long and provocative analyis, the *New York Daily Mirror* said the riot grew out of a struggle for control of "Black Dollars."

> Chicago Negroes [the *Mirror* said] adopted a slogan: "Don't Spend Your Money Where You Can't Work!" and compelled the capitulation of hundreds of merchants in the Negro section of that city....
>
> This excursion to the Chicago scene has been necessary to clear up what seems to be the most perplexing feature of Harlem's outbreak of March 19, when 5,000 Harlemites went beserk up and down Harlem's avenues, smashing and looting and assaulting, and all to the tune of a cryptic rallying cry: "Down with the ofay stores!"
>
> To those who think in such simple black-and-white terms as race wars the riot and its war-cry made no sense at all. What was all this talk about "Negroes to wait on Negroes?" What a remote issue to cause spilling of blood!
>
> But it was not a remote issue. It is the sole issue existing in Harlem today. For Harlem has still to face the crisis which Chicago's Black Belt met and fought out to solution in 1917. Harlem has no "black economics." In a very painful as well as symbolic sense, Harlem is "bled white." Harlem's dollars—even the few that circulate now in these times of a few jobs—do not stay in Harlem, scarcely over one night.
>
> The white storekeeper and the white rent collector take the dollars away. There have been two conquests of Harlem by infiltration since the end of the war. The first was the invasion of the district by colored residents. The second has been just as complete as the first—a white re-conquest of the area the Negroes won. Block by block, store by store, house by house, white profit seekers have infiltrated back into the district which became black by common consent in the decade after the war.
>
> It is for the "Black Dollar" that Harlem fights now, because it has to. The process whereby the wealth of Harlem is sucked out as soon as made, has gone so far that it is now an elemental matter of survival that it should be stopped.

This elemental struggle for survival dominated the dialogue of the thirties and was a key factor in the organized efforts which prevented a total collapse of the black community. It is also important to remember that many black-owned businesses (North Carolina Mutual, Atlanta Life, Supreme Life, Golden State, etc.) weathered the storms of the Depression. In a 1937 report on the causes of Negro insurance company failures, the U.S. Department of Commerce said, "This report centers attention on the failures which the insurance business, as conducted among Negroes, has experienced. However, the contribution which Negro operated companies have made to the economic development of the race should not be overlooked. During the past twenty years their services have caused them to be regarded as financial reservoirs from which funds may flow in times of stress. Today, after weathering the most serious depression in the nation's history, thirty odd Negro companies justify this confidence."

The survival of black retail stores also justified a certain confidence. By 1939 there were 57,195 black-owned retail and service establishments with a total annual income of $108,119,000 and 27,958 employees. The total income of these retail outlets, however, was less than two-tenths of 1 percent of the national total, and the proportion of black-owned stores among all retail outlets was smaller in 1939 than in 1929. Moreover, the total sales in black-owned stores and restaurants dropped 28 percent from 1929 to 1939, as compared with a 13 percent loss for all retail stores.

The meaning of these figures was plain and ominous: the relative position of the black entrepreneur had declined sharply. The war boom of the forties changed this picture slightly, but the same process that characterized the Civil War was at work. In other words, white businesses improved their position so dramatically on war profits that the net result was a relative impoverishment of the black entrepreneur. Nevertheless, internal progress was evident everywhere, as blacks made their most significant economic gains since World War I. To take one clear point, the war years changed the occupational profile of the black community and brought a dramatic increase in the number of black technicians and white-collar workers. This change, in turn, stimulated the real estate market and created new opportunities for realtors, financiers, and advertisers. The black movement of the fifties and sixties accelerated these changes by raising the consciousness of blacks and forcing substantial government intervention. By the late sixties there was a flurry of activity by a number of government agencies, including the Small Business Administration. Critics said this government action was a classic example of "too little given too begrudgingly too late." They said, in general, that none of the programs dealt with the imperatives of fundamental change, the imperatives of redistributing the national income and transforming the black community by massive doses of capital controlled by blacks. They were especially critical of the ambiguous Black Capitalism program of the Nixon Administration. This program seemed to many critics to be based on an imitation of the dying small business ethic. In support of their views, the critics cited alarming figures which indicated that the number of black-owned businesses declined by more than a fifth in the sixties, faster than the similarly declining rate of white-owned small businesses.

If the new climate of the fifties and sixties did not, as the critics charged, change the economic position of blacks, it did at least change the morale of black entrepreneurs, who seized and held new ground. A good deal of light is thrown upon the temper of the new entrepreneurs by the careers of five men who heralded the new age and played central roles in it. The first man is Dr. Meredith C. Gourdine, who pioneered in the commercial development of electrogasdynamics and created the multi-million dollar New Jersey firm, Gourdine Systems, Inc. At the other end of the spectrum is Elijah Muhammad, the leader of the Nation of Islam. Like Martin Delany, like Marcus Garvey, the leader of the Nation of Islam preached the gospel of self-reliance and self-assertion. By 1973 he and his followers had created a multi-million dollar economic empire which incuded 4,200 acres of farm land, a weekly newspaper, and a nationwide chain of supermarkets, barber shops, restaurants, and clothing stores.

No less successful is another Chicago-based entrepreneur, George E. Johnson, president of Johnson Products Company. Johnson began his career as a chemist for Fuller Products, which was a successful black-owned cosmetics firm of the sixties. In 1954 Johnson borrowed $250 from a finance company and started his own firm. The story of how he got this loan is very instructive, for it illuminates the continuing problems of black entrepreneurs. Johnson first applied for a loan and stated frankly that he was going to use the money to start a business. The loan was rejected. Three days later he went to another branch of the same loan company and applied for a loan to take his wife on a vacation. Within a few minutes, the loan was approved. "This was a peculiar but devastating expression of racism," Johnson said later. "The loan company turned me down, not because I was a poor credit risk, but because I wished to borrow money for a serious business venture. But the company made the loan to me, a black man, when I said it was for frivolity." The limitations of the loan company did not limit George E. Johnson, who used the money not for frivolity but for economic development. In 1971 his company became the first black-owned firm to be listed on the American Stock Exchange.

Another loan, $700 from a credit union, was the catalyst which enabled Berry Gordy Jr., a young Detroit automobile assembly worker, to start Motown Records. Under Gordy's leadership, Motown Records soon became a leading force in the entertainment industry, creating and promoting stars like Smokey Robinson and the Miracles, the Supremes, the Temptations, Stevie Wonder, Marvin Gaye and the Jackson Five.

John H. Johnson, the fifth and final example, also began his career with a small loan and a big idea. In 1942 he borrowed $500 on his mother's furniture and started *Negro Digest* and Johnson Publishing Company. Three years later, in 1945, he produced the first issue of *Ebony*, the most successful black publication in history. By 1974 *Ebony* had achieved the highest monthly paid subscription of any black magazine, and Johnson had been honored by numerous organizations as a leader of the publishing and business worlds. By that time Johnson had expanded his operation to include other magazines (*Jet, Black Stars, Ebony Jr., Black World*), a cosmetics company, Supreme Products, and a radio station, WJPC. He is also chairman and chief executive officer of Supreme Life Insurance Company, the largest black insurance company in the North.

These men indicated the new possibilities of an age which witnessed important changes in the position of the black entrepreneur. According to the first comprehensive survey of the black business field, there were 163,000 black-owned businesses in 1969 with total receipts of $4.5 billion and 151,996 employees. This compared favorably with the total number of black-owned businesses reported in 1930 and unfavorably with the total number of American businesses (7,489,000), of which black-owned businesses constituted a tiny 2.2 percent. As in 1920 and 1930, most black-owned businesses in 1969 were small and marginal with heavy concentrations in retail trade and service outlets. The ten most important industries for black-owned firms were 1) automobile dealers and gasoline filling stations, 2) food stores, 3) wholesale trade, 4) eating and drinking places, 5) personal services, 6) special sales contractors, 7) miscellaneous retail stores, 8) general building contractors, 9) trucking and warehousing, 10) insurance carriers.

Although black-owned firms accounted for only 1 percent of the total sales of America businesses, they were the focus of considerable attention in the sixties, which was characterized by an evangelical business spirit roughly comparable to the mood of the twenties. There was a dramatic rise in the number of black banks and savings and loan associations. There was a resurgence of the Black Consumer movement under the leadership of Jesse Jackson, who added a new twist by negotiating covenants requiring major white corporations to use black banks and black insurance companies and to employ a higher proportion of black workers and black executives. Less dramatic but no less relevant was the revival of the ideological debate on the possibilities of an independent black economy. There was also talk—but little else—of quasi-public development corporations, cooperative black merchants' associations and the use of location subsidies and other incentives for corporate ventures in the black community.

*ALL* these currents reflected different aspects of the problem, and all attempted, in one way or another, to deal with the paradox of internal colonialism. And as America approached the two hundredth anniversary of the Declaration of Independence, the forces shaping this paradox pushed the black colony and the white metropolitan center toward another fateful fork in the road.

Foremost perhaps among these forces was the simple fact of growth. By 1972 the twenty seeds of Jamestown had become millions. No one can say with certainty how many blacks were in America in 1972—blacks are traditionally undercounted in census surveys—but official figures listed 23.4 millions, 11.3 percent of the population as compared with 10 percent in 1940, and 11 percent in 1950. The black population, as these figures indicate, was growing faster than the white population. In the 1960–1970 decade, the rate of growth for blacks was 20 percent, compared to 11.9 percent for whites.

The rate of growth for the black population was dramatic; so also was the direction of growth. Between 1950 and 1970, the proportion of blacks living the South declined markedly, from 68 percent in 1950 to 52 percent in 1972. In each of the three decades leading up to 1970, the South lost about 1,500,000 blacks through net out-migration. In

1970, 39 percent of the black Americans were living in the North and 8 percent were living in the West. Most of the blacks in the North and West were congregated in major metropolitan areas. Almost four out of ten were living in twenty-six cities with a black population of one hundred thousand or more. Of these twenty-six cities, three (Washington, D.C., Atlanta, Newark) had a black majority, six (Baltimore, Detroit, New Orleans, St. Louis, Birmingham, Richmond) had a black population of between 40 and 50 percent, and five (Chicago, Philadelphia, Cleveland, Memphis, Oakland) had a black population of between 30 and 40 percent. By 1974 six of these cities (Detroit, Washington, Los Angeles, Cleveland, Atlanta, Newark) had elected black mayors.

The black presence in these cities—the urban heartland of America—was real and challenging. In only one of the twenty-six cities—Indianapolis—was the proportion of black children enrolled in public elementary schools less than one-fourth. In one—Washington—more than 93 percent of the public elementary school children were black. In thirteen, black children represented a majority of the public elementary school children.

In the major metropolitan areas, as elsewhere, the work relationship was central, and it is significant that the three cities with black majorities had the highest proportion of blacks in their employed labor forces—68 percent in Washington, 48 percent in Newark, 47 percent in Atlanta. Washington also had the highest proportion—15 percent—of blacks employed in professional, technical, and managerial occupations, followed closely by Los Angeles, Boston, New York, and Columbus, Ohio. At the other end of the spectrum, Oakland, California, had the highest unemployment rate—12 percent—in 1970, and Washington and Richmond had the lowest—4 percent. As for income, blacks in Washington and Detroit led the list, with family median incomes of $7,600 and $8,500, respectively. The per capita income for individual blacks was $2,700 for Washington and $2,500 for Detroit. For reasons of perspective and balance, these figures should be compared with the data on continuing deprivation. About four out of every ten black persons were living below the poverty line in New Orleans, Memphis, Birmingham, and Jacksonville, and the percentage of blacks below the poverty line was 32 percent in Pittsburgh and Cincinnati, 31 percent in St. Louis, 30 percent in Richmond, Dallas, and Houston, 28 percent in Boston, 25 percent in Chicago, and 19 percent in Washington.

These figures*—figures of growth, concentration, and continuing deprivation—cast a revealing light on the shape and structure of black America in the third quarter of the twentieth century. Like other data cited here, the figures and the forces behind the figures point to a critical watershed, whose streams run in one direction back to the Jamestown landing, in another forward to a shore shrouded in mist. The shape of that shore will be determined in the last analysis by the responses of black and white Americans to two paradoxes, the first of which is the central paradox of the political economy of whiteness: the fact that the fate of America is inextricably intertwined with the fate of the black fragment imbedded in its urban spine. The second is the paradox of the political economy of blackness: the fact that black Americans have an annual income larger than India, Australia, or Sweden, and the further fact that African-Americans are demonstrably poor and do not control 3 percent of any thing worth having in America. Poor, yet making many rich; deprived, yet providing capital for many; empty-handed, yet possessing in the mass enormous productive and consumptive potential: this was the paradoxical profile of black America in the seventies. With an annual income of $55 billion, with 7.7 million living below the poverty line and millions more unemployed and underemployed, black America in the seventies was a symphony of contradictions in search of a theme and creative conductors. It was not clear at the end of this period whether the enormous potentials of this community would be orchestrated and focused on "the great ends toward which black people move." But there were signs of progression as well as retrogression, and it was clear that Black America was groping toward some new equilibrium, as yet undefined.

---

* See *Characteristics of the Black Population for Cities With 100,000 or More Blacks: 1970*, page 340.

## Characteristics of the Black Population

| | Black Population | % of Total Population | % of Total Voting-Age Population | No. Black Children in Public Schools | % Black Children in Elementary Schools | No. Blacks in Labor Force | % of Total Employment |
|---|---|---|---|---|---|---|---|
| New York, N. Y. | 1,668,000 | 21 | 18 | 414,000 | 37 | 588,000 | 18 |
| Chicago, Ill. | 1,103,000 | 33 | 28 | 316,000 | 56 | 364,000 | 26 |
| Detroit, Mich. | 660,000 | 44 | 39 | 174,000 | 64 | 224,000 | 40 |
| Philadelphia, Pa. | 654,000 | 34 | 30 | 173,000 | 61 | 232,000 | 30 |
| Washington, D. C. | 538,000 | 71 | 64 | 134,000 | 93 | 227,000 | 68 |
| Los Angeles, Calif. | 504,000 | 18 | 16 | 126,000 | 25 | 176,000 | 15 |
| Baltimore, Md. | 420,000 | 46 | 41 | 121,000 | 67 | 150,000 | 43 |
| Houston, Tex. | 317,000 | 26 | 23 | 86,000 | 32 | 120,000 | 23 |
| Cleveland, Ohio | 288,000 | 38 | 35 | 81,000 | 57 | 100,000 | 35 |
| New Orleans, La. | 267,000 | 45 | 39 | 78,000 | 68 | 79,000 | 38 |
| Atlanta, Ga. | 255,000 | 51 | 46 | 66,000 | 65 | 99,000 | 47 |
| St. Louis, Mo. | 254,000 | 41 | 35 | 72,000 | 65 | 82,000 | 36 |
| Memphis, Tenn. | 243,000 | 39 | 34 | 73,000 | 51 | 77,000 | 32 |
| Dallas, Tex. | 210,000 | 25 | 21 | 58,000 | 34 | 82,000 | 22 |
| Newark, N. J. | 207,000 | 54 | 48 | 58,000 | 72 | 66,000 | 48 |
| Indianapolis, Ind. | 134,000 | 18 | 16 | 37,000 | 23 | 49,000 | 16 |
| Birmingham, Ala. | 126,000 | 42 | 38 | 35,000 | 53 | 41,000 | 36 |
| Cincinnati, Ohio | 125,000 | 28 | 24 | 34,000 | 46 | 42,000 | 24 |
| Oakland, Calif. | 125,000 | 34 | 29 | 36,000 | 57 | 41,000 | 29 |
| Jacksonville, Fla. | 118,000 | 22 | 20 | 34,000 | 28 | 39,000 | 20 |
| Kansas City, Mo. | 112,000 | 22 | 19 | 32,000 | 32 | 42,000 | 20 |
| Milwaukee, Wis. | 105,000 | 15 | 11 | 33,000 | 28 | 34,000 | 11 |
| Pittsburgh, Pa. | 105,000 | 20 | 18 | 28,000 | 42 | 32,000 | 16 |
| Richmond, Va. | 105,000 | 42 | 37 | 29,000 | 57 | 40,000 | 39 |
| Boston, Mass. | 105,000 | 16 | 13 | 27,000 | 32 | 34,000 | 13 |
| Columbus, Ohio | 100,000 | 18 | 16 | 28,000 | 26 | 36,000 | 17 |

Source: *U.S. Department of Commerce, Social and Economic Statistics Administration, Bureau of the Census.*

### Ten Leading Metropolitan Areas for Black-owned Firms

| Metropolitan Area | Firms | Gross Receipts |
|---|---|---|
| Chicago, Ill. | 8,747 | $332,197,000 |
| Detroit, Mich. | 5,442 | $227,494,000 |
| Los Angeles-Long Beach, Calif. | 8,318 | $210,950,000 |
| New York, N. Y. | 7,753 | $200,153,000 |
| Philadelphia, Pa. | 6,246 | $151,866,000 |
| Washington, D. C. | 7,768 | $123,184,000 |
| San Francisco-Oakland, Calif. | 3,358 | 90,791,000 |
| Cleveland, Ohio | 3,208 | 90,410,000 |
| St. Louis, Mo. | 2,986 | 87,815,000 |
| New Orleans, La. | 2,723 | 86,594,000 |

Source: *Minority-Owned Businesses: 1969*, U.S. Department of Commerce, Bureau of the Census, issued August, 1971.

## or Cities With 100,000 or More Blacks: 1970

| % in Professional, Technical, Managerial | % Craftsmen, Foremen | % Self-employed | % Labor Force Unemployed | % High School Graduates | % College Graduates | Per Capita Income | Median Family Income | % Below Low-Income Level | % of Occupied Units Owned | Median Value Owner-Occupied Units |
|---|---|---|---|---|---|---|---|---|---|---|
| 13 | 9 |   | 5 | 41 | 4 | $2,402.00 | $7,150.00 | 24 | 16 | $22,000.00 |
| 11 | 10 |   | 7 | 39 | 4 | 2,321.00 | 7,883.00 | 25 | 24 | 19,400.00 |
| 10 | 10 |   | 10 | 37 | 4 | 2,534.00 | 8,645.00 | 22 | 51 | 13,900.00 |
| 10 | 10 |   | 7 | 32 | 3 | 2,243.00 | 7,883.00 | 26 | 47 | 8,500.00 |
| 15 | 9 |   | 4 | 44 | 8 | 2,734.00 | 8,488.00 | 19 | 27 | 18,700.00 |
| 14 | 9 | 1 | 10 | 50 | 6 | 2,435.00 | 7,200.00 | 26 | 32 | 18,500.00 |
| 11 | 9 |   | 6 | 28 | 4 | 2,056.00 | 7,289.00 | 27 | 30 | 9,400.00 |
| 11 | 10 | 1 | 5 | 35 | 6 | 1,812.00 | 6,392.00 | 30 | 45 | 10,700.00 |
| 9 | 10 |   | 7 | 35 | 3 | 2,255.00 | 7,617.00 | 27 | 38 | 15,900.00 |
| 10 | 9 | 1 | 8 | 26 | 4 | 1,458.00 | 4,745.00 | 44 | 27 | 16,400.00 |
| 11 | 8 |   | 5 | 34 | 7 | 2,077.00 | 6,742.00 | 29 | 37 | 14,700.00 |
| 10 | 6 |   | 9 | 31 | 4 | 1,912.00 | 6,534.00 | 31 | 31 | 11,200.00 |
| 9 | 9 | 1 | 8 | 24 | 4 | 1,438.00 | 5,177.00 | 41 | 42 | 9,700.00 |
| 9 | 9 | 1 | 5 | 37 | 5 | 1,828.00 | 6,311.00 | 30 | 44 | 11,300.00 |
| 8 | 10 |   | 8 | 33 | 2 | 2,077.00 | 6,742.00 | 27 | 16 | 17,100.00 |
| 10 | 9 | 1 | 8 | 36 | 4 | 2,210.00 | 7,849.00 | 22 | 49 | 11,400.00 |
| 9 | 9 |   | 7 | 29 | 4 | 1,522.00 | 5,184.00 | 40 | 42 | 10,400.00 |
| 9 | 7 |   | 8 | 29 | 3 | 1,979.00 | 6,504.00 | 32 | 27 | 14,800.00 |
| 11 | 10 |   | 12 | 43 | 4 | 2,365.00 | 7,700.00 | 25 | 40 | 18,500.00 |
| 9 | 9 | 1 | 6 | 29 | 5 | 1,502.00 | 5,122.00 | 40 | 55 | 8,500.00 |
| 12 | 7 |   | 6 | 40 | 5 | 2,090.00 | 7,247.00 | 25 | 55 | 9,500.00 |
| 9 | 10 |   | 8 | 34 | 3 | 1,974.00 | 7,491.00 | 27 | 33 | 12,100.00 |
| 11 | 8 |   | 9 | 35 | 3 | 1,993.00 | 6,097.00 | 32 | 33 | 10,400.00 |
| 9 | 7 |   | 4 | 26 | 4 | 1,881.00 | 6,179.00 | 30 | 41 | 11,600.00 |
| 13 | 10 |   | 7 | 45 | 4 | 2,054.00 | 6,346.00 | 28 | 17 | 14,200.00 |
| 13 | 9 |   | 6 | 41 | 5 | 2,293.00 | 7,556.00 | 26 | 43 | 13,900.00 |

*Ten Leading Industries for Black-owned Firms*

| Industry Group | Firms | Receipts |
|---|---|---|
| Automotive dealers, gas stations | 6,380 | $631,000,000 |
| Food stores | 11,268 | $438,000,000 |
| Wholesale trade | 1,660 | $385,000,000 |
| Eating and drinking places | 14,125 | $360,000,000 |
| Personal services | 33,906 | $288,000,000 |
| Special trade contractors | 13,477 | $284,000,000 |
| Miscellaneous retail stores | 6,412 | $278,000,000 |
| General building contractors | 2,359 | $140,000,000 |
| Trucking and warehousing | 7,252 | $134,000,000 |
| Insurance carrier | 104 | $133,000,000 |

Source: *Minority-Owned Businesses: 1969*, U.S. Department of Commerce, Bureau of the Census, issued August, 1971.

# BIBLIOGRAPHY

Ames, Susie M. *Studies of the Virginia Eastern Shore in the Seventeenth Century.* Richmond, 1940.
Andrews, Charles C. *History of the New York African Free Schools.* New York, 1830.
Aptheker, Herbert. *American Negro Slave Revolts.* New York, 1943.
———, ed. *A Documentary History of the Negro People in the United States.* New York, 1951.
Baker, Henry E. "The Negro in the Field of Invention." *Journal of Negro History* 2 (1917).
———. "Benjamin Banneker, the Negro Mathmematician and Astronomer," *Journal of Negro History* 3(1918).
Ballagh, James C. *White Servitude in the Colony of Virginia.* Baltimore, 1895.
———. *A History of Slavery in Virginia.* Baltimore, 1902.
Baron, Harold M. "The Web of Urban Racism." In *Institutional Racism in America.* Edited by Louis Knowles and Kenneth Prewitt. New York, 1969.
———. "The Demand for Black Labor: Historical Notes on the Political Economy of Racism." *Radical America* 5(1971).
Baron, Harold M., and Hymer, Bennett. "The Negro Worker in the Chicago Labor Market." In *The Negro and the American Labor Movement.* Edited by Julius Jacobson. New York, 1968.
Barnes, Gilbert H. *The Antislavery Impulse, 1830–1844.* New York, 1933.
Bauer, Raymond, and Bauer, Alice. "Day to Day Resistance to Slavery." *Journal of Negro History* 27(1918).
Becker, Gary S. *The Economics of Discrimination.* Chicago, 1957.
Bell, Howard H. "National Negro Conventions of the Middle 1840s: Moral Suasion vs. Political Action." *Journal of Negro History* 42(1957).
———. "Expressions of Negro Militancy in the North, 1840–1860." *Journal of Negro History* 45(1960).
Bennett, Lerone, Jr. *The Negro Mood.* Chicago, 1964.
———. *Confrontation: Black and White.* Chicago, 1965.
———. *Black Power, U.S.A.: The Human Side of Reconstruction.* Chicago, 1967.
———. *Pioneers in Protest.* Chicago, 1968.
———. *The Challenge of Blackness.* Chicago,
———. "Black Bourgeoisie Revisited." *Ebony,* August, 1973.
Benson, Adolph B., ed. *The America of 1750: Peter Kalm's Travels in North America. The English Version of 1770.* 2 vols. New York, 1937.
Bentley, George R. *A History of the Freedmen's Bureau.* Philadelphia, 1965.
Bernstein, Barton J. *Towards a New Past.* New York, 1968.
Beverley, Robert. *The History and Present State of Virginia.* London, 1705.
Blauner, Robert. "Internal Colonialism and Ghetto Revolt." *Social Problems* (1969).
Bloch, Herman D. "Craft Unions and the Negro in Historical Perspective." *Journal of Negro History* 43(1958).
———. "Labor and the Negro, 1866–1910." *Journal of Negro History* 50(1965).
Bond, Horace Mann. *The Education of the Negro in the American Social Order.* New York, 1934.
———. "Social and Economic Forces in Alabama Reconstruction." *Journal of Negro History* 23(1938).

Boskin, Joseph. "The Origins of American Slavery: Education as an Index of Early Differentiation." *Journal of Negro Education* 35(1966).
———. "Race Relations in Seventeenth Century America: The Problem of the Origins of Negro Slavery." *Sociology and Social Research* 49 (1965).
Botkin, B. A. ed. *Lay My Burden Down*. Chicago, 1945.
Boxer, C. R. *Race Relations in the Portuguese Colonial Empire, 1415–1825*. Oxford, 1963.
Brackett, Jeffery R. *The Negro in Maryland*. Baltimore, 1889.
Brazeal, B. R. *The Brotherhood of Sleeping Car Porters*. New York, 1946.
Brewer, William M. "John B. Russwurm." *Journal of Negro History* 13(1928).
Bridenbaugh, Carl. *Myths and Realities: Societies of the Colonial South*. Baton Rouge, 1952.
Brimmer, Andrew. "The Negro in the American Economy." Speech delivered at Memorial Dedication Festival, North Carolina Mutual Life Insurance Company, April 1, 1966. Mimeographed.
———. "An Economic Agenda for Black Americans." Speech delivered at Atlanta University, October 16, 1970. Mimeographed.
Brodie, Fawn M. *Thomas Jefferson*. New York,1974.
Brown, Sterling A., *et al*, eds. *The Negro Caravan*. New York, 1941.
Browning, James B. "The Beginnings of Insurance Enterprise Among Negroes." *Journal of Negro History* 22(1937).
Bruce, Philip A. *Economic History of Virginia in the Seventeenth Century*. 2 vols. New York, 1896.
———. *Social Life of Virginia in the Seventeenth Century*. Richmond, 1907.
Buck, Paul H. *The Road to Reunion*. Boston, 1937.
Butcher, Margaret Just. *The Negro in American Culture*. New York, 1956.
Calhoun, A. W. *A Social History of the American Family*. 3 vols. New York, 1917.
Cantor, Milton, ed. *Black Labor in America*. Westport, 1969.
Catterall, Helen T. *Judicial Cases Concerning American Slavery and the Negro*. 5 vols. Washington, 1926–37.
Cayton, Horace R., and Mitchell, George S. *Black Workers and the New Unions*. Chapel Hill, 1939.
Chastellux, Marquis de. *Travels in North America in the Years 1780, 1781 and 1782*. Translated and edited by Howard C. Rice, Jr. 2 vols. Chapel Hill, 1963.
Clark, Kenneth B. *Dark Ghetto*. New York, 1965.
Chicago Commission on Race Relations. *The Negro in Chicago*, 1922.
Clarke, John Henrik, ed. *Marcus Garvey and the Vision of Africa*. New York, 1963.
———, ed. *Harlem, A Community in Transition*. New York, 1964.
Courlander, Harold. *Negro Folk Music, U.S.A*. New York, 1963.
Cox, Oliver C. *Caste, Class, and Race*. New York, 1948.
Cromwell, John W. *The Early Negro Convention Movement*. Washington, 1904.
Cronon, Edmund David. *Black Moses: The Story of Marcus Garvey*. Madison, 1955.
Cross, Theodore L. *Black Capitalism*. New York, 1969.
Daniels, John. *In Freedom's Birthplace*. Boston, 1914.
Davis, John P., ed. *The American Negro Reference Book*. Englewood Cliffs, 1966.
Davis, David B. *The Problem of Slavery in Western Culture*. Ithaca, 1966.
Davis, John W. "George Liele and Andrew Bryan, Pioneer Negro Baptist Preachers." *Journal of Negro History* 3(1918).
Davis, T. R. "Negro Servitude in the United States." *Journal of Negro History* 8(1923).
Degler, Carl N. "Slavery and the Genesis of American Race Prejudice." *Comparative Studies in Society and History* 2(1959).
Delaney, Martin R. *The Condition, Elevation, Emigration, and Destiny of the Colored People of the United States*. Philadelphia, 1852.
Detweiler, Frederick G. *The Negro Press in the United States*. Chicago, 1922.

Donnan, Elizabeth. *Documents Illustrative of the History of the Slave Trade to America*. Washington, 1930–35.
Drake, St. Clair, and Clayton, Horace R. *Black Metropolis*. New York, 1945.
Douglass, Frederick. *The Life and Times of Frederick Douglass*. Hartford, 1881.
Du Bois, W. E. B. *The Philadelphia Negro*. Philadelphia, 1899.
———. *The Souls of Black Folk*. Chicago, 1903.
———. *Black Reconstruction*. New York, 1935.
———. *Dusk of Dawn*. New York, 1940.
———, ed. *The Negro Artisan*. Atlanta, 1902.
———, ed. *The Negro in Business*. Atlanta, 1899.
———, ed. *The Negro Church*. Atlanta, 1903.
Dunbar-Nelson, Alice. "People of Color in Louisiana." *Journal of Negro History* 1(1916).
Eaton, John. *Grant, Lincoln and the Freedmen*. New York, 1907.
Edwards, Bryan. *The History, Civil and Commercial, of the British Colonies in the West Indies*. 3 vols. London, 1801.
Fanon, Frantz. *The Wretched of the Earth*. New York, 1966.
———. *Studies in a Dying Colonialism*. New York, 1967.
Federal Writers' Project, WPA. *The Negro in Virginia*. New York, 1940.
Fleming, Walter L. *The Freedmen's Savings Bank*. Chapel Hill, 1927.
Foner, Phillip S. *The Life and Writings of Frederick Douglass*. 4 vols. New York, 1950.
Force, Peter. *Tracts and Other Papers*. 4 vols. Washington, 1836–46.
Forten, Charlotte. *The Journal of Charlotte Forten*. Edited by Ray Allen. Billington, 1953.
Fortune, T. Thomas. *Black and White*. New York, 1884.
Franklin, John Hope. *From Slavery to Freedom*. New York, 1947.
———. *The Free Negro in North Carolina*. Chapel Hill, 1943.
Frazier, E. Franklin. *The Negro in the United States*. New York, 1957.
———. *Black Bourgeoisie*. Glencoe, 1957.
Garfinkel, Herbert. *When Negroes March*. Glencoe, 1959.
Garrett, Romeo B. "African Survivals in American Culture." *Journal of Negro History* 51(1966).
Godwyn, Morgan. *The Negro's and Indians Advocate.* . . . London, 1680.
Goodell, William. *The American Slave Code in Theory and Practice*. New York, 1853.
Gossett, Thomas F. *Race: The History of an Idea in America*. Dallas, 1963.
Gray, Lewis. *History of Agriculture in the Southern United States to 1860*. 2 vols. Washington, 1933.
Greene, Evarts B., and Harrington, Virginia D. *American Population before the Federal Census of 1790*. New York, 1932.
Greene, Lorenzo J. *The Negro in Colonial New England, 1620–1776*. New York, 1942.
Greene, Lorenzo., and Woodson, Carter G. *The Negro Wage Earner*. Washington, 1930.
Gross, Bella. "The First National Negro Convention." *Journal of Negro History* 31(1946).
Hammond, John. *Leah and Rachel*. London, 1656.
Handlin, Oscar, and Handlin, Mary F. "Origins of the Southern Labor System." *William and Mary Quarterly* 7(1950).
Harmon, J. H., Jr. "The Negro as a Local Business Man." *Journal of Negro History* 14(1929).
Harris, Abram L. *The Negro Capitalist*. Philadelphia, 1936.
Harris, Marvin. *Patterns of Race in the Americas*. New York, 1964.
Haynes, Elizabeth Ross. "Negroes in Domestic Service in the United States." *Journal of Negro History* 8(1923).
Haynes, George Edmund. *The Negro at Work in New York City*. New York, 1912.
Haywood, Harry. *Negro Liberation*. New York, 1948.
Hening, William W. *The Statutes at Large Being a Collection of All the Laws of Virginia*. 13 vols. Richmond, New York, Philadelphia, 1809–23.

Herskovits, Melville J. *The American Negro: A Study in Racial Crossing*. New York, 1928.
———. *The Myth of the Negro's Past*. New York, 1941.
Hiestand, Dale L. *Economic Growth and Employment Opportunities for Minorities*. New York, 1964.
Hill, T. Arnold. *The Negro and Economic Reconstruction*. Washington, 1937.
Hirsch, Leo H., Jr. "The Negro and New York, 1783-1865." *Journal of Negro History* 16(1931).
Hotten, John C. *The Original Lists of Persons of Quality*. New York, 1881.
Howison, Robert R. *A History of Virginia*. 2 vols. Richmond, 1848.
Hurd, John Codman. *The Law of Freedom and Bondage in the United States*. 2 vols. Boston, 1858-62.
Jeltz, Wyatt F. "The Relations of Negroes and Choctaw and Chickasaw Indians." *Journal of Negro History* 33(1948).
Jernegan, Marcus W. *Laboring and Dependent Classes in Colonial America, 1607-1783*. Chicago, 1931.
Johnson, Charles S. *Shadow of the Plantation*. Chicago, 1934.
———. *Patterns of Negro Segregation*. New York, 1943.
Johnson, James Weldon. *Black Manhattan*. New York, 1930.
Johnston, Sir Harry H. *The Negro in the New World*. New York, 1910.
Johnston, James Hugo. "Race Relations in Virginia and Miscegenation in the South, 1776-1860." Ph. D. dissertation, University of Chicago, 1937.
Jones, Hugh. *The Present State of Virginia*. New York, 1865.
Kaplan, Sidney. "Jan Earnst Matzelinger and the Making of the Shoe." *Journal of Negro History* 40(1955).
Katz, William. *The Black West*. New York, 1973.
Kesselman, Louis C. *The Social Politics of FEPC*. Chapel Hill, 1948.
Kingsbury, Susan M., ed. *Records of the Virginia Company of London*. 4 vols. Washington, 1906-35.
Klein, Herbert S. *Slavery in the Americas*. Chicago, 1967.
Krogman, Wilton Marion. "The Racial Composition of the Seminole Indians of Florida and Oklahoma." *Journal of Negro History* 19(1934).
Lacy, Dan. *The White Use of Blacks in America*. New York, 1972.
Lauber, Almon W. *Indian Slavery in Colonial Times*. New York, 1913.
Light, Ivan H. *Ethnic Enterprise in America*. Berkeley, 1972.
Lincoln, E. Eric. *The Black Muslims in Amercia*. Boston, 1961.
Lindsay, Arnett G. "The Economic Condition of the Negroes of New York Prior to 1861." *Journal of Negro History* 6(1921).
———. "The Negro in Banking." *Journal of Negro History* 14(1929).
Litwack, Leon F. *North of Slavery*. Chicago, 1961.
Loggins, Vernon. *The Negro Author*. New York, 1931.
Lofton, Williston H. "Abolition and Labor." *Journal of Negro History* 33(1948).
———. "Northern Labor and the Negro During the Civil War." *Journal of Negro History* 34(1949).
Logan, Rayford. *The Negro in American Life and Thought: The Nadir, 1877-1901*. New York, 1954.
———. "Estevanico, Negro Discoverer of the Southwest." *Phylon* 1(1940).
[Long, Edward]. *The History of Jamaica*. 3 vols. London, 1774.
McCormac, E. I. *White Servitude in Maryland*. Baltimore, 1904.
MacCrone, I. D. *Race Attitudes in South Africa*. London, 1937.
McKee, Samuel. *Labor in Colonial New York, 1664-1776*. New York, 1935.
McKinley, Albert E. "The Suffrage Franchise in the Thirteen English Colonies in America." *Publications of the University of Pennsylvania Series in History* 2(1905).

McManus, Edgar J. *A History of Negro Slavery in New York*. Syracuse, 1966.
McPherson, James. *The Struggle for Equality: Abolitionists and the Negro in the Civil War and Reconstruction*. Princeton, 1964.
———. *The Negro's Civil War*. New York, 1965.
Mandel, Bernard. "Samuel Gompers and the Negro Workers, 1886–1914." *Journal of Negro History* 40(1955).
Marshall, Ray. *The Negro and Organized Labor*. New York, 1965.
Mason, Philip. *Patterns of Dominance*. Oxford, 1970.
Mazyck, Walter H. *George Washington and the Negro*. Washington, 1932.
Meier, August. *Negro Thought in America, 1880–1915*. Ann Arbor, 1964.
Memmi, Albert. *The Colonizer and the Colonized*. Boston, 1967.
Moore, George H. *Notes on the History of Slavery in Massachusetts*. New York, 1866.
Morris, Richard B. *Government and Labor in Early America*. New York, 1946.
Morse, W. H. "Lemuel Haynes." *Journal of Negro History* 4(1919).
Nash, Gary B. *The Great Fear: Race in the Mind of America*. New York, 1970.
National Advisory Commission on Civil Disorders. *Report of the National Advisory Commission on Civil Disorders*. Washington, 1968.
Nell, William C. *The Colored Patriots of the American Revolution*. Boston, 1855.
Noel, Donald L., ed. *The Origins of American Slavery and Racism*. Columbus, 1970.
Nordhoff, Charles. *The Cotton States in the Spring and Summer of 1875*. New York, 1876.
North, Douglass C. *The Economic Growth of the United States, 1790–1860*. Englewood Cliffs, 1961.
Northup, Herbert R. *Organized Labor and the Negro*. New York, 1944.
Northup, Solomon. *Narrative of Solomon Northup*. Auburn, 1853.
Nugent, Nell M. *Cavaliers and Pioneers, A Calendar of Virginia Land Grants, 1623–1800*. Richmond, 1929.
Olmstead, Frederick Law. *The Cotton Kingdom*. Edited by Arthur M. Schlesinger. New York, 1953.
Oak, Vishnu, V. *The Negro's Adventure in General Business*. Yellow Springs, 1949.
Palmer, Paul C. "Servant into Slave: The Evolution of the Legal Status of the Negro Laborer in Colonial Virginia." *South Atlantic Quarterly* 65(1966).
Payne, Daniel A. *History of the African Methodist Episcopal Church*. Nashville, 1891.
Penn, I. Garland. *The Afro-American Press*. Springfield, 1891.
Piore, Michael J. "Public and Private Responsibliity in On-the-Job Training of Disadvantaged Workers." *Department of Economics Working Paper 23*, M.I.T. Press (1968).
Platt, Orville H. "Negro Governors." *New Haven Historical Society Papers* 5(1900).
Ploski, Harry A., and Brown, Roscoe C., Jr. *The Negro Almanac*. New York, 1967.
Porter, Dorothy B. "David Ruggles, an Apostle of Human Rights." *Journal of Negro History* 28(1943).
———. "The Organized Educational Activities of Negro Literary Societies, 1828–1846." *Journal of Negro Education* 5(1936).
Porter, Kenneth Wiggins. "Relations between Negroes and Indians Within the Present Limits of the United States." *Journal of Negro History* 17(1932).
———. "Florida Slaves and Free Negroes in the Seminole War, 1835–1842." *Ibid*. 28 (1943).
———. "Negro Guides and Interpreters in the Early Stages of the Seminole War." *Ibid*. 35(1950).
———. "Negroes and Indians on the Texas Frontier." *Ibid*. 41(1956).
———. "Negroes and the Seminole War, 1817–1818." *Ibid*. 26(1951).
Quaife, Milo M. *Checagou*. Chicago, 1933.
Quarles, Benjamin. *The Negro in the Civil War*. Boston, 1953.
———. *The Negro in the American Revolution*. Chapel Hill, 1961.

Quillin, Frank U. *The Color Line in Ohio.* Ann Arbor, 1913.
Read, Allen Walker. "The Speech of Negroes in Colonial America." *Journal of Negro History* 24(1939).
Reimers, David M. *White Protestantism and the Negro.* New York, 1965.
Richardson, Joe M. *The Negro in the Reconstruction of Florida.* Tallahassee, 1965.
Rose, Willie Lee. *Rehearsal for Reconstruction: The Port Royal Experiment.* Indianapolis, 1964.
Ross, Arthur M., and Hill, Herbert. *Employment, Race, and Poverty.* New York, 1967.
Ruchames, Louis. *Race, Jobs and Politics: The Story of FEPC.* New York, 1953.
Rudwick, Elliott M. *Race Riot at East St. Louis.* Carbondale, 1964.
Russell, John H. *The Free Negro in Virginia.* Baltimore, 1913.
Saunders, Doris, ed. *The Ebony Handbook.* Chicago, 1974.
Savage, W. Sherman. "The Influence of William Alexander Leidesdorff on the History of California." *Journal of Negro History* 38(1953).
Schorr, Alvin L. *Explorations in Social Policy.* New York, 1968.
Seeber, Edward D. "Phillis Wheatley." *Journal of Negro History* 24(1939).
Sherwood, Henry Noble. "Paul Cuffe." *Journal of Negro History* 8(1923).
Simmons, William J. *Men of Mark.* Cleveland, 1887.
Simpson, George E., and Yinger, J. Milton. *Racial and Cultural Minorities.* New York, 1953.
Smith, Abbot Emerson. *Colonists in Bondage: White Servitude and Convict Labor in America.* Chapel Hill, 1947.
Somers, Robert. *The Southern States since the War.* New York, 1871.
Spero, Sterling D., and Harris, Abram L. *The Black Worker.* New York, 1931.
Stampp, Kenneth M. *The Peculiar Institution.* New York, 1956.
Steiner, Bernard C. *History of Slavery in Connecticut.* Baltimore, 1893.
Stewart, Austin. *Twenty-two Years a Slave.* Rochester, 1857.
Stuart, Merah S. *An Economic Detour: A History of Insurance in the Lives of American Negroes.* New York, 1940.
Tabb, William K. *The Political Economy of the Black Ghetto.* New York, 1970.
Tate, Thad W., Jr. *The Negro in Eighteenth-Century Williamsburg.* Williamsburg, 1965.
Taylor, A. A. *The Negro in the Reconstruction of Virginia.* Washington, 1926.
———. *The Negro in South Carolina During Reconstruction.* Washington, 1924.
Thompson, Edgar T., ed. *Race Relations and the Race Problem.* Durham, 1939.
Tindall, George Brown. *South Carolina Negroes, 1877–1900.* Columbia, 1952.
Towner, Lawrence W. "'A Fondness for Freedom'": Servant Protest in Puritan Society." *William and Mary Quarterly* 19(1962).
Trent, William J. *Development of Negro Life Insurance Enterprises.* Philadelphia, 1932.
Turner, Lorenzo D. "African Survivals in the New World with Special Emphasis on the Arts." In *Africa Seen by American Negroes.* Paris, 1958.
Turner, Edward R. *The Negro in Pennsylvania.* Washington, 1911.
U.S. Commission on Civil Rights. *1961 Commission on Civil Rights Report.* 5 vols. Washington, 1970.
———. *Racism in America.* Washington, 1970.
U.S. Bureau of the Census. *Negro Population 1790–1915.* Washington, 1918.
———. *Negroes in the United States, 1920–32.* Washington, 1935.
U.S. Department of Commerce, Bureau of the Census. *The Social and Economic Status of Negroes in the United States, 1970.* Washington, 1971.
———. *Minority-owned Businesses: 1969.* Washington, 1971.
———. *The Social and Economic Status of the Black Population in the United States, 1971.* Washington, 1972.
———. *The Social and Economic Status of the Black Population in the United States, 1972.* Washington, 1973.

U.S. Department of Labor. *The Economic Situation of Negroes in the United States.* Washington, 1962.
U.S. Department of Labor. *Negro Migration in 1916–17.* Washington, 1919.
Wade, Richard S. *Slavery in the Cities.* New York, 1964.
Washington, Booker T. *Up from Slavery.* New York, 1901.
———. *The Negro in Business.* Boston, 1907.
Weare, Walter B. *Black Business in the New South.* Urbana, 1973.
Weaver, Robert C. *The Negro Ghetto.* New York, 1948.
———. *Negro Labor.* New York, 1946.
Wertenbaker, T. J. *Patrician and Plebeian in Virginia.* Charlottesville, 1910.
Wesley, Charles H. *Negro Labor in the United States, 1850–1925.* New York, 1927.
———. *Richard Allen.* Washington, 1935.
———. "The Negroes of New York in the Emancipation Movement." *Journal of Negro History* 24 (1939).
Wharton, Vernon L. *The Negro in Mississippi.* Chapel Hill, 1947.
Wiley, Bell Irvin. *Southern Negroes 1861–1865.* New Haven, 1938.
Williams, Eric. *Capitalism and Slavery.* Chapel Hill, 1938.
———. *The Negro in the Caribbean.* Washington, 1942.
Williamson, Joel. *After Slavery: The Negro in South Carolina During Reconstruction.* Chapel Hill, 1965.
Wolfe, Bernard. "Uncle Remus and the Malevolent Rabbit." *Commentary,* July, 1949.
Wish, Harvey. "American Slave Insurrections Before 1861." *Journal of Negro History* 22(1937).
———. "Slave Disloyalty Under the Confederacy." *Journal of Negro History* 23(1938).
Wood, Peter H. *Black Majority: Negroes in Colonial South Carolina.* New York, 1974.
Woodson, Carter G. *A Century of Negro Migration.* Washington, 1918.
———. *The Education of the Negro Prior to 1861.* Washington, 1919.
———. *Free Negro Heads of Families in the United States in 1830.* Washington, 1925.
———. *The History of the Negro Church.* Washington, 1945.
———, ed. *The Mind of the Negro Reflected in Letters Written During the Crisis, 1800–1860.* Washington, 1926.
———. "The Negroes of Cincinnati Prior to the Civil War." *Journal of Negro History* 1(1916).
———. The Beginnings of the Miscegenation of the Whites and Blacks. *Ibid.* 3 (1918).
———. "The Relation of Negroes and Indians in Massachusetts." *Ibid.* 5 (1920).
Woodward, C. Vann. *Origins of the New South, 1877–1913.* Baton Rouge, 1951.
Wright, James M. *The Free Negro in Maryland.* New York, 1921.

# INDEX

## A

Abbott, Robert, 320
Abolitionists. *See* Antislavery movement
Abraham (black Seminole leader), 106
Africa, 16, 64, 117–18, 208, 210, 212–15, 216–18; culture of, in America, 29–32, 152–53, 286
African-Americans, first generation: academic controversy over, 9–10; arrival, 5–9, 12, 27, 28; culture of, 29–32; deterioration of position in colonies, 33–34, 57, 63–66; in Massachusetts, 27, 32, 33; in New York, 25, 27–28, 32; number of, 11, 12, 13–16, 29; occupations, 33; origin, 6–8, 12, 27–28, 29–30; resistance of, 28, 31; status, 10–11, 16, 22–23, 26; in Virginia, 5–27, 30, 31, 32
African Colonization movement, 132–34
African Methodist Episcopal Church, 126, 138, 185, 320. *See also* Church, black
African Methodist Episcopal Zion Church, 126, 138, 320. *See also* Church, black
Allen, Richard, 124–26, 127, 129, 130, 136, 138–40, 141, 294
American Colonization Society, 131, 132–33, 136
American Federation of Labor, 264–65, 270, 273, 277
American Negro Academy, 219
American Negro Labor Council, 277
American Revolution, 98–99, 115; and black protest, 120–21; and black soldiers, 121; ideology of, 118; postwar reaction, 121–24
Antislavery movement, 118, 131–32
Atlanta, Ga., 338, 342
Atlanta Life Insurance Company, 313, 315, 334
Attucks, Crispus, 138

## B

Ballagh, James C., 7, 11, 43, 65
Baltimore *Afro-American*, 320, 329
Baltimore, Md., 338, 342
Banneker, Benjamin, 138, 141–42
Baraka, Amiri, 163
Baron, Harold, 222–23, 272
Beckwourth, James, 94–96
Binga, Jesse, 329–30

Birmingham, Ala., 338, 342
Black artisans, 269; displacement of, 258–59, 266, 271; free, 122; significance of, 237–38, 258; slave, 76, 238; and white opposition, 76, 240
Black businesses, 139, 291–92, 294–300, 307, 320–21, 335–37; banks, 187, 302–5, 312, 313, 324, 327, 329, 330, 337; catering and restaurant, 287–89, 295, 309, 334; farming, 268, 285–86, 305–6; insurance companies, 313–15, 320, 322, 323–24, 325, 326–29, 330, 334, 337; manufacturing and building, 289, 293, 299, 335–36; money-lending, 298; real estate, 321; retail stores, 296, 308, 325, 330, 334; tailoring and clothing, 297. *See also* Economic development, black
Black colleges, 199, 253
Black family, 12–13, 32, 197–98
Black labor, 276; in Colonial America, 239–40; in ante-bellum period, 240–43; in Reconstruction period, 243–48; in post-Reconstruction period, 248–53, 255–69; during World War I, 268–69; in 1920s, 269; in 1930s, 273–75; in 1940s, 275–76; in 1950s, 276; in 1960s, 277–78; in 1970s, 278–82; and automation, 277; and development of capitalism, 74, 234, 236; displacement of, 258–59; and dual labor markets, 235, 271; and economic discrimination, 239–40, 266–67, 273; role of, 222, 234–35, 238–39, 253; and sharecropping, 248–50; significance of, 234, 237, 251; and slavery, 236–38; strikebreaking, 243, 267–68; unions, 241, 246–47, 261–65, 272–73; and white immigration, 134, 240–41; and white labor, 76, 134, 238–40, 243, 260–62, 265–67, 271–72, 274. *See also* Economic development, black
Black Muslims. *See* Nation of Islam
Black mutual aid societies, 126, 128, 290–91
Black pioneers, 136–41; and American Revolution, 118–19, 120; and black education, 127; and black identity, 115–16, 120, 140; create Protest movement, 118–19; culture of, 115–18, 136–37; and development of black America, 113–14; elect Negro governors, 27, 119–20; and founding of black

351

Black pioneers—*cont.*
  Church, 117–18, 120, 124–26; and mutual aid societies, 126, 128; leaders, 137–41; organize institutions, 121, 125–29; resistance of, 79–80; significance of, 114–15, 142; social life, 122; and white founding fathers, 115; and white missionaries, 116–17, 127
Black population, 12, 13, 16, 29, 77–78, 121, 337–38
Black power: political, 245–46, 274, 305–7
Black press, 128–29, 320–21
Black protest movement, 28, 118–19, 124–26, 129–34
Black servants, 12, 23, 24–27; resistance of, 19–20, 28, 31–32; status of, 10–11, 16, 18, 22–23, 26–27, 28; treatment of, 11, 17–23, 28, 53; and white servants, 17–22
Black servitude, 16, 18, 23, 28, 34; beginning of, 9–11, 27–28; development of, 16, 33–34, 61–66. *See also* White servitude
*Black Stars*, 336
*Black World*, 336
Blacks: contributions of, 145–46, 194, 234, 236–38, 250–51; with French and Spanish explorers, 84–87, 93–94; as inventors, 315; and meaning of America, 114–15, 141–42; and quest for identity, 115–16, 120, 128–29, 136–37, 145–46, 197–98, 225–26, 270, 339
Bogle, Robert, 289
Boston, Mass., 116, 126, 127, 295, 338
Brimmer, Andrew, 281
Brotherhood of Sleeping Car Porters, 272
Browne, William W., 313
Bruce, Blanche Kelso, 305
Bruce, Philip, 12, 18, 21, 54, 56–57, 70
Bryan, Andrew, 120, 138
Bush, George W., 93
Butler, B. F., 176, 180

## C

Capital Savings Bank, 313
Cardozo, F. L., 307
Carey, Lott, 140–41
Chase, Mary, 185
Chesapeake Marine and Dry Dock Company, 307
*Chicago Defender*, 320, 330
Chicago, Ill., 94, 96, 98, 338, 342
Christian Methodist Episcopal Church, 320
Church, black: origin of, 117–18, 120, 124–26, 163; growth of, 219, 310–11; and black business, 313, 315, 323–24
Cincinnati, Ohio, 134, 135, 295, 338
Civil rights: demonstrations, 124–25, 132; legislation, 191–92, 194, 221, 244, 278; movement, 220–21, 276–77, 330–33, 334
Civil War: beginning of, 171–74; and black soldiers, 194; Jubilee, 169–71, 177–78, 181–84, 192–98; and Lincoln Administration, 172–73, 184, 190; and Northern racism, 172–74, 243; responses of free blacks, 185; responses of slaves, 173–84; and U.S. Congress, 191–92, 194
Clark, Kenneth, 221
Cleveland, Ohio, 338, 342
Coker, Daniel, 133, 137, 138, 140–41
Colonialism, internal, 209, 215, 218–20, 221, 309–10; in Africa, 213, 216–17; definition of, 209, 218; development of, 213–15, 218–19, 253; mechanisms of, 211, 214–15, 222–29, 248, 253–56; origin of, 210, 213; and violence, 254–55
Colored Merchants Association, 325
Communists, 271
Compromise of 1877, 218, 252, 270, 275, 316
Congress of Industrial Organizations, 273, 274, 277
Cornish, Samuel E., 128, 131, 132, 134, 138
Cox, Oliver Cromwell, 210
Cromwell, John W., 139
Cuffee, Paul, 92–93, 132, 133, 137, 138, 139, 300

## D

Dallas, Tex., 338, 342
Daniels, John, 131
Davis, David B., 146
Davis, Jefferson, 172, 186
Declaration of Independence, 121, 124, 135
Delany, Martin R., 241, 294, 295, 297, 299, 317, 335
Depression, the Great, 272, 275, 330, 334
Derham, James, 138, 139
Detroit, Mich., 97, 98, 99, 338, 342
Disenfranchisement, 134, 253, 255
Dorantes, Stephen, 85–86
Dorsey, Thomas, 296, 300
Douglass, Frederick: on economic development, 244, 294, 299, 303–4; on emancipation, 169, 170, 172, 193; as protest leader, 219, 317; on racism as a system, 207, 256; on slavery, 151, 154, 161–62
Douglass National Bank, 329, 330
Du Bois, W. E. B., 122; on African heritage,

# INDEX

Du Bois, W. E. B.—*cont.*
29; on black business boom of 1920s, 323; on black caterers, 288, 296, 309; on black Church, 117; on black economic development, 317, 319–20, 332; on Free African Society, 123; on Freedmen's Bank, 305; on Jubilee, 170; as protest leader, 219
Du Sable, Jean Baptiste Point, 94, 96–101, 138

## E

Eaton, John, 183, 184, 185–86
*Ebony*, 336
*Ebony Jr!* 336
Economic development, black, 286, 293–94; in Colonial period, 286–88; in ante-bellum period, 290–92, 294, 299; during Civil War, 300–2; in Reconstruction period, 305–8; in post-Reconstruction period, 268–70, 308–15, 320; in 1920s, 322–29; in 1930s, 329–34; in 1940s, 334; in 1950s, 275–76; in 1960s, 334–35, 337; in 1970s, 337–38, 342–43; barriers, 287, 292–93, 308–10, 335–36; Black Buying Power movement, 274–75, 330–32; and "Black Capitalism," 335; and black Church, 310–11, 323–24; and fraternal orders, 311–13, 314; land ownership, 24–26, 28, 286–87, 299; and black middle class, 122, 139, 316–20; and mutual aid societies, 289–90, 311; ideology of, 316–20, 299–300, 316–20, 323, 332
Education: discrimination, 254–55; for free blacks, 116, 117, 127–38, 199; of freedmen, 185, 199–201; and white missionaries, 116–17, 127–28, 199
Elks, Order of, 311
Elliott, Robert Brown, 263
Emancipation Proclamation, 171, 172, 192–94, 201
Estevanico. *See* Dorantes, Stephen

## F

Fanon, Frantz, 135
Forten, Charlotte, 185, 198–99
Forten, James, 132, 138, 139, 198, 290, 300
Free African Society, 126, 133, 138, 140, 290–91
Free blacks, 10, 14, 22, 24, 27, 33, 115, 121–22, 124, 136–37, 199
Freedmen, 121–22, 198; and black family, 197; camps and colonies, 186–90; and crisis of emancipation, 192–94, 196–98; demand land and education, 187–91, 198–200; and new roles, 197–98; organize semi-autonomous black governments, 186, 189–90; and white opposition, 200–2
Freedmen's Bank, 302, 303, 304, 316
Freedmen's Bureau, 158, 191, 194, 199, 260
*Freedom's Journal*, 128–29

## G

Garnet, Henry Highland, 299
Garrison, William Lloyd, 131
Garvey, Marcus, 269, 325–26, 335
Gibson, Truman K., 323
Gillespie, Frank L.
Golden State Guarantee Fund Insurance Company, 324, 334
Gompers, Samuel, 270, 271
Gordy, Berry, Jr., 336
Gourdine, Meredith C., 335
Grant, Ulysses S., 185
Great Lakes Mutual Life Insurance Company, 324
Greene, Lorenzo J., 27, 75, 91

## H

Hall, Prince, 117, 118, 121, 126–27, 132, 137, 138–39
Handlin, Mary F., 34, 64
Handlin, Oscar, 34, 64
Handy, W. C., 325
Harlem Renaissance, 219, 269
Harlem Riot of 1935, 333
Harris, Abram L., 289, 301
Haynes, Lemuel, 121, 137, 138
Haywood, Harry, 316–17
Herndon, Alonzo F., 313–15, 326, 327
Herskovits, Melville, 84, 108
Hope, John, 317–18, 285
Houston, Norman O., 32–34
Houston, Tex., 338, 342
Howard, Oliver O., 191
Hurston, Zora Neale, 162–63

## I

Income, black, 276, 277, 279, 280, 338, 339, 342
Indians: adoption of white racial attitudes, 90, 101–2, 108; and blacks, 79, 83–109; and English settlers, 8–9; and freedmen, 107–8; as indentured servants and slaves, 10, 13, 22, 40, 41, 44, 51, 53, 65, 67, 87–89; and national decision on slavery, 63–64;

Indians—*cont.*
    Seminoles, 101–7; wars of, 31, 88, 101, 103–7
Integration, 19–22, 74–76, 255–56

**J**

Jackson, Andrew, 105, 134, 293
Jackson, Jesse, 337
James, C. L. R., 236
Jamestown, Va., 5–14, 44, 45, 176
Jefferson, Thomas, 69, 115, 121, 141–42
Jernegan, Marcus W., 48
*Jet*, 336
Johnson, Andrew, 190, 191, 201, 243
Johnson, Anthony, 14, 15, 24–26, 287
Johnson, George E., 335
Johnson, James Weldon, 28, 127, 163, 293
Johnson, John H., 336
Johnson Products Company, 335
Johnson Publishing Company, 336
Johnston, James Hugo, 20–21, 69–70, 88, 102
Jones, Absalom, 124–26, 130, 138, 139
Jones, John, 297, 299, 300
Jordan, Winthrop, 72, 77, 78

**K**

King, Martin Luther, Jr., 220
Klein, Herbert S., 66, 70
Knights of Labor, 259, 264
Ku Klux Klan, 247

**L**

Lacy, Dan, 235, 250–51
Leadership, black, 130–31, 219
Leidesdorff, William Alexander, 299
Lewis, Edmonia, 102
Liele, George, 120, 138, 140
Lincoln, Abraham, 172, 184, 190, 191
Los Angeles, Cal., 288, 339, 342
L'Ouverture, Toussaint, 141

**M**

Masons, black, 119, 126–27, 138–39, 311, 312
Matzeliger, Jan E., 315
Memphis, Tenn., 338
Merrick, John, 313–14
Migration, Great, 220, 269
*Mirror of Liberty*, 128
Mississippi Life Insurance Company, 320, 328–29

Morgan, Albert T., 305–6
Morgan, Garrett A., 315
Moton, Robert Russa, 175, 211
Motown Records, 336
Muhammad, Elijah, 335
Murphy, Carl J., 320
Myers, Issac, 261–62, 263

**N**

Nation of Islam, 335
National Association for the Advancement of Colored People, 219, 270, 277, 332
National Baptist Convention, 320, 324
National Benefit Insurance Company, 330
National Business League, 318–19, 325
National Labor Union, 259, 264
*Negro Digest*, 336
Negro National Labor Union, 262–64
New Orleans, La., 296, 299, 338, 342
*New York Daily Mirror*, 333
*New York Herald*, 202, 240
New York, New York, 76, 122, 126, 294, 299, 338, 342
*New York Times*, 247
Newark, N. J., 338
Niagara movement, 219
Nickerson, William, 324
Norfolk *Journal and Guide*, 320
Nordhoff, Charles, 176, 310
North Carolina Mutual Life Insurance Company, 313–14, 334
Northeastern Life Insurance Company, 323, 325
Northup, Solomon, 148, 151–52, 157, 160

**O**

Oak, Vishnu, 322–23
Oakland, Cal., 338–42
Odd Fellows, Order of, 311, 312
Olmstead, Frederick L., 147, 159
Osceola (Seminole Indian chief), 105–7
Ottley, Roi, 27–28
Overton, Anthony, 329

**P**

Pace, Harry, 323–24, 325
Paul, Nathaniel, 138
Peake, Mary, 185
Peonage, 214, 248–49, 253, 254
Perry, Heman E., 326–29

# INDEX

Peters, Thomas, 121, 141
Pettiford, W. R., 313
Philadelphia, Pa., 45, 116, 122, 294, 295, 299, 338
Phillips, Wendell, 172
*Pittsburgh Courier,* 320
Poor, Salem, 92, 121
Populist movement, 255–56
Porter, Kenneth W., 84, 93, 102, 108
Powell, Adam Clayton, Jr., 277, 331–32
Prince, Abijah, 287
Prosser, Gabriel, 130, 132, 138
Purvis, Robert, 299, 300

## Q

Quaife, Milo M., 97
Quakers, 116, 118
Quarles, Benjamin, 116

## R

Race riots, 135, 239, 243, 293, 333
Racism: origin of, 62, 63–73; development of, 68–69, 73–79, 134; as functional requirement of the system, 71–72, 211, 217, 223, 256; national decisions on, 61–66, 68, 69, 79, 253, 271; and poor whites, 64, 76–78; and white identity, 78–79
Rainey, J. H., 307
Randolph, Asa Philip, 272, 274, 277
Ransier, A. J., 307
Rapier, J. T., 305
Reconstruction, 218; and economic conflict in South, 245–46, 248–51; and Northern industrialization, 242, 243; end of, 252, 308
Reimers, David M., 255
Religion: of African-American slaves, 117–18, 162–63; and development of racism, 66–68, 73, 123–26, 254; as ideological prop of slave regime, 10, 22, 66–67, 73, 216
Remond, Charles Lenox, 138
Revolutionary War. *See* American Revolution
Richmond, Va., 338, 342
Rillieux, Norbert, 296
Roosevelt, Franklin Delano, 274
Rose, Edward, 93–94
Ruggles, David, 128, 130, 132, 138
Russell, J. H., 26, 88
Russwurm, John B., 128, 133–34, 137–38, 139, 140–41

## S

St. Louis, Mo., 338, 342
St. Luke, Order of, 312
Salem, Peter, 121
Savings Bank of the Grand Fountain United Order of True Reformers, 313
Saxton, Rufus, 185, 187, 188, 189
Schurz, Carl, 201, 247
Segregation, 124, 248, 253, 254
Seminoles, 101, 102–9
Sherman, William T., 187–89, 190
Slave codes, 55, 66–68, 72–73, 123, 147, 287
Slave Trade, African, 7, 40, 46, 50, 65, 146
Slave community: art and folklore, 145–46, 163–65; and black family, 156–58; characteristics of, 150–51, 155; culture of, 146, 152–53; 161–63; leaders of, 159–61; morale, 153–55; sanctions, 155–56, 158; significance of, 166; social life, 156–57; values, 158–59
Slave revolts, 79, 135–36, 180–81
Slavery, 145–66, 236; beginning of, 62–70, 74, 194; and cultural control, 148; development of, 74–78; impact of, on poor whites, 76–78; Indian, 10, 44, 64–65, 67; legacy of, 71; and rise of capitalism, 74, 146; significance of, 146–48; white, 44
Slaves: legacy of, 149–50; as overseers and drivers, 160; relations between house and field, 159–60; resistance of, 88–89, 118, 147, 150, 154–55
Smalls, Robert, 176, 307
Smith, Abbott Emerson, 50, 54–55, 77
Somers, Robert, 198
Southern Tenant Farmers' Union, 274
Spaulding, C. C., 314
Spero, Sterling, 266, 270
Stampp, Kenneth, 32, 62, 149
Standard Life Insurance Company, 326–29
Stevens, Thaddeus, 191, 244
Steward, Austin, 136, 148
Stuart, M. S., 310, 313, 326–27
Suffrage, 26–27, 245, 274
Supreme Liberty Life Insurance Company of Chicago, 325, 334
Supreme Life Insurance Company of Chicago, 336
Supreme Life and Casualty Company of Ohio, 322, 323, 325
Supreme Products, 336

## T

Tabb, William K., 221

Taylor, Susie King, 174, 185
Trent, W. J., Jr., 311
True Reformers, Order of, 311, 312, 313
Tubman, Harriet, 185
Turner, Henry McNeal, 185, 192–93
Turner, Nat, 130, 135–36, 138, 139, 177

## U

Unity Mutual Life Insurance Company, 324
Universal Life Insurance Company, 324
U.S. Constitution, 123
U.S. Government: and racism, 147, 184, 277
U.S. Supreme Court, 220, 249, 252

## V

Valdez, Maria Rita, 288
Vann, Robert L., 320
Varick, James, 129, 138
Vesey, Denmark, 130, 132, 138, 153
Victory Life Insurance Company, 324, 329

## W

Walker, Madame C. J., 321–22
Walker, David, 129, 130, 135, 138, 139, 140, 294, 299
Walker, Maggie, 312
Washington, Booker T.: on Civil War, 175; on education, 254; as middle-class spokesman, 316–20; organizes National Business League, 318–19; as slave, 169
Washington, D. C., 138, 299, 338, 342
Washington, George, 51, 69, 115, 120–21, 289
Weiner, Leo, 84
Wertenbaker, T. J., 52, 69–70, 78
Wheatley, Phillis, 120, 138, 139
Whipper, William S., 128, 134, 136, 138
White servants, 39–40, 53; and black servants and slaves, 19–22, 74–77; number of, 13, 40, 45; occupations, 53; origin of, 45–46; recruitment of, 46–49; resistance, 19–20, 54–56; sale of, 50–52; status, 52; treatment of, 11, 18, 53–54
White servitude, 8, 10, 11; and black slavery, 40–41; development of, 43–44, 52, 76; origin of, 41–42, 44–45; significance of, 40–41, 56–57; and white servant trade, 44–50
Wiley, Bell I., 178
Williams, Eric, 40
Williams, L. K., 324
Williams, Peter, Sr., 129, 138
WJPC Radio, 336
Woods, Granville, 315
Woodson, Carter G., 219, 243, 257, 298
Wright, Richard, 220

## Y

Young, P. B., 320

E
185
.B43
1975

3 3312 00015 9368
ASHEVILLE-BUNCOMBE TECHNICAL COLLEGE

75-155

Bennett, Lerone
The shaping of Black America

DATE DUE
1- 3 '94

DISCARDED

AUG 25

Asheville-Buncombe Technical Institute
LIBRARY
340 Victoria Road
Asheville, North Carolina 28801